BISON
BOOKS

Buchen meisteri.

From Hans Wegener, Küchenmeisterei, *facsimile of the book printed in Nuremberg by Peter Wagner in 1490, Leipzig 1939*

THE
FOOD AND COOKING
OF
EASTERN EUROPE

Lesley Chamberlain

With a new introduction by the author

UNIVERSITY OF NEBRASKA PRESS
LINCOLN AND LONDON

Library of Congress Cataloging-in-Publication Data
Chamberlain, Lesley.
The food and cooking of Eastern Europe / Lesley
Chamberlain; with a new introduction by the author.
p. cm.
Reprint. Originally published: London: Penguin Books, 1989.
Includes bibliographical references and index.
ISBN-13: 978-0-8032-6460-1 (pbk.: alk. paper)
ISBN-10: 0-8032-6460-7 (pbk.: alk. paper)
1. Cookery, European. 2. Cookery—Europe, Eastern. I. Title.
TX723.5.A1C48 2006
641.5947—dc22 2005028777

Books on food can be many things to their authors, and more things
again to their readers. Conceived as a successor to *The Food and Cooking
of Russia*, *The Food and Cooking of Eastern Europe* was presented to the
public in 1989 as a collection of recipes from countries whose cuisines
were little known as a consequence of the Cold War. It was ironic then
that, having been a while in preparation, this volume should appear in
exactly the year when the Iron Curtain was lifted after having divided
Europe for almost half a century. As Communist authority finally lost
its hold over millions of people, most spectacularly with the fall of the
Berlin Wall, the old "Eastern Bloc," and with it the terms in which
the book was conceived, disintegrated overnight. The term "Eastern
Europe"—for Westerners, always a political term rather than a matter
of geographical accuracy—was even an insult now that the old Moscow
satellites were suddenly free nations again. It was more fitting to speak
of a "Central Europe" that included Czechoslovakia, Slovenia, Croatia,
Hungary, and western Poland, and an "East Europe" comprising the
remainder of Poland, Ukraine, Belorussia, and parts of Russia. The
three Baltic States—Estonia, Latvia, and Lithuania—and the Balkan
countries, which also once formed part of "Eastern Europe" were also
now liberated to be themselves. The Balkan group included Bulgaria,
Romania, and the southern republics of Yugoslavia—Serbia, Montenegro, Macedonia, Bosnia, Kosovo—together with neighboring Albania.

Here were many distinct nations, to be freshly defined by their
particular languages, ethnic makeup, and shifting historical borders. The
process continued when Czechoslovakia disappeared, and the Czech
Republic and Slovakia emerged, and when Yugoslavia broke up. Equally,
from the moment the Soviet Union no longer existed, Ukraine, Belorussia, and the Baltic States, whose food had been covered in *The
Food and Cooking of Russia*, were now geopolitically, and again perhaps

offensively, misplaced as cultures on the Russian periphery and might better have been included in a book making them culinary neighbors of Poland and Germany. Germany, now one large country again, had itself to be reassessed. It evidently qualified for a place in Central Europe, even if it remained a unique amalgam from a culinary point of view. Still, I took exception to the reviewer who called *The Food and Cooking of Eastern Europe* "a museum piece." Here evidently was a reviewer who neither cooked nor understood the continuity of food across political borders, nor, most important, the diverse functions of food writing.

I began writing the present book at the tail end of a grand tradition in postwar English cookery writing, in my mind created primarily by Elizabeth David and Jane Grigson. These women were practical cooks who were also writers. Their familiarity with ingredients and kitchen equipment was both essential and not quite the point of the enterprise. M. F. K. Fisher was another *éminence grise*, and though I had not read her work, she surely helped create the cultural impulse that was reflected in a newspaper column I read sometime in the early 1980s. "If you can't think of a plot, write a cookbook," said the writer, whose famous name escapes me. She made me aware of some of the motivation behind my first book. Nevertheless, the cookbook genre was a fine choice in my view, precisely because its best postwar exponents were travelers. In Grigson's case, they were also translators of note. And on top of all this, they were intrepid notetakers of their daily experience. This was exactly what I wanted to be.

I had been a Reuter correspondent in Moscow for a bit over a year (1978–79) and had published a translation of a Tolstoy story when I began work on *The Food and Cooking of Russia*. Subsequently, *The Food and Cooking of Eastern Europe* emerged out of travels in Europe I undertook privately when based back in London. I knew Russia, and I felt I knew Germany too, having studied German and spent time there. What I wanted to understand now were all the countries that, for the whole of my lifetime and much longer periods in their history, had found themselves squeezed between these two cultural giants. My former partner was living in Poland, so I began there. Our daughter, born in 1980, became caught up in the increasingly impassioned project that took me in succession to all the "East European" countries in turn. The original aim, to write the occasional feature article about my travels and discoveries, soon gave way to a projected book about what this semi-banished world meant to me. The region had powerful links to the great nineteenth-century continental empires and a fate determined by two world wars. I wanted to approach that history through the stories of people and places that came my way, and through literature.

The result, *In the Communist Mirror*, with its passionate involvement in a now lost world, was a book too personal for some tastes. But I think what it did fairly was set down a marker for the classic experience of a "Westerner" in a divided Europe. I and the book I projected were part of the history being described. I divided my role between introspective traveling and the archeology of cultural remains. But because out of sheer joy I always kept notes on the food I encountered along the way, there was material left over for a second book, and that was how *The Food and Cooking of Eastern Europe* came to be written. *In the Communist Mirror* was actually published a year after *The Food and Cooking of Eastern Europe*, but they were written in the reverse order. Food was interesting to market-minded publishers, my ruminations less so—until they could be presented as reflecting the end of Communism, which was not their import at all.

The Food and Cooking of Eastern Europe was more honestly marketed. Much as I had done in Russia, I matched my personal experience of food and cooking in Central and Eastern European countries to the information I could find in classic Polish, Hungarian, Romanian, and other cookbooks. I consulted with more or less difficulty these invaluable sources in the round reading room of the British Museum and in the London Library, and on my own shelves. An eminent Russian of my acquaintance, who had lived in London since he was a boy but retained his native language, used to claim he could get by across a whole swath of the European continent by employing "basic Slav." So now did I. This was a shaky linguistic principle on which to proceed: once my eminent acquaintance tried to request three return tickets from Prague to Kishinev and found himself with six singles and a watermelon. Nonetheless, with a knowledge of Russian and suitable dictionaries I confronted recipes in Polish, Czech, Slovenian, Serbo-Croat (as the official language of Yugoslavia was then known), and Bulgarian. My experience of Romance languages helped with Romanian. All I can say is that friends and family were repeatedly invited to taste the results of my culinary-linguistic adventures and to advise me on whether the pleasure of eating had been lost or found in translation.

I still cook from the many lovely recipes I collected up to a quarter century ago. Indeed, they created my culinary style. Romania taught me to make my own *tarama* and supplied a much-loved recipe for chicken with apricots. *Cholent*, a gorgeous cassoulet-like concoction of beans and goose and barley, entered my repertoire from Jewish traditions. Stuffed eggplants and wonderful sticky cakes were borrowings for life from the Balkans. Another South Slav recipe, *ajvar*, stewed peppers left whole and with just a shot of vinegar, regularly plunges visitors to my table into ecstasy. Bulgarian rice puddings, Fugger's lemon cake from Warsaw, Serbian bean soup, soup with yogurt and barley . . . I could go on. This is real food requiring the best, freshest ingredients, and like all excellent cooking, it is best made lovingly at home. In fact, the value of home-cooked food is probably one I owe almost entirely to Eastern Europe. I found it a joy to come across a world in which, although dented by shortages in an ill-managed economy, the culture of food was still intact. Above all, the food industry was innocent compared with its Western counterpart, and the link between town and country persisted more or less unbroken from before the war. Markets were still more frequent than supermarkets, and there was no need to go to "health" shops to buy whole grains, jam that was actually made of fruit, and superb dairy products at honest prices.

But when I encounter this book again as a book, rather than a collection of recipes, I see that it was at heart a diary devoted to my sensual response to traveling in mentally difficult places. To note through their food the pleasures and frustrations of millions of people not free to come and go across the world was intended as a gesture of sympathy and not meant to be condescending. It was perfectly clear that a morally and materially satisfying life could be led without political freedom. And yet in the end my food travels had the opposite political function— namely, to celebrate diversity. I set out to look for differences from the ideological norm, from the standards of official institutions, and also for deviations from uninformed Western expectations. I wanted at home to make better known the ordinary daily lives of "faraway" Europeans who had been propelled out of the common orbit. One has to remember how little cultural interest there was in points east during the Cold War years. This was especially the case in the Anglo-Saxon world. Far less Russian, Polish, Czech, and Hungarian art and music were available in our media, and what was broadcast, staged, exhibited, or published very often had an anti-Communist political point. My aims were different, and I like to think that, alongside living recipes, they are now on mummified display in this "museum" of a book.

CONTENTS

LIST OF MAPS

CONVERSION TABLES

Liquid measures

British

I quart	= 2 pints	= 40 fluid oz
I pint	= 4 gills	= 20 fl oz
½ pint	= 2 gills	
	or one cup	= 10 fl oz
¼ pint	= 8 tablespoons	= 5 fl oz
	I tablespoon	= just over ½ fl oz
	I dessertspoon	= ⅓ fl oz
	I teaspoon	= ⅙ fl oz

Metric

I litre = 10 decilitres (dl) = 100 centilitres (cl) = 1,000 millilitres (ml)

American

I quart	= 2 pints	= 32 fl oz
I pint	= 2 cups	= 16 fl oz
	I cup	= 8 fl oz
	I tablespoon	= ⅓ fl oz
	I teaspoon	= ⅙ fl oz

Approx. equivalents

British	Metric	American
1 quart	1·1 litre	2½ pints
1 pint	6 dl	1¼ pints
½ pint	3 dl	10 fl oz (1¼ cups)
¼ pint (1 gill)	1·5 dl	5 fl oz
1 tablespoon	15 ml	1½ tablespoons
1 dessertspoon	10 ml	1 tablespoon
1 teaspoon	5 ml	⅓ fl oz

Metric	British and American
1 litre	35 fl oz
½ litre (5 dl)	18 fl oz
¼ litre (2·5 dl)	9 fl oz
1 dl	3½ fl oz

American	British	Metric
1 quart	1½ pints + 3 tbs (32 fl oz)	9·5 dl
1 pint	¾ pint + 2 tbs (16 fl oz)	4·7 dl
1 cup	½ pint − 3 tbs (8 fl oz)	2·4 dl

Solid measures

Approx. equivalents

British	Metric
1 lb (16 oz)	450 g
½ lb (8 oz)	225 g
¼ lb (4 oz)	110 g
1 oz	25 g

Metric	British
1 kg (1,000 g)	2 lb 3 oz
½ kg (500 g)	1 lb 2 oz
¼ kg (250 g)	9 oz
100 g	3½ oz

Oven Temperatures

Fahrenheit	Gas Mark	Centigrade	Heat of Oven
225°F	$\frac{1}{4}$	110°C	Very cool
250°F	$\frac{1}{2}$	120°C	Very cool
275°F	1	140°C	Cool
300°F	2	150°C	Cool
325°F	3	160°C	Moderate
350°F	4	180°C	Moderate
375°F	5	190°C	Fairly hot
400°F	6	200°C	Fairly hot
425°F	7	220°C	Hot
450°F	8	230°C	Very hot
475°F	9	250°C	Very hot

*Mother sent me into the fields with food for some gypsies
who were hoeing corn for us . . . they fell upon their food,
as silent as eels.*

Ion Creanga, Recollections

*One happiness remains: when in a grey hour you sit by the
fireside with a few of your friends and lock the door against
the uproar of Europe, and escape in thought to happier
times, and muse and dream of your own land.*

Adam Mickiewicz, Prologue to Pan Tadeusz

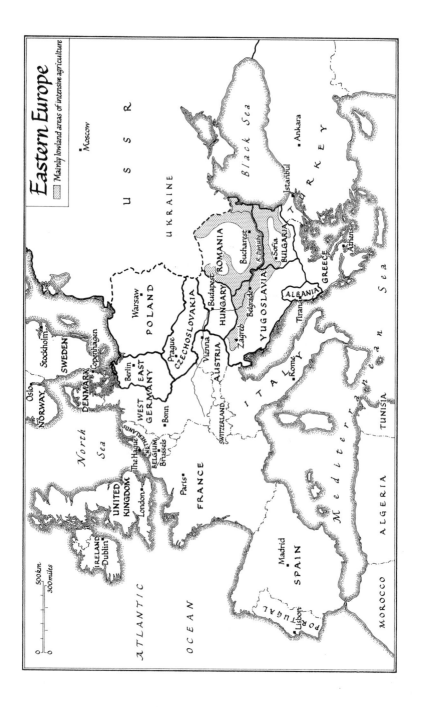

Eastern Europe

▨ Mainly lowland areas of intensive agriculture

INTRODUCTION

The food and cooking of Eastern Europe cover more than half the gastronomic globe, from Paris to Moscow, and from the Adriatic to the Baltic. Take any dish from north or south Europe and you will almost certainly find its equivalent in Eastern Europe, adapted to local tastes and conditions. Many dishes that have migrated across the Atlantic can also be traced back to their East European origins. Within the half-continent the choice of food styles is so abundant it would be vain to try to define the cuisine of a single country. The points of contact are sometimes buried from immediate sight, but they exist with cuisines as different as Chinese, British and French. There are signs – dating back to the early Roman influence as far afield as Germany and Romania – of an affinity with Italian food, though only in the flavours, not in the meal patterns; but ultimately East European cooking is adaptable. It is that which has kept it independent of the international style dominated by the French, and yet hugely receptive to the foremost cuisines of West and East.

At its most solid it is the food of Central Europe, heavily influenced by Germany and Austria; at its most exotic it is the food of the Balkans and the Near East; and these different food cultures modify each other to give huge variety. In the babble of dishes it is sometimes difficult to say which dish belongs where. Polish *barszcz* and Hungarian *gulyás*, for instance, seem distinctive, but what is the real home of beetroot soup, considering the Russians, Lithuanians, Ukrainians and Jews all lay claim to it? And what nationality is 'goulash' today, when it is found in Romania, Czechoslovakia and every East German railway buffet? For reasons of national pride most countries

3

would willingly take the borderline recipe as their own, but the whole business of nationality in food, particularly in a part of the world so ill-served by natural geographical borders, is generally unhelpful to the cook. In Bulgaria the food resembles that of Turkey and Lebanon with touches of Russia and Vienna, while in East Poland it is close to the staple Russian diet. On the Baltic coast it reflects Scandinavian tastes.

For these reasons the recipes in this book come only nominally from the eight countries on the present political map: East Germany, Czechoslovakia, Poland, Hungary, Bulgaria, Romania, Albania and Yugoslavia. In practice each 'country' represents the food and cooking of many more nations and peoples which do not show up as independent entities today, among them Bohemia, Moravia, Slovakia, Lithuania, the Ukraine, Transylvania, Macedonia, Serbia, Croatia, Moldavia. The recipes also take into account the kind of cross-fertilization that the cooking habits of Turks in Bulgaria, Albanians in Yugoslavia, Saxons and Georgians in Romania, and Muslims, Armenians and Jews everywhere have brought. Besides being sets of instructions for making this or that dish, the recipes are symbols of food at work.

The small, historically less than mighty nations have been greatly affected in their cooking as in everything else by migrations, movable borders and occupation. From the sixteenth century Turkey left its Middle Eastern gastronomic stamp on over half the area covered in this book. From the eighteenth century Austria exerted considerable Germanic influence in Hungary, Czechoslovakia, Slovenia and Croatia and Transylvania. Russia was an influential neighbour in Bulgaria and a conqueror in Romania and Poland. Germany, which had little influx of foreign settlers and no major shifting of its frontiers, was unusual in having a cuisine virtually free of the marks of an outside hand, showing an affinity with Poland and Russia only towards its eastern borders. The faint trace of Soviet influence in East German food today is a rare sign of outside intrusion, one might say capitulation. East Bloc, especially East German, restaurants are also inclined to put on Russian specialities and Russian cooking weeks. The Germans used to be adamant that they would retain their own food and their own language at the table. When the reign of Paris was at its height they refused even to write their menus in gastronomic French, so that diners had to come to recognize '*Seezungenfilet auf normannischer Art*' as *sole normande*.

What the cuisines in this book have in common, beyond this or that dish, is the fact that their cooking has been greatly affected by politics in the last forty years. They are more old-fashioned than they need be, having remained out of contact with Western fashions, and without the material plenty and leisure they need to flourish. The gastronomic story is similar to that of the higher arts. Otherwise two books, one on Central Europe and one on the Balkans, might have been more natural.

To look at the countries themselves, however: within borders, social class has played a weighty part in setting up a tension between outside influences and native ways, which has inevitably been enriching. In over half of the countries in this book, two parallel systems of cooking developed in the early modern era. The feudal class structure divided aristocracy from peasantry, and the foreign-influenced monarchies increased the food gap. Exceptions were Bulgaria and Albania, which until the late nineteenth century were wholly subjugated peoples without monarchies; also Germany, where foreign refinements in food did not attract even those who could afford them. But in the other countries, while simple cooking continued to rely on local ingredients and handed-down ideas, from about the fifteenth century a more elaborate cuisine, demanding imported ingredients and foreign techniques, grew up alongside. The gastronomic influences effected through royal courts and international diplomacy were mainly French and Italian, but the courts also helped circulate food ideas within the eastern half of the continent, for example between Hungary and Poland.

I'm underplaying the idea of nationality in food, to try to keep passionate partiality out of this book. The differences in the finished food products are often not as marked as the various ministries of tourism would like. But each country has its gastronomic history and character, as much as it has its peculiar general history and position in the world.

Poland

The Polish cuisine, which should be praised for its resistance to foreign influence, became, in a way that has perhaps been underestimated by historians, the mainstay of what was Polish in a period of particular difficulties.

> Maria Lemnis, *Old Polish Traditions in the Kitchen*, 1979

From the eighteenth century to the First World War, Poland was partitioned into non-existence by alien powers, which is one reason why its food has been neglected as an international attraction. At the same time, the annihilation of the state encouraged Poles to become more self-consciously national and find a source of unity and continuity in religion, and both these overtones are strong in the food. They reach right up to the present day. Polish exiles abroad speak Polish and eat Polish food as if the continuity of their culture depended upon it. I was struck while reading Maria Lemnis, whom I have just quoted, to find her lamenting the loss of so many precious handwritten collections of family recipes in the sacking of Poland during the last war. Food history is taken as seriously as any aspect of national history, the Polish table being the product of centuries of political upheaval, cultural yearning and vulnerable geography.

Poland is a northern, Slavonic country, bordering Germany, Russia and Czechoslovakia, with a Baltic Sea coast and aspirations towards the Latin cultures of France and Italy. The severe winter climate has enforced a traditional reliance on mainly root vegetables and cabbage, dried mushrooms and pickles, alongside heavy rye bread and barley, millet and buckwheat, but outside influences have introduced a few lighter touches.

The shared subjection to intense cold brings Polish closer to Russian food than any other country in the East Bloc. The sweet-sour taste of many basic Polish dishes, whether prepared with meat or only vegetables, would be familiar in Moscow, and the Poles share the Russian fondness for sour cream and the taste of dill and horseradish. Both peoples enjoy pancakes and gruels (*kasha*), thick soups and curd cheese, and like the Russians the Poles begin a formal meal with a spread of small cold and hot dishes (Polish *zakaski*, Russian *zakuski*) away from the main table. In both cases the accompanying drink is vodka. They share a taste for game and pork and carp. Even the dishes the national poet Adam Mickiewicz singles out in his epic of Lithuanian life at the time of the Napoleonic campaigns: meat *zrazy*, sauerkraut, the potato-starch sweet known as *kisiel*, mushrooms, sausages and an iced soup of beetroot leaves and cream, are equally associated with Russia and the Ukraine – the Ukraine having been both Polish and Russian.

'Oh, but Polish food is not Russian! It is somehow different,' say the least nationalistic spirits, and their protests can be justified if the full extent of Polish cooking is taken into account. The Poles are known, distinctly from the Russians, for their pork, ham and sausages and their sweet-and-sour sauces with carp and game. In the fourteenth century Poland and Lithuania, then distinct and rival political entities, although neighbours, pooled their gastronomic resources and the Poles found themselves shareholders in luxury. The finest smoked ham and rye-wheat bread has ever since born a legendary Lithuanian tag. Poland's Baltic tradition in cured fish also means that herring in every form is relished. Smoked eel counts as a special delicacy. The Poles have French-style sauces and are also *pâtissiers* in a way the Russians have never been. Moreover, Poland owes its most important early cookery book to France. *The Perfect Cook*, which appeared in 1786, was a Polish translation from the French, replacing the pioneering Latin-language *Compendium Ferculorum* of 1682.

The subsequent history of *The Perfect Cook* says much about the position of Polish cooking, and culture, at the beginning of the nineteenth century. New editions added old Polish recipes and it was here that Mickiewicz looked for the dishes to be eaten at 'the last Old-Polish banquet' of 1812 in the final book of *Pan Tadeusz*. It is not a gastronomic distinction, but one of cultural spirit, that the edition of this cookbook in that same year was imbued, as was Poland generally – in stark contrast to Russia – with the spirit of the French Revolution. It addressed itself to 'citizens and citizen housewives'. At the same time a leading intellectual journal cautioned against excessive imitation of all things French and the omission of Polish dishes from the diet. Polish cosmopolitanism and nationalism have continued to be creative combatants at the table to this day.

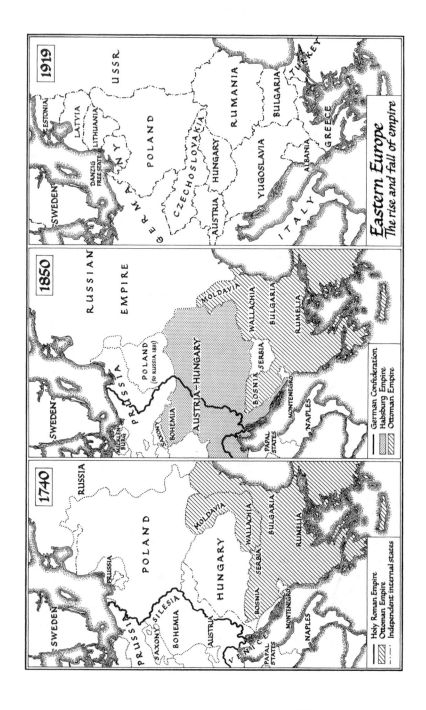

Eastern Europe
The rise and fall of empire

1740

SWEDEN
RUSSIA
POLAND
PRUSSIA
PRUSSIA
SILESIA
BOHEMIA
SAXONY
AUSTRIA
HUNGARY
VENICE
MOLDAVIA
WALLACHIA
SERBIA
BOSNIA
BULGARIA
MONTENEGRO
RUMELIA
PAPAL STATES
NAPLES

Holy Roman Empire
Ottoman Empire
Independent internal states

1850

SWEDEN
RUSSIAN EMPIRE
MECKLENBURG
PRUSSIA
POLAND
(to RUSSIA 1831)
BOHEMIA
SAXONY
AUSTRIA–HUNGARY
MOLDAVIA
WALLACHIA
SERBIA
BOSNIA
BULGARIA
MONTENEGRO
RUMELIA
PAPAL STATES
NAPLES

German Confederation
Habsburg Empire
Ottoman Empire

1919

SWEDEN
USSR
ESTONIA
LATVIA
LITHUANIA
DANZIG FREE STATE
GERMANY
POLAND
CZECHOSLOVAKIA
AUSTRIA
HUNGARY
RUMANIA
YUGOSLAVIA
BULGARIA
ALBANIA
GREECE
TURKEY
ITALY

Western influences have helped put a distance between Polish and Russian styles. A combination of French and Italian culinary techniques and the dietary dictates of the Roman Church as compared with the Russian Orthodox have made Polish dishes more thoroughly 'composed' than Russian. The essential plainness of Russian food preparation, not stripping meat from the bone and not combining ingredients before they reach the table, sprang from the Orthodox control over the traditional diet. The converse, a highly 'concentrated' quality, belongs to Polish food. This, however, is something for which Western palates have most often expressed reproach. It is precisely what does not team well with wine. It may have come about when Italian sauces were powerfully remade with Polish ingredients. Thus, when the French nineteenth-century chefs looked to Poland, as they did to Russia and other alien cuisines, for new inspiration, they had to soften the texture and the flavour, just as they did with Russian food. Walter Bickel, in his list of international dishes at the beginning of this century, describes as the primary '*sauce polonaise*' 'veal *velouté* mixed with sour cream, grated horseradish and chopped fennel, seasoned with lemon juice . . .' which is extraordinary. Many of the ideas pervading not only Polish food but the present book – the sour cream, the sharp horseradish relish, the piquant dash of sour juice and the fresh, faintly aniseed taste of fennel (better known to the French than the Central European dill, though not the same) – are enshrined in that sauce which represents a half-continent.

But Poland suffered the same constraints of the religious calendar as the rest of Europe and Russia as far as the frantic pattern of feasts and fasts was concerned. It has long shared with Orthodox Russia a lavish celebration of Easter, with tables of roast meat and decorative butter and sweetened cheese, to be eaten with rich bread and cakes, and a rumbustious Carnival week full of heavy eating and drunken socializing at the advent of Lent.

Unlike Russia, however, because of the different emphases of Orthodoxy and Catholicism, the most important Polish feast is Christmas Eve. The number of courses served that night may run into two figures, to equal the number of Apostles. A typical festive meal may include three soups, among them a beetroot consommé and a potage of mushrooms; three fish preparations, including herring and, famously, carp baked in a dark sweet-and-sour sauce with rye bread and vinegar and raisins; a dish of braised red or green cabbage; cheese-filled pastries; and various sweet things, such as noodles with poppy seeds and honey, stewed dried fruit and heart-shaped biscuits. The occasion is surrounded by Christian and pre-Christian rites, though these are dying away. Remnants from the meal used to be left outside to placate the wolves, and blades of hay were laid under the tablecloth for the girls to tell their fortunes. The meal began at dusk, as soon as the evening star appeared, with the children posting themselves outside to look for it:

Slowly the village was vanishing in grey snowy shadows, melting away; neither huts nor fences nor orchards could be made out; only a few lights twinkled, more thick than usual, because everyone was busy preparing the meal of Christmas Eve.

In every cabin, from the richest to the very poorest of all, preparations were being zealously made; in each family room, at the corner next the east, they had placed a sheaf of corn; the tables were strewn with hay beneath blanched linen napery; and they looked out eagerly through the windows for the appearance of the first star.

The sky, as is often the case when it freezes, was not very clear when evening began to fall; and it seemed to veil itself as soon as the last glow had burned out, and was hidden in the gloom of many a dusky wreath.

Yuzka and Vitek, terribly chilled, were standing outside the porch. . . .

'There it is!' Vitek suddenly exclaimed. 'There it is!'

Boryna and the others, and Roch last of them all, came out to see.

Yes, it was there, and just in the east, having pierced through the sombre curtains which hung round about it: it shone forth from the dark-blue depths, and seemed to grow larger as they gazed upon it; gleaming brighter and brighter, nearer and nearer, till Roch knelt down in the snow, and the others after him.

'Lo, 'tis the star of the Three Wise Men,' he said; 'the Star of Bethlehem, in whose gleaming our Lord was born. – Blessed be His Holy Name!'

. . . Their hearts throbbed with tender gratitude and glowing faith, while they received and absorbed into their hearts that pure light, the sacred fire – the sacrament to fight with and to overcome all evil!

... 'And now that the Word is made Flesh,' said Roch, 'it is time to take our meal.'

Wladislaw Reymont, *The Peasants*

As the Christmas menu shows, the Poles like sweet food even when the meal is nominally savoury. They share a predilection with the Czechs, Germans and Hungarians for fruit with everything: in soup, in sauces and in *Mehlspeisen* like dumplings and pancakes.

The idea of lightness flits across Polish food and quickly vanishes. The Poles like sweetish, copious and substantial food, which is the view many of us have generally of Central European cooking. Many traditional Polish recipes overlap with and have influenced Jewish cooking. Not being averse to bulk in noodle and dumpling design they closely resemble the Czech. Waverley Root writes that the Central Europeans are people 'living in a continental climate, receptive to bulky, filling foods with scant regard for coarse or insipid flavour'. (To clarify, they hardly care if their food is coarse.) It is one weight of cooking, if not one style. Predominantly, what has become known to us is the cooking of the middle classes, whose recipes were set down in huge tomes early in the last century. The Mrs Beeton of Poland was Lucyna Cwierciakiewiczowa. 'Her recipes were aimed at the abundant eating habits and ostentation of the Polish gentry and well-to-do urban classes,' I am reliably told.

The Polish idea before a battle, a hunt or celebration, for amusement, for company or for show, was to eat a lot. In Falstaffian medieval days big eaters were considered the healthiest men. A related practice of excess amongst the old nobility was the use of spices. According to a proverb, 'more expensive the seasoning than the food', they showered pepper and cloves, saffron and cinnamon and raisins on everything, in order to display their wealth.

The Poles like a lot of meat, and their high requirements have become politically controversial in recent times of austerity. Many of us could exist quite happily on what a Pole would consider meagre rations. The excess has deep roots. When the Italians came to Poland in the sixteenth century, in the wake of the marriage of their princess, Bona Sforza, to

Central Europe

Leningrad

Baltic Sea

Gdansk

Vilnius
Smolensk

EAST
Berlin
GERMANY

Poznan
Warta

Vistula
Warsaw

Neman

POLAND

Odra

U S S R

BOHEMIA
Prague

Cracow
GALICIA

Kiev
Dnieper

Danube

CZECHOSLOVAKIA

MORAVIA

UKRAINE

Carpathians

Dniester

Chernovtsy

The Alps

Vienna

Bratislava

SLOVAKIA

Tisza

BESARABIA

Budapest

Drava

HUNGARY

Szeged

TRANSYLVANIA

Cluj

ROMANIA

Prut

Odessa

Po
Venice
Trieste

SLOVENIA

Zagreb

Mures

Transylvanian Alps

Galati

Rijeka

Sava

Belgrade

Rome

CROATIA
Zadar

Sarajevo

Adriatic

Mostar

Sea

Dubrovnik
Cetinje

YUGOSLAVIA

SERBIA

Nis

Durres
Tirana

Skopje
MACEDONIA

Iron Gate

Bucharest

Danube

Sofia

BULGARIA

Plovdiv

THRACE

DOBRUDJA

Constanta
Black

Varna
Sea

Balkan Mts

Istanbul

Aegean

Sea

Athens

Mediterranean   Sea

0   300km
0   200 miles

Sigismund, the Polish heir to the throne, they could not believe
how much meat these people ate. To be fair the Italians, who
tend in the opposite direction, were more likely to be surprised
than the British or the French. Our standard lies somewhere
in the middle.

The Poles, though, listened to the Italians, and a marked
southern influence came into Polish cooking from that time, at
the same time as the idea of eating in small courses arrived. Bona
Sforza from Milan brought southern vegetables that were
planted in the gardens of the Royal Court in Cracow, and ever
since all green vegetables have been known in Polish as
wloszczyzna, 'things Italian'. This much-appreciated queen also
introduced the Poles to pasta and probably to ice-cream and to
the rich pastries in which they now excel. The famous Polish
'baba' is based on the Milanese *pannetone*. The Poles' marked
Latin taste, distinguishing them from Russia and Germany
either side, is also perhaps underlined by the passion with which
all sections of the population took to coffee in the first hundred
years of its arrival from the East in the mid-eighteenth century.
It was accompanied by a positive hatred of tea. As a fanatical
priest of the day put it: 'If China sent us all her poisons, she
could not harm us as much as with her tea.' Tea only slowly
made its way, encouraged by the Russian partition. Chocolate
was a high-class alternative.

Nowadays one of the most pleasant ways to while away time
in Warsaw is to sit in a café over black coffee and strudel or
cheesecake or a poppy-seed roll. It is quite legitimate in such
boudoir-like establishments to read or write and to be in no hurry
to move on, and the same may be said for the tea-rooms that
dispense glasses of various steaming black and green teas with
cinnamon, cream or lemon.

Since so much of the Polish tradition in food has been
continued in exile, it is worth observing the Polish cafés of
London. Daquise in South Kensington has been serving 'Polish
and Russian specialities' and good coffee since the war. Here and
in the various cafés and restaurants exiled Polish communities
abroad so carefully maintain to preserve the national spirit, the
management and the language and much of the food remain
Polish. Daquise, however, is exceptional in having always
invited in addition a non-Polish, often distinguished and

fashionable London clientele. It has that cosmopolitan spirit which has always accompanied Polish nationalism. Manager for over twenty-five years, Serge Ganjou, now in his eighties, remembers in the 1950s and 1960s offering 'the best pastries in London', baked by his Polish chef, which 'had the Rolls-Royces and Bentleys queueing up outside'. It is a nice twist of food history that when the original chefs became too old, Ganjou, a man who made his international career as a dancer and acrobat and prides himself on a refined, well-travelled palate, turned to London's Italian bakers to provide Daquise with 'Polish' rye bread and cakes.

The Poles export a lot of food, and anything to do with cakes and preserved fruit, jam, honey, pickles, ham and other pork products is worth pursuing for the quality. At home Poland produces excellent yoghurt and fermented-milk products. There is not much scope for drinking wine, except imported, though there is a tradition of wine bars, such as Fukier's in Warsaw, where wine is drunk Italian-café style in large tumblers, without food. Here again you may feel the force of the old, lingering cosmopolitanism which is nowadays so frustrated. The true Polish national drinks though are vodka and beer, or, as a speciality, mead. The prevalent sweetness or sweet-sourness at the Polish table does not complement the grape, and wine does not naturally belong in its cooking.

East Germany

East German food is traditional German food without the American and immigrant influences that have changed the face of West German culture since the last war. The result is an old-fashioned, solid cuisine made of rich ingredients and served in some quantity. German cooking everywhere is workmanlike and of a consistently high quality and tends to sit on its laurels. It has a homely quality, even in restaurants. Communism has not much dented this tradition, for East Germany has a thriving economy that can supply a cornucopia of foodstuffs. Every

German town has laden shops and busy traditional takeaway stalls selling sausages and doughnuts and, latterly, pizza, and stand-up snack bars, *Imbissstuben*, for those who cultivate the industrious life from breakfast to early evening. Nourishing, solid sit-down food during the day and evening is to be found in the taverns and excellent station restaurants, and wherever there is a town hall one can be sure the catering in the cellar restaurant will be exemplary. Something distinct about East as opposed to West German cooking however is that it is not a wine-based cuisine. There is a definite gastronomic partition of greater Germany where wine begins to come second to beer. That part east of the Elbe, which has been the German Democratic Republic since 1949, produces some wine, in the south, but the product is greatly inferior to the wines of the Rhine and the Mosel and the Neckar in the Federal Republic. My experiences of Algerian red and GDR white were equally dire.

The menus in the town-hall restaurants are typical of good daily middle-class fare. These *Rathauskeller* are as vast, cavernous and dark as their name suggests. The atmosphere is warm and busy at the long trestle tables. One can drink beer, or wine, or tea or coffee, or have a meal. This will usually be one course, served on a laden plate and accompanied by a sweetish dressed salad on a separate dish. The most popular fare is some variety of fried or poached sausage or fresh or cured pork (*Eisbein*), with fried potatoes (*Bratkartoffeln*) or sauerkraut. It is said the Germans probably learned from the Romans, who also brought them Christianity, how to make sausages. Sauerkraut, prepared with many different liquids and spices, and served cold and hot, sweet and sour, was a very early borrowing from the Slavs, who in turn learned the habit from the Chinese. The Germans have made themselves such modern masters of *la choucroute* that even the French have been forced to concede its good-value tastiness. As for pork, Berlin specializes in a yellow-pea purée with bacon, and much use is made of bacon fat and lard in all cooking. Schnitzels of pork, either in breadcrumbs or a sauce, are also popular, as is veal and sometimes game. For those who want soup, the *Rathauskeller* always have on their menus *Gulaschsuppe* and *solyanka*, a very popular borrowing from the Soviet Union. In the north, under the Scandinavian influence, close to the Baltic coast, one can usually eat good fish in restaurants and station buffets.

Interestingly, because of a similar confinement to root vegetables such as one finds in Poland, and made worse by poor soil, fruit long ago became the most popular accompaniment to meat, poultry, game and even fish. Cooked fruit is either incorporated in the recipe or served as a tart side dish. Home cooking meanwhile favours thick soups with lentils and beans. Padding comes from dumplings, pancakes, noodles and rice, but most important of all in the north and centre is the potato. The Germans share with the Czechs something approaching a passion for this import from the New World, foisted upon them in the late 1700s by Frederick the Great at a time of famine. Scepticism among the eighteenth-century peasantry rapidly gave way to enthusiasm when it was found the new vegetable not only grew well in the poor soil and cold climate of the North European Plain, but tasted so fine it positively warranted the name *Kartoffel*, adapted from the Latin and meaning 'little truffle'. Recipes came into being for the various potato salads, with sour cream or oil and vinegar, with various herbs and vegetables, which are still considered ideal festive fare whatever time of the German day or evening. Of this kind of fare, produced between meals as well as at them, all healthy men and women wishing to remain slim should beware. As a young teenager I was unable to squeeze back into my jeans after a fortnight of such rich and kind German hospitality. Food is produced at all times, at meals and between them, especially over Easter, when I made my first enlarging stay.

No one goes hungry later on, but as a rule of thumb German catering tends to emphasize the importance of food in the early part of the day. Breakfast anywhere is an unrivalled spread, with yoghurt and buttermilk, warm boiled eggs, hard cheese and cheese spreads, many varieties of sliced or spreading sausage, jam and the Germans' uniquely flavoured curd cheese, Quark. Accompanying these will be dark pumpernickel, perhaps leavened black bread, and certainly the daily staples, grey bread, mixed bread and white rolls. Hotels and private houses also offer cake for breakfast, and fruit, with tea, coffee or cocoa to drink. Children are often given cocoa for breakfast, and since it was introduced to the rest of Europe in the eighteenth century, when for many years it was only afforded by the rich, it has counted as a most sustaining source of nourishment. Goethe, poet, dramatist, novelist, scientist, artist and wanderer, did not spend much of his waking time considering food, but accepted from a friend the tip of drinking cocoa in the morning before travelling. He discovered it was the one substance which kept him going through the day. It is not uncommon to see people taking alcohol for breakfast, beer for the men, brandy for the women. Bismarck once said: 'If a German wants to be properly conscious of his strength he must first have half a bottle of wine inside him – or better still a whole bottle.' How much one is expected to eat at that hour may be gauged by the average allowance for a Western tourist in the German Democratic Republic, which in 1986 was eight East German marks. A pot of standard coffee, typically with evaporated milk in a separate jug, together with an egg and several slices of bread, butter and honey, barely took up half the allotted sum. In hotels all the breakfast items are priced individually and one serves oneself. The remaining four marks was enough to make sandwiches for lunch.

 The generally cold evening meal, taken early, is but a shadow of breakfast, with bread and cold-cuts and cheese and pickles. A formal meal would, it is true, take such a cold spread as only its first course of *Vorspeisen*, to be digested with short draughts of neat spirits such as *Schnaps* (German eau-de-vie). But in daily practice there is usually nothing of more moment to follow than soup. In home circumstances the spirits too may be tamed by being poured into a cup of black tea.

German food has stubbornly resisted French influence. One result is the large breakfast, another is the peculiarity of not serving coffee after meals, a third is the persistence of German in all menus at every level, so that typically the diner is faced with the prospect of *Brandteigkrapfeln*, not *profiteroles*. The German, though, is invariably more graphic a description of the food in question. *Brandteigkrapfeln* immediately makes clear that a special dough is involved, namely one cooked on top of the fire, or, in our own opaque French words, *choux* pastry. The coffee business can be more vexing. Often one has to leave a restaurant and find a café if coffee is an immediate digestive requirement, for it may not be available in the same establishment. The Germans congregate in cafés and *Konditoreien* a couple of hours after lunch, when they enjoy their celebrated gâteaux, strudels and cheesecakes with their two-cup *Kännchen* on a tray. Regular German coffee is strong filter coffee, but made with plenty of water. *Mocha*, closer to an after-dinner espresso, or to an unsweetened Turkish coffee, is sometimes available in hotels. For those with a sweet tooth an alternative to the café is the *Eisdiele*, which serves ice-cream topped with whipped cream. The pleasure of such a visit is sometimes reserved for the evening, after a cold supper.

The afternoon institution, of coffee and a chat (*Kaffeeklatsch*), not restricted to women, reaches its acme in the chic cafés in the centre of rebuilt East Berlin. These warm and cosy public parlours, best described by the untranslatable word *gemütlich*, attract huge custom with their newspapers on sticks and little alcohol. It may be an odd feeling to sit in upholstered luxury alternately reading the state-controlled pro-proletarian press and staring out of immaculately polished plate glass at the Alexanderplatz, which teems with commuters, anti-Fascist memorials and flowers, but this is the new Communist order with a vengeance, and prosperous East Germany is unique in representing it. It combines affluence with hard-line politics. On my first visit to East Germany, in Leipzig, I was struck by the degree of what I would call middle-class sentiment that went into the partaking of food. This is not to register disapproval. There, out of Goethe's *Faust*, and with life-size statues of the master and Mephistopheles at the door, alongside 'the Enchanted Tipplers' was *Auerbachs Keller*, a historic subterranean establishment serving everything from a cup of 'Lady Milford' tea to a full meal. Tea is associated with the English eighteenth-century aristocracy, while the history of coffee in Germany is celebrated at the famous *Zum Kaffeebaum* coffee-house, with a painted three-dimensional sign of a Turkish imbiber outside and the reputation of having gathered great names in literature and music, not least Liszt, Schumann and Wagner, within.

In food matters the sound economy affords GDR citizens leisure and money to spend on inessential interests like culinary history. The six provinces that now make up East Germany, Brandenburg, Mecklenburg, Pomerania, Saxony, Silesia and

Thuringia, date from the time when Germany was a conglomeration of principalities, and they all have their regional gastronomic specialities. At the time of writing these are being officially revived and encouraged in the GDR and the varied ingredients needed are amply available in ordinary shops, health shops and specialist herb-and-spice shops.

German food history is not, I think, exceptional. Like everyone else who could afford it, the Germans ate and drank too much in the Middle Ages, and indulged in lavish ceremonies, despite the counsel of the Minnesänger, which was 'discipline and moderation'. At lavish weddings and to show off the wealth of traders, meals of many courses were served; there are instances in the fourteenth century of the dishes being brought in on horseback. Singing was a feature of the merry table and also the clinking of glasses, a habit Germany gave to Europe. It is a cuisine that has never undergone a Latin renaissance.

Czechoslovakia

Czechoslovakia, never a country to lose touch with Western Europe, or to seem too exotic, nevertheless has an inimitable Slav character. Its cuisine needs modernizing to make it lighter and healthier and less time-consuming, but it is a source of good and economical new ideas for those interested in plain, nourishing cooking. The food is a mixture of northern and southern ideas, with a strong concentration on beer. Bohemia industrialized rapidly and prosperously in the nineteenth century, leading to the emergence of a middle class well versed in the arts of pleasurable routine. The soil is rich, yielding exceptionally good grains and pasture land everywhere. Czech food reaches its traditional, solid, bourgeois best with an extravagant expenditure of meat and butter, eggs and cream. Without modification it can prove impossibly fattening.

The flavours are strong, with one recurrent pair, bacon and caraway, used the way the Italians employ olive oil and basil and the Russians sour cream and dill, to characterize many dishes.

Cabbage is richly complemented by the sweetness of marjoram. Anchovy is used to heighten the flavour of beef, and all dishes abound in sour cream. As in the other Central European countries, Poland and Germany, root vegetables are widely used and mushrooms are dried and pickled as winter delicacies. Beer and yeast are prominent flavours in composite dishes.

Habits and flavours change as one goes south, however, and properly one should speak of the individual cooking of Bohemia, Moravia and Slovakia, rather than of Czechoslovakia, a political creation that only came into being in 1918.

Bohemia was a sophisticated, enlightened state that lived through a Golden Age in the 1300s, when it boasted one of the earliest and finest universities in Europe. Its food developed under Austrian influence. By contrast, the lands to the south, whilst speaking a virtually identical language, spent 1,000 years, until the First World War, under Hungarian and, indirectly, Turkish dominance, and their food took a different course. Dishes now popular all over Czechoslovakia, like goulash and stuffed peppers, entered the cuisine through Slovakia, as did cooking with wine, while the grand tradition in baked goods and tortes (layer cakes) came from Bohemia, modified by the style of Middle Eastern pastry-making from the south. The north was responsible for the passion for dumplings of every conceivable size, filling and variety, held to be a national food today, while the south flourished on rice, cornmeal and pasta.

The eating day throughout the country begins with breakfast, which, whilst not as lavish and well-organized as in Germany, can still be a substantial meal, with eggs and sausage and cheese. Therefore, for many people away from home, just as in Germany, lunch may be only a snack from a takeaway stall, sausages with mustard or a hot filled doughnut. These pavement snacks are generally taken outside, even in the depths of winter. The habit chimes oddly with our French-influenced idea of a picnic as a highly organized *déjeuner sur l'herbe* and the British don't find street eating entirely good manners. But probably no Czech would think sitting on a cold, windswept beach or at a busy roadside, eating sandwiches suffused with sand or exhaust fumes, superior. There again the contemporary Czechs seem to me to have that rushed attitude to food we in Britain dislike about ourselves and I am inclined to agree with Escoffier:

Czech students revel in Vienna, 1840. Bibliothèque des Arts Décoratifs, Paris (photo: J.-L. Charmet)

The culinary art depends on the psychological state of society ... wherever life is easy and comfortable, where the future is assured, it always experiences a considerable development. On the contrary, wherever life and its cares preoccupy the mind of man he cannot give to good cheer more than a limited place. Oftener than not, the necessity of nourishing themselves appears to persons swept up in the hurly-burly of business not as a pleasure but as a chore. They consider lost the time spent at table and demand only one thing: to be served quickly.

In Czech restaurants soups, casseroles and schnitzels are always good, and if you feel like something plain it is invariably possible to order a plate of bread, preserved salads and pickles and cheese and cold meat. The cheese is either a yellow all-purpose cheese of slight maturity but considerable firmness or the Carpathian brine cheese called *bryndza*, which is like Greek feta. Clear beef soup with liver dumplings has been declared the national favourite. Other good soups are made with mushrooms, with beer and egg, and with dried beans. The Czechoslovaks share with traditional Jewish cooking a taste for goose and beef and carp in sweetish sauces, and a liking for pancakes and beans and *latkes*, which are fried cakes of grated raw potato. Being a land-locked country their fish cookery is not the best, except in the Slovakian capital Bratislava, when the trout is fresh from the Danube.

All Czechoslovakia drinks beer. As in Germany and Poland the predominantly sour-sweet food, consisting of dense, whole-grain dark bread and rich pork, sausage and sauerkraut dishes, requires beer to accompany it. The famous Pilsen brew comes from Bohemia and the taste of it endures in the many soups and casseroles made directly with beer or flavoured with yeast. But it is important to note, as in Germany, where the beer line falls. The grape, accompanied by a marginally lighter, spicier food, comes into its own on the slopes of Moravia and Slovakia. The white wine is light and flowery in the neighbouring Austrian style, and probably best enjoyed away from the table. Both regions also produce a red. Locally, wine is served from the cask.

In general, peasant food has prevailed throughout the country. The typical dishes are robust, poor man's food, supplemented by the over-rich food poor men like to eat on feast days. Czech dumplings, *knedliky* (the word is closely related to the German *Knödeln*), are served both sweet and savoury, in soups, or sliced with meat and gravy, or with melted butter or a sweet coating of honey, nuts, poppy seeds or cinnamon. It is a mark of the peasant diet still predominating in all the Central European countries that the staple foods are interchangeably served sweet or savoury, with sugar or with animal fats, as a main course or a second dish, day or evening, to fit in with whichever foodstuffs are available to provide the necessary calories to work. These basic foods, mainly made with flour, are called *Mehlspeisen*, literally 'foods with flour', in German and the term applies throughout the old Austro-Hungarian Empire. The sweet or fat pattern applies, for instance, to the East European treatment of pasta. A far cry from today's Italian practice, noodles are as likely to appear for pudding with honey and poppy seeds as they are as an accompaniment to meat and sauce. There is a similarly hazy line drawn between sweet and savoury porridge, gruel and soup. The tradition in rural districts of Bohemia is still to eat soup, albeit perhaps a milk or grain-and-water soup, at all times of the day, including the early morning. Some soups included in modern Czech cookery books still betray the impoverished peasant life in being little more than caraway seeds or garlic and bread and water. Old habits evidently die hard, even if more affluent conditions apply for most people.

At the sweet end of the scale both Czechs and Slovaks are devoted to cakes and pastries, many of which are also categorized as *Mehlspeisen*. In Bohemia the tea-rooms and coffee-houses are the places to eat strudels, puffs, biscuits, yeast buns called *kolacky* and other confections made with apple, plums, chocolate, nuts, honey, curd cheese, spices and poppy seeds. Most cafés nowadays offer either normal or sugarless cakes, which is a blessing. Cakes are also available in the child-and female-oriented milk-bars all over the country, along with ice-cream and soft-drinks, and the elderly often go there too. In fact in this self-segregating country everyone seems to congregate in these bright little oases of sobriety except working men. The spear side is to be found in the packed, smoky, canteen-like atmospheres of unpretentious restaurants and pubs.

As in Poland, an intense nationalism attached itself to Czech food in the nineteenth century. The author of the best-known Czech cookbook, Bohemia's answer to Mrs Beeton, Magdalena Dobromila Rettigova (1785–1845), was a key literary figure in the National Revival. She also wrote children's fiction and generally on social topics. A different personality in the same spirit, and another pioneering woman writer, was Bozena Nemcova (1820–62) whose best-known work, *The Grandmother* (1855), chronicled, against the tide of fashionable foreign habits, some of the customs attaching to food in daily life in Bohemia. Nemcova's 'novel' was a semi-autobiographical account of life divided between the gentry manor and the peasant hut in the Sudeten Mountains of north-east Bohemia. The grandmother was the repository of the sound old ways which were expounded to the countess, a benevolent, Austrian-educated painter who represented her class in being privy to the drinking of coffee and chocolate and being removed from the wisdom of the soil.

This, dear Countess, is some caraway and some agrimony. The caraway is dried, the seeds used in cooking and in bread, and the straw for the children's bath; the agrimony is very useful as a gargle for a sore throat . . .

Nemcova, the illegitimate daughter of servants to the nobility, with a book-reading father who encouraged her education, had lived as a teenager with the educated family of the steward of the manor. There she immersed herself in German and Czech literature and felt the tension between native Bohemian and incoming Austrian ways, which went deep enough to threaten the steward's marriage. It was the steward, also a reading man, who did much to encourage her intellectual progress, and for Nemcova their friendship was the first of numerous love affairs. She wrote of that marriage, into which she injected the dissension dividing her own parents:

His wife was in no way congenial to him . . . She was a Catholic, he a Protestant who hated priests . . . Then too he preferred Bohemian cookery, while she prepared everything according to an Austrian cookbook. When he would not eat, her eyes filled with tears as she said: 'Aber, August, es ist ja gut, iss nur!' ['August, please, just try it, it's good, honestly!'] to which he usually replied, 'Ich glaub's, liebe Netti, habe aber keinen Appetit.' ['Dear Netti, I'm sure it is, but I'm not hungry.'] Then he smiled grimly, arose, drank a glass of wine and went into the fields . . .

It is often emotion rather than major culinary distinctiveness that separates one cuisine from another in Central Europe, emotion that makes quarrels and principles out of matters of taste. On the other hand, exactly what Nemcova's father objected to in her mother, whom city life in Vienna had changed from being a bright peasant girl into a stiff lady of few words and great austerity of morals and behaviour, made Austrian food different: it was a more refined and cosmopolitan cuisine than the Czech. Vienna was the place where in food terms Slav habits were smoothed out for Western consumption and Western ways brought new richness and variety to the table, with salads and vegetables and a French emphasis on beef. Nemcova *père* wanted the food of the land in which he lived.

The Grandmother discusses many foods and food customs: bread, sour soup, poppy-seed buns, cabbage and dried peas; the picking and drying of young leaves for soup in spring, of fruit in summer and the killing of the goose in autumn; the wearing of rosemary by the bridegroom and his horses on the day of the wedding; the old custom of greeting strangers to the house with bread and salt going out of fashion with the smarter classes, and the elaborate baking with honey done for Christmas and Easter. These are festivals followed with some intensity, with many similar rituals to the Poles, concerning the importance of the Christmas Eve supper (which was not, however, meatless) and the table laid around the Paschal lamb. Children were told that if they fasted the day before, they would see golden pigs flying through the room on Christmas Day. The emphases and flavours of food today have not greatly changed, except that there is very much more meat in the average diet and less ceremony.

It is curious to see Nemcova described by a modern Czech historian as being a convinced disciple of Rousseau's teachings, for the back-to-nature organic-food movement in the West is of course similarly inspired. Because of the slow pace of social and economic change in the East Bloc, the retarded ways of one half of the continent have come to meet the advanced fashions of the other. Natural-food addicts are regularly delighted to find most whole grains and many unprocessed foods on general sale in East European grocers.

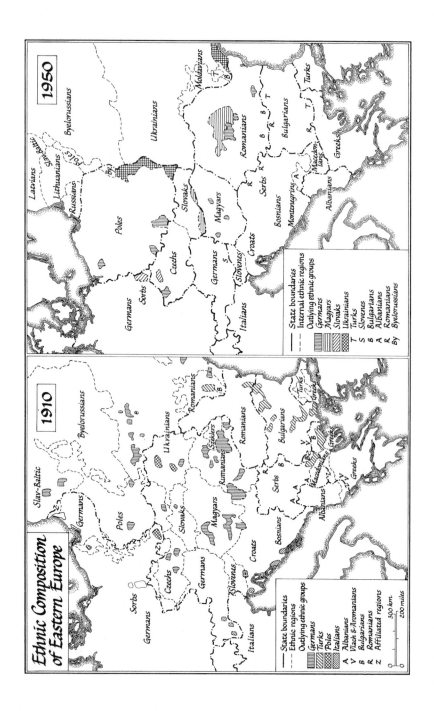

Ethnic Composition of Eastern Europe

1910

1950

Hungary

The French must always be our masters.   Károly Gundel

Hungary lays claim to being one of the great cuisines of the world, and it certainly has been in the past: once in the fifteenth century and once between 1870 and 1939, its *belle époque*. The cooking of this small country of 10 million people has however greatly diminished since the arrival of Communism. The Hungarian-born connoisseur Egon Ronay has located the lowest point in the 1970s:

When I visited Hungary in 1983, 37 years after I had emigrated, most of the restaurants were state-run. The once-brilliant catering standards had sadly deteriorated. So much so that when a friend of mine took her English husband on his first trip to Budapest in the seventies and patiently asked an old waiter to suggest a dish that *wasn't* 'off', he gave her a lugubrious look and said, 'Lady, if I were you I wouldn't eat here.'

Ronay noted however that some restaurants were returning to private ownership with spectacular results. We can only wait and see.

Yet on a lower scale of things, compared with its neighbours, Hungary is still the gastronomic treat of the East Bloc. It has a grand cosmopolitan tradition in food, has long enjoyed better stocked markets than most of its Communist neighbours and produces its own plentiful good wine. Menus are lengthy and varied. The Magyars' political fate of having been carved up by the Ottoman and Habsburg Empires, and ruled by a cosmopolitan elite, has led to a wide spectrum of dishes which has not been obliterated and is sure of having some appeal to outsiders of all tastes. In 1985 my student friends were unqualifiedly enthusiastic about the stuffed peppers, pancakes, sauerkraut and so on they could rely on in a bustling, thriving inn with checked tablecloths down a narrow side street in central Budapest. They were happy to take me there and indicated it would be my lack of discernment if I didn't enjoy

27

Leaving for the puszta, *1870* (photo: J.-L. Charmet)

the meal. Certainly I saw no better-furnished market in the whole East Bloc than the central covered market in Budapest, with its vast range of vegetables and spices, wines and spirits, meat and cheese, poultry and game and flowers.

A glance at George Lang's *The Cuisine of Hungary* (Penguin 1985), the classic gastronomic history in English, shows the diverse culinary influences of Germany and Austria, Turkey, Italy and France on the Magyar table. The very early, pre-Christian cooking had an Oriental-cum-Turkish aspect with its roast lamb, fermented mare's milk and glutinous meatballs, and these features coexisted with sour soups, associated with both the Turkish and the Slav kitchens, with creamy curd cheese, roasted fish on a spit, game and fish soups. With sauerkraut, sour cream and yoghurt in addition, Old Hungary was already drawing on a wide range of ideas. To drink, there was a most ancient, sweet fermented sap, known as birch water. (Birch-sap cordial is still found as a soft-drink in vending machines in Russia.) Original ways of preserving meat by drying also existed in early Hungary, and these as practised by the cowboys and shepherds have been seen as the origin of techniques used in *gulyas*. On these good native foundations therefore, and encouraged by a viticulture the Roman Emperor Probus established in the third century AD, Hungarian cuisine was set to grow.

Hungary embraced Christianity early in the eleventh century and was subjugated by the Mongols in 1241. There was some enrichment of the food repertoire in the later period at the expense of a vast deterioration in national well-being. Lang suggests the Mongols taught the Hungarians to stew lamb dry to release the meat juices, which was a significant new idea. But the cuisine did not emerge as distinctive and excellent until Hungary recovered politically and attained its greatest status in history as an international power, helped on its way by a fifteen-year-old. The boy who came to the throne in 1458, Matthias, was an exemplary noble, with wide, cultivated interests and a tireless zest for life. His favourite country was Italy, where he travelled and returned with a bride, Beatrice, the daughter of the King of Naples. When he was thirty-three, in 1475, they married, with a wedding feast whose plenty did not go unrecorded. It was a great event and also a watershed. Beatrice brought Italian chefs with her and they brought pasta, unusual cheeses, pastries, ice-creams, chestnut, anise, dill and capers. Beatrice asked her sister to send onions and garlic too. The royal household's refined and broad tastes improved Hungarian food and gave impetus to an entirely new cultural chapter in everyday life. Fine faience plates were produced, dining became formalized, table ornaments entered a new dimension of decorative craftsmanship, edible and inedible, and chefs were appreciated as masters in an acknowledged field of expertise.

When Hungary once again fell into political decline in the next century the foundations of the modern table – a blend of Asiatic, Italian and French ideas as served to the lords of the land, with weaker versions handed out to commoners at the manor – remained in place. The Hungarians were already cooking extensively with wine. They had the Chinese habits of combined cooking methods, e.g. boiling then roasting. They produced variations on the same ingredients by serving them in a 'long' or 'short' broth, akin to the distinction today between a *pörkölt* and a *gulyás*. And travellers talked of the fine natural resources of the country. Hungarian wheat fields on the *Puszta* or Great Plain yielded an excellent white bread of memorable flavour and texture.

In the seventeenth century the territory of Hungary was split between Habsburg Austria, independent Transylvania and Ottoman Turkey. The first two provided continuing contacts with the West, which generally had a mellowing effect on the native cooking, while the Turks brought techniques and ingredients inseparable from our understanding of the modern Hungarian table. They included flaky pies with their strudel pastry folded in layers, stuffed vegetables (though not stuffed cabbage, which was already known and had probably been received very early from China), also maize, cherries, coffee, tomatoes and paprika. These were vital new ideas, though paprika was slow to catch on, except among the common people. Meanwhile in 1686 the defeat of the Turks at Buda provided the chance for the Austrians to redouble their political and gastronomic influence over a greater part of Hungary. The influence was two-pronged: middle-class food became more and more Germanized, with a number of cookbooks in German, while upper-class food, because it imitated the food of the Viennese court, was Austro-French and very lavish. The first of the modern Hungarian chefs stepped in to establish order.

The first cookery book in Hungarian, subsequently reprinted many times, appeared in 1826. The quantities suggested in it look large to us, but the dishes are as familiar as in other European books of the day: sausages, roast chicken, dumplings, rich beef stews, sauerkraut, pike and oysters. Meanwhile the potato came into its own as a favourite staple food. Middle-class Hungarian food established a strong identity, and what also grew around it was an unaffected culture of eating out. Town and country inns were famous for their good, solid, traditional dishes, wine in earthenware pitchers, gypsy music and lively atmosphere. Much would be made of this in more self-conscious later days.

The Dual Austro-Hungarian Monarchy dates from 1867. The close coalescence of the partners meant Hungarian dishes began travelling to Vienna as well as vice versa. The two countries quickly came to share many cakes and a number of meat dishes

Engraving from Joseph C. Dobos, Livre de Cuisine Franco-Hongrois,
Budapest 1881 (photo J.-L. Charmet)

and Austrian cookbooks still often claim Hungarian specialities
such as Lipto cheese spread (they call it Liptauer), chocolate
salami and *palacsinták* (pancakes) as their own. It was through
Hungary that Austria acquired a taste of the Orient and through
Austria that Hungary renewed contact with Italy, four centuries
after the death of King Matthias. This juncture takes us more or
less to the present day.

Today Hungarian cooks' ubiquitous, characteristic use of
paprika, long ignored by the cultivated classes, is a mainstay of
the national cuisine. All Hungarian cooks feel they must explain
this powder to foreigners labouring under misconceptions.
Paprika is the sweetish, red, powdered seasoning, obtainable in
varying degrees of hotness, not necessarily hot at all, which
gives the many varieties of Hungarian casseroled meat their
distinctive flavour. I am assured by Joanna Labon, who lived for
a year in Hungary recently, that Hungarian food indeed only
tastes Hungarian when it is made with paprika from Hungary.

What reaches Britain is the sweeter, softer variety of paprika. The powder is made from the paprika plant, that is, from peppers strung up to dry by the hundred thousand from the roofs of houses in the areas around Szeged and Kalocsa. Forty thousand tons of fresh peppers give 7,000 tons of powdered spice. The Turks who brought the paprika habit to Hungary probably acquired it from Bulgaria. By the time paprika was discovered by the first theoreticians of national cuisine its popularity was widespread and genuine. It spiced the most famous offering in the Hungarian repertoire, the copious and fairly liquid meat casserole, *gulyás*. It turned up in the drier, oniony *pörkölt* casseroles and cream-based casseroles called *paprikás*. Hungarians sprinkled paprika over vegetables and salads to add flavour and they also liked the look of it. Dishes dressed with yoghurt or sour cream habitually acquired a few grains as a final picturesque garnish.

Hungarian food is also imbued with the flavour of tomatoes, but most characteristic is what it does with all the wine, paprika, onions and tomatoes it shares with other cuisines: this is where the very condensed, highly flavoured sauces such as those of the *pörkölt* become most representative of a soft, concentrated style of food preparation. These sauces add an almost Mediterranean touch, recalling the texture of a pulp of sweet tomatoes and peppers. Meanwhile the Magyar table is neither so yeasty nor so tart as much Central European food, and relies less heavily on pickles. It maintains the half-continent's predilection for sweet and sour, but has allowed a Parisian balance and smoothness of tastes to modify it. At the same time it has rejected from France the introduction of 'outside' sauces not formed from the main ingredients of the meal. A gastronomic spirit close to the Austrian shows in the use of well-flavoured dripping to thicken soups. The Hungarians also remain as keen as any country in Eastern Europe on sour-milk products and brine cheese, share in the Central European fondness for sausages and salami and use caraway seeds as a basic seasoning, along with flat parsley and dill. For centuries their staple padding was millet, which is still popular, but like Poland they supplemented it with pasta, the habit acquired from Italy some three hundred years before.

At the sweet end of Hungarian eating comes the superlative *pâtisserie*, influenced by both Middle Eastern and Viennese baking, and traditionally enjoyed at its best in two famous Budapest cafés. Gerbaud's, on the Pest side of the river, has been renamed Vorosmarty, but both it and the Café Russwurm, in hilltop old Buda, have been preserved as national institutions for the consumption of cake with strong black coffee, German–Austrian style, in the afternoon. Both these *confiseurs* were foreigners, Gerbaud from Switzerland and Russwurm from Austria.

Lang has a nice way of suggesting the faint decadence of heightened attention to food which took Hungary into the twentieth century. The people lost revolutions (in 1848 and again in 1918, the time of the short-lived first Hungarian Communist administration) while they won gastronomic battles. Hungary's share in Austrian political power, to help bolster Austria against the rising might of Prussia, led to the rise of important new dynasties at home – in the restaurant and hotel industry. The father of Károly Gundel ran the dining room in the Archduke Stephen Hotel, serving oysters from the Adriatic, sturgeon from the Danube, salmon from the Rhine, crabs from Lyublyana and Hungarian specialities, already well mellowed by the Austro-French influence. The menu reflected the size of the new Hungarian Empire, embracing Croatia as far as the sea and up to Austrian-ruled Slovenia. It was a far larger country than today, extending north into present-day Czechoslovakia and east into Romania.

The generation after the Austro-Hungarian *Ausgleich* produced three superlative chefs: József Dobos, who ran a delicatessen shop crammed with extraordinary edibles and drinkables from all over the world, prepared with painstaking attention to detail and window-dressing; József Marchal, chef to royalty through Europe and who became head chef of the Budapest National Casino; and Karoly Gundel, following in his father's footsteps and going on to write magisterial books. Now, as in France and Romania, writers and poets declared their interest in cooking and stationed themselves among peasant communities seeking the secrets of this or that dish. This was the gastronomic epoch that inspired the British monarchy and carried its charms to the cities of the world in Hungarian restaurants with gypsy music. Nothing seemed kitsch or overdone and the public watched spellbound as the beautiful princess Chimay eloped with the famous gypsy fiddler Rigo Jancsi. Hungary still trades on this reputation and of all the East Bloc countries one is still most likely to find a Hungarian restaurant abroad, encouraged to survive by enthusiastic local patronage. Yet Hungarian food never conveyed a deeper idea of nationality, unlike the food in Poland or, to a lesser extent, Bulgaria. It conveyed a playboy's way of life.

Substantial, rich Hungarian dishes of many subtly blended ingredients clearly appealed to Edwardian and Georgian England for their culinary quality, but the image of gastronomic Hungary soared way beyond the food. It was simply chic. The Italian-born chef Joseph Vecchi who had worked in two great hotels, the Kaiserhof in Berlin and the Astoria in St Petersburg, survived the Russian Revolution to return to London and open a restaurant in Regent Street. He had acquired a passion for Russian cooking, and served mainly Russian and French dishes with only a sprinkle of paprika here and there, but with an eye for fashion he called the establishment the Hungaria. The Hungarian government provided money, on condition only Hungarian wines were sold, and a Hungarian cellarmaster and Hungarian or Romanian gypsy musicians were brought over. Patrons included George V, who had a taste for vintage Tokai, and the future Edward VIII. The talk was, in Vecchi's own words, of current affairs and society. Whether consciously or not, what a slight that decorative, superficial use of paprika was!

No wonder the Communists were pleased to see this life come crashing down, at least in Hungary where they took power. Gundel lived through the upheaval and maintained a detachment which declared he would never be more or less than a gastronome who was not interested in politics whatever the ideologues might say. He was critical of lack of taste wherever it occurred. One year he was catering in the grand style to a Habsburg Archduke and the next to followers of the early Hungarian Communist Béla Kun, 'who would only eat the white stems of asparagus, because they considered the green tips inedible'. The right-wing politicians of a subsequent era, 'the White Terror', were no more refined: 'We had guests who ordered roast goose and ate only the wings and legs, because they thought the breast wasn't good enough.' Gundel was official caterer to this Horthy government and also cooked for

King Carol of Romania. During the war he served German officers at the front of his restaurant and Jewish friends in the back. In the battle for Budapest in 1944 he lost his fortune: gold tableware to serve 120 and a great collection of rare cookery books, not to mention a huge quantity of wine. Another consequence of the siege was the shedding of eighty pounds in weight. He watched as the good hungry citizens of Budapest began eating animals from the zoo next door to his restaurant. After the Communist takeover the almost normal-sized, impoverished Gundel, with two books on Hungarian cooking behind him, was allowed to leave and he retired to Austria in 1952, the year after his restaurants were nationalized. Thirty years later his restaurant has been revamped and his recipes reprinted. The desire to return to the old ways, culturally at least, is marked, but the economic reality makes it hard. Prices at the new Gundel's are way out of the price range of ordinary Hungarians, consequently too many waiters and not enough customers fill an uneasy, beautifully decorated circular room. Most of the diners are inevitably foreign. The zoo is still next door.

Romania

Bucharest is Babylon of the Apocalypse . . .

Florence K. Berger, 1877

Romania, next door to Bulgaria, sharing movable borders and the Danube basin, is an intriguing mixture of Latin and Slav culture. The straitened circumstances of the 1980s conceal a sophisticated Francophile cuisine grafted on to the Balkan habits of the people. As Sacheverell Sitwell expressed it after a good dinner, part of a rich visit in 1938:

There were little trout, fried like fresh sardines and eaten as an hors d'oeuvre, and a Romanian dish of chicken breast, minced and served in breadcrumbs with a sauce of sour cream. The white wine of the country was delicate and appropriately refreshing. This was, in fact, our introduction to the Romanian cuisine, a style of national cooking which is as distinct as the Russian and offering the same contrast of half-barbaric with sybaritic pleasures.

The French leaning matches Bucharest's long-standing desire to be a second Paris and has produced some notable Romanian gastronomists. More than anywhere, in Romania one can speak of a self-conscious, literary food culture which is most concerned with food and not at all with nationality. One of the first cookery books in Romanian, in 1841, with over 200 recipes, was the work of two writers, Mihail Kogalniceanu and Constantin Negruzzi. Aesthetic considerations have continued to bridge the gap between food and the written arts. The playwright, journalist and humorist Ion Luca Caragiale, always short of money, ran in turn a café, a theatre and the brasserie of the Romanian Academy, where he inevitably drew material for his stage satires on the ways of the emergent Romanian middle classes. Alexandru Teodoreanu was another journalist and humorist who became a leading gourmet between the wars, as well as a hotel manager and a poet; he wrote many short essays on food. The famous cafés and restaurants of Bucharest early this century enshrined the marriage between high-class Romanian-cum-foreign food and the middle-class interest in Romanian-cum-foreign newspapers, novels and avant-garde art. Capşa (pronounced 'Kapsha'), on the corner of Calea Victoriei, was the gilded, cushioned public salon where the best people ate the best cakes and ice-creams and the best writers and critics exchanged words.

Capşa is a Frenchman who has learned his duties as a cook-confectioner in some of the best houses of Paris, and coming to Bucharest he has brought French taste to bear upon the cookery of the country, and at his restaurant there is always a choice of dishes of Bulgaria [sic!] and of French plats ... The walls of the restaurant are painted to resemble green and yellow marble, and the pillars which support the roof are green with gilded capitals. A great white stove is the only un-Parisian object in the restaurant. There is a show-table on which cold delicacies and fruit are placed ... Many of [the clientele] are elderly, all are smart, and on race-meeting days the talk is of horses, for these well-groomed gentlemen are mostly owners of race-horses and members of the Jockey Club. Capsa, sharp-featured, wearing a little moustache and frock-coated, goes from table to table taking with him a dish of some cold delightful meats or a plate of exceptionally fine fruit to show his favourite customers. The prices are . . . Parisian.

Newnham Davies, *The Gourmet's Guide to Europe*, 1908

Freedom from Turkish suzerainty in 1877 was perhaps responsible for the very rapid acceleration of the city's capacity for sophisticated pleasure. Twenty years before Davies, the Austrian Rudolf Bergner described a typical dinner menu in Bucharest as being much the same as in Vienna or Berlin, but cheaper: pilaf with chicken, spit-roasted chicken, baked sweetcorn, baked cascaval cheese with eggs, *sarmale* (stuffed cabbage leaves), *ghiveci* (vegetable stew), stuffed courgettes, chicken with okra. The meal would begin with *mastica* or *tuica* and end with Turkish coffee. For an elegant man, breakfast was at midday, lunch at five, leaving him free to enjoy the evening before supper.

It says much about the food culture of Romania that one needs to begin by talking about restaurants. The accent is away from home, the very opposite of Germany. Travellers curious about the extravagant atmosphere that had become a legend in Europe feared pickpockets and, as Miss Berger said, Babylon; they came to see gypsies and dancing bears and people who were 'on holiday about 210 days of the year'. Of the many injustices and imbalances built into this extraordinary cosmopolitan, quasi-Oriental society at the end of the nineteenth century, the gypsies were the cooks and music-makers and virtual slaves to the Romanian well-to-do. The simple folk did the dancing and had on their side the legends of the *haiduks*, the bandit heroes celebrated in national song, who took food and wine without paying for it. Meanwhile in reality the rich men and princes owned the shops, which they stocked with luxury foreign items and the produce of their estates. The peasants acquired what they needed from the land and by barter. The situation continued into the first three decades of the twentieth century.

Then the war came, followed by the arrival of Communism and the abdication of the king. The social bottom dropped out of the literary-cum-gastronomic market, began to rise again in the late 1960s and early 1970s, but has sunk again today. Romania is poor as poor, albeit stylish in poverty. It is sad that neither the general lot nor the state of the cuisine and general culture have improved. Contemporary circumstances are no clue to past culinary achievements.

The immediate post-war period was fascinating. The Hungarian restaurateur Károly Gundel was working in Bucharest where Anna Pauker, the only woman in the new Communist government, used to dine. Both sides were critical of the new social style this woman seemed to represent, and she herself was described as afraid of the revolution she was helping to impose. The men who supported her in politics rejected the style of femininity she brought with her. Albanian leader Enver Hoxha criticized her for having her hair boyishly short. Gundel's verdict, regarding every sphere of life to which she might apply herself, was that she lacked good taste. The young Jack Lindsay and Maurice Cornforth were more sympathetic. Their description of the affected, posturing past that had to go evoked the most sordid splendour:

As the bourgeois Rumanian state unsteadily developed, with foreign capital flowing into the exploration of the oil resources, the new City of Pleasure expanded – with its violent contrasts of extreme poverty and luxury, its famous nightclubs and confectionery shops, its bitter roadways of ragged workers and bony horses; Lipscani Street with its litter of merchandise, lacemaking, banks, and, past the planes of Sf. Gheorghe Square, wretched starveling workers with no work, lost Hungarian servant-girls, dwarf houses sunk under advertising signs, gypsies with lupus-eaten noses ... while in Capşa's or Zamfiresco's *confiserie* actresses, police spies, rich ladies, amiably nibbled honeycakes.

In 1953, when it had gone, their view of Bucharest was no less imaginative on the progress of social equality:

Now, while the Attenée Palace hotel remains as splendid, the guests and diners are not like those who gleamed, scandalmongered, committed adultery and spied here from 1910 to 1944 – delegates of all countries (who range from factory workers to poets and philosophers, from housewives to women scientists), intellectuals and stakhanovites of Rumania itself, young couples out for a specially fine dinner. One night there is a huge dinner celebrating some Hungarian journal's anniversary, the next day one sees a large group of Chinese youth. In what was the smart Cina restaurant, where once a worker would not even dare to peer through the glass, one now sees a Pioneer lad come in and say he wants to use the lavatory, or a peasant woman sit down for a *sirop*. Outside the red flowers burn in the gardens, but the bronze of Carol I is gone. The *Bonjouristes*, who did not deign to speak their native tongue, are gone . . . Bucharest belongs to the people and they love and enjoy it.

Rumanian Summer, 1953

For hundreds of years Romanian territory was ruled by the Phanariot Greeks on behalf of the Ottoman lords. The Phanariots inspired the love of France but, as in Bulgaria, the influence of the Turks was also profound. They introduced to Romania the habit of eating appetizers, called *meze*. Bean salads, raw salad vegetables, baked and dressed aubergines, yellow and brine cheeses, ham and sausage, vegetables preserved in oil and herbs and, above all, fish delicacies, provide the opening to a Romanian meal. Most celebrated is carp's roe paste (*icre*), a kind of caviare, served alone with bread or with marinated cold fish.

In other dishes the abundance of vegetables and fish is pronounced. Fish is baked, stuffed with vegetables, or embedded upon vegetables; or it is braised in a casserole with onions, peppers and tomatoes, or made into a thick soup. Carp, pike, tuna, bream, perch, sterlet and sturgeon are all found in the Danube. A dish similar to the Bulgarian vegetable casserole, with an almost identical name, *ghiveci*, is a ratatouille-style medley of vegetables, sometimes including meat, or mushrooms, and potatoes, and eaten hot or cold. It is said each family has its own *ghiveci* recipe and all good cooks know instinctively what is the right combination of vegetables in the right proportion. Vegetables are eaten fresh in season or baked and stuffed, and they are preserved in winter.

In the cold weather Romanian cuisine takes a Slavonic turn. Soups often have a tart flavour from lemon juice, beer, vinegar, sour cream or fermented fruit or vegetables. A sour soup is made from lamb and flavoured with lovage. The prized dish of stuffed cabbage leaves, *sarmale*, as in Bulgaria, uses fermented or fresh leaves. Fresh and fermented cabbage are also braised with sour cream, for which there is some fondness, leading to its being used to bake meat, fish and poultry, thicken sauces and soups and dress salads. But Romanian food is not generally as heavy as Slav cooking and is well-accompanied by the excellent local red and white wines and 'champagne'.

Romanians are proudest of their grilled meat, of which they consider *mititei*, garlic-flavoured skinless beef sausages, traditionally served with preserved peppers in oil, the finest example. *Mititei* are equally welcomed in informal eating and on the grand table. Some lamb or mutton is eaten, and chicken is popular, roast and served with preserved fruits and vegetables, or stewed in a casserole with vegetables, or fresh fruit, or with olives and wine. Chicken livers are easily come by and often served fried. Duck is also appreciated, treated in the same way as chicken. Hungarian influence has brought in goulash-style stews of beef. But the most widespread red meat cooked and eaten is pork, whether in steaks, in casseroles or in the form of spiced sliced sausage. In the case of pork one finds the Romanians doing a rare thing for them and cooking in beer. Pork fat is also often used in cooking instead of oil.

By way of padding Romania shares with Italy a virtually unique passion in Eastern Europe for boiled cornmeal. This is *mamaliga*, better known to us under its Italian name, polenta. For more than two centuries it has been the peasant staple. The fluffy yellow mixture, cooked firm and left to set, is eaten with dishes with plenty of sauce or with a topping of cheese, butter, tomato, fried onion or bacon. Or it can be formed into balls stuffed with ewe's cheese and baked, as in *balmus*. Alongside rice and potatoes *mamaliga* supplements or takes the place of Romania's white and dark breads. Romanian cheese, although good in salads, is not distinguished, but baked on top of or inside *mamaliga* to give the Romanian cooked equivalent of a pizza or toasted cheese it proves very satisfying.

Fruit – plums, cherries, apricots, peaches, berries, apples – is plentiful in season and well preserved in syrup or made into jam. Plums are used to make the national cakes, *cozonaci*, and the famed eau-de-vie, *ţuica*. Olives add a Mediterranean touch to *meze*, salads and cooked dishes.

Fruit, nuts, excellent local honey, jam and cottage cheese go to make many sweet preparations. Romania finds itself at the crossroads of Austro-Hungarian and Middle Eastern influences and has taken the best of both worlds. Sweet dishes served after a meal include pancakes (*clatite*) filled with cottage cheese or jam, or eaten with sour cream, noodles with nuts or jam, sweet omelettes with fruit sauce, dulceata and fritters. The use of eggs in these light fried dishes reflects French influence, but the same cheese may also be baked into cheesecakes, Central European style. The Romanians are particularly proud of their flaky pastry, used to make both savoury and sweet pies, called *placinta*. In the cafés tortes and strudels rub shoulders with very sweet oily pastries made with honey, nuts and poppy seed. Coffee, sometimes a sweetened cappuccino, is drunk with cakes and pastries, and between or after meals Romanians also drink a great deal of Turkish coffee and sweet tea. Much business used to be conducted in the dark, crowded coffee-houses of provincial towns over this strong sweet black brew. They were centres of Jewish life in Romania before the war.

Transylvania

The steep, narrow Street of Grape-Sellers led to the new town [Sibiu] which had grown at the foot of the hill. It was market day and the street was lined with women standing or squatting by their grape-filled baskets. Above them the market place was crowded with *carute* [wagons or two-wheeled carts] before which were mountains of vegetables, brilliant splashes of colour rising from the cobbles. The Saxon peasant women were easily distinguishable by their flat straw hats with immense brims and their rather sombre clothes . . . Buying some grapes from them was my first introduction to them. They were not free and easy in their bargaining; they joked little and prospered exceedingly.

D. J. Hall, *Romanian Furrow*, 1933

This former kingdom, for a long time part of Hungary and now in Romania, in the sixteenth and seventeenth centuries performed an independent balancing act and held the key to

Street coffee vendor, from Jacques Le Hay, Recueil de Cent Estampes
Representant Differentes Nations du Levant, *Paris 1714*

unsteady stability when Vienna and Constantinople were the
vying superpowers in Europe. Though more famous for its
connections with Dracula, it forms a distinct gastronomic
region, made up chiefly of Hungarian, Romanian, Saxon
German, Jewish and Armenian influences. Unlike Hungary, it

knew independence under the Turks and for two centuries had greater international standing than the Magyar kingdom. It rose and fell, whereupon its rich lands passed to the Austrian crown and were later administered by Austro-Hungary. After Hungary's defeat in the First World War they were ceded, on the basis of a persistent claim dating back more than 2,000 years, to Bucharest. Not surprisingly, Hungary and Romania are inveterately hostile to each other's view of Transylvanian history, and this shows up in food as much as anywhere. Both staunchly include Transylvanian recipes in their national collections, quite rightly. An American *émigré* restaurateur, born in present-day Cluj, Paul Kovi, has, with his *Transylvanian Cuisine*, done his best to put the gastronomic historical record straight.

Both countries are right to claim Transylvanian recipes, because in practice one finds the different cooking styles side by side, along with a rich legacy of outside influences. Amongst the earliest foreign settlers, in the Middle Ages, were the Saxon Germans, and Germans came again from Schwabia in another wave of emigration in the late eighteenth century. The main Transylvanian towns show considerable German cultural influence, strengthened by the nearly two centuries spent under Austro-Hungary, and some regions, around Brasov and Timisoara, are partly German-speaking. Apart from Romanians and Hungarians, and even leaving aside the ethnic Germans (now a dwindling community), the Transylvanian population today is made up of at least twelve tiny minorities, all of which affect the food. Kovi defends the attractive theory that a very early and still palpable influence on Transylvanian cuisine came from China via the spice trade. He cites the coincidence of dishes like pork, cabbage and crayfish and the abundant use of ginger and saffron. The food is hot, but not nearly as fiery as in Romania nor so pervaded by paprika as in modern Hungarian cooking. An additional style of cooking and preserving came in with the Armenians and with the Turks, and it is the Turks who are said to have set the Transylvanians drinking black coffee sooner than the Viennese. Meanwhile the influence from the Near East is not as pronounced as elsewhere in the Balkans. And lastly, on an independent note, Transylvania being a rich agricultural land (hence the early arrival of Western settlers and the many quarrels over possession), its cuisine most often reflects abundant local resources: corn, aubergine, fruit. Nowhere else has quite the taste in seasoning for tarragon, caraway, savory and mustard. The favourite meat is pork, except among the Jews, who have helped enrich the repertoire of vegetables, fish and goose. Sour cream is used, but no yoghurt; wine, but little beer; wheat, rye, maize and barley, rice at the encouragement of the Armenians; cabbage is a most important vegetable. The Armenians have encouraged a liking for nuts and honey, which inevitably means Oriental-style pastries have their place, and they also favour beef; the Saxons cultivate bacon and dumplings, and insist on leavened bread. Yet in the end it is not actually a matter of ingredients, more one of spirit. Transylvanian cuisine is far removed from the cuisines either side of it, the Mediterranean and the Slav, and its variety can only be rivalled by that of Eastern Europe as a whole.

Bulgaria

I have memories of scrambling into the top bunk of the sleeper train from Sofia at midnight, clutching my daughter in one hand and a warm packet of boiled sausage, bread and cucumber in the other. Not much is known about Bulgarian food beyond the reputation of its yoghurt, but actually, when one is not dependent on the station buffet, it is one of the world's simplest, healthiest and most naturally elegant styles of cooking, akin to the cuisines of Turkey and Lebanon. The seasoning is light and the accent on preserving natural flavours. It is the very opposite of the 'concentrated' food of Poland. The mountainous country of 8 million, bordered by Greece, Romania, Yugoslavia, Turkey and the Black Sea, is hot, with fertile valleys, and broad plains. The land, which the Ancients called Thrace, yields abundant green vegetables and fruit; Thrace was believed to be the home of the god of vegetation and fertility, Dionysus. The Black Sea is rich in fish, providing both the livelihoods and the staple diet of the conglomeration of nationalities living along the Dobrudja

A meal by the Bosphorus. From Antoine Ignace Melling, Voyage Pittoresque de Constantinople, *Paris 1819*

strip. The famous Valley of the Roses, planted at Turkish instigation in the 1600s, traverses central Bulgaria west to east, and is the home of the highly precious oil, rose attar, giving rise to a small industry in soap and rose liqueur.

Among the many features of the modern Bulgarian table likely to appeal to Western tastes are the appetizers or *meze*. The word comes from the Turkish and many of the dishes have a Middle Eastern flavour, including white beans and preserved vegetables in olive oil, peppers, olives, tomatoes, spicy sausage (pasterma), hot pastry and deep-fried savouries in batter, green onions, cucumber, yoghurt, pickled cucumbers and a white, very salty, fresh cheese like the Greek feta. Herbs – thyme, tarragon, basil, savory, mint, dill – are widely used, both fresh and dried, to flavour salads and in curing or preserving cheese and meat. Flat and leavened bread, white and brown, accompany *meze*.

The sausage, salami, cheese, yoghurt, vegetables and fruit that characterize this very natural table first appear at breakfast, along with yellow cheese and a number of other excellent fermented-milk products that confirm Bulgaria as a worthy home of the supposedly life-enhancing *bacillus bulgaricus*. Meat, often lamb, is simply prepared, by grilling on charcoal or spit-roasting. Out of minced meat the Bulgarians make spiced meatballs and rissoles which are baked or grilled, and cubed meat (*kebap*) is cooked in the same way or baked with vegetables. The results avoid undue greasiness.

Chicken and game are relished, and a festive speciality is stuffed white fish with nuts and raisins. Probably the best-known dish outside the country, and one promoted as national, is *gyuvech*, a sealed casserole of up to twelve different vegetables, with or without the addition of meat or fish, and sometimes with a garnish of grapes. When one lifts the lid on this dish and takes in the aroma and the rich, natural taste, no more vital contrast with the cooking of Central Europe to the north is imaginable. To think of Poland in winter and Bulgaria in late spring is like comparing Siberia with the Garden of Eden.

Because of the fertility of the soil both the Scandinavian and the African floras flourish. Rye, barley, wheat, corn and oats grow alongside abundant soft and hard fruits and green and root vegetables. The list of produce from the Bulgarian vegetable garden is long and celebrated: aubergines, tomatoes, peppers, onions, garlic, okra, green beans, cucumbers, courgettes, beets, potatoes, corn, spinach, radishes, lettuce, sorrel. The French Romantic poet Alphonse de Lamartine, in his *Journey to the Orient*, quickly sensed the natural prosperity of a garden land whose single disadvantage was to be under a foreign yoke for 500 years.

The land inhabited by [the Bulgarians] would have promptly been transformed into a fine garden but for the ruthless and stupid yoke which did not allow them to cultivate their fields with a greater degree of security. They have a passion for their land.

A Mexican visitor after the last war, in the years when Bulgarian agriculture was being boosted with modern equipment and new investment, was rightly struck by the similarities with his own country. He noticed the maize and paprika which 'can only suit the palate of a man steeled by a fiery sun and a land of bronze . . . all this is offered to us under the blue sky of a landscape blessed by the light of the Mediterranean and the mildness of the Black Sea.'

Once again, food, and in Bulgaria's case the natural favours bestowed upon the land, have not failed to enter the national consciousness as a source of unity and consolation in the face of lack of national autonomy:

. . . with all its hardships bondage has yet this one advantage: it makes a nation merry. Where the arena of political and scientific activity is closely barred, where the desire of rapid enrichment finds no stimulant, and far-reaching ambition has no scope for its development, the community squanders its energy on the trivial and personal cares of its daily life, and seeks relief and recreation in simple and easily obtainable material enjoyment. A flask of wine sipped beneath the cool shade of the willows by some clear murmuring rivulet will make one forget one's slavery; the native guvetch with its purple egg-plants, fragrant parsley and sharp pepper-pods, enjoyed on the grass under the spreading branches overhead, through which peeps the blue distant sky, constitutes a kingdom, and if only there be gipsy pipers present, is the height of earthly bliss. An enslaved nation has a philosophy of its own which reconciles it to its lot. When a man is irretrievably ruined, he often puts a bullet through his head or ends his life in some equally rapid and decisive manner. But a nation, however hopeless its bondage, never ends its own existence: it eats, drinks, begets children. It enjoys itself. If one but looks at the poetry of a nation, one finds clearly expressed the national spirit, the nation's life, and its views of existence. There, amid cruel torments, heavy chains, dark dungeons, and festering wounds, is yet interwoven the mention of fat, roasted lambs, jars of red wine, potent raki, interminable marriage feasts, and mazy dances on the green sward beneath the shade; these form the subject of a whole anthology of national songs.

Ivan Vazoff, *Under the Yoke*, 1889–90

This joyful materialism of a land of politically emasculated epicures is abundantly evident under Communism. Since the early 1980s private plots have been encouraged by the otherwise collective-minded government, and Bulgarians relish the opportunity to grow and harvest their own produce. Let a Bulgarian buttonhole you in the street and he will tell you about his garden. The abundant soft fruit of early summer – cherries and strawberries – ripens in May, and is followed by the seasons for peaches, apricots, plums, apples, grapes, figs, quinces and, finally, olives. Nuts, especially walnuts, are widely cultivated to add to soups and sauces and cakes. Out of them is also pressed a high-quality culinary oil often preferred to sunflower and olive oil.

A special preparation is *banitsa*, consisting of wafer-thin layers of buttery pastry enclosing a filling of spinach and cheese or ground meat and cheese with herbs. Savoury, it is like a pastry version of lasagne; sweet versions come with nuts and cheese or jam and cheese, or pumpkin. *Musaka* is another well-known composite dish of baked meat and vegetables and herbs, sometimes topped with a savoury custard or yoghurt, which the Bulgarians share with the rest of the Balkans. For padding they enjoy pilaf, the rice staple of the Middle East, in both sweet and savoury forms, with raisins and with poultry stock and onions. Rice, which since the First World War has been intensely cultivated, is also baked into milk puddings, another style shared with the Turks and the Lebanese.

Restaurant fare is generally as simple as the food made at home. Eggs and vegetables can be ordered from most menus, separately or together, and it should always be possible to have some vegetables served raw. Though fish is little-known inland, and not popular because the river fish tend to be very bony, on the coast pike is a firm white fish worth looking out for. It may be used to make a casserole with white wine, paprika, garlic and a lot of onions, called *yakhnya*, or a fish *gyuvech*. In the open-air taverns in small, non-tourist-oriented Black Sea towns, however, probably all that will be available at lunchtime will be plates piled high with small fried fish, to be eaten with chunks of white bread and washed down with beer or wine.

Bulgaria has one of the lowest per capita meat consumption figures in Europe, akin to Greece and, beyond Europe, to Egypt. The habit of making cold 'continental' sausages and salamis to eat with bread was learned from the Germans. The association of ideas is sufficiently understood that it is quite natural for a Bulgarian to refer in song to 'Deutschland' as 'Wurstland'. A pig is slaughtered for Christmas eating, along with venison, and through the year pork, veal, beef and lamb are eaten in moderation. It is not uncommon for meat to be cooked with fruit, for example veal with quinces, but the result is far from the sweet-sour products of Central Europe. To continue sounding the note of simplicity, one of the most surprising aspects of traditional meat cookery and Bulgarian cuisine in general is the absence of sauces. Thus, when the venison is cooked for Christmas it is only marinated and roasted and then served dry with cooked vegetables.

The Slavonic influence in Bulgarian cuisine is not pronounced, despite the proximity to Russia and a strong cultural affinity, since Bulgaria gained freedom from the Turks with Russian help in 1876. The affinity is most marked in the shared customs of the Orthodox Church at Easter. The Bulgarians bake a yeast-leavened cake, *kozunak*, the equivalent of the Russian *kulich*, and likewise serve with it a sweetened cream cheese. Orthodox Bulgarians also kept the pre-Christmas fast and the Great Fast through Lent. A Bulgarian friend in London remembers the pain that faith exacted: three foodless days before Christmas and seven before Easter. But generally the food is not at all Russian; neither caviare nor *kasha*. These extremes can be taken literally as points of comparison. Sturgeon swim up the Danube and in some Bulgarian rivers, but for many years, while caviare became a luxury commodity in Europe, exported from Russia and from neighbouring Romania, Bulgarian peasants shunned those black eggs as unacceptable to eat. What *kasha*-like grain porridges are eaten are either of un-Russian cornmeal, as in Romania, Hungary and Serbia, or of leftover bread. My Bulgarian acquaintance, Pashanko Dimitroff, describes his version of the latter, *popara*, in such rich terms that it seems most like a cheese fondue in which several of the guests have lost their bread, and not at all like a bowl of pap.

The Bulgarians share a passion evident throughout the Balkans and the Slav countries for stuffed fresh or fermented cabbage leaves, and they also stuff every other kind of vegetable and fruit from quinces to peppers, tomatoes to aubergines. The Slav element is perhaps more evident in the sweet-sourness of traditional soups, though in Bulgaria the souring agent tends to be lemon juice or yoghurt, which gives a lighter and more delicate flavour, closer to Middle Eastern taste. There is hardly a sign of the vinegar, pickling juices and sour cream used in Central Europe and Russia, except in winter food such as dried-bean broths. Traditional all-year Bulgarian soups are made with predominantly southern ingredients like spinach, lamb, olives, rice and lemons. The most famous is *tarator*, made with cucumber and yoghurt, thickened with ground walnuts and served cold.

Albania

Like Bulgaria Albania until the twentieth century had no royal court to introduce foreign eating habits to the ruling class for the sake of prestige. Up to 1912 the rulers of this diverse country at the lower end of the Adriatic, opposite Italy and wedged between Yugoslavia and Greece, were the Turks. From that date until the arrival of Communism in 1946, the country was prey to Italian invasions. Much of the country is mountainous, though more and more land has been brought under cultivation in recent years, by means of irrigation and the draining of marshes. The narrow strip of plain along the sea coast is a naturally rich, arable area, with the greatest density of population and agricultural and industrial yield. According to official figures, the land under cultivation has increased two and a half times since 1938 and agricultural production multiplied by five. Today, with a population of 3 million, Albania declares itself self-sufficient in food. Realistically this means some belt tightening towards the end of winter and into mid-spring, for the cuisine is wholly dependent on the seasons rather than imports, but it remains primarily an agricultural country. I happened to visit Albania in September, which was, at the opposite end of the scale, the high season of locally harvested food. Peppers, tomatoes and aubergines abounded, with goat's-milk brine cheese, eggs, pasta, rice, dried beans and unadulterated bread. There was yoghurt, a wonderful green olive oil, some passable red meat and chicken, good fish – we ate grey mullet from the sea and carp from Lake Shkodra – and to highlight the Turkish legacy wonderful sweet Oriental pastries and *lokum* (Turkish delight) followed at the table and in the streets with fat bunches of green grapes and slices of refreshing watermelon.

Albania produces its own citrus fruit, also wheat, maize, barley, oats, rye; and sheep and goats graze in its fields. I am outlining a cuisine which, like a house in the same condition, has the appeal, but also the disadvantages, of being wholly unmodernized. Coffee Turkish-style is as likely to be off in a café as on, and there is no guarantee of getting even a sandwich. Communal cooking is still practised. The women take their pans of stuffed peppers and bread to the bakery, which functions like a community centre, with pictures from Albanian magazines and photographs of the late leader, Enver Hoxha, around the walls.

The faith of the people is, or was until official atheism was declared in 1967, predominantly Muslim, with some Catholicism in the north and Orthodoxy nearer Greece. Much cooking is done with yoghurt and milk, little with alcohol; more lamb and beef are eaten than pork. Good wines are produced in collective vineyards everywhere, however, and an eau-de-vie and a raki which have some appeal abroad. There are one or two hot spiced pork dishes favoured and developed by the non-Muslims, with plenty of paprika, garlic and onions – and some similarly seasoned rich bean dishes shared with the Serbs. A hallmark of savoury dishes as well as sweet is the use of cinnamon. Much rice is eaten and *kabuni* is a pilaf thus flavoured. As in Bulgaria, there is a liking for skewered meat or meat braised in small chunks, and for lemon juice to flavour soups and sauces. The herbs most often used are mint, followed by dill and parsley. The art of preparing stuffed vegetables may have been learned from Greece, though it is equally shared with Yugoslavia to the north. Flaky *boreks* sold in *borek* cafés everywhere are the equivalent of the Turkish pies of the same name, and the Bulgarian *banitsa*. *Borek* is one of the few words I managed to recognize on a three-day trip, along with the beautiful-sounding *ushqimore*, meaning grocers. Albania is a place to eat Middle Eastern pastries: with sugar syrup, with nuts, with raisins, honey, occasionally with sweet soft cheese; with fruit preserves. The ice-cream is very sweet and may be flavoured with cinnamon.

The nearly thirty years of this century when Albania was virtually an Italian province have left their mark on architecture and food and probably on other aspects of the culture which I cannot appreciate. The recent influence redoubles the effect of contact with the Venetians 400 years earlier. You can sit in the Daiti Hotel in Tirana, which was built for Mussolini and remained for many years under Italian management, and enjoy coffee and pastries in cool, airy lounges that have lost their glamorous top polish but remain elegant with their wood panelling and high ceilings. The garden is tall, dark and lush and the entrance is hidden from the road, in stark contrast to the more modern international hotel in the centre of Tirana, open to the world. Yet there is nothing unrefined about the service and atmosphere of the newer hotel, where you or anyone else can sit on the terrace with fresh orange juice and watch Tirana go by, mostly on foot or by bicycle. The relaxed Italian and Middle Eastern cultures here have naturally coalesced. Only, don't stir the orange juice, for you will find several tablespoons of undissolved sugar at the bottom of the glass.

The Italian gastronomic influence is most apparent in the pasta, the sauces of wine and tomatoes, and the seafood soups and fish stews. Albania probably first encountered tomatoes, potatoes and maize via Italy.

It is difficult to find Albanian recipes, for there is no book on Albanian food in English, nor (that I have come across) in any other foreign language. 'Albanian dishes have just enough to distinguish them from those of their neighbours and former foes,' writes Kay Shaw Nelson, in which case the style of food seems to be imbued with the same pride and desire for independence in fairly hopeless circumstances as the style of Albanian politics. Though Communist and officially atheist, the national ethos is still inspired by a Muslim grace and aesthetic restraint. Hoxha once said: 'Even if we have only bread we will still decorate the plate we serve it on.'

Yugoslavia

The food and cooking of Yugoslavia contain the exciting variety of the whole continent and could form the basis of a delightfully varied gastronomic tour. Like Czechoslovakia, it is a composite country that only came into existence in this century, but the diversity of peoples and cultures is far greater. Three separate languages, two alphabets and three primary religions span its six republics and two autonomous regions. Mountainous and rugged, where communication is still difficult, it contains extremes of climate from Alpine uplands to the Pannonian continental plain and is bordered by Italy, Austria, Hungary, Romania, Bulgaria, Greece, Albania and the Adriatic. On the Adriatic coast the climate is Mediterranean, a host to olives and lemons and cacti. Childhood sweethearts carve lasting initials on these prickly pears. In the south the Mediterranean influence continues inland, following the rivers, into Macedonia, giving rise to a special climate suited to growing Oriental plants such as sesame, aniseed and peanuts.

Beyond geography the republics tend to take their characteristics from the culture that ruled over them before independence: Austria in Slovenia, Hungary in Croatia and Turkey in Serbia, Montenegro, Macedonia and Bosnia Herzegovina. Intermittently for hundreds of years the Italians have also played an important part in the fate of the Yugoslav seaboard, and all along the coast from the Istrian Peninsula to Montenegro their influence is strong. The Italian style in food persists into Slovenia, the Alpine republic next door to Austria, where it blends with the Central European tradition. The Serbians in the east cook Balkan fashion, but with the addition of some originally Hungarian dishes. Their preference is for pork, whereas further south-west in Bosnia Herzegovina and Macedonia the Islamic religion and Turkish legacy favour lamb.

The Yugoslavs follow the general Turkish-inspired Balkan habit of preparing *meze*, which they eat with their famous plum brandy, *slivovica*. These appetizers include small pieces of fried liver, cheese, nuts, raw and pickled vegetables, spiced preserved meat, small cheese-filled flaky pastries. A special delicacy is

A Montenegrin interior, 1858. Bibliothèque des Arts Décoratifs, Paris (photo: J.-L. Charmet)

Dalmatian *prsut*, a dark smoked ham, like the Italian *prosciutto*, sliced very thinly and eaten on bread. As throughout the Balkans, all cooks delight in the abundance of vegetables like green beans, corn, peppers, tomatoes, beets, green onions and aubergines, to which are added goat's-, ewe's- and cow's-milk brine and various yellow cheeses.

Composite Balkan dishes range from pilaf and *musaka* to stuffed vegetables (*dolma*), including cabbage *sarma*, stuffed vine leaves and stuffed onions, a ratatouille-style *djuvec*, related to the Bulgarian and Romanian dishes, and goulash. There are also Middle Eastern influenced casseroles consisting of lamb and green vegetables very slowly cooked, a special Bosnian stew of meat and vegetables called *ionac* and an intriguing composition of minced veal flavoured with lemon and hibiscus and pepper. Meanwhile everywhere one finds grilled spiced meatballs, *civapcici*, and *raznjici* and *sis kevap* are ubiquitous popular varieties of meat grilled on a skewer. ·Slovenia specializes in a preparation of roast beef with onions and spices called *stajerski kostrun*, and various cutlets and schnitzels of pork and veal. Turkey with pasta is a holiday speciality in Croatia, while a fine Dalmatian dish, *pasticada*, simmers beef in wine with bacon, garlic, spices and prunes.

Generally the Yugoslavs like food highly seasoned with hot peppers, garlic and onion. Dried beans are made into soups and casseroles, but most happily of all are eaten with pork and hot red peppers. The Slavonic contribution to their cooking is most noticeable in the soups, which have the familiar sour finish. These are generally made with sauerkraut, dried peas and beans, barley, meat and poultry, and mushrooms. Yoghurt, sour cream, buttermilk and the Serbian speciality *kaimak* (thick cream made from boiled milk) are used alone or to accompany various sweet and savoury salads and cooked dishes. A fine savoury combination of pastry and meat or cheese and vegetables is to be found in the flaky pie borrowed from the Turks, *burek*.

Cornmeal is cooked as in Romania and in the Croatian capital Zagreb it is baked into a layered delicacy called *koruzna potica*. In Slovenia because of the mixture of cuisines, one sees *calamari* (stewed squid) and sauerkraut offered side by side. The Italians have also made pasta and pizza, albeit made with brine cheese, very popular. Meanwhile the Pannonian Plain is a bread-basket. If one travels to Belgrade by train from the north, the bright yellow sea of corn and rye, dotted with the coloured garments of workers, seems to stretch for hundreds of miles in each direction. The country can also boast every variety of light and dark bread, from the whole-grain mixtures, sometimes including buckwheat, of Slovenia, to the flat white bread of the south.

Yugoslavia probably offers the best fish cookery of Eastern Europe. Croatia specializes in seafood, most simply mixed and deep-fried in batter, Italian style, and served with lemon. Further south the influence of Venice, which once ruled Dubrovnik, has made itself felt over 500 years with seafood soups and grilled specialities. *Brodet* is a stew of several kinds of fish in oil, wine, onion, garlic and parsley. Inland in Croatia and Slovenia substantial dishes are built around freshwater fish from the lakes and rivers. There is also a strong tradition, less within reach of the casual visitor, of eating large and small game, thanks to the rich stocks of the forests, mountains and valleys.

It is a tribute to Yugoslav viticulture that a wine can be found to suit most of these diverse dishes, from the excellent Teran red of Istria to the powerful black wine of Dalmatia and the light, Austrian-style Rieslings, which also come from the Alpine republic. Dalmatia produces a famed dark red and powerful wine called Dingac. From Herzegovina comes the excellent dry white Zilavka, while Dalmatia produces the more flowery and sweeter Traminac and Silvaner, close to their German namesakes Gewurztraminer and Silvaner. Prosek is an excellent dessert wine. Istria, the peninsula next door to Italy, has poor soil, but one of the few good things to come from it is wine. Besides *slivovica* there are many different liqueurs, including Travarica, *vinjak, lozovaca* and *maraschino*, and to the last various healing properties are attributed.

The Slovenes meanwhile claim they are the country's cake-makers, with a pride to rival Bohemia. Their tortes, and also their sweet noodles, fruit dumplings, doughnuts and biscuits belong to the Austro-Hungarian tradition and rival the Turkish-style pastries of Serbia. Sugar, dried fruit, fresh fruit and local honey are all used as sweetening agents. The Slovenian speciality is *potica*, a rich sweet strudel made with a leavened dough and baked, or sometimes boiled like a pudding. Fillings vary, but among the most interesting is soft white cheese with sugar and herbs, either dill or tarragon. Sometimes the flour used for boiling is buckwheat, also employed in little boiled cakes called *strucli*. Further south the typical dessert would more likely be *kadaif* (threads of sweet, fried pastry, coated with sugar), or *baklava* (flaky pastry with nuts and honey), or Turkish delight, or halva made from pulped sesame seeds, or a pudding of sweetened pumpkin. Thin pastry layers filled with sweetened soft cheese make up the well-known Yugoslav strudel pie called *pita*, which seems to combine ideas from various regions. Sufficient to say that everywhere baked goods are excellent. The ice-cream is also good, though very sweet. In Slovenia they have the German habit of topping it and cakes and modestly strong coffee with huge dollops of whipped cream, *Schlag*. Down south, where as elsewhere in the Balkans, the Turkish habit is practised of giving guests a little heavily sweetened stewed fruit and a glass of water to revive them in the heat, Turkish coffee is served more commonly than German-style or espresso.

Good food needs some freedom to flourish, whether it be the licence granted to a professional chef in a kitchen where no expense is barred and the diners are adventurous, or the scope of a whole country to refine and self-consciously enjoy its eating habits. Yugoslavia does not belong to the Moscow-centred East Bloc, which leaves it freer to decide its economic and political fate, and one can immediately see the benefits for gastronomy. While still nominally Communist, its borders are open and private enterprise is moderately encouraged. In public enjoyment of food this leads to a bearable tension between state and privately-owned establishments. It is usually resolved in the marked preference of the locals for the latter. Modern times have probably seen an improvement in the standard of restaurant cooking too, unlike any other country discussed in this book. While Newnham Davies described standards as dire at the turn of the century, after the war Lovett Edwards spoke of Belgrade as a city of gourmets. His theory could be tested by, as always, avoiding the big international tourist-oriented establishments and looking for smaller *kafanas* where the locals ate.

The East Bloc countries are perhaps not quite the uncivilized, grey and awful lands they are sometimes taken to be from afar. As a Czech housewife and free-thinker said to me while she was making the mutton and vegetable stew and washing the lettuce, having just got in from a French class and fed the baby, while her husband looked on approvingly: 'I often don't recognize Czechoslovakia in what gets written abroad. Daily life simply isn't that bad.'

When Communism has passed it may be remembered as a political outlook that cares little for, or attributes in theory a low priority to, the art and pleasures of the table, but the memory will be ironic. Its leaders have been satirized as being amongst the great eaters of the world, and quite representative of the older cultures out of which they emerged.

SOME NOTES ON INGREDIENTS

Bacon. Bacon is essential to the cooking of Central Europe, everywhere except central and southern Yugoslavia, Albania, Bulgaria and parts of Romania, where the Turkish-inspired tradition was to eat fowl and lamb, to add flavour with hot peppers and to cook in butter (Romania) or olive oil. D. J. Hall, an inspired English traveller in Romania before the war, described being shown round a Saxon German village in Transylvania. This was one of the southernmost points of bacon-based cooking and seemingly it was still defending itself against the encroachment of Oriental ways:

Hans Lienz showed us the fortress [built to fend off the Turks]. Nearly every Saxon village possesses one, and in many cases it is part of the church. . . . Inside were four stories, wooden ladders connecting them. Each one was filled with sides of bacon hanging from the rafters. Every piece had a label indicating the villager to whom it belonged. The tower was kept locked, and anyone wishing to cut a piece off his bacon went to the custodian, who came along to see that he did not take a piece from someone else's store.

The local style of cooking in Transylvania, as elsewhere, required however the flavour and fat of smoked bacon rather than the slab of lean meat the word bacon conjures up to us. If you intend to cook a lot of East European food it is worth saving bacon fat and rinds to flavour soups, cabbage, sauerkraut, dumplings, potatoes and home-made pasta. In Germany various kinds of *Speck* are sold for the purpose, these being solid blocks of pork fat with a rind and a thin stripe of meat running through them. *Speck*, found elsewhere under different names, is

59

A Polish market. Drawing by Daniel Chodowiecki, published 1770 (photo: Hulton Picture Library)

sold in a piece and cut into small cubes or chips about 1 cm ($\frac{1}{2}$ inch) long to fry and use to start a casserole or garnish a finished dish. There is no British equivalent and some of the subtlety of the different kinds of *Speck* is inevitably lost. Most economical are so-called bacon 'misshapes' or 'pieces'.

Buckwheat. Buy both the groats and the speckled flour in a health-food or whole-food shop, where you can also get **pot barley, millet groats, cornmeal, dried beans** and **rye flour**. Cypriot delicatessens also commonly stock **cornmeal** in a coarse or fine grind.

Chard. This is spinach beet, *beta vulgaris*, with a broad white leaf-stalk often eaten separately, and a dark-green leaf less acid than spinach. There is no real substitute.

Cheese. For the soft mild curd cheese used everywhere in sweet and savoury dishes, most British cookery books used to specify cottage cheese, but there was always the chore of beating this smooth first and at only 4 per cent fat it needed the addition of cream cheese. East European cooking in Britain has become much easier now that the ideal, medium fat (12 per cent) curd cheese, which can be frozen, is sold in many supermarkets. Failing that, Italian ricotta is wonderful, in many recipes rather too good, for curd cheese is a very routine ingredient. Yoghurt drained and dried a little or home-made milk cheese are other alternatives, though time-consuming and cumbersome to produce in sufficient quantities.

In the Balkans particularly, also further north, white ewe's-milk cheese is preserved in brine to make the kind of very tangy crumbly cheese known in Britain as Greek or Danish feta. This cheese has a different generic name (*sirene* in Bulgarian, *brindza* in Romanian) to distinguish it from hard yellow cheese and it is ideal for salads, pie fillings and for combining with spinach, potatoes, courgettes and other vegetables. Maude Parkinson, a gifted Irishwoman who taught English in Bucharest in the early part of this century, saw it being made:

The sheep were driven into a small enclosure at one corner of which was a flap-door. When the flap was raised, the sheep nearest the door saw a means of escape from its uncomfortable surroundings and made a dash for it, only to be caught by the hind leg by the man seated near, who did not let go till he had got every available drop of milk from the animal. On an average one could count upon half a glass of milk from each sheep. But the dexterity of the man in catching his prey, his skill in the quick milking of the animal in spite of all its struggles, then its final rush for freedom, were all very amusing to witness.

The cheese from this milk was packed oblong-shaped in bark, which gave it flavour, and sold in small quantities at a price reflecting the difficulty of its provenance. When the cheese reached the table it was sliced through the bark. Any feta can be substituted for *brindza*, or in salads try *ricotta salata*, which has a different taste but is very enjoyable. The trouble with such substitutions, however, is that they turn inexpensive everyday cooking from one country into showpieces in another. Given the risk of disappointment at the ordinariness of the dish demanding 'special' ingredients and effort, at a relatively high cost, a local equivalent would often be better. For brine cheese a white Cheshire, Caerphilly or Wensleydale cheese can be a good replacement, though these cheeses are far milder and less moist, not to mention less salty.

Still made from ewe's milk, but matured in the air, is the general Balkan yellow cheese, *kashkaval*. The word is originally Turkish and the same basic distinction between types of cheese applies throughout the Middle East. Kashkaval can be rubbery and bland, but at its best it is a whitish cheese of almost pearly appearance with a piquant taste. Buy it from Greek, Cypriot and Middle Eastern delicatessens. It is excellent for grating, toasting and frying. Thick slices can be coated in egg and breadcrumbs and fried. Fresh Italian *pecorino*, which is also made with ewe's milk, is an excellent substitute, though relatively expensive. A mixture of Cheddar and grated dry *pecorino* or parmesan (the cow's-milk equivalent) is a better solution for everyday purposes.

In both Central Europe and the Balkans the style of eating cheese is remote from the French and therefore from the English. There are few soft-ripened cheeses and no blue cheeses, except for the imitation Camembert, Brie and Roquefort which are now industrially produced. No hostess or restaurant would produce a cheese board towards the end of a meal. At most the cheese would appear as a first course or, most likely, as a snack during the day. But many regions have their ewe's- and goat's-, occasionally cow's-milk-cheese specialities. In Yugoslavia Pag produces a renowned fresh white cheese. In Romania some fine cheeses used to be made by the monasteries and were remarked upon by travellers. In Rucar, in the scenic Dimbovita valley between Bucharest and Piteşti, Sacheverell Sitwell came across 'a goat's cheese of indescribable delicacy that makes its appearance in round boxes of pine bark. A smoky, acrid, resinous, pinewood taste is the result of this.' No doubt this was a special goat's-milk version of *brindza*. Hungarian Liptó cheese, named after the region where it originated, is also a speciality ewe's-milk brine cheese, best-known as the chief ingredient in a spread made with butter, paprika, caraway and onion. The now commercially produced Liptauer, as Lipto was called when it was adopted by the Austrians, is based upon it and many other variations have sprung up. George Lang observes that the citizens of Trieste, which belonged to Austro-Hungary until 1920, used to make *their* Liptó by mixing gorgonzola with mascarpone and adding the onion and spices. That must be one of the finest examples of substitution by local equivalent.

Herbs. Fresh dill is essential to all East European cooking. Ask for it in ethnic-food markets, delicatessens and even the local greengrocer till you track down a source, then freeze whole what you don't need, for later use. An alternative is to grow dill on the window-sill or in the garden, though I have had little success with either growth or flavour in London. Dried dill weed is a third-rate alternative in soups and stews, but if it is used, it should be added at the last minute, before serving. My Bulgarian friends swear that the authentic taste of Bulgarian food depends on *chubritza*, which is the savory that grows wild in the Balkans. This is a sturdy bush quite easy to grow. The leaves can be picked fresh almost all year round and the plant gives white flowers and good ground cover. What savory is to Bulgaria, another lesser-known herb, lovage, is to Romania. Again, it is possible to grow these leaves, which smell like fenugreek, one of the ingredients in curry powder.

Kaimak. A rich cream/cheese that has a very mild taste when fresh. Aficionados describe it as margarine-and-honey-and-cream. It is made by skimming the layers of cream off fat boiled milk, salting them and letting them dry. Clotted cream or cream cheese with a few spoonfuls of sour cream can be substituted. Use it to moisten Balkan flaky-pastry pies or as a starter. Elsewhere in the Middle East it is known as *eishta*.

Mushrooms, dried. Available in any Polish food shop and other delicatessens, also the larger supermarkets. The price is shockingly high everywhere.

Sauerkraut. Buy Central European brands in jars from supermarkets and Central European delicatessens. **Pickled cucumbers** from the same stores should also be the East European variety wherever possible, for French brands are much saltier and have no dill.

Sour cream. Good sour cream is now so widely available that it should no longer be necessary to 'sour' fresh cream with a few drops of lemon juice. Anyway, the result is not the same. So-called sour cream is a culture like yoghurt and cream treated this way has a special fresh taste, hence the nearest French equivalent, *crème fraîche*. Both sour cream and *crème fraîche* also have fewer calories than ordinary cream of the same density, because their thickness comes from the culture. Polish and some other delicatessens and supermarkets sell *smatana*, which is specifically Polish sour cream. It is slightly thinner than the standard British dairy variety and most suitable for East European cooking. In some recipes where sour cream is used as a dressing, thick Greek yoghurt can be substituted. Romanian *smintina* is traditionally made with buffalo milk.

Spring onions. Use the whole onion, green part included.

Yoghurt. This is very widely used in Balkan cooking as a sauce either included in dishes of baked meat and vegetables, or to eat with them at the table. It is also delicious on its own for breakfast or with bread and raw vegetables as a starter or made into *airan*, a cooling, nourishing drink with soda water, like the *lassi* found in India and *laban* in Lebanon. In 1963 May Mackintosh described entering a Romanian village at dusk and seeing the whole village serenely drinking by lamplight, beer at the beer carts, yoghurt in the taverns.

The *bacillus bulgaricus* has drawn attention to the prominence of yoghurt, particularly in Bulgarian cuisine, since a French bacteriologist discovered it there in the nineteenth century. Its many rivals the world over have acquired enormous popularity in the last decades as much because of the health tag as the taste.

All the recipes in this book call for plain yoghurt. Greek ewe's-milk yoghurt, which has a fashionable following, will cater for them very well, but so will many supermarket products as long as they are not stabilized with gelatine. Most economical for otherwise simple recipes calling for a cup of yoghurt or more is to make it yourself, using a live starter and fresh milk. Heat 600 ml (1 pint) or more of semi-skimmed or whole milk for a few minutes and leave to cool until it is just warm to a finger. Mix a couple of teaspoons of ready yoghurt with a little cold milk, combine with the warm milk in a thermos flask, seal it, shake to mix again and leave for 18–24 hours. Turn the yoghurt into a pot with a lid and refrigerate. Home-made yoghurt is particularly suitable as a pouring sauce. The fatter the milk the less sour the yoghurt is likely to be, provided it has been made at a low temperature. Extra heat also increases sourness.

APPETIZERS
AND THE COLD TABLE

In Central Europe hors d'oeuvres, instead of or in addition to soup, betoken some formality. They signify an affluence, sophistication and leisure far removed from peasant tables. The case is different in the Balkans, where taking a little of several contrasting dishes is a common Oriental habit encouraged by the debilitating heat of the sun. But everywhere starters emphasize the ideal character of the meal: spacious, copious and unhurried in the centre and north, delicately balanced, sensual and comforting in the south and east.

Many starters are miniatures of main dishes, which help bring a range of tastes, textures and colours to the table without exhausting the appetite. They are time-consuming to prepare as part of a larger meal, but a chance to show *savoir-faire*. Home cooks will probably find different uses for them. Many people seem to enjoy several small dishes in place of a well-flanked main course. The recipes here are mostly traditional lunch or dinner overtures, but they are infinitely adaptable as brunches, light lunches, high teas, bar snacks, 'theatre' suppers, even picnics.

Romanians have a particular love of their *mezelicuri*, eaten with *tuica*, dry plum brandy. An English traveller before World War II discovered the custom when he dined in the company of the poet Mihai Codreanu:

We began, of course, with glasses of tuica, that plum liqueur whose colour is so deceptively white [sic], for as it gallops down your throat, a gorgeous herald of the meal to come, it flashes on its way in dazzling colours, crimson and azure and gold. We divided one glass of tuica from the next with delicious little meatballs that we seized with a toothpick, and among other items claiming our attention were pickled mushrooms, pale brown and a delicate pink, olives of the right oval shape, caviare direct from [the Danube Delta fishing port of] Valcov and beyond all praise, thirst-producing anchovies so that we drank more tuica, tiny hot sausages, little cheese wafers made by the fairies and homely radishes to bring us back to earth and other things and slices of hot goose-liver on toast ... Mr Codreanu, who sat next to me, declaimed a sonnet while the soup was being brought ... then came a dish of minced meat wrapped up in very young vine leaves, during which Codreanu was good enough to declaim for me another sonnet ... next came some stuffed veal ...

Henry Baerlein, *In Old Romania*, 1940

The Romanian cold table should be refined and tantalizing. Typical seasonal ingredients include nuts, black and green olives, goat's- or sheep's-milk cheese, kebabs of minced or unminced meat, round and sausage-shaped rissoles, pieces of fish or small whole fish, fish roe, liver, brains, white and brown beans, young vegetables, raw and cooked, little flaky-pastry pies (*borek*), and various purées, usually fish or vegetable, into which bread is dipped. Ready additions might include garlic sausage, salami, sunflower or watermelon seeds, fresh or pickled cucumber, tomatoes and grapes.

Bulgarian *meze* are generally less elaborate, with the accent on the goodness and variety of local vegetables and fruit, and on milk products. Bowls of plain yoghurt are usually available on café and hotel menus for breakfast or as an impromptu appetizer.

In Yugoslavia a meal might start with yoghurt or salad or brine cheese or cold meat, more or less spicy, depending on the region. President Tito's former chef Olga Novac-Markovic suggests cheese or *charcuterie* specialities like *prsut*, salami and brawn, or melon. Every region has its way of preparing the lean, dark pink Dalmatian prosciutto, usually made from pork, which after smoking is dried in the air. Good bread and salt, pepper and paprika powder are the only necessary accompaniments. Mixed sweet melon and watermelon in a dressing of white wine, sugar, lemon and vanilla is a light summer hors d'oeuvre, as is the familiar Italian-style melon with smoked ham or shrimps.

A traditional tablecloth edging from Eugène Pittard, La Roumanie,
Paris 1917

Moving into Hungary one is more likely to encounter single
appetizers, elaborately prepared and bought ready-made. Except
in dire necessity the Hungarian would no more make hors
d'oeuvres at home than a German would make his own layer
cake, except perhaps for a few slices of salami with some fresh
grated horseradish. To cater for advanced Hungarian tastes
Jozsef Dobos ran a famous delicatessen in Budapest at the end of
the last century, selling all kinds of prepared first courses. It
stocked over sixty different cheeses and twenty-two kinds of
champagne. The range of dishes included duck pâté, Casino
eggs, pastry horns with ham, beet salad and *croquettes à la palota*,
which were artfully-created meat and mushroom patties made
into little sticks, dipped in egg and breadcrumbs, fried and
served with a green or Tartar sauce. The sauces too could be
bought from Dobos.

In Czechoslovakia, Germany and Poland the pre-table mainly
consists of cold meat, fish, sour vegetables and eggs. Polish
zakaski, related to the Russian *zakuski* and Scandinavian smörgas-
bord, are generally taken with vodka before the main meal and
are at their best when they include smoked eel. Vegetables will
include mushrooms, cucumbers, beetroot and dried beans. The
zakaski table comes into its own at Easter, with sides of roast ham,
sucking pig and other meats on display with various pickled salads
and horseradish, decorated eggs and the Paschal butter lamb.

In Czechoslovakia, as in Poland, a cold spread may be put on for Easter, but generally there is little tradition of eating hors d'oeuvres. Magdalena Rettigova, who wrote the bible of Czech food in the 1820s, described hors d'oeuvres as belonging to the high nineteenth-century table, with exceptions to the common man's expectations only beginning on feast days and holidays. At Christmas carp was often prepared in aspic as a beginning to the festive meal, and goose liver in aspic was enjoyed on other occasions. Some starters are eaten nowadays, but the national taste remains oriented to robust foods. The Czech club in London, a re-creation of a pre-war gastronomic reality for permanent exiles, offers a simple pre-menu of spicy *klobas* (sausage) from Moravia, Matjes herring, rollmop herring or liver pâté with very garlicky fried bread. As a starter its fat-laden *topinki* – toast-sized croûtons of fried bread – further topped with pâté, are only for gargantuan appetites. Popular home-made dishes are stuffed tomatoes, served cold, and potato salad.

In Germany the cheese, ham, boiled eggs, sausage and yoghurt have already been eaten before lunch. At best a herring starter, particularly if taken in a restaurant, might replace the soup at lunch. The best German cold preparations are reserved for the evening cold table, the *Abendbrot*.

Leeks and mushrooms

Romanian *meze* include this deluxe version of vinaigrette leeks.

6 leeks, whites only	¼ teaspoon dried thyme
salt, fresh black pepper	1 teaspoon fennel seeds
24 button mushrooms	1 bay leaf
24 ripe olives	3 tablespoons fresh parsley,
12 tablespoons olive oil	chopped
½ lemon, sliced	

Wash the leeks and cook covered in a little salted water for about 10 minutes, until just tender. Drain well and cool. Wipe the mushrooms and simmer whole in salted water for 5 minutes.

Combine leeks and mushrooms with all the remaining ingredients except the parsley. Leave covered in a cool place for two days, turning occasionally. To serve, remove the lemon slices and bay leaf and garnish with parsley.

Serves 6.

Variations There is a similar recipe I have adapted to our green celery, which is not found in Central Europe. Wash a bunch of celery carefully, chop into pieces 2–4 cm (1–2 inches) long and cook covered in a little salted water for 5 minutes. Drain, pour over a mixture of 3 parts olive or sunflower oil to 1 part wine vinegar and garnish with black olives and chopped parsley. This salad is especially good served while the celery is still warm.

Aubergine purée

Bake some aubergines whole, then, without using a metal implement, which would discolour them, pound the soft flesh with as much crushed garlic as is desirable, slowly adding olive or sunflower oil and finishing with lemon juice and black pepper. This paste may also be used as a dip for meat or fish.

Aubergines baked in white wine

The simplicity of Bulgarian cooking is very appealing and quite took me by surprise when I first met it. Even under contemporary circumstances it is excellent in the round, and further researches amongst printed sources have proved amply worthwhile. This recipe, for instance, tops my list as a way of using up leftover white wine. The texture and flavour together would defeat any blindfold test.

3 aubergines, about 180 g (6–8 oz) each
juice of 1 lemon
salt
3 tablespoons flour

50 g (2 oz) butter
3 onions, thinly sliced
1 glass white wine
parsley

Wash the aubergines and bake or grill them whole for 15 minutes, then peel them, split them lengthwise and cut them into fillets about 2½ cm (1 inch) thick, sprinkling with lemon juice and a little salt. After 10 minutes blot up any moisture, dip fry them in the butter for 4 minutes on each side. Lay them side by side in an ovenproof dish, cover with the onion rings, sprinkle on the parsley and pour over the wine. Bake covered in a medium oven 20–30 minutes, or until the wine has been absorbed. Serve cold.

Raw onion salad with garlic

Not all Bulgarian food is delicate. This salad is unusually blatant and unlikely to be served to tourists, but is certainly worth trying as an accompaniment to good bread or alongside a rice salad. It is also prepared in Albania.

Peel and slice 500 g (1 lb) large mild onions into thin rings and dress them with equal parts of olive or sunflower oil and white-wine vinegar. Sprinkle over 2 finely chopped cloves of garlic, turn the salad carefully and serve at room temperature.

Onions are a likely salad in winter and early spring, when fresh produce is not available.

White beans in olive oil

Dried beans are another winter standby. This preparation is one all those with a half-hearted appreciation of beans should try. It is the best bean salad from anywhere. Essential features are the sugar (the reason why baked beans are so popular) and the oil included in the cooking. It can also be served as an accompaniment to roast or grilled meat.

500 g (1 lb) white beans	2 medium carrots, diced
4 cloves garlic, crushed	1 cup olive or sunflower oil
2 medium onions, chopped	1 teaspoon salt

2 tablespoons sugar
2 tablespoons wine vinegar
   or lemon juice

3 tablespoons chopped
   parsley

Soak the beans overnight, then cook for 45 minutes in plenty of fresh water. Add the garlic, onions, carrots, oil and salt and cook until the beans are soft. Add the sugar, vinegar or lemon juice and return to heat for 5 minutes more. Serve cold, garnished with parsley.

Bean salads are found throughout the Balkans, sometimes with festive import. Albanians in former Catholic areas serve them in oil at the end of Lent.

Black olive paste

You may find this in Bulgaria or Romania or any olive-producing country. Mash or pound stoned olives with a little oil and lemon juice, or with butter and herbs (fresh fennel or dill and parsley), or onion and black pepper, and spread on bread.

Cucumber and walnut salad

This kind of salad, bound into a thick mixture with ground walnuts, also has several countries of origin. This recipe comes from Albania, which shares with Bulgaria an ideal of simple food. Its starters mainly comprise yoghurt and vegetables.

1½ long cucumbers, peeled,
   diced and lightly salted
2 cloves garlic
4 tablespoons walnut pieces

1 tablespoon wine vinegar
4–5 tablespoons olive oil
black pepper
fresh mint (optional)

After 30 minutes drain the cucumber. Roughly crush the garlic with the nuts, combine with all the other ingredients except the mint and mix well. Chill and serve, garnished with fresh mint, and with good dark bread.

The Romanian recipe uses a thick slice of bread, soaked in water and squeezed dry, instead of the nuts.

Garlic aubergines

Albania is still largely a feudal society, and the greater part of the economy is agricultural. The fields are dotted and clustered with manual workers, planting, sowing, tending and harvesting. The most common summer vegetables produced in quantity on collective farms for Albanian domestic consumption are the aubergine and the green pepper. Since enjoying a meal at Mussolini's old hunting lodge in the northern inland town of Lezhe I have often made these garlicky Albanian chunks. Complete with their identifying purple skins, they are my favourite aubergine recipe.

Allowing about 175 g (6–8 oz) aubergine per person, wash and cut the aubergines into rough chunks without peeling, salt them lightly and leave for 30 minutes. Squeeze out any juice before frying gently in olive oil in a covered pan with as much crushed garlic as you can cope with, at least one clove per aubergine. These garlic aubergines can be served Italian-style alongside other *antipasti*, or with grilled meat. They can be served either warm or cold, but room temperature is best.

Robin Howe suggested in his *Balkan Cooking* some years ago that *meze* may have been introduced first to the region by Genoese traders, which is perhaps why this preparation makes one think of Italy. On the other hand Albania, on the Adriatic coast, and because of close political contacts, has long been susceptible to Italian influences. The Albanian way is to drink aniseed *raki* or one of the many similar drinks from Greece and the Middle East, like *ouzo*, with small portions of tempting, well-flavoured food like this.

Asparagus with green sauce

This recipe shows international cooking – the green sauce comes from France, probably via Germany – being given a unique touch in Yugoslavia by the use of locally plentiful ingredients. It makes an eye-catching statement as well as being a very fine start to a meal.

Clean a bunch of asparagus and simmer gently in salted water with a slice of lemon and two tablespoons of milk until tender, leaving the asparagus to cool in the water. Garnish with a green sauce made by blending 3 tablespoons mayonnaise with 1 tablespoon sour cream, a hard-boiled egg, an ounce of spinach, cooked and drained, plenty of fresh parsley and chives, a chopped shallot and the leaves from one or two sprigs of fresh tarragon. Diced red peppers may be added to the finished sauce for colour.

Pepper and tomato salad

Salads with tomatoes and peppers are amongst the easiest Balkan salads to reproduce. Throughout the Balkans combinations of tomatoes, green peppers and onions, dressed with olive oil and vinegar, are ubiquitous in season, as are preparations of tomatoes, peppers and cooked aubergines. The peppers are skinned to make them less indigestible. To decide whether or not to do this, by grilling or baking, then cooling under a cloth or dipping in cold water, toss up between the risk of mild gastric discomfort and the value of saving 20 minutes. A compromise would be to resort to tinned whole red peppers. *Pimientos* of Spanish origin have an excellent flavour. They could be used in this Yugoslav recipe, though the pleasant colour contrast would be lost.

3 green peppers	olive or sunflower oil
500 g (1 lb) tomatoes	lemon juice or wine vinegar
1 onion	sugar (optional)
salt, ground black pepper	fresh parsley

Cook at an oriental court. Jacques Le Hay, Recueil de Cent Estampes Representant Differentes Nations du Levant, *Paris 1714*

If the peppers are to be skinned, grill or bake them until their skins wrinkle and char, then proceed as above, making sure your hands are wet when you handle them. Cut the skinned peppers into about 8 pieces each, removing the core and seeds, then slice

75

the tomatoes and the onion finely, mix all the vegetables together with the seasoning and add a few tablespoons of oil and vinegar. If the tomatoes are not sweet it is a good idea to add a sprinkling of sugar. Garnish with chopped parsley and serve at room temperature.

Pindzur

One theory goes that as well as the Turks the Serbs did much to excite the passion for peppers amongst the neighbouring Hungarians, who then came to prefer their peppers cooked or ground into various paprika powders. The best of all cold pepper recipes is a tribute to Serbian good taste. It has a chunky but well-integrated texture and an irresistible amount of garlic. Serve it chilled with warm bread, garlic bread or with roast or grilled lamb.

500 g (1 lb) each sweet peppers, red tomatoes, aubergines	salt
	6 tablespoons oil
	3–4 tablespoons vinegar
at least one whole bulb of garlic	chilli peppers (optional)

Grill or bake the vegetables until soft. Dip in cold water or leave to cool under a cloth before skinning. Chop coarsely and lightly crush with a wooden pestle or the end of a rolling pin. Add the garlic, chopped, the salt, oil and vinegar. Leave to chill for a few hours, add the finely minced hot pepper if liked and serve.

Serbian salad

This mixture of southern vegetables with raw onion and raw cabbage is like a combination of a north European cabbage salad with a tomato salad from southern Europe. The sulphuric bitterness is removed from the cabbage and onion by several days' steeping in a sweet-sour solution. Only afterwards comes the dressing with oil.

500 g (1 lb) green peppers
250 g (½ lb) green tomatoes
500 g (1 lb) red tomatoes
500 g (1 lb) cucumber
375 g (¾ lb) onions
500 g (1 lb) white or red
 cabbage

1–2 teaspoons sugar
3 tablespoons mild vinegar
salt, peppercorns, bay leaf
 and herbs
4 tablespoons olive oil

Clean the vegetables and slice the peppers, tomatoes, cucumber and onions into rounds. Shred the cabbage finely. Combine all in an earthenware or glass bowl. Bring the vinegar, sugar, seasonings and a bouquet of herbs – dill, savory, tarragon, or basil, oregano and thyme – to the boil in 1½ litres (2½ pints) water and pour this over the salad while still boiling. Cover the bowl with foil for 4–5 days and keep in a cool place. Sprinkle each portion with olive oil before serving.

The technique of pre-steeping recalls some methods for coleslaw designed to enhance the awkward digestibility of raw cabbage. From nearly 1,000 miles north of Serbia, in Bohemia, emigrants to America in the mid-nineteenth century took recipes for their compound salads and copied them out for later generations. Mary Rosicky, who collected recipes for Bohemian-Americans who risked losing the ancestral way with food, in the last century called her cabbage salads Cold Slaw. The first word was American and the second an Americanized version of the Czech *hlavka*, cabbage. Normally the derivation is regarded as coming from the Dutch for cabbage salad, *koolsla*. It may be a case of two tributaries, one stream.

Warsaw salad

150 g (6 oz) haricot beans
2 tablespoons lemon juice
1 teaspoon ready-made
 mustard
salt, black pepper, sugar to
 taste

2 hard-boiled eggs
1 apple
60 g (2 oz) pickled cucumber
1 onion
2 tablespoons sour cream

Soak the beans overnight, then cook them in fresh, unsalted water till tender. Drain. Combine the lemon juice, mustard, salt, pepper and sugar and pour over the beans. Toss and leave to stand an hour. Chop the eggs, the peeled apple, the cucumbers and the onion and mix in with the beans. Stir in the sour cream before serving.

Stuffed tomatoes

6 medium tomatoes (about 750 g [1½ lb])
salt, pepper, ½ teaspoon paprika
1 medium onion, chopped fine
2 tablespoons butter
1 clove of garlic, crushed

75 g (2½ oz) fine fresh breadcrumbs (2 thick slices of bread)
2 tablespoons parsley
2 anchovy fillets, minced
50 g (2 oz) tuna fish, cooked chicken or chopped ham (optional)

Cut the tops off the tomatoes, scoop out the pulp and set both tops and pulp aside. Sprinkle cavities with salt and invert to drain. Sauté the onion in butter, add garlic and tomato pulp, season with salt, pepper and paprika and cook for a minute, stirring, then add the remaining ingredients. Mix well, remove from heat, fill tomatoes and replace caps. Bake in a buttered dish in a medium oven about 30 minutes and allow to cool before serving.

Potato salad

From an abundance of Czech and German recipes this one without mayonnaise is excellent, especially when served with other salads. Its great virtue is to show off the flavour of the potato, not the dressing. The best potatoes to use are the mealy and absorbent varieties.

1 kg (2 lb) freshly boiled potatoes

Scant 300 ml (½ pint) hot stock

115 g (4 oz) onion
2 tablespoons vinegar
salt, pepper
1 teaspoon mustard

½ teaspoon sugar
2 tablespoons oil
parsley

Slice the potatoes while they are hot. Mix together all the other ingredients except the parsley and pour over the potatoes. Garnish with parsley before serving at room temperature. Fried bacon and its fat can be substituted for the oil, though the result is not pleasing cold.

Variations Mayonnaise can swamp the delicate flavour of potatoes. One creamy dressing which avoids this is made with hard-boiled egg yolks mashed and diluted with sour cream and sharpened with a dash of vinegar and a little ready-made mustard, also a pinch of sugar. Try it on boiled, unpeeled new potatoes.

Autumn potato salad

The following Czech salad, though, benefits from the inclusion of mayonnaise to bind its various vegetables.

750 g (1½ lb) potatoes
½ onion
1 large green pepper
250 g (½ lb) firm tomatoes
2 sour apples

½ cucumber
150 g (6 oz) mayonnaise
lemon juice, pepper, sugar
2 hard-boiled eggs (optional)

Boil the potatoes in their skins and when cool cut in slices or large dice with all other vegetables and fruit. Flavour the mayonnaise to taste with lemon juice, pepper and sugar, and mix into the salad, which may be garnished with sliced hard-boiled eggs. A home-made mayonnaise here would turn a predictable dish into an excellent one. An alternative is to mix equal parts of mayonnaise and sour cream, or mayonnaise and yoghurt. In the last case the dressing will not need further sharpening with lemon. Beetroot is a possible additional ingredient, and would certainly replace the green pepper in hard Czech times.

I used to wonder when I was in Germany what that slightly sweet-tasting pale vegetable was that came crinkle-cut and marinated out of glass jars, delicious with bread or as an accompaniment to bread and cold meat for *Abendbrot*. It turned out to be celeriac, which is used in most Central European countries where our green celery is not. It looks like a very large, round, knobbly parsnip and needs very little attention to produce a vegetable dish full of texture and taste. Unpeeled and raw, or cooked and dressed with oil and vinegar or in a marinade it will keep for weeks without spoiling or wilting. This is a basic recipe from Hungary.

Celeriac salad

750 g (1½ lb) celeriac
1 tablespoon lemon juice
1 onion, thinly sliced
1 tablespoon parsley
½ tablespoon sugar

½ tablespoon salt
½ cup white-wine vinegar
white pepper
1 tablespoon olive oil

Peel and slice the celeriac, cover with water and lemon juice and cook gently until just tender. Strain, and keep the cooking liquid, which should be about 1½ cups. Put the onion slices and parsley on the bottom of a serving dish. Bring the cooking liquid to the boil, then add the sugar, salt, vinegar and pepper, and pour this dressing over the onion and parsley. Add the celeriac slices, sprinkle with olive oil and serve cold.

Celeriac salad with ham

The Czech taste in vegetables is often sweet, or sweet and sour, and preparations can be cloying. Here, though, the dense mixture of textures and tastes is appetizing. Czechs would probably eat this with white bread, though I would serve it as one of several salads for lunch.

1 medium celeriac, about 600 g (1¼ lb)
salt, lemon for cooking
up to 150 g (6 oz) ham
1 scant teaspoon horseradish (fresh, grated or sauce)
1 tablespoon stewed cranberries or cranberry sauce
2 tablespoons mayonnaise
1 tablespoon lemon juice

Boil the peeled celeriac in large pieces in salted water with a dash of lemon juice for about 10 minutes, when it should be just tender. Drain, and cut it into cubes, with the chopped ham. Mix the remaining ingredients together and fold into the ham and celeriac. Serve at room temperature or chilled.

Pickled vegetables, sour salads and relishes

These provide a good contrast in texture and taste with fresh vegetable salads, cheese and meat.

Muraturi

1 kg (2 lb) vegetables, including green tomatoes, red cabbage, carrots,
celery or celeriac, cauliflower, chilli peppers, small sweet

green and red peppers,   sprigs of fresh fennel
garlic   100 g (3½ oz) sea salt
a few peppercorns, bay leaf,   100 ml (⅙ pint) vinegar

Clean and prepare the vegetables, selecting them with one eye
on the intended colour and variety in the jar: divide the cabbage
into wedges and the cauliflower into florets, slice the carrots into
rounds, the celeriac into thin slices, the peppers into long strips.
Peel the garlic but leave the cloves whole. Place the vegetables
in a sterilized, wide-necked glass jar or jars, alternating varieties
and colours and dividing the herbs and spices between the jars.
Stand in a tray of cold water. Bring ¾ litre (1¼ pints) water to
the boil with the salt and vinegar and pour over the vegetables
while still boiling. Cover, seal and keep in a warm place till
the liquid clears, then store in a cold, airy spot. These are
Romanian pickles. In Bulgaria similar preserves are called *turshia*.

Ajvar

Serbia as much as Hungary is the home of peppers, and the taste
for them is hot. A highly spiced, sweet-and-sour Serbian
mixture of peppers, tomatoes and aubergines is sometimes given
as a salad, but being fierce and concentrated it more resembles a
relish. It can be served with raw vegetables as a dip, or to spice a
plate of cold meat or fish. I have also found it good with cheese.

1 kg (2 lb) sweet green, red or yellow peppers
1 very hot chilli pepper
500 g (1 lb) aubergines
2 cloves garlic, crushed with salt
9 tablespoons oil
4 tablespoons wine vinegar, or more or less to taste

Set the oven to hot and bake the washed peppers and aubergines
till soft. Dip in cold water and remove skins with wet hands,
also seeds and ribs from the peppers. Mince the flesh finely in a
stainless steel, glass or earthenware bowl, add the garlic, oil and
vinegar, then cook in a stainless steel or earthenware pan until

the mixture is thick and homogeneous, like a fine chutney. Put the hot mixture into glass jars, wipe the edges of the jar, cover with a layer of oil and seal with cellophane and an elastic band or a clean, tight-fitting lid. Use immediately or store in a cool place.

Variations A less hot version of *ajvar* adds twice as much garlic, omits the hot pepper and uses lemon juice instead of vinegar. The mixture is not returned to the pan to thicken, simply chilled and garnished with parsley before serving. In this form it is sometimes called 'vegetable caviare' and eaten like the aubergine purée on p. 70.

Pickled mushrooms

500 g (1 lb) button mushrooms
6 tablespoons wine vinegar
2 cloves garlic
salt, a few peppercorns, a bay leaf
1 clove
3 tablespoons oil

Wipe the mushrooms clean and bring them to the boil in a scant cup of water with the vinegar, peeled whole cloves of garlic, salt and spices. Cook for 10 minutes without covering, then allow to cool. Pour into a sterilized glass jar, pour oil over the top, cover and seal. Leave for at least a week in a cold place. Use as a garnish or as part of another salad, or hand round with ice-cold vodka.

Compare this Polish recipe with the Romanian pickled vegetables on p. 81–2. The difference between Balkan and Central European salads more often concerns the vegetables used than the technique for serving them. Both gastronomic spheres enjoy pickling their particular vegetables in season and then serving them with neat spirits to encourage appetite and thirst.

Mikolai Rej's beetroot salad

Bake the beets, peel and slice them and put them in a cask with some grated horseradish, shake them and sprinkle with vinegar and season with salt. 'The juice is tasty and the lady *cwitka* herself will be very tasty and will smell very nicely,' wrote Rej, one of Poland's great writers and public figures in the sixteenth century. A modern method is to marinate 500 g or more (1– 2 lb) cooked beets in the juice of a lemon, half a cup of raw beet juice and a glass of dry red wine. As many beets may be used as will just be covered by the liquid. Leave them covered for two days in a cool place to mature.

Rej was an admirer of his country's food and language, and anxious to set their attractiveness alongside foreign ways. He was the first eminent writer to abandon Latin and write a colourful, expressive, vernacular Polish, describing, amongst other things, his love of good simple food and his hatred of excess and affectation. He was a copious eater himself.

Pickles to buy

Choose pickled cucumbers of Hungarian, Polish or Bulgarian origin (not French, because they don't use dill and there's no sweetness in the result). With the tinned *pimientos* suggested on p. 74, drain them, dress with oil and vinegar and sprinkle with paprika, or serve them plain, with chopped garlic, black olives and white cheese.

Cheese and yoghurt

Soft white cheese, a very common and convenient starter throughout Central Europe and the Balkans, is a marvellous vehicle for other flavours, but deserves to be treated delicately. The Czechs make a creamy Znojmo spread by combining curd cheese and Swiss cheese with cream, onions, gherkins and paprika. Another mixture attributed to Olomouc and, ideally, made with the region's strong-flavoured Kvargli soft cheese, adds butter, onion, gherkins, capers, anchovies, parsley and garlic, all in small quantities.

Meanwhile Germany, Czechoslovakia, Austria, Poland and Hungary all lay claim to the most famous spread, called in German Liptauer. The original took its name from the unripened sheep's-milk culture of the region of Lipto, northern Hungary, and from there it became the most celebrated cheese in the Austro-Hungarian Empire.

Liptó cheese

60 g (2 oz) butter
120 g (4 oz) curd cheese
1 tablespoon cream
salt

caraway seeds
1 teaspoon paprika
grated onion or chives

Beat the butter till it is light, add the cheese and cream, combine well and add the remaining ingredients. The proportions are only suggestions and may be varied according to taste. Serve in a smooth mound on a plate, with bread, toast or raw vegetables. If sheep's-milk curd cheese is used, the Lipto will be stronger and benefit from being mixed with fresh cream. Blander cow's-milk curds should be mixed with sour cream. A third possibility is to use a brine cheese like feta, which is close to the original Lipto. In that case beware of adding additional salt. Some recipes also include as a sharpener $\frac{1}{2}$–1 tablespoon ready-made mustard and/or $\frac{1}{4}$ teaspoon anchovy paste; others replace the butter and cream with half as much butter again and 3 tablespoons beer. Inevitably the anchovies give way in some households to the more readily available sardines. The sardines in her mother's Lipto were the reason the young gourmet George Lang had to give up an otherwise charming girlfriend. The same kind of overdressing occurred in the last century at the other end of the scale, when Lipto spread was suggested as a vehicle for caviare, to encourage jaded aristocratic palates. Best to stick to the basic recipe.

Shopska salad

This salad will be particularly well-known to anyone who has holidayed on the Black Sea coast, where it has become ubiquitous in tourist establishments. It has obvious affinities with Greek feta-cheese salads. Neither fact detracts from its goodness.

4 medium red or green
  peppers, sliced
1 medium cucumber, sliced
500 g (1 lb) tomatoes, sliced
2 medium onions, finely
  sliced
olive or sunflower oil,
  vinegar

chopped parsley, fresh dill,
  salt, black pepper
120 g (4 oz) crumbly white
  brine cheese, or substitute
  a cheese such as Cheshire,
  Wensleydale or Caerphilly

Arrange the vegetables in overlapping circles, sprinkle with the oil, vinegar, seasoning and fresh herbs, and crumble the cheese over the top. The peppers can be omitted, and more or less cheese added, according to taste. In summer Shopska salad makes a light lunch in itself. Soak up the sauce with plenty of rough bread. The name derives from the village of Shopka near Sofia.

Kaimak or cream cheese

A popular Yugoslav and sometimes Bulgarian starter which may also be found in Albania is *kaimak* (see p. 63) with fresh warm bread, with new potatoes or as a dip with green and red peppers.

Thick yoghurt with pickled cucumber

A Bulgarian starter which is exactly what it says it is. Drain the yoghurt until it is very thick and creamy and add very finely minced pickled cucumber. Serve in a flat dish with good brown or, even better, black bread.

Fish and fish salads
⚭

Tarama

A couple of little wooden sheds are the centre of the caviare industry. In each, an old white-bearded fisherman presides. The sturgeon are immense fishes, ten or twelve feet long, from whose bodies the sacks of eggs, or caviare, is quickly removed with the knife, while the wretched creature tries to defend itself, lashing out with its tail. The caviare is then passed through a sieve, washed in the muddy river water, a pinch of salt is added, a round tin is taken down from a shelf, the caviare pressed into it and trimmed down with a spoon, and the caviare is ready for sale, at anything from twenty-five shillings to two pounds ten the tin; cheap, compared with the prices obtaining in Western Europe, but becoming expensive when the extreme simplicity of the operation is considered. The process is, to be frank, more than a little horrifying. On seeing it, I felt that the only course was to eat some caviare at the next meal, on the same principle that an air pilot

will fly again, the same day after a bad landing, in order to restore his nerve.
Sacheverell Sitwell, *Roumanian Journey*

Romania specializes in processing large quantities of various kinds of fish roe. The best is black sturgeon caviare (*icre nere*), but this delicacy being out of reach of most Romanians today, carp and pike roe from the Danube Delta are also very popular. They are made into a thick paste and eaten with bread. In Britain smoked cod's roe is an expensive equivalent of *icre nere*. Lumpfish roes come nowhere near it in taste but make a not unpleasant mild paste for everyday consumption. The carp-roe paste I ate in Romania was grey, but most people will probably prefer to use orange roe to produce the familiar pink of supermarket taramasalata. In the case of lumpfish, the taste is identical.

90 g (3 oz) soft white bread without crusts
25 cl (8 fl oz) olive or sunflower oil
100 g (3½ oz) roe, either smoked cod's or lumpfish
juice of 1 lemon (3 tablespoons)
chopped chives, or finely chopped raw onion, or spring onion (optional)

Soak the bread in a little cold water, squeeze out excess and break into pieces. Gradually add a third of the oil, working with a fork to make a paste, or put in a liquidizer. Add the roe, mix again until smooth then add the rest of the oil and stir until you have a thick purée. Add the lemon juice, a little water if the *tarama* is too thick and the chives or onion if desired. Serve with good bread, melba toast or *crudités*.

Purée of anchovies

In Poland and Germany, anything salty goes. This anchovy purée is not particularly original, but it has the virtue of not using butter as a base. I offer it therefore as a potential refuge for slimmers.

Pound 12 drained, flat anchovy fillets. Moisten 3 slices of white bread with water and squeeze dry. Mix the two thoroughly, with enough sour cream and vinegar or lemon juice to make a smooth, sharp purée, and serve spread on small pieces of black bread.

Cured herrings

There are many herring recipes attributed variously to Germany, Poland, and Czechoslovakia within a limited range. The first one is an old-fashioned Polish recipe, for purists.

Herrings in oil

8 salt herrings	2 bay leaves, lightly crushed
about 1 cup boiling wine	2 onions cut in fine rings
vinegar	sunflower oil
8 peppercorns	pickled mushrooms and
4 grains allspice	radishes, to garnish

Soak the herrings as on p. 90 and skin them. Bring the vinegar to the boil with the spices, and pour it, still boiling, over the onions. Leave to cool. Drain the onions and arrange them over the herrings in a shallow dish. Dress with oil and decorate the plate with radishes and pickled mushrooms. Again, dark bread is the best accompaniment, or plain potato salad. Rollmops straight from the jar are a fair substitute.

Herring salad

Herrings combine excellently with boiled eggs, sour cream, raw onions and fresh dill, and also with potatoes. Make this salad with or without incorporating boiled sliced potatoes. Either way, it is a robust starter needing perhaps only the complement of a soup. I prefer to avoid mayonnaise, but many people don't.

500 g (1 lb) potatoes
diced herring
1 large cooking apple
2 pickled cucumbers
4 tablespoons each sour cream and mayonnaise,
or 8 tablespoons sour cream
1–2 teaspoons ready-made mustard

Boil the potatoes in their skins, peel when cooked. When cool, combine with the herring, finely sliced or grated apple and the chopped cucumbers. Combine remaining ingredients to make a dressing.

Salt herrings in cream

This is a modern German herring salad.

8 salt herring fillets or rollmops	1 small carton (5 fl oz) sour cream
2 sour apples	tomato ketchup
2 onions	parsley
2 tablespoons mayonnaise	

Soak the salt fillets in cold water for 12 hours, changing the water twice. Drain and dry them carefully. Peel and core the apples, peel the onions and slice both thinly. Mix the mayonnaise and sour cream, fold into the apple and onion and pour over the fillets. Decorate with a trickle of ketchup and a scattering of parsley and eat with black bread or *Vollkornbrot*. For the sweeter rollmop herrings, choose an unsweet mayonnaise and decorate with sliced gherkins.

Once one gets into the eating of cured fish in central and north-east Europe, it is difficult to avoid an overwhelmed palate. The over-use of salt goes back to Frederick the Great's salt monopoly, which forced Prussians to consume more salt than they wanted. It also had to do with the need to preserve foods through long harsh winters, before the advent of large-scale canning. But there is so much vinegar around, alongside brine, that even when both of these are softened with sugar, they leave one longing for the subtler, drier, savoury flavours of the south, which enhance wine. How pleasant to feel a blending of flavours on the palate instead of a battle. This Romanian treatment of herring, perhaps developed by the large German community in Romania, brings an unaccustomed touch of the south to Matjes fillets.

Romanian gourmet herring

8 salt herring fillets
3 tomatoes or 2 tablespoons tomato purée
salt, 1 tablespoon sugar
sprigs of dill and tarragon, or $\frac{1}{4}$ teaspoon each, dried
1 cup black olives

1 teaspoon capers
1 stalk celery
1–2 spring onions, or a piece of leek
1 tablespoon wine vinegar
4 tablespoons olive oil
parsley

Soak, rinse and dry the herrings as in the foregoing recipe. Cook the tomatoes until soft in a little water with a pinch of salt and the sugar. Separately bring to the boil a little water containing the herbs, olives, capers, chopped celery, onions, vinegar and oil. Simmer for 5 minutes, mix with the tomato and pour warm over the herrings. Serve cold, sprinkled with parsley. Eat with white bread, cornbread or warm *mamaliga* (p. 330).

Another step back in the direction of more luxurious eating comes with this dish, which would have graced Hungarian aristocratic tables in the last century. It is a smooth, elegant salad originally made with Hungarian freshwater crayfish, and made easily digestible by the cooking of the peppers.

Delicate shellfish salad with peppers

375 g (¾ lb) boned
monkfish, or crayfish, or
large prawns (weight
after shelling)
250 g (½ lb) green peppers,
diced
2 tomatoes, diced

1 tablespoon tarragon
vinegar
½ tablespoon grated onion
salt, white pepper
¼ teaspoon paprika
3 tablespoons olive oil
2 hard-boiled eggs,
separated
parsley

Boil the fish for a few minutes in lightly salted water, and drain. Cut the monkfish into bite-sized pieces. In fresh water bring the green peppers to the boil, drain and add to the fish, together with the diced tomatoes. Mix the vinegar, grated onion, salt, pepper and paprika to taste, then add the oil drop by drop, stirring. Mix a little of this dressing with the mashed egg yolks to make a smooth paste, then combine both mixtures. Use to coat the fish and vegetables in a small serving dish. Decorate with the finely chopped egg whites and chopped parsley.

For the best starters one comes back to the Balkans, where cold fish salads are still found everywhere, but without the combined harshness and sweetness of preparations further north. The use of mustard in the next two recipes, from Yugoslavia, is characteristic of Central Europe at a junction with the Adriatic.

Cold fish salad

375 g (¾ lb) cod
lemon juice for cooking
2 tablespoons oil
2 teaspoons ready-made
mustard
salt and pepper to taste
3 tablespoons lemon juice

250 g (½ lb) green peppers,
diced
250 g (½ lb) tomatoes, diced
1 medium lettuce, shredded
170 g (6 oz) cooked green
peas

1 bunch spring onions, sliced, including green parts

1 bunch of radishes, grated
parsley

Poach the fish in a little water with lemon juice for about 8 minutes, covered. When cool, drain, cut into cubes. Make a dressing with the oil, mustard, salt and pepper and lemon juice and mix with the green peppers, tomatoes, lettuce, peas, spring onions and radishes. Add the fish and turn very gently to coat. Garnish with parsley and serve at room temperature with good bread.

Squid salad

750 g (1½ lb) squid
salt
55 g (2 oz) soup vegetables
white pepper seeds, bay leaf
85 g (3 oz) boiled potatoes
30 g (1 oz) onion
55 g (2 oz) pickled cucumber
4 olives, stoned

2–3 tablespoons olive oil
1 tablespoon white-wine vinegar
4 capers
mustard
chopped parsley, salt and pepper
lettuce leaves, lemon slices, sprigs of rosemary

Clean the squid and cook in salted water with the cleaned, cubed soup vegetables and seasonings. Discard soup vegetables and seasonings. When cool, drain, dice the squid, peeled boiled potatoes, raw onion, cucumbers and olives and mix together with a dressing made with oil, vinegar, chopped capers, a pinch of mustard, parsley, salt and pepper. Serve in small glass dishes lined with lettuce leaves. Decorate with a lemon slice and a sprig of rosemary.

Meat dishes

There are few of these as such, because most meats on the cold table are bought cooked and sliced.

Mititei

The centrepiece of the Romanian *meze* table is the little sausage offered as a national dish, *mititei*. These sausages are less mysteriously good than they are made out to be, though they are certainly worth the effort to give variety to the hors d'oeuvres table and ensure an excellent contrast in texture to the pastes and purées above. The best taste comes, as with the closely related hamburger, from a mixture of pork and beef. The same recipe is also used to make *mititei* for a main course, as part of the classic Romanian mixed grill (p. 229) and to make the meat stuffing for sour cabbage leaves, *sarmale*.

500 g (1 lb) each minced beef and pork
4 cloves garlic, crushed with ½–1 teaspoon salt
½ cup water or stock
½ teaspoon dried savory or thyme
¾ teaspoon ground allspice
plenty of fresh black pepper
2 teaspoons bicarbonate of soda

If possible, mince the meat at home, as finely as possible, which will ensure high quality and a good texture. Mix in all the remaining ingredients, knead like bread with a few tablespoons of water until very smooth and leave the mixture to stand, if possible overnight. Before cooking, brush the grill rack with oil. With wet hands, shape the mixture into cocktail-sized sausages. Cook under a high heat or over charcoal for about 7 minutes on each side. This recipe makes about 32 sausages. *Mititei* are served with *muraturi* (see p. 81) dressed with oil, and are equally welcome in informal eating as on the grand table.

Meanwhile, how basic can one go?

This recipe is a curiosity, from the days when it was common to disguise one food as another to get round shortages and fasting rules.

Polish caviare

1 onion
250 g ($\frac{1}{2}$ lb) goose dripping
1 teaspoon salt
1 teaspoon each fresh ground pepper and marjoram

Grate the onion into the cold dripping, add the salt, pepper and marjoram and mix thoroughly. Chill well and eat spread on dark bread.

This is Polish bread and dripping. Every nation, here and there, has its inventiveness forced into a straitjacket.

> If wishes were horses
> Beggars would ride;
> If turnips were watches
> I would wear one by my side.

Eggs

The best egg hors d'oeuvres are generally the simplest. With boiled eggs the egg-yolk paste can be used as a vehicle for a single strong flavour, onion, garlic, fish or herb. As with so many other preparations in Central Europe, the treatment can be fine or robust, under the influence of foreign aristocratic or local traditions. Richness can be added with butter or (to my outsider's mind) subtracted with yoghurt.

Casino eggs

In Hungary this name covers a range of fillings, more or less expensive. The original took its name from the National Casino in Budapest, where the director-chef in the 1870s was József Marchal, former chef to Napoleon III of France and to Tsar Alexander II. This establishment, founded in the eighteenth century, was a point of repair for the cream of Hungarian political and military society. Its menus were in French and it served the best Franco-Hungarian cuisine. For its stuffed eggs it used butter, sour cream, capers and anchovies, with a little mustard, and set them on a cooked-vegetable salad dressed with a rich sauce, thickened over heat, of egg yolks, sour cream, lemon juice and sugar. The full recipe will be found in George Lang, *The Cuisine of Hungary*. This is my adapted, low-cholesterol and less overwhelming version, which was liked by both adults and children who tested it.

8 hard-boiled eggs	2 teaspoons finely chopped
4 tablespoons mayonnaise	capers
4 tablespoons yoghurt	salt, pepper
1 tablespoon parsley, plus a	black olives (optional)
little for the garnish	

Halve the eggs lengthwise, mash the yolks with half the blended mayonnaise and yoghurt and add the parsley and capers with a pinch of seasoning. Pile the mixture into the egg-white cavities, arrange on a dish, pour over the remaining dressing and strew a little more finely chopped parsley. You could top each egg with a black olive.

Polish eggs

Ways with eggs are endless, as this most unpretentious recipe from Poland shows. It is not the most common recipe, but an interesting one.

4 hard-boiled eggs
85 g (3 oz) goose fat
1 onion
dill, parsley, chives
salt and pepper to taste

Mash the yolks with a fork, chop the whites, and mix both with the remaining ingredients. Eat with bread. For a hot version, stuff the mixture back into well-washed egg shells, sprinkle cheese and breadcrumbs over the surface and place in a hot oven for 10 minutes.

A recipe for pickled eggs, more accurately eggs in brine, is shared by the Germans and the Czechs, who call it *Bohemian eggs*. The eggs are hard-boiled, then the shells cracked all over without being removed. Water boiled for five minutes with 115 g (4 oz) salt to every 1 litre (two pints), peppercorns, caraway seeds and onion is then poured over the eggs in a bowl, where they are left to stand for 24 hours. To serve these the Czech way, peel them, cut them into quarters and serve with black bread and butter, perhaps alongside a cucumber salad or with raw or pickled vegetables and gherkins. The habit in Berlin, however, where these eggs evolved as yet another way of using up the Emperor's salt, was to cut off the top, remove the yolk, put oil and pepper in the cavity, then replace the yolk and eat the egg with beer. It oozed oil all over the drinker's fingers and clothes.

Yeast and egg spread

This homely but delicate spread from a modern Czech manual goes well with toast.

115 g (4 oz) fresh yeast
55 g (2 oz) butter
1 onion
125 cl (4½ fl. oz) milk
4 eggs

chives, salt
1 teaspoon mustard
fresh breadcrumbs, as
   necessary

Melt the yeast in the butter and when it starts to brown add the finely chopped onion and fry lightly, stirring, taking care the yeast does not burn. Add the milk off the heat and mix to a smooth cream, then add the eggs, chives and seasoning. Return to a low heat and stir while the spread thickens. If it does not reach the desired consistency, add a tablespoon of fine fresh breadcrumbs. Turn into a small serving dish and serve spread on squares of bread or toast. Try it also in children's sandwiches.

Eggs combine well with the southern vegetables, to show off their colour and sweetness. Here is a Yugoslav recipe that anoints a firm omelette with a richly flavoured spicy sauce of barely cooked vegetables. As a variation on the omelette and salad theme, it is both original and decorative.

Montenegro omelette

For the sauce:
3 tablespoons olive oil
1 tablespoon butter
2 cloves garlic, crushed
1 medium onion, 1 green
    pepper, 2 sticks celery,
    all finely chopped
1 500 g (16 oz) tin tomatoes,
    drained and chopped
1 teaspoon salt
$\frac{1}{8}$ teaspoon cayenne
    or ground dried chillies

$\frac{1}{2}$ cup red wine
2 tablespoons brandy

For the omelette:
8 eggs
3 tablespoons milk or light
    cream
$\frac{1}{2}$ teaspoon salt
white pepper
$\frac{1}{4}$ teaspoon thyme
3 tablespoons butter

Make the sauce first by heating the oil and butter in a large frying pan and adding the garlic and all the vegetables except the tomatoes. Cook for a few minutes, add the tomatoes and seasonings and continue cooking for another 5 minutes. Add the wine, stir and simmer, covered, over a low heat for a further 10 minutes. Uncover, add the brandy, and cook for a final 15 minutes, stirring occasionally.

    Make the omelette by beating together the eggs, milk or

cream and seasonings, then pouring the mixture into a large hot omelette pan in which you have melted the butter. When the underside is golden brown, remove the pan from the heat, slide the omelette out on a plate, re-butter pan if necessary and return the omelette, uncooked side down, to finish. Alternatively, set the top of this thick omelette by putting the pan under a hot grill for a few minutes. If you intend to serve the omelette warm, turn it out on to a warm plate, and cut it into 6 wedges (though this dish is very good, and less trouble, served cold). On individual plates coat each wedge with sauce.

SOUPS

❦

The soups associated with Eastern Europe are of several distinct types, quite different from the Franco–British style of 'cream of'. They include Polish *barszcz*, Hungarian *gulyás*, Romanian fish or chicken *ciorba* and Bulgarian *tarator*. German or Hungarian cold fruit soup, thick pea soup from Germany, Poland or Czechoslovakia, fresh- and dried-mushroom soups, sour-bean soup from the Balkans and many thickened, liquid combinations of sauerkraut, bacon and sour cream make up the range. Soups are served at the high and low table, and at all stages in between. They are recommended for every debilitated state, lack of appetite, nervous tension or hangover. At heart they are the common man's food, warming, revivifying and generally inexpensive. But rich, well-travelled men and women in love with their native cuisines have developed luxury versions.

Breakfast soups and pottages

❦

Before the arrival of coffee in Central Europe, the first cup of soup was drunk at breakfast and the habit continued well into the nineteenth century, not only amongst the poor. Magyar peasants first thought of coffee as 'black soup', while in Poland, though coffee quickly became a passion in the towns, the breakfast soup, *gramatka* or *farmuszka*, made with beer, was still enjoyed in country manors little more than a hundred years ago. Sweetened beer soups, which were also drunk during Lent,

Joseph C. Dobos, Livre de Cuisine Franco-Hongrois, *Budapest
1881* (photo: J.-L. Charmet)

continue to be included in contemporary Czech, German,
Polish, Hungarian and Romanian recipe books. The taste is
difficult to acquire for most Westerners, and I don't exclude
myself.

One of the reasons why beer evolved as a breakfast
accompaniment, as it did in England in pre-coffee and tea days,
was the relative shortage of any other well-flavoured liquid or
fat to moisten the bread or cooked grain. The reversible identity
of soup and alcoholic beverages may be seen in the Polish word
krupnik, which usually means a thick, creamy, mildly sour
barley soup, but is also used to describe a wine punch. A sad
story was recorded by a member of the first short-lived
Hungarian Communist government after the First World War
who was a sympathizer with the hard lot of the still feudally
tied peasants. In the region of Eger, during the frequent

shortages of food, he saw infants wending their way to school, drunk on a breakfast of wine dregs. No doubt this beverage was called soup by those whose social consciences were less well primed than his.

An alternative to alcohol as a breakfast liquid in Europe was a thin flour-and-water porridge. In the Steiermark, eastern Austria and towards the Hungarian border, the upland farming community ate a rough maize porridge, flavoured and diluted with what most readily came to hand: pork fat, sour milk, ersatz coffee. The habit lasted into the 1950s. A seasonal alternative to moisten the porridge was fruit must or the local rosé wine. The same farmers later took a second breakfast of sour soup: water, vinegar, flour, salt and caraway. Today all through Central Europe and the Balkans recipes persist for such very thin 'soups' whose flavours depend on caraway seeds, or garlic, or bread, and these would seem to derive directly from the breakfast and second-breakfast soups.

The thin soups are poor men's standbys, and during Lent a means of self-punishment. The Polish *zur* is based upon a fermented solution of warm water and oat or rye meal with a starter of a small piece of yeast dough, rye bread or a spoonful of the previous batch of *zur*. The emulsion is left in the warm for three days, when it should be ready for use. Modern recipes suggest combining it with vegetables, dried mushrooms, sour cream, bacon fat, sausage and so on, in other words, treating it just like any other soup stock. The technique is the same as for Romanian *bors* (see p. 129) based on bran and Russian *kvas* based exclusively on rye. In practice *zur* was served in a far plainer form, being the staple food, partnered with herring, of Polish Lent. After six weeks of misery, the vile brew was ceremoniously buried on Easter Saturday:

Outside the church there was a great noise and tumult: for, according to immemorial custom, on that day (which brought Lent to its close) they had come together in the early morning to give a funeral to the *zur* and herrings on which they had been feeding all Lent through . . . the youngsters arranged the funeral, with Yasyek Topsy-Turvy at their head. They had got, somewhere or other, a big pot of *zur*, to which they had added certain filthy matters besides.

Vitek let himself be enticed into carrying the pot, which dangled from his shoulder in a net, whilst another little fellow at his side dragged along the ground a herring cut out of wood and attached to a string. They went foremost, the others trooping behind with a deafening noise of rattles and shouts . . . They went in procession round the pond and church, and turned off to the poplar road where the funeral was to take place . . . when suddenly Yasyek struck at the pot with a spade and shivered it to pieces! And the *zur*, with all its filth, poured over Vitek's clothes!

Wladislaw Reymont, *The Peasants*

The principles for making *zur* may be revived for dietetic reasons, also for economic ones, though the modern tendency is to use an unfermented liquid based on similar ingredients, which is quicker and more bland. In 1985 one quarter of the soup recipes in a book on Czech cuisine consisted of either bread or potatoes, or flour or oatmeal, cooked in water or milk with herbs, sometimes thickened with cream or egg. The only thing that appeared to have changed was the base liquid. In Albania in 1987 I came across a white soup that must have been a near relative of modern *zur*-type soups. It was so plain and bland we dubbed it 'cream of cream'. The following recipes are for something better.

Potato soup with rolled oats

70 g (2½ oz) butter
225 g (8 oz) potatoes,
   peeled and diced
115 g (4 oz) rolled oats

salt
300 ml (½ pint) milk
1–2 egg yolks
parsley or chives

Melt the butter in a heavy pan, add the potatoes and oats, cook, stirring for a few minutes, then add 1½ litres (2½ pints) water with a pinch of salt and simmer until tender. Sieve or liquidize before adding the milk beaten together with the egg yolks. Add fresh herbs before serving.

This is a Czech recipe.

Thin spring soups are often made out of the tender new leaves of food plants and herbs.

Bulgarian thyme soup

1 large bunch of fresh thyme
2 tablespoons vinegar
½ cup pudding rice
pepper
2 cloves garlic, crushed with salt
yoghurt

Wash the thyme thoroughly and soak it in cold water and vinegar for several hours. Set aside a sprig for garnish. Strip the leaves from the remaining twigs by running your fingers against the growth, and cook them in fresh water, covered, for 5 minutes. Add the rice, pepper and garlic and cook until the rice is soft. Add a few tablespoonfuls of yoghurt before serving, and garnish with a sprig of thyme. This recipe may be used for other suitable fresh herbs: tarragon, parsley, dill, basil; there are many similar recipes with different thickenings.

Variations Another Bulgarian recipe is to make a light roux of butter, flour and water with equal handfuls of parsley, dill and mint, and to thicken it with 1 cup yoghurt and 2 egg yolks, beaten together, before serving.

The Czechs make a spring herb or Easter soup using parsley, chives, young nettles, lettuce leaves, strawberry leaves, flavoured with a pinch of nutmeg. Stock replaces the water and the yoghurt and eggs are omitted, though sour cream could be added.

The Romanians and Hungarians similarly make very light soups of dill and of caraway.

With herbs as the main ingredient, or garlic, these soups approach being thickened *tisanes*, except for the occasional appearance of bacon fat or butter, away from the influence of the Church.

Garlic soup

1 bulb garlic, finely
  chopped
2 large onions
2 tablespoons parsley and
  chives

2 tablespoons oil or bacon
  fat
1 tablespoon flour
squares of buttered toast
1 tablespoon fresh dill

Bring the garlic and whole onions to the boil in 1 litre (2½ pints) of lightly salted water and simmer covered for 15 minutes. Cook the parsley and chives in the melted fat or oil for a few minutes in another pan, add the flour and brown it, then add the onion, garlic and onion liquid gradually, stirring. Cook for 10 minutes. Liquidize, return to the boil, adjust seasoning and serve the soup poured over the squares of buttered toast and sprinkled with fresh dill.

This recipe is from Romania.

Variations A nineteenth-century Bohemian garlic soup begins with rye bread cut in thin slices and fried in butter. A few cloves of garlic crushed with salt and mixed with butter are brought separately to the boil in a few cups of water and the hot liquid, once it has taken the flavour, is poured over the bread. A garnish might be fresh marjoram, a herb of which the Czechs are fond.

A less elaborate garlic soup is made in Albania by frying half a dozen cloves of garlic in a tablespoon of olive oil, sprinkling on a teaspoon of paprika and a few cups of water. When the soup boils, add a few handfuls of vermicelli, season with salt to taste and garnish with parsley.

Generally these thin soups are quickly and cheaply made for everyday family consumption. They are cleansing and they take the edge off keen appetites. Bread soup, though not nominally thin, I think belongs in the same category because of its low nutritional value. Without the addition of some fat it will not stay long in the stomach. During Lent the Poles and Czechs made bread soup, flavouring it now with caraway, now with nutmeg, and expected to be hungry. When the rules relaxed again, and in less rigorous modern times, they added cream or cheese. The Albanians have a recipe for the simplest bread soup: with paprika, onion and potato. This probably has more to do with poverty than piety.

Luncheon soups

These soups have more flavour and subtlety and do not immediately speak of humble origins and limited ingredients. Their popularity in Germany, Czechoslovakia and Hungary is high, with soup generally preferred to hors d'oeuvres as the everyday first course at the main meal.

Sour cream soup from the Giant Mountains

This soup uses fresh yeast for extra flavour, a frequent habit in Bohemia.

30 g (1 oz) dried
   mushrooms
1 heaped teaspoon caraway
   seeds
salt
30 g (1 oz) fresh yeast

1 medium onion
1 tablespoon butter
4 hard-boiled eggs
500 g (1 lb) potatoes
1 carton (5 fl oz) *smatana* or
   sour cream

Boil the mushrooms with the caraway seeds in 1 scant litre ($1\frac{1}{2}$ pints) water, adding a little salt to taste, until you have a well-flavoured stock. Mix the yeast with a little warm water to a smooth paste and add it to the soup, together with the onion, chopped and lightly fried in butter. A lid on the pan or frequent stirring will stop the onion browning. Shell and chop the hard-boiled eggs, boil the potatoes in their skins and cut into quarters.

To serve, dilute the cream gradually with a little of the stock, then add it to the soup in the pan. Check seasoning. Reheat the soup without boiling and pour over some potato and egg in each soup plate.

The Giant Mountains are a group of peaks in north-east Bohemia within the Sudeten range.

Many soups for daily consumption are made from potatoes and from grain, using water or white stock as a base. Green rye (spelt) and barley are traditionally used in Germany, Czecho-slovakia and Poland, with barley almost achieving the status of a national food in Poland.

Krupnik

250 g (8 oz) mixed vegetables without cabbage
250 g (8 oz) soup bones
2 dried mushrooms
½ cup pearl barley
3 tablespoons butter

3 potatoes, boiled and cubed
salt
parsley, chopped
fresh dill, chopped
sour cream or egg yolk, lightly beaten (optional)

Make a stock with the vegetables, bones, mushrooms and 1½ litres (scant 3 pints) of water. Wash the barley, then cook separately in ½ litre (1 pint) water, together with half the butter. Remove the bones from the stock, add the potatoes and combine with the barley and any remaining cooking liquid. Bring to the boil and season. Add the fresh herbs and remaining butter just before serving. A little sour cream is an excellent addition, as is an egg yolk. The barley can be replaced by buckwheat to give a meatier flavour.

I first had this soup, made with chicken stock, in the Lublinianka Hotel in Lublin, close to the Russian border. It paved the way for a strapping, well-cooked lunch of ox-tongue goulash and was served with large glasses of beer. The hotel, a stately nineteenth-century civic building painted deep blue-grey with only a few remaining scrapes of red, was poor, dimly lit, yet thriving. The atmosphere was rather enviable, made up of stiff white tablecloths, a grand staircase, overworked waitresses and an unassuming, hungry clientele.

Rumford soup

This is a poor man's version of *krupnik*. The philanthropist Lord Rumford (1753–1814) invented it on behalf of poor German peasants, and it retains its place in a modern Polish cookery book. It uses peas instead of meat bones and no sour cream. According to the West German novelist Günter Grass, much of whose inspiration is culinary, stale bread and flat beer also went into this pottage, which was so thick it would not part from the spoon.

Kapusniak

This is the classic Polish sauerkraut soup, the equivalent of the Russian *shchi*.

250 g (8 oz) mixed vegetables
2 dried mushrooms
250 g (8 oz) pork bones
1 450–500 g (16 oz) jar sauerkraut
caraway seeds

1 medium onion plus one small, both finely chopped
3 tablespoons bacon fat
4 tablespoons flour
salt, pepper
peas (optional)

Make a stock with 1½–2 litres (3–4 pints) water, the vegetables, mushrooms and bones, and strain it, reserving the mushrooms. Drain off the sauerkraut juice (reserve it for another recipe, such as one of the sour soups below, or for seasoning the soup before serving). Chop the sauerkraut and cook it in a little water with the caraway seeds and the medium-sized onion, until tender. In another pan, brown the small onion in the bacon fat, add the flour, cook for a few minutes, then gradually add some of the stock, stirring until the soup thickens. Add the rest of the stock, chop and add the mushrooms, and also the sauerkraut and onion. Bring to the boil and season. Some of the raw sauerkraut juice will increase the piquancy of this soup, which is pleasant. It looks better when it is garnished with sweet green peas.

Abroad, the best-known Polish soup is *barszcz*. In Reymont's novel *The Peasants* one of the chief male protagonists returns from prison crying for homely *barszcz* and potatoes to relieve him of the town food he has had to endure. *Barszcz* qualifies as an Old Polish, i.e. medieval, preparation, which became a mainstay of the burgher cuisine of the nineteenth century. There are many varieties, hot and cold, clear and thick. This modern Polish recipe for the unstrained, hot vegetarian version is attributed to what is now western Russia, just over the border from Lublin. It would be at home in the town of Lvov, known to the Poles as Lwow and to the Germans as Lemberg. In fact, therefore, it is Ukrainian. Moreover, I can see no fundamental difference between it and Russian *borshch*. Poles, Ukrainians, Russians and Jews have this kind of soup in common, either with meat or meatless, and with small variations in the type of stock and herbs used.

Barszcz

150 g (5 oz) dried white beans

250 g (8 oz) mixed vegetables – onion, carrot, parsnip, leek etc.

150 g (5 oz) fresh beets, or, second best, bottled

3 medium potatoes

1 large tin tomatoes, puréed, or tomato purée made up to 1 cup with water, or five fresh tomatoes, cooked and puréed

3 tablespoons flour

1 small carton (5 fl oz) sour cream

salt, sugar to taste

fresh dill, chives

Soak the beans overnight, then cook until nearly tender. Add the finely chopped vegetables, fresh beets and potatoes, and when all are tender add the tomato purée. Mix the flour to a paste with the sour cream and dilute with a little hot soup before adding to the pan. Bring to the boil, stirring, and add salt and sugar to taste. Garnish with the fresh herbs. In need, bottled beets can be used. Add them finely chopped when the other vegetables are already tender. The juice from pickled beets is also often used to improve the colour of beetroot soups, and to give them a final piquancy, as with the *kapusniak*.

Traditionally *barszcz* is served with cooked buckwheat or potatoes. A fictitious meal of Polish flavours to suit Western tastes might consist of this soup followed by one of the buckwheat or potato dishes on pp. 304–5, 314–15 and 318–19, or you might simply serve it, for a wholesome vegetarian lunch, with buckwheat bread (see p. 353) and a plate of Lipto cheese (see p. 85).

A recipe for clear *barszcz* will be found on p. 132, and for the cold *chlodnik* on p. 134.

Potato soup

The classic homes for potato soup are Germany, Czechoslovakia and Transylvania, though recipes abound from everywhere. The Czechs like to flavour their soup with caraway, or with garlic and marjoram, or by including slices of sausage. Often, as in the Polish manner attributed to the Western town of Poznań, the taste is brought out with a final dash of vinegar. My favourite remains this soup from Romania.

1 kg (2 lb) potatoes	chives, chopped
350 g (12 oz) onions, chopped, plus one small onion	2 heaped tablespoons chopped parsley
2 tomatoes, quartered	1 clove garlic, crushed
120 g (4 oz) carrots, diced	salt, pepper
½ leek, or a few spring onions, or a handful of	2–3 bacon rashers, diced
	1–2 tablespoons flour
	1 teaspoon paprika

1 egg yolk
1 small (5 fl oz) carton sour
    or fresh cream

chopped fresh dill

Wash the potatoes, cut them coarsely and bring to boil in 2½ litres (4 pints) water. Add the vegetables, parsley and garlic, reserving the small onion. Cook for 15 minutes, then season lightly. In a separate pan, fry the small onion, chopped, with the bacon. Stir in the flour and paprika and dilute with a few drops of soup. Add this mixture to the soup and cook until potatoes are soft. Mix the egg yolk with the sour cream, dilute with a little soup and return to the pan. Heat through, stirring carefully. Add the dill just before serving. Serve rough bread and extra sour cream. This soup is *maigre*, tastes thoroughly of potato, and is very satisfying both to eat and to reflect upon. Don't be tempted to liquidize it.

Here is another Balkan recipe, from Yugoslavia. It is more sophisticated and has an encitingly rich caramel colour.

Potato soup with chanterelles

500 g (1 lb) potatoes
250 g (8 oz) fresh
    chanterelles, or 30 g
    (1 oz) dried
fresh or dried savory, dried
    marjoram
bay leaf
2 cloves garlic

salt, pepper
50 g (2 oz) butter
50 g (2 oz) shallot
30 g (1 oz) flour
fresh chives
4 tablespoons sour cream
a few tablespoons tarragon
    vinegar

Peel and cube the potatoes, add the sliced mushrooms and cook in 1½ litres (2½ pints) water with the dried herbs, bay leaf, garlic, salt and pepper for 30 minutes. In a separate pan, make a roux with the butter, shallots and flour, and dilute with a little stock before adding to the large pan. Boil the soup well. Before serving add the chives, sour cream and vinegar to taste.

A few sprigs of tarragon kept in a bottle of vinegar for a month will flavour the vinegar.

An ounce of dried mushrooms substituted for the fresh chanterelles will produce a soup which would be equally at home in Poland.

Pea soup

The Germans, the Poles and the Czechs are famous for their pea soup. In the pea-soup capital, Berlin, this generally thick broth is served with bacon, in Prague with sausage. Polish *grochowka* is with *barszcz, krupnik, grzybowka* (mushroom soup) and *kapusniak* one of the classic national five. This basic recipe, which I have chosen from among various recipes as the lightest, can either be adapted to meat or served in a vegetarian version with a little thin cream.

90 g (3 oz) dried peas	½–1 teaspoon paprika or a
30 g (1 oz) butter or bacon fat	good pinch of cayenne pepper
30 g (1 oz) flour	1 diced frankfurter, or 60–
½ teaspoon sugar	90 g (2–3 oz) bacon in a
1 small onion, grated	piece, diced and fried, or
2 cloves garlic	the same quantity of
salt	garlic sausage, or similar

Soak the peas in unsalted water overnight, then cook until tender in 2 litres (scant 3 pints) water. Purée the peas in the cooking liquid. Make a roux with the fat and flour, add the purée and cook for 15 minutes. Add the sugar, the raw onion, grated, the garlic, crushed with salt, and paprika or cayenne. Before serving add the bacon or sausage.

The same recipe can be followed using lentils.

A meatless *grochowka*, with a stock based on dried mushrooms and thickened with potato and flavoured with garlic and marjoram, sometimes appears on the Polish Lenten Christmas table.

Fruit traders from Montenegro. Engraving after Valerio, 1864,
Victoria and Albert Museum

Kempinski soup, named after the famous Berlin hotel of Bismarck's day, is a purée of green peas and carrots, garnished with rice. It is one of the register of international dishes established by Richard Henry, *chef de cuisine* at the Hotel Metropol in Vienna in 1907.

Chestnut soup

In Dalmatia, where chestnuts are an important food crop, a sweetish soup is made from a chestnut purée diluted with stock, to which egg yolks and a little sugar are added.

Almond soup

This is considered rather old-fashioned even in Poland, where it used to be one of the choices for Christmas Eve. Normally soup is served as the second course of this large Lenten meal, but this one is suggested to follow the fish course, which would make it the fourth or fifth course and a way of cleansing the palate before the sweet courses.

200 g (7–8 oz) ground almonds
6 cups milk
$\frac{1}{2}$ cup rice, cooked separately
sugar to taste
1 teaspoon almond extract
$\frac{1}{2}$ cup raisins

Mix the almonds with a little cold milk, bring the rest of the milk to the boil, combine, and add all other ingredients.

Albanian summer-vegetable soup

1 tablespoon butter or oil
225 g ($\frac{1}{2}$ lb) tomatoes, chopped
225 g ($\frac{1}{2}$ lb) green peppers, chopped
1 onion, chopped
1 tablespoon flour

1 litre (2 pints) stock – white, vegetable or made with chicken stock cubes
$\frac{1}{3}$ cup rice
1 egg
$\frac{1}{2}$ cup yoghurt

Heat the fat in a heavy pan, add the tomatoes, peppers and onion, cook for a few minutes, sprinkle with the flour and cook for another few minutes, then slowly, stirring, add the stock. Simmer for 20 minutes, then strain. Return the strained soup to the pan, add the rice and cook for 10–15 minutes more. In a warmed serving bowl beat the egg and the yoghurt together and slowly pour in the hot soup, stirring constantly. Alternatively, mix a little of the hot soup with the egg and yoghurt and return this mixture to the pan, stirring. This soup, like all egg-based liquids, should be reheated very carefully and not allowed to boil, otherwise it will congeal.

Rice, which the Turks encouraged as a food crop in southeast Europe, is used widely in Balkan soups, but yoghurt is peculiar to two countries: Albania and Bulgaria, which learned their eating habits from the Orient. Yoghurt takes the place of sour cream or, occasionally, whey, in Central Europe.

Sorrel soup

Sorrel soups are popular wherever sourness is liked, but perhaps mainly in Hungary and Poland. Paul Kovi writes that the flavour used to be particularly favoured by Transylvanian Jews. In Britain, sorrel divides the sheep from the goats as far as kitchen management is concerned, because its tart green leaves, related to rhubarb, are virtually unavailable in shops, though an easy perennial to grow. When you make a sorrel soup for the first time, you may be surprised how close it comes to being a fruit soup, because of the rhubarb connection. It needs either sweetening or blunting (puréed white beans are excellent for this) and cream is often added, which produces something not dissimilar to a rhubarb fool. Get someone to try it blindfolded. This recipe comes from Hungary.

500 g (1 lb) sorrel	a pinch of sugar
1 large onion, chopped	2 tablespoons flour
50 g (2 oz) bacon fat or butter	4–5 tablespoons sour cream
	$1\frac{1}{2}$–$1\frac{3}{4}$ litres ($2\frac{1}{2}$–3 pints)

good stock, made with vegetables and meat bones	4 eggs salt

Remove the stems of the sorrel and wash it. Sauté the onion in the fat, add the sorrel and sugar and braise covered for about 10 minutes. Combine the flour and cream, mix in the strained stock and pour onto the sorrel. Simmer for about 5 minutes. Drop the eggs singly into the soup to poach with a pinch of salt on top of each. Serve immediately.

Cauliflower soup

This is a Czech recipe for a soup that also belongs to Berlin.

1 large cauliflower salt 4 tablespoons butter 4 tablespoons flour a pinch of mace	1–2 egg yolks ¼ litre (½ pint) single cream chopped parsley

Boil the cauliflower in 1½ litres (scant 3 pints) lightly salted water, till nearly tender. Make a roux with the butter and flour and dilute with some of the cooking water before adding to the pan and continuing cooking with the seasoning till smooth and soft. The soup can be puréed if a very smooth result is desired. Finish it either by adding an egg yolk or two, beaten with up to ¼ litre (½ pint) cream, and garnishing with parsley, or, better, by serving with dumplings.

Dumplings To make these, combine an egg with 80 g (3 oz) fresh breadcrumbs moistened with milk, a teaspoon of butter, a pinch of salt and some fresh parsley. Form small balls and poach in the soup for 3–5 minutes.

Soup with pasta

Especially in Hungary and Yugoslavia, pasta, traditionally home-made, is a likely addition to soup. In Poland it is commonly added, pre-cooked, to fruit soup. Some of the savoury pasta 'soups' from the Balkans are so thick I have reclassified them as pasta dishes, but the German variety is always very light, in effect just a consommé with a garnish. The same savoury idea is also to be found in Poland. I like the German name for beef-tea, *Kraftbrühe* ('strength broth'), more than I like the result, which tends to be dull even when it is enhanced with that ubiquitous liquid-meat extract in a bottle so beloved of German cooks, Maggi. If you have time to make fresh pasta, however, the effort makes all the difference.

Riebelesuppe

The name means 'rubbed' or 'grated' soup, from the very quick technique used to make the pasta.

4 tablespoons flour

1 small egg

salt

1 litre (1¾ pints) beef or chicken or other well-flavoured stock

fresh parsley (optional)

Mix the flour, beaten egg and salt together and rub between the hands to form little crumbs. These should be as dry as possible. Add water only in real need. Add the 'crumbs' to the boiling stock, remove it immediately from the heat and serve plain, or garnished with parsley. I prefer a sprinkling of parmesan cheese, though this is not an idea from Germany or Central Europe.

At Christmas Poles sometimes serve a mushroom consommé for *Wigilia*. The mushroom broth is made by simmering an ounce of dried mushrooms in a good vegetable stock with more onions and parsley. Strain off all the vegetables except the mushrooms, which should be chopped and returned to the soup. Check seasoning and serve with egg noodles.

Omelette soup

Using 2 eggs per person, beat together the whites until stiff. Separately, beat the yolks with a teaspoon of flour and a pinch of salt per person. Combine the whites and the yolk mixture. Meanwhile, bring to the boil a well-flavoured stock to which you have added a piece of lemon rind or some tarragon or dill. Pour the egg mixture into the hot soup, cover, and simmer gently for a few minutes, until the eggs are firm. Turn the soup into a warm bowl, cut the omelette into individual pieces and serve with the liquid in soup plates, garnished with chopped parsley. This soup seems rather Chinese or Japanese.

Is not yonder fat, German-speaking Falstaff one of our most cherished friends, the apple of our eye, the prince of innkeepers and the very embodiment of large-hearted hospitality? How many times has he not brought us our egg soup with his own nimble fingers and lighted up the family flambeaux in our honour in that little low, dark room, with its framed engravings of French *grisettes* and the Hungarian patriots of '49.

Florence K. Berger, *A Winter in the City of Pleasure*, 1877

Wine soup

A rather different kind of egg soup is made by beating the yolks with sugar and alcohol. This really is a pick-me-up, and generally takes the name 'wine soup', not 'egg soup'. In effect it is an egg-nog, or a French *chaudeau*, or a more dilute version of an Italian *zabaglione*. Ms Berger, making her way down the Danube from Pest to Bucharest, staying in wayside inns, strong but appearing frail, would have been a good candidate to be offered and to receive wine soup most gratefully on behalf of the weaker sex.

Bring to near boiling 1 litre (2 pints) white wine with a cup of water, a cinnamon stick, 2 cloves and 3 allspice corns and allow to simmer for a few minutes. Strain off the spices and slowly add the hot wine to a mixture of five egg yolks beaten with two tablespoons of sugar, stirring all the while. A thick foam should form on top. Serve in cups, with sponge wafers.

Lemon soup

The Dalmatians make a similar soup, but replace the wine above with water flavoured with the juice of two lemons and their peel, cinnamon and salt. Beat this liquid into three yolks beaten with two tablespoons of sugar. Bring to the boil and drop in by the spoonful the stiffly beaten egg whites, as if cooking dumplings.

Pasulj

A standard Yugoslav dish is pasulj, which merely means beans. The beans are cooked with smoked pork and a flavouring of hot red paprikas, for a very long time, until all the flavours become pleasantly fused. But it is too heavy for a hot climate such as that of Dalmatia. Pasulj is frequently served in the Serbian and Macedonian monasteries, though the amount of hot paprika is sometimes surprisingly high. I recall being 'honoured' with pasulj at the very isolated monastery of Matejic on the mountains overlooking the plain of Kumanovo in Macedonia. It was very good pasulj and I was very hungry. But it was so highly seasoned that the sweat poured down my forehead in streams as I ate it, much to the amusement of the sole resident monk and a group of the monastery's Albanian goatherds.

Lovett Edwards, *Introducing Yugoslavia*, 1954

300 g (11 oz) white beans	2 cloves garlic
250 g (9 oz) onion	350 g (12 oz) smoked pork
carrots	bay leaf
parsley	1 tablespoon flour

50 g (2 oz) fat

1–2 tablespoons tomato
purée

1 sliced chilli pepper, or

cayenne, or chilli powder
to taste

salt

Soak the beans overnight. Drain. In 1½ litres (3 pints) water, cook the beans with the vegetables, garlic, meat and bay leaf until tender. Make a roux with the flour and fat, dilute with some soup, add the tomato purée and the sliced chilli pepper and return all to the pan to finish cooking. Check seasoning and serve with a piece of meat in each bowl.

Hungarian bean soup is cooked with bacon, seasoned with paprika and finished with sour cream. See also the sour Serbian bean soup on p. 127.

Gulyás

Many meat soups are closer to casseroles in the modern sense in that they constitute filling, one-pot meals. Goulash, which takes its name from that of a cowboy on the Great Hungarian Plain, is certainly better known in Britain as a stew and has become, like so many foreign dishes, a catch-all for restaurants and institutions to use up their leftovers. My daughter swears the school kitchen puts aubergines in the dreaded goulash. In Central Europe goulash is better cared for and is at least as well known as a soup. As a warming, filling savoury item it often appears on café menus in Austria, Czechoslovakia and Germany for consumption at any time of day. For home eating, packet versions are widely available.

Gulyás is essentially a way of cooking meat with plenty of unthickened liquid flavoured with paprika and caraway, tomato, green pepper and garlic, plus potatoes. In the beginning the puszta cowboys made a dish by adding water to meat they had preserved by cooking it with onions and drying it in the sun. This meat they carried in their sheep's-gut saddle-bags until needed. The recipe here is flexible: for stew, with potatoes, or with more liquid, for a soup worthy of a dinner-party. The soup

Cowherds of the puszta. Engraving after Valerio, 1885, Victoria and Albert Museum

should be strained. George Lang constructively suggests the removed meat be used to stuff peppers.

200 g (7 oz) onion, chopped
50 g (2 oz) bacon dripping
　or oil
1 teaspoon paprika powder,
　Hungarian if possible
pinch of chilli powder
750 g (1½ lb) lean beef,
　cubed (a mixture of
　different cuts, e.g. chuck,
　shin) will give maximum
　flavour

1 clove garlic, crushed with
　salt
½ teaspoon caraway seeds
2 green peppers, chopped
2 tomatoes, chopped
salt

For the stew only:
1 kg (2 lb) potatoes, peeled
　and diced

Fry the onion lightly in the fat, sprinkle with the paprika and chilli powder, cook 1 minute, then add the meat and mix well. Add the garlic and the caraway seeds. Add a few tablespoonfuls of water and simmer covered, stirring frequently, adding more water as necessary. After 10 minutes add the peppers, tomato, and for a stew, the potatoes, and simmer until meat and potatoes are tender. Check seasonings. For the stew use just enough water to stop the dish from becoming dry, about 2 cups in all. The soup calls for another cup of water at most, and should be strained before serving.

Variations The Yugoslav version of goulash soup, *bograc*, is hotter and breaks all the classic rules established in Budapest, such as not using either wine or flour. It is nevertheless very good. Following the recipe above, take 350 g (12 oz) onions for every 500 g (1 lb) beef, add another clove of garlic, ½ teaspoon marjoram and 2 tablespoons red wine. Add extra chilli powder or hot red peppers to taste. This soup is traditionally made in Pannonia and served in small, highly spiced portions from the traditional cast-iron cauldron which gives it its name. A version is also made with venison.

Solyanka

A latter-day competitor for the central place of *Gulaschsuppe* on the standard all-day East German menu is *solyanka*, which is a mainstay of the Russian repertoire. In the East Bloc it is sometimes called a Ukrainian speciality and sometimes included in a mini-festival of Russian cooking. Its cultivation in Germany smacks of political brown-nosing, less so in neighbouring Bulgaria, but gastronomically it cannot be denied that it is worth copying. The German version I had just inside the border at Berlin's *Ostbahnhof* was made with pork and sour cream, olives, capers and sour cucumbers. This cup was not only satisfying and warming, it was as evocative as it was intended to be. The last time I had *solyanka* in a restaurant was in the buffet car of a Soviet express train.

Czech pork soup

A soup which has a special place in Carnival week.

350 g (12 oz) pork – a pork head, a tongue and a piece of liver are recommended, but any cheap cuts will do
120 g (4 oz) soup vegetables
1 onion

salt, pepper
2 or more cloves garlic, crushed
dried marjoram
a few spoonfuls of cooked barley or rice

Make a stock with the meat, vegetables, onion and $1\frac{1}{2}$–$1\frac{3}{4}$ litres ($2\frac{1}{2}$–3 pints) water. Strain the stock, strip the meat from the bones, chop the meat and return it to the stock. Season and flavour with garlic and marjoram and serve over a spoonful of cooked grain. If the stock is fatty it may be cooled, skimmed and reheated. It may also be reduced before returning the meat, to strengthen the flavour.

Polish festive soup of beef and duck

500 g (1 lb) stewing beef
bay leaf, juniper berry, clove, allspice, marjoram
500 g (1 lb) duck portions
2 tablespoons oil
1 onion
180 g (6 oz) carrots
90 g (3 oz) parsnip

90 g (3 oz) celery
1 leek
salt
1 small carton (5 fl oz) sour cream
1 tablespoon flour
dill and parsley

Stew the beef in 1 litre (2 pints) water, together with the spices, which may be tied in muslin. Brown the duck pieces on both sides in a little oil, add a little water and roast in the oven. Sauté the vegetables in the rest of the oil. Bone the duck and add the flesh and the vegetables to the beef and cook together for a further $\frac{1}{2}$ hour. Remove the meat, cut into small pieces as necessary, place it in a tureen and pour over the soup, which has been thickened with the cream and flour mixed to a paste, adding the parsley and the dill.

A Polish royal consommé is made by combining beef with chicken. The two are simmered together with soup vegetables, spices and a sautéd onion. The stock is then strained, skimmed of fat and served with savoury pastries, strips of tomato omelette or other garnishes. These little onion tarts are also very suitable.

Kotaczynski with onion

Dough:
15 g (½ oz) yeast
¼ cup warm milk
2 egg yolks
350 g (12 oz) flour
⅓ teaspoon salt
45 g (1½ oz) melted butter

Filling:
250 g (8 oz) onion
50 g (2 oz) butter
½ teaspoon sugar
ground black pepper

Sprinkle the yeast on the warm milk and leave for 10 minutes in a warm place. Add the egg yolks, the flour sifted with the salt and the melted butter, and form into a firm dough. Break off small pieces, round them into buns about 6 cm (2 inches) in diameter. Place them on a greased baking sheet about 6 cm (2 inches) apart, and leave to rise, covered with a tea towel or plastic bag. Meanwhile, slice the onion and braise it in the butter over a very low heat, covered, until very soft. Take care not to let the onion burn. When done, add sugar and black pepper. Make small hollows in the top of the buns with a finger, fill with the mixture and bake in a preheated medium oven for about 20 minutes, or until golden brown. Serve warm.

In peasant societies in Central Europe, when the conventions were still clearly defined, very hearty soups were used to speak the language of matrimonial commerce. Young lovers in Hungary faced the prospect of a 'matchmaker soup', followed eventually by a 'nuptials soup'. The recipes I have seen for these are rich in various meats, vegetables and dumplings; real show-stoppers. Conversely, the young Pole who received a 'black' slaughterhouse soup (see p. 130) knew his chances were lost. This was the fate of Jacek Soplica, hero of Mickiewicz's epic, *Pan Tadeusz*, who was suing for the hand of a much younger girl. The story echoed the poet's own rebuff in love. According to another disturbing custom, the prospect of a bowl of pea soup would keep a lover in suspense until it was set before him. If the pig's tails inside were lying down, the answer was no, if they were standing up, yes.

Tarragon lamb soup

Recipes for this excellent soup are found in Hungary, Romania and in Transylvania.

approx. 750 g (1½ lb) inexpensive cuts of lamb on the bone	1 tablespoon flour
	1 tablespoon or more sour cream
150 g (5 oz) carrot, celery and parsley root mixed, as available	salt
	1 egg yolk
1 onion	approx. 1 tablespoon wine vinegar
peppercorns	toast
1 bunch fresh tarragon	

Bring the meat to the boil in plenty of water, skim off any scum and cook with the vegetables, peppercorns and tarragon until tender. Strain, discard the vegetables and bone, and dice the meat. Mix together the flour and sour cream, dilute it with a little stock, then return to the pan. Heat the soup through. Season, remove from the heat, add about a tablespoon of wine vinegar, then pour onto the egg yolk, which has been put in a tureen. Return the meat and add squares of toast just before serving.

Fred Macnicol says this soup was originally made with a lamb's head which was served on a separate plate. The skull was broken open and the brains eaten on bread with the soup.

Sour Soups

From my childhood, I have been accustomed to eat soup, mostly sour; in the mountains we like that the best. Sour soup and potatoes for breakfast, potatoes and sour soup for dinner, supper the same; Sundays we usually had, in addition to soup and potatoes, a slice of oaten bread. This is the usual fare of people living in the Giant Mountains and they are thankful they have enough of it; for in hard times they are glad to get a little bran. Further in the interior people have peas, whiter flour, cabbage, and sometimes a little meat; they live well! But the poor must not accustom themselves to dainties, else they would soon be at the end of their means. Besides, such things are not nourishing.

Bozena Nemcova, *The Grandmother*, 1855

The path to 'sour soup' has been paved by many of the preceding recipes. The thin breakfast soups and the *zur* are sour because of their fermented 'beer' bases. Soups with sauerkraut speak for themselves, but many soups like *barszcz* and tarragon lamb soup are, less obviously, finished with a dash of vinegar or sauerkraut or pickled beet juice. *Solyanka* is based almost wholly on pickling brine, as its name suggests. (*Sol'* is the Russian for salt.) The sour theme applies to both thin and thick soups. Sour semi-liquid combinations of sauerkraut, beans, smoked meat and sour cream are popular in Yugoslavia and Bulgaria and Hungary, 'Vipava soup' and 'Alföld Reaper's soup' among them. A traditional Transdanubian soup is made with sauerkraut and fish roe.

In relation to these sour soups from Central Europe, the Balkan *ciorbas* are a kind of sub-genre, sometimes using the same souring agents, sometimes preferring lemon or yoghurt. In general, though, they are part of a different gastronomic world, more centred on Istanbul than on Vienna. The word *ciorba* comes from Turkish.

Serbian bean ciorba

250 g ($\frac{1}{2}$ lb) dried white
   beans
2 carrots
1 parsnip
1 onion
1 tablespoon salt
1 tablespoon dripping, lard,
   bacon fat or oil

2 tablespoons flour
3 or more garlic cloves
1 tablespoon paprika, plus
   $\frac{1}{4}$ teaspoon cayenne
   pepper
1 cup yoghurt
1 teaspoon white-wine
   vinegar

Soak the beans overnight, and cook in plenty of fresh water until almost tender. Peel and dice the vegetables and add to the cooked beans in their liquid. Cook together for 10–15 minutes or until the beans and the vegetables are both quite soft. Season with half the salt. In a separate pan, melt the fat, stir in the flour and cook for a few minutes. Add the garlic, crushed with the rest of the salt, and the paprika and cayenne. Dilute into a smooth sauce with half a cup of cold water and add to the beans and vegetables, mixing well. Simmer, adding water or stock if the soup is too thick, for 10–15 minutes more. It may be left as it is or half of it puréed in a blender to give a thicker and more homogeneous texture. Just before serving, dilute the yoghurt with a little hot soup and add to the pan, then add the vinegar and adjust the seasoning. This is one of the tastiest bean soups I have ever made. The use of well-flavoured dripping to make the thickening is basic to simple Hungarian cooking, as is the sour finish to contrast with the sweetness of the vegetables. Both devices add bite.

Romanian fish ciorba

An English visitor to south-east Europe before the war described the Romanians as amongst the best and most prodigious eaters in the world. This fish *ciorba* is a luxurious example of their cuisine at its best. Carp, pike, tuna, bream, perch, sterlet and sturgeon are all found in the Danube.

1 scant litre (1½ pints) fish
stock
1 cup pickled cucumber or
sauerkraut juice
6 spring onions
1 tomato
1 small green pepper
3 tablespoons each parsley
and fresh fennel or dill

2 tablespoons fresh lovage
or 1 teaspoon fenugreek,
crushed
500–750 g (1–1½ lb)
sturgeon, carp, salmon or
halibut, filleted
salt, pepper

Mix the liquids, which are the secret of this simple soup, in a
large pan (not aluminium), add the chopped vegetables and
herbs and simmer gently for 10–15 minutes. Add the fish in
chunks and continue cooking another 10 minutes. Check
seasoning and serve. The traditional accompaniments are hot
peppers and a glass of *tuica* – plum brandy. The sourness of the
soup does not flatter wine.

Soup always fits well with bread, but in the countryside the old
preference was for *mamaliga*, that yellow cornmeal porridge
better known to us by its Italian name, polenta. To try it, cook
cornmeal (maize) grains to a thick mush with water and either
serve this stiff mixture direct from the pot or bake it so the top is
crisp and cut it into squares. Variations on the *mamaliga*-and-
sauce theme underlie much Romanian peasant cooking. If there
is no soup, almost anything else will do: melted butter, dripping,
cheese, or sour cream, or fried onion or hot pickles. Legend has
it the devil will work for man if he can eat his fill of cornmeal.

Ciorba with meatballs

bones for stock
2 carrots
½ celeriac, or a few sticks
of celery and some
parsnip
2 onions, studded with a
clove

1 green pepper
1 clove garlic
thyme, bay leaf
parsley
fresh dill
2 tomatoes

salt, freshly ground black pepper	lamb, veal or pork, or mixed as for *mititei* (see p. 94)
1 litre (2 pints) sauerkraut or pickled cucumber juice	a good slice of bread, moistened with milk or 2 tablespoons cooked rice
1 egg yolk	1 egg
2 tablespoons sour cream	salt, pepper
For the meatballs:	
500 g (1 lb) minced beef,	

Bring the bones to the boil, skim the surface and add the vegetables, garlic, thyme and bay leaf. Simmer gently for 40 minutes, remove the bones, add the fresh herbs and tomatoes. Check seasonings. Combine all the ingredients for the meatballs, form with wet hands into balls the size of walnuts and poach in the soup liquid, which should be just simmering. Warm the sauerkraut liquid and add to the soup just before serving. Thicken the soup with the egg yolk and cream, which have been beaten together and first diluted with some of the liquid from the pan. Serve as above, with sharp peppers and *mamaliga*.

A rich *ciorba* known as *bors* (sounding like the Russian *borshch*) is also made in Romania with lamb and based on fermented bran. Other less well-known *ciorbas* are made with veal and with tripe. The other Balkan countries also make soups of lamb or mutton soured with vinegar.

Bulgarian chicken ciorba

This mild, light recipe is specifically Bulgarian in using yoghurt as the souring agent. Cook two tablespoons of rice in about a litre (2 pints) chicken stock and season with salt and black pepper to taste. Separately mix a cup of yoghurt with two cups of water, one or two beaten egg yolks and two tablespoons of flour, and heat gently, stirring all the time to prevent curdling. Add the stock and rice slowly, stirring, and cook five minutes. Garnish just before serving with fresh mint and a knob of butter.

Albanian lemon chicken soup

Cook rice in stock as in the previous recipe and, when tender, combine carefully with a well-beaten egg and about two tablespoons lemon juice. Heat through carefully and serve with plenty of freshly ground black pepper.

Slaughterhouse soups
🙭

At Christmas father would kill a pig and singe it and scald it and quickly wrap it in straw to make it sweat, in order that the hair would scrape off easier. I used to sit astraddle the pig and make a tremendous racket, knowing that I would be given the pig's tail to fry and the bladder to fill with grain, to blow up and drum upon once it was dry . . .

Ion Creanga, *Recollections*

When the boy who would become one of Romania's greatest modern story-tellers went Christmas carol-singing, he beat time on this drum made from the bladder of the freshly killed pig. At home his father jointed the carcass and his mother made soup, lard, sausage and bacon. The boy knew how to count the family blessings at this time of the year, before the onset of the worst of the winter. There were logs in the shed, flour and bacon in the loft, a barrel full of cheese and a tub full of pickled cabbage; and his parents were happy. The Christmas slaughter that capped this plenty, was, though hardly consciously, a ritual celebration of affluence over adversity. Wladislaw Reymont in *The Peasants* describes killing the pig for Easter. Children and women crowd around eagerly; the catching of the steaming, spurting blood in a bowl is a triumphant moment. We no longer make these soups nor understand these emotions.

Modern East European cookery books still include a number of 'slaughterhouse' recipes for domestic use. Polish *czarnina* incorporates the blood of freshly killed ducks, geese or a pig into a rich stock made with giblets and bones, vegetables and dried mushrooms, spiced with vinegar, a piece of gingerbread and sweetened with dried prunes and sugar. Hungary has *tszantul*, pig-killing soup, which makes a rich stock from the liver, lungs, heart and bones of the pig, flavours it with mixed vegetables and savoy cabbage, thickens it with a roux of flour and lard and laces it with sour cream and a little lemon juice, the creamy piquant finish of so many Hungarian recipes. All these soups were by origin ritualistic dishes, sometimes imbued with a special function in connection with love and fertility, like the matrimonial soups mentioned on p. 124.

In the second rank, less significant but equally nourishing, are the soups made of entrails. Yugoslavia has a sour pork broth made from trotter, tail and ear, thickened with flour, made spicy with hot paprika, finished with sour cream.

The food writer Joseph Wechsberg, born in Moravia at the turn of the century, remembered the bowl of calf lungs he enjoyed for second breakfast. This too was a soup, which has its counterpart all over Eastern Europe.

Some affinities with Italy

🙚

Rice in soup with fresh sausage

This is a simple idea, but since I came across the idea in Yugoslavia I have found it a very useful standby. All the difference is made by adding the parmesan cheese, so don't be tempted to omit it or substitute another cheese.

Cook 200 g (7 oz) rice in 1 litre (2 pints) well-flavoured stock. When half-done, add diced fried sausages, ideally home-made, and finish cooking. Check seasoning, sprinkle each bowl with grated parmesan and serve.

Dubrovnik minestrone

Cook mixed vegetables – sprouts, potatoes, courgettes, French beans – in a good meat stock and when half-tender add pieces of garlic sausage, or other continental sausages, and chopped bacon. Before serving, mix together some olive oil, parsley and crushed garlic and stir into the soup, which should not be too thick.

Dalmatian fish soup

If you trust sea water, use $\frac{2}{3}$ sea water to $\frac{1}{3}$ fresh water, otherwise take about $1\frac{1}{2}$ litres (3 pints) fresh water, lightly salted. Lightly fry a large onion in plenty of olive oil until transparent, add 1 kg or more (2–$2\frac{1}{2}$ lb) mixed sea fish, about 200 g (7 oz) fresh tomatoes, 100 g ($3\frac{1}{2}$ oz) rice, $\frac{1}{4}$ litre ($\frac{1}{2}$ pint) white wine, the water, crushed garlic, peppercorns, parsley and a bay leaf. Simmer until the rice is cooked. The problem with this soup, as with so many fish dishes, is the bones: a problem rarely acknowledged in books. The original recipes are undoubtedly full of bones, to which those who grow up with them become accustomed. Filleted fish is a must for most of us. Use the bones and scraps to make a fish stock for another recipe.

Two soups for a dinner-party
☙

Barszcz with little mushroom pies

This is the most common Polish choice for Christmas Eve. A well-flavoured, rich-coloured beetroot consommé is worth taking the trouble to prepare for a special occasion.

250 g (8 oz) fresh raw
  beetroot, sliced
½ celeriac, sliced, or a few
  sticks of celery
15 g (½ oz) dried
  mushrooms

parsley
1 large clove of garlic
1¼ litres (2½ pints) water or
  stock
beetroot juice or *zur*
salt

Simmer all the vegetables including the parsley and the garlic in the water or stock. Strain, add the beetroot juice, for a touch of sourness and colour, and adjust seasoning. Pour over the mushroom pies and serve garnished with more parsley.

To make the pierogi, combine 75 g (3 oz) flour and 1 egg yolk and a pinch of salt, form into 4 cm (2 inch) squares. Make the filling by frying a small onion in 15 g (½ oz) butter with 120 g (4 oz) fresh chopped mushrooms. Add a tablespoon of fresh breadcrumbs, some parsley and, most essential, some fresh dill. Season with salt and pepper and bind with a beaten egg white. Put some filling in each square, fold into triangles and press the edges together. Lower into boiling water and simmer for 5 minutes. Drain.

Tarator

Bulgaria is the home of the yoghurt culture *bacillus bulgaricus*, made with lamb glands. It has acquired legendary status as a means to longevity. Home-made yoghurt would suit this recipe, though if it is already thin, dilute it with less water than given below.

1 large cucumber, peeled, diced, salted and drained
3 cups yoghurt
3 cups iced water or mineral water
2 tablespoons olive oil
85 g (3 oz) walnuts, crushed
3 large cloves garlic, crushed with salt

Combine all the ingredients in a blender and serve chilled.

Chlodnik

Mickiewicz in *Pan Tadeusz* describes a soup of young beet leaves with cream, served with ice. This is the embellished recipe Polish *émigrés* took with them to the United States, very much resembling the Russian cold beet-leaf soup, *botvinya*, and the cold buttermilk and dill pickle soup, *okroshka*.

500 g (1 lb) fresh beets with greens	1 pickled cucumber, finely chopped
1½ litres (3 pints) water or chicken stock	3 tablespoons chopped fresh dill
salt	pepper
1 large fresh cucumber, diced	1 lemon, sliced
6 radishes, sliced	2 hard-boiled eggs, chopped or sliced
6 spring onions, chopped	12 large shrimps, cooked and peeled (optional)
2 tablespoons lemon juice	
2 cups sour cream or buttermilk	

Clean the beets and leaves well, but do not peel. Set to cook in plenty of lightly salted water, simmering gently until tender. Drain, reserving the liquid. Peel and chop the beets and the greens. Combine with the liquid and all other ingredients, using the lemon, eggs and shrimps as a garnish. Chill well before serving with black bread and chilled lager. For a meal with a thoroughly Polish flavour, follow with an entrée of boiled sausage and lentil purée and a dessert of warm apple strudel.

Fruit soups

From savoury sourness it is a small step to fruit soups. The fruit-soup tradition is especially popular in Germany, Hungary and Poland. These are best made with fresh soft fruit in season, sweetened with sugar or dried fruit. Outside these boundaries, both apples and rosehips are possible. A few years ago a good restaurant in Warsaw had strawberry soup on the menu – but only on the menu – in December, evidence that the grand intention was at least there. The Hungarian Gay Hussar restaurant in London is famous for its cherry soup. The function of these soups is to sharpen the palate for more savoury flavours to come, but it is perhaps misleading to find them most often offered in restaurants only as first courses. Like sorbets, they also cleanse the palate, and are assimilated into the French meal pattern by being served after the entrée and before the cheese. In Poland at this point in the meal they would be followed by dessert. Fruit soups also make excellent summer snacks and soothing pick-me-ups, as a change from coffee and biscuits.

Cherry soup

1½ kg (3 lb) fresh cherries
½ teaspoon or a stick of cinnamon bark
2 cloves
½ cup sugar or to taste
¾ cup sour cream

Cook the washed, stoned fruit and the spices in 1¼ litres (2 pints) water. Remove the cinnamon bark and cloves, purée the liquid and add sugar to taste. When cool, beat in the cream and serve chilled. The Polish recommendation is to serve it with noodles or croûtons.

Apricot soup

500 g (1 lb) fresh apricots
1 tablespoon potato flour
  or cornflour
⅓ cup sugar

peel and juice of ½ lemon
¼ teaspoon salt
600 ml (1 pint) sour cream

Cook the apricots in $1\frac{1}{4}$ litres (2 pints) water, remove the stones and purée with some of the cooking liquid. Mix the flour to a paste with the rest of the liquid, bring to the boil and stir until thick. Add the fruit, sugar, lemon and salt and cook for a few minutes. Serve hot or cold, with the sour cream spooned on top of each serving. This recipe can also be made with plums.

Cold berry soup

Purée three cups of fresh berries – strawberries, raspberries, blackberries or blackcurrants. Add two cups of water and simmer 15 minutes. Mix a tablespoon of potato or cornflour with a little water, stir into the soup and continue stirring over heat until thick. Add the peel and juice of half a lemon, plus sugar to taste and about $\frac{1}{2}$ teaspoon cinnamon. Chill, beat in 600 ml (1 pint) sour cream and garnish with a cup of uncrushed berries.

Prune and sour cream soup

350 g (12 oz) dried prunes, stoned
250 g ($\frac{1}{2}$ lb) rhubarb
$\frac{1}{2}$ teaspoon cinnamon
2 cloves
sugar to taste
1 tablespoon cornflour or potato starch (optional)
$\frac{3}{4}$ cup sour cream

Soak the prunes in 3 cups hot water for 1 hour, then cook in the same water for 5 minutes. Cook the rhubarb in 2 cups boiling water for 10 minutes. Purée both and combine. Add the spices, sugar and the cornflour mixed with a little water if desired, bring to the boil, stirring, then remove from the heat. When warm, stir in the cream. The recommendation is to serve this at room temperature with macaroni or croûtons, after a rich meat course.

FISH

The major waterways of Eastern Europe are the Adriatic, the Danube Delta and Black Sea and the Baltic. Add to these the thousands of rivers, beginning with the Danube itself, and lakes such as Ohrid, Shkodra and Balaton, and you have a picture of a half-continent with rich local traditions in fish cooking. The preparations vary not only from country to country but from region to region, which is wonderful for the culinary traveller, though frustrating in the confinement of a British kitchen. The recipes here are for those dishes most successfully reproducible outside their native habitat.

The Adriatic

Excellent fish is prepared on the Istrian Peninsula and all along the Adriatic coast, from Dalmatia to the southern tip of Albania. The great variety of fish in the sea and the simple preparation, by grilling, frying in batter and stewing in wine, are shared with Italy. Thus, to the Italian *brodetto* corresponds the Dalmatian *brodet* and to *fritto misto* the heaped plates of mixed deep-fried fish and shellfish served by Yugoslav waterside restaurants to lure tourists. It is said the deeper waters of the eastern Adriatic produce a higher quality catch than on the shallow Italian side of the sea, and that discriminating Venetian restaurants buy their fish from across the water. There again the maritime and fish-eating cultures of Venice and Dalmatia have been rivals for a thousand years.

Halászcsárda

Hungarian fishermen's tavern (J.-L. Charmet), c. 1930

Dalmatian originality is most readily found in the distinctive flavours that come from its local wines and olive oils, and also from its herbs. Rosemary, a herb Pliny the Elder noted growing on the island of Solta, is much in evidence. It grows prolifically on the islands of Vis and Brac, together with wild mint and sage. Another unusual Dalmatian characteristic is to eat fish with chard, that green leaf vegetable so rightly prized by the Italians and so difficult to find in Britain, where it hides under the misleading name of sea-kale.

The eastern Adriatic catch has been praised since antiquity. Pliny wondered if it were not the food of Split as well as the sulphur springs that in the third century AD lured the Roman emperor Diocletian into retirement on the narrow seaboard at the foot of the sheer, dark and arid Dinaric Alps. The available catch in the area, potentially a different fish for every day of the year, includes tuna, mackerel, sardines, anchovy, whitebait, oysters, squid, octopus, sea bass, sole, dentex, hake, eels, Dublin Bay prawns (scampi) and freshwater crayfish (spiny lobster). This maritime harvest set a standard for fish in all Romance Europe. The French word for the spiny lobster, *langouste*, derives from Lagosta, the ancient Illyrian name for the Dalmatian island of Lastovo. The connection between the south Slavs and the eastern Mediterranean coasts was established 2,000 to 3,000 BC, in the Late Stone Age, thanks to the widespread belief in the curative powers of the 'sea gold' dug up from the Baltic shores. One of the famous amber trade-routes led from the eastern Baltic south, overland and down the eastern Adriatic coast towards the Mediterranean. Time and again travellers and passing traders stopped to praise the quality of Dalmatia's fish from the river mouths and the sea.

The eighteenth-century Venetian traveller Alberto Fortinis, in his *Viaggio in Dalmazia* (1774), particularly enthused about the sea-perch caught at the mouth of the river Cetina, between Split and Makarska. He also apologized for the piracy, which alone – alongside their fishing trade, rosemary and olive-oil production, viticulture and handicrafts – allowed the coastal Slavs to live. The poorest were the islanders, with little agricultural land and no livestock except high in the mountains. To the islanders' further disadvantage, centuries of foreign domination in Dalmatia, successively by the Turks, the Austrians, the French, the Hungarians and the Italians, had hindered cultural development.

Not surprisingly the diet of these communities, though naturally well endowed, remains simple. The tourism that has now come to relieve the Dalmatian economy has in the last hundred years turned Dalmatia into a treasure-trove for romantic travellers. The rich natural resources, the instinctive aesthetic of those whose lives are predominantly physical and spent in sunshine, and the classical heritage are immensely attractive. The appeal of the islands has in the past been enhanced by the songs of the fishermen and the taste of their stews, as well as by the truly clear water, mild air and blue sky which are still there. Even native spirits have not been immune. Petar Hektorovich, a Serbian poet, gave Croatia its oldest written record of national melodies when he collected *Fishing and Fishermen's Tales* (1568) from along the coast.

Fresh sardines

Sardine fishing, for the onlooker, is a fascinating sight. For here, as on other parts of the [Dalmatian] coast, the catch is made by the aid of acetylene lamps, a dozen very powerful ones being fixed in a glass case on the bows of the boats. At the start a cloth is thrown over them, and the boats row out in darkness except for a starlit sky, over waters that in daylight are as clear and transparent as crystal, but a crystal of ultramarine.

When a likely spot for a haul is reached, the boats draw apart, with the enormous nets stretched between them, and then the lamps are uncovered, transforming the sea into a fairyland of twinkling lights piercing down below the water in long quivering shafts. Attracted by these, sooner or later the shoal comes swimming to its death, but meanwhile the silence is unbroken, until the time comes for testing the weight of the nets. Soft calls are now exchanged and the boats begin to draw together again. It is a wonderfully picturesque sight, the quiet moon above, and the lights below flickering over the lines of dark figures as they sway backwards and forwards in the steady rhythmic motion of hauling in the nets length by length, singing the while soft lilting songs, whose rhythm times with that of their bodies.

It is customary for the sardine catchers to carry spears mounted on long poles, and with these they do deadly work upon the great octopi which lurk in the innumerable coastal caves and prey relentlessly upon the shoals, thus giving the fishermen nights of toil with little result.

Nora Alexander, *Wanderings in Yugoslavia*, 1936

Fresh sardines and anchovies are plentiful and the air of the islands smells not unpleasantly of the canning industry. Eaten on the spot, they are cleaned, rolled in flour and deep fried, served hot or cold with a slice of lemon, some bread and red wine. *Girice*, matchstick-sized sardines – the equivalent of whitebait – are dipped whole in flour, seasoned with salt and paprika, fried crisp in oil and served with lemon.

Mackerel with tomato

Mackerel does not have a romantic image, but when it is very fresh it is good to eat. In Dalmatia it is often marinated before being barbecued, grilled or fried.

4 mackerel, about 200 g (7 oz) each
3 lemons
½ cup olive oil
salt, pepper
fresh parsley
500 g (1 lb) tomatoes, sliced

Rub the cleaned and gutted mackerel inside and out with a mixture of the juice of 2 lemons, the oil, salt, pepper and chopped parsley. Cook flattened under a hot grill for 6–8 minutes each side, then finish for 2 minutes with the sliced tomatoes laid on the inside. Serve on warm plates with wedges of lemon.

Barbecued spicy mackerel

4 mackerel, about 200 g (7 oz) each
3 tablespoons wine vinegar
salt, pepper
8 olives, stoned and chopped
6–8 tablespoons oil

Wash and gut the fish, removing the heads, then halve and fillet them. Add the vinegar, salt, pepper and olives to half the oil and marinate the fish in this mixture for two hours. Barbecue on a griddle, turning and basting with the remaining oil. When cooked, serve on a warm plate with the marinade poured over.

Alternatively, wrap each fish, well soused with oil, in a packet of aluminium foil and bake it in the fire or in the oven.

Marinated grilled or barbecued mackerel is also served with plenty of finely chopped garlic strewn over it.

Kvarner mackerel with fresh sardines

4 mackerel, about 200 g (7 oz) each
1 dessertspoon salt
150 g (6 oz) fresh sardines
3 tablespoons oil
1 onion, chopped
1 tablespoon vinegar, 1 bay leaf, pepper

Traditionally, the washed, gutted mackerel is cooked for 10 minutes in sea water. For fresh water, add a dessertspoon of salt to a large pan of water and bring it gently to the boil with the fish immersed in it. Remove the cooked fish, cut off the heads, remove the bones and cut into fillets. Meanwhile, clean the sardines, remove the heads and cut into thin strips. Sauté these in the oil with the onion. Sprinkle with a tablespoon of vinegar, add a bay leaf, fresh black pepper and a scant cup of water and cook for 10 minutes. Pour the mixture over the mackerel fillets and chill before serving.

Against conventional wisdom the Dalmatians recommend boiling mackerel heads and bones with soup vegetables and seasoning to make a rich fish stock. This is a matter of taste.

Tuna and bonito

Some of the same excitement aroused by the sardine catch also surrounded the giant silvery tuna fish. Travellers fifty years ago described the fish being spied on at night by fishermen on 'tuna ladders' way above the water. Once the shoal was sighted the nets were closed and a haul of great commercial value netted.

Succulent fresh tuna steaks can be grilled or braised like beef in a rich sauce, and have often proved succour to the hungry male traveller. Alan Davidson quotes a delicious tuna *pasticada* in his *Mediterranean Seafood*. The fresh tuna is briefly fried on both sides in abundant olive oil, then two cloves of garlic, two spicy cloves, salt and pepper and three tablespoons of wine vinegar are added per pound of fish. Cook gently for an hour, gradually adding, per 500 g (1 pound), half a glass of red wine, a teaspoon of sugar and a little water if necessary.

The recipe also suits other meaty fish steaks like shark and swordfish, which, though deep-frozen, are often available in Britain in better condition than 'fresh' tuna. The fish may be served with chard and boiled potatoes, that combination being regarded as the basic diet of the Dalmatian people. *Pasticada* is normally made with beef (p. 198), which emphasizes the substantial way tuna is regarded.

Tuna fish patties

This recipe is *intended* to be made with tinned fish.

250 g (8 oz) puff pastry
50 g (2 oz) cooked rice
200 g (7 oz) cooked or
    tinned tuna with oil
1 clove garlic, crushed
120 g (4 oz) curd cheese,
    mild cream cheese or
    thick sour cream

120 g (4 oz) red pepper,
    chopped, or substitute
    another crisp vegetable
    like celery
1 tablespoon capers
salt, pepper
2–3 hard-boiled eggs, sliced
beaten egg to brush pastry

Roll out the pastry thinly and cut into rectangles. Size will depend on the function of the dish, but for a hot starter 5 cm × 5 cm (2 inches × 2 inches) will be about right. For convenience, if these pies are to make the body of a light meal, cut them twice as big. In a bowl mix the rice, tuna and oil, garlic, cheese or cream, red pepper and capers, and season lightly. Reserving half the rectangles as tops, spread the filling in two layers on each of the others, with a layer of egg between. Marry top and bottom of the pies and press the edges together. Brush the pastry with beaten egg, especially along these seams, and bake for 40 minutes in a medium oven. Serve as hot starters wrapped in a warm cloth, with white wine, or on a plate with salad.

White fish

The white fish of the Adriatic, along with the crustaceans, are its gastronomic glory. Delicacies like sea bass and dentex, however, are expensive even on the menus of waterside restaurants. The fish are grilled, baked whole or barbecued. The local speciality is to brush them or baste them with olive oil impregnated with rosemary or crushed juniper. Use a sprig of fresh rosemary for garnishing. Dried rosemary can be used in cooking, being one of the few herbs effective in that state, though when improvising beware of its strong flavour. The gilt-head bream, known locally as *orad* (the French *daurade*), is poached. Dalmatian sole, once it has been filleted, fulfils all the usual functions asked of it in an Anglo-French kitchen, though when home-caught it is simply turned in batter and fried, or spit-roasted, any leftovers being served cold with mayonnaise.

Hake or cod with prsut and anchovy in pastry

750 g (1½ lb) filleted hake or cod, or cod steaks
2–3 tablespoons each lemon juice and olive oil
500 g (1 lb) puff pastry
4 thin slices of prosciutto
4 anchovy fillets
beaten egg to brush pastry

For the sauce:
120 g (4 oz) onion or shallots, chopped
2 tablespoons butter
1 tablespoon red peppers
2 tablespoons flour
½ cup fish stock
salt
1 small carton (5 fl oz) cream
1 egg yolk (optional)

Buy the fish in eight thin fillets if possible, and sprinkle these with lemon juice and steep them in the oil for up to two hours. In the case of steaks, leave in one piece, together with the central bone, and proceed in the same way. Roll out the pastry and divide into four rectangles big enough to envelop the fish. Place a fillet on each rectangle, top it with a slice of prosciutto and chopped anchovy, and where applicable cover with a second fillet. Fold the pastry over the fish, seal the edges and brush with egg. Bake 50 minutes in a medium oven or until golden grown and serve immediately. While the fish is cooking, make a sauce by browning the onion in butter. Add the red peppers, stir and cook for a minute, add the flour, cook another minute, then slowly pour in the stock, stirring. Season. Simmer for 10 minutes, then add the cream. Serve warm, poured over the pies or separately. The sauce may be strained and an egg yolk beaten into the cream before adding to make it more luxurious, but to my taste this is unnecessary. Better to liquidize the sauce to give it more body, then add cream as desired.

Dalmatian eels

1 kg (2 lb) eels
salt, pepper
a few sprigs of parsley
3 cloves of garlic
juice of ½ lemon
¼ cup olive oil

Make deep cuts to the bone along the backs of washed whole eels, or cut conger eel in slices about 2 cm (1 inch) thick. Place in a fireproof dish, sprinkle with salt, pepper, parsley, crushed garlic and pour over the lemon juice and oil, plus just enough water to cover. Bake slowly for 30 minutes and serve with boiled potatoes. Wine may be used instead of the water and a sprig of rosemary included for flavour.

Salt fish

At the other end of the scale from the best white fish, but a very popular item in the Dalmatian diet, is salt fish. This fish was once white too. It may be cod, whiting, hake or something similar, which has been heavily salted before drying and now looks to be an unappetizing yellow block. It is liked all through the Mediterranean. A Dalmatian dish sometimes identified as 'sailor's cod', normally called *bakalar*, is very similar to the famous Languedoc *brandade*, and also sounds like the Venetian *baccala mantecato*. The Adriatic term comes from the Greek for less distinguished members of the cod family. The salt fish is soaked for half an hour in warm water, drained and pounded with a wooden mallet, replaced in fresh water for another 24 hours, pounded again and the scales removed. The fish is then washed and cooked in cold water without salt, drained, sliced or flaked and returned to the pan with lashings of olive oil, garlic, pepper, parsley and a little of its own stock. This mixture is then tightly covered and simmered gently, shaking the pan from time to time but not stirring. In Yugoslavia it would be fitting to serve *bakalar* with chard and potatoes or another staple carbohydrate, polenta (see p. 330).

Eels and octopus are also dried in Dalmatia, mainly for use in soups.

If fish has to be preserved today, most Western palates would probably prefer it deep-frozen, but recipes for salt fish can be a good guide to making the best of the cheaper fresh white fish, like coley and ling. The worst aspect of the following recipe is its name.

Codballs

500 g (1 lb) salt fish or fresh coley	3 small eggs
	50 g (2 oz) onion, chopped
180 g (6 oz) cooked mackerel	chopped parsley
	salt, pepper
oil for frying	50 g (2 oz) flour
100 g (3½ oz) salted anchovy fillets, chopped small	1 cup tomato juice
	½ teaspoon sugar
100 g (3½ oz) bread without crusts	

Poach the coley in a little seasoned water if it is not already cooked, fry the mackerel, then skin and bone both fish and chop the flesh, together with the anchovies. Add the bread, soaked in water, squeezed dry and chopped, the beaten eggs, the onion, which has been lightly fried in a little oil, plenty of chopped fresh parsley, and salt and pepper to taste. Shape into small balls, roll these in flour, fry them in oil, drain them and put them in a shallow baking dish. Pour over the tomato juice seasoned with the sugar and bake for 30 minutes.

Squid and octopus

The octopus is a tentacled night-hunter, with a brain, that eats oily little fish. The sardine fishermen only like him when he arrives crisp or succulent on the table, alongside the less threatening squid. The dish may be a risotto, a *fritto misto*, a stew or a mayonnaise-based salad.

Stuffed squid

12 medium-sized squid
2–3 tablespoons chopped onion
2–3 tablespoons olive oil
2 cloves garlic, crushed
375 g (12 oz) overall weight of squid tentacles, shelled prawns, tinned or fresh shrimps or boned monkfish
50 g (2 oz) breadcrumbs, soaked in fish stock

1 egg
parsley
salt, pepper

For the sauce:
3 tablespoons olive oil
2 cloves garlic
200 g (7 oz) tomatoes
1 glass white wine
fish stock
fresh parsley
rosemary or sage

Clean the squid by pulling gently at the head until it comes away from the tubular body. Cut off the tentacles and discard the head. Pull out the transparent quill from the tube and discard, along with the white innards. Wash the tube under running water. The tentacles should also be washed before chopping, though not under a tap, for they tend to slip down the drain. Brown the chopped onion in oil, add the garlic, tentacles and prawn, shrimp or monkfish flesh. Cook lightly, then add the breadcrumbs and, off the heat, the egg, parsley and seasoning. Stuff the squid tubes with the mixture, secure the ends with toothpicks and fry gently in olive oil. Add all the sauce ingredients and simmer covered, or bake, for 30 minutes. Serve with boiled potatoes or polenta (see p. 330). Sage is another herb that grows wild in Dalmatia.

Crustaceans

The prized flesh of lobsters and salt-water crayfish is boiled or grilled, then sliced and eaten with a salad or tartar sauce. The fish are grilled by splitting them down the middle and sprinkling them with lemon juice, butter and curry powder. Cooked crab is included in composite salads, or the crabs are stewed whole in layers with potatoes, oil and garlic, water and vinegar. Dublin Bay prawns (scampi) are threatened with the usual bread-and-deep-fry treatment and are nicer stewed in wine, garlic and tomato, or skewered with smoked bacon and brushed with olive oil and cooked on a spit. Oysters are eaten cooked, raw with lemon or in a soup: make a fish stock, season with lemon juice and white wine and pour the whole over dry toast.

Fish, shellfish and mixed stews

These dishes abound all along the coast, from Kvarner Bay in the north to Kotor in the south. The ratio of taste to cost is extremely favourable. The shellfish stews often combine mussels, prawns, shrimps, etc. in a rich fish stock with tomatoes, white wine, garlic and lemon, and with the traditional flavouring of rosemary. Here is a slightly more unusual recipe, however, associated with the famous cheese of the island of Pag.

Shellfish stew with a cheese topping

1 kg (2 lb) mussels or other
  shellfish
100 g (3–4 oz) onion
3 tablespoons olive oil
6 cloves garlic
100 g (3–4 oz) green pepper,
  chopped

200 g (7 oz) tomatoes, fresh
  or tinned
1 cup dry white wine
salt, pepper
80 g (3 oz) grated cheese

Scrub the shellfish, discard any open mussels. Pour over $\frac{1}{2}$ litre (1 pint) boiling water and cook covered for 10 minutes. Remove fish from shells. Brown the chopped onion in oil, add the garlic, peppers and tomato, then the white wine and the shellfish cooking liquor. Stew for 10 minutes, then add the shellfish and season. Pour the soup into warm ovenproof bowls, sprinkle the cheese on top and put under the grill until bubbling. Serve with rough or crusty white bread.

Istra brodet

This is the staple fish stew, the Dalmatian bouillabaisse.

1 kg (2 lb) any variety of
  fish or shellfish
1 tablespoon flour
$\frac{1}{2}$ cup olive oil, or more to
  taste
250 g (8 oz) onion
1 cup wine
3 cloves garlic

1 tablespoon wine vinegar
1 cup fish stock or water
peppercorns, rosemary,
  juniper berries
a few olives, capers and
  slices of lemon
1–2 tomatoes or 2–3
  tablespoons tomato juice

Clean the fish, cut into pieces, roll in flour and brown in oil. Drain off the oil or the fish, whichever is easier, and fry the onion in the same oil. Return the fish with all the remaining ingredients and simmer gently for 20–30 minutes covered. Red mullet included with white fish, shellfish and squid will give a good flavour to this stew, though it may also be made with mackerel. Of commonly available white fish in Britain, I have used a mixture of conger eel, cod and skate, which gives a good taste. The bones of these fish are all large, which is not as good as none at all, but not as discouraging as many small ones. Stews like this are sometimes served with chard and polenta dressed with olive oil (p. 330). The combination of flavours is excellent.

Variations An interesting nameless variant of the Dalmatian fish stew may be made with red wine and rice. An onion is sautéd in oil, then 1 kg (2 lb) cleaned fish is added, along with 150 g (6 oz) tomatoes, a scant cup of wine, 60–80 g (2–3 oz) rice, a bay leaf and other seasonings, and enough water to cover. The soup, in the pan in which it is to be served, is gently heated uncovered for 25 minutes. The soup is not stirred, but sprinkled with parsley before it is brought to the table. Red wine best enhances mackerel and tuna. It tends to drown the flavour and will obviously discolour white fish and shellfish.

Other Dalmatian fish

The possibilities for trout include baking, barbecueing, marinating and poaching in vegetable broth. Around the marshy mouth of the River Neretva, south of Split, a delicacy that Dalmatians travel miles to enjoy is frog. Frogs' legs are fried in breadcrumbs and eaten with lemon, or the whole frog is stewed with potatoes or noodles, herbs, lemon and juniper, finished with a roux, to thicken the sauce, and a dash of vinegar.

Serbian and general Balkan fish cookery

Away from the coast, the Yugoslav cuisines change. Italian influence gives way to Serbian in the centre and the south, and to Austrian and Hungarian in the north. The general treatment of the many varieties of freshwater fish in the rivers and lakes of Bosnia-Herzegovina, Serbia, Macedonia and Montenegro is spicy rather than delicate and often involves large quantities of vegetables, which French-educated Western taste tends to shun. The vegetables may be sweet, as essentially they are in *djuvetch*, or sour, as in fish with sauerkraut. These two ideas are the mainstay of Balkan fish cookery, supported by the use of sour cream and paprika. They extend the length of the Danube from Budapest through Belgrade and western Romania and into Bulgaria, and through the mountains of Montenegro to the Albanian coastal plain. There contact is restored with the sea, olive oil, rosemary and Italy. The predominant inland fish are carp, river trout, sturgeon and sterlet, pike, river perch, river bream, freshwater crayfish, eels, catfish (sheatfish) and, in specific localities, bleak.

Lake Shkodra, dividing low-lying Yugoslav Montenegro from Albanian Montenegro, is rich in fish, most of all carp and bleak, though its political position bars it from being the travellers' destination it might be. The border between Albania and Yugoslavia runs through the middle of this large, serene expanse of water set in flat, marshy countryside, and it is marked by staves and chicken wire. Roads either side are deserted. The sole Han-i-Hottit crossing point, adorned with Albanian political proverbs, affords an excellent view over the unadorned, unpeopled landscape. Fishing from both sides continues. The Yugoslavs regard bleak, a white fish typically weighing four or five pounds and with an untroublesome bone structure, as a good candidate for barbecueing with oil and garlic, and as a delicacy when smoked. It belongs to the Alburnus family, whose members are to be found in parts of England and across Europe from France to the Caspian Sea. Shkodra carp, which I ate in the Albanian town of the same name, was served Mediterranean-style, with wine and tomatoes. It would have been a wonderful dish, for the flesh was very sweet, except for the hundreds of tiny bones.

Tipsy carp or salmon trout

This recipe can be used for any firm white fish, or for trout, but best of all for salmon trout. It gives carp a less meaty treatment than elsewhere in Central Europe and the Balkans.

I large fish, weighing about 2 kg (4 lb)
salt
3–4 cloves garlic
$\frac{2}{3}$ cup olive or sunflower oil
fresh black pepper
I cup white wine

Clean the fish, salt it and leave for 2 hours. Put the garlic cloves inside the carp and sew it up. Put the fish in a greased, ovenproof dish, brush with oil, dust with pepper and pour over the wine. Bake at 375°F (190°C, Gas Mark 5) for 20–30 minutes, basting frequently. Serves 8–10.

Lake Ohrid, 2,000 feet above sea-level, is the centre of a tourist region and area of outstanding natural beauty on Yugoslavia's Macedonian border with Albania. The exceptionally warm water attracts bathers as well as local and visiting anglers who catch eel, carp and Ohrid's famous red-spotted trout. The stock is carefully controlled by artificial insemination. Where the River Crnu Drim enters the lake at Struga the eels abound every spring after spawning and every autumn when the elvers return. The carp in the so-called 'Macedonian Sea' are so large and plentiful they have occasionally been reported to have been caught by hand. But pride of place goes to Ohrid's salmon trout, related to a rare and similarly appreciated species in the far-away Siberian lake, Baikal. Since potentates often have a care for their stomachs, it is not surprising to find that the medieval

Serbian emperors dined upon this *pastrmka*, and that when the Turks took over in Macedonia a courier service was organized to bring Ohrid trout to the sultan's table in Istanbul.

The town of Ohrid has a rich Slavonic and Oriental heritage, with traces of Mediterranean influence. Disciples of Saints Kiril and Methodius, who brought Christianity to the Slavs of Bulgaria and Moravia, spread the faith to Macedonia in the ninth century and built several monasteries here. The region then formed part of the two successive medieval Bulgarian empires, before emerging as a mighty Balkan dynasty in its own right. From the beginning of the twelfth century until the mid fourteenth century, it ruled over Serbia, Montenegro, parts of Albania and Bulgaria and present-day northern Greece. Ohrid, an important staging-post on the road connecting the Adriatic and the Aegean, then accumulated the wealth and enlightenment to build its memorable churches. Masterpieces by Byzantine and Serbian-Macedonian fresco artists survive in Ohrid Cathedral after centuries under Turkish whitewash. The atmosphere in this no-longer-rich part of Yugoslavia is slow, one of faded Byzantine mystery, but the views remain panoramic. A traditional street trade in leather and fish continues.

Lake Ohrid stuffed trout

1 salmon trout about 1 kg (2 lb) in weight	oil for frying
salt	150 g (6 oz) cooked rice
250 g (8 oz) onions, chopped	parsley, salt and pepper
	2 lemons
120 g (4 oz) green peppers, chopped	2 tablespoons flour

Clean the trout and remove the backbone. Sprinkle with salt and chill for 30 minutes. Make the stuffing by sautéing the vegetables in oil, covered, making sure they do not burn. When soft, add the rice, parsley, seasoning and the juice of one lemon. Stuff the fish with this mixture, sew it up and roll it in flour.

Budapest. From Johann Georg Kohl, Die Donau, Trieste 1854

Bake in a greased dish in a hot oven for 30 minutes. Serve the fish whole, with slices of lemon and a salad garnish.

Trout from Ohrid and elsewhere may also be smoked and served with a dressing of whipped cream, fresh fennel, horseradish and lemon juice.

Eels from Struga are smoked, or prepared as *Dalmatian eels* above.

The Danube

We made for the enchanting glade, where a group of fishermen sat round a fire and where it was proposed we should lunch ... Under the branches which met overhead delicacies of the most appetizing nature were spread on an impromptu table made of a board laid across two upturned boats. The banqueting board was flanked at each end with batteries of bottles of amber-coloured wine which tasted deliciously cool. Little black olives piquant in taste and caviare had been kept on ice. The soup was prepared from fish, and had a peculiar but attractive flavour tasting something like the Hungarian *goulas*. Sterlet was grilled on a spit over the open fire. The salad, made of tender roots, and very grateful to the palate, is called *ardei grassi* [green peppers] ... Ice-cooled tuica, with sugar melons and pears and black Turkish coffee crowned a wonderful repast.

E. O. Hoppé, *In Gipsy Camp and Royal Palace*, 1924

Fish cookery along the Danube has some unity imposed by the uniformity of the catch, language and political style, and mobility up and down the river. The Habsburgs at their eighteenth-century peak ruled the Danube from Linz in Austria to Giurgiu in Wallachia, where the river marks the present-day border between Romania and Bulgaria. After they defeated the Turks, who laid siege to Vienna in 1683, they began to gather along the Danube an empire that briefly included Belgrade. The language and cultural expectations of imperial bureaucrats on distant postings forged gastronomic and cultural links between Slovakia, Hungary and what is today known as the Vojvodina, the strongly Hungarian part of Yugoslavia north-west of the capital. The Vienna-centred culture widened to embrace the Banat of south-western Romania, adjacent to Serbia, a region intermittently colonized since the Middle Ages by German settlers from Saxony, Schwabia and Alsace. It also took in the lands of the Wallachian Plain. On the fringes of the empire Austrian influence met that of Turkey and Russia, while wherever they traded the very mobile Serbs were bearers of mixed Oriental and Slavonic ways. This was the cultural map of the Danube before the First World War.

The chief fish of the river are sterlet and sturgeon, pike, perch, catfish, carp and trout. A Viennese dignitary in Serbia might well have had his sterlet, a creature highly valued on most tables, cooked with lemon and butter, or poached and served cold. His carp Belgrade-style might have been with garlic, oil and lemon. Having been caught in the river, these fish would go on sale in long wooden tanks in the streets of this or that town, or be hawked about on the end of strings. The most likely table presentation of the more modest fish would have been in a sauce of sour cream. The Serbs and Hungarians are fond of this method, and use it for catfish and carp. The Hungarians make a rich, spicy sauce for carp by adding fresh horseradish. They share the habit with the Czechs, north Germans and Poles. The Vojvodina might have come up with pike or perch in a sour-cream sauce with mushrooms. In 1897, however, Herbert Vivian, the otherwise enthusiastic, Brighton-based author of *Servia, the Poor Man's Paradise*, declared the quality of fish nothing to write home about. He had eaten more delicate sterlet in Moscow and regarded the plentiful Serbian fish as coarse. Danube fish do lack tenderness because of the turbulence of the river as it merges with the River Sava and approaches the Iron Gate. A hundred years ago the proximity of the river was also no guarantee that fresh fish would be available, because of the difficulty of storing it. At Ruse, situated on the Danube and today in Bulgaria, no fresh fish was to be found, though every variety of salted fish was sold by silent, cross-legged, chibbuk-smoking Turkish street merchants, as Vivian described them.

For all these reasons, perhaps the best, most imitable and certainly most famous preparation along the Danube is the fresh stew, attributed for hundreds of years to the fishermen. Such a simple, tasty dish was probably not available except very locally, and even then not in commercial establishments. I would guess that circumstances would be similar today, and that under Yugoslav Communism's dual system of state and private catering, only the latter would cultivate fish broth as a speciality. It would take a local to show a visitor the back entrance to good eating.

Danube fish paprikás

This modern version of the fishermen's broth, with the Hungarian name *paprikás*, comes from the Yugoslav riverside town of Apatin, just south of the Hungarian border.

375 g (12 oz) small river fish, such as roach	250 g ($\frac{1}{2}$ lb) tomatoes, chopped
250 g ($\frac{1}{2}$ lb) catfish	1 green pepper, chopped
750 g (1$\frac{1}{2}$ lb) carp	1 chilli pepper, chopped
120 g (4 oz) pike	generous $\frac{1}{2}$ cup wine
2 onions, chopped	paprika, salt

Clean the roach and cook in 1 scant litre (1$\frac{1}{2}$ pints) water until they fall apart. Remove the heads and bones and liquidize the remaining stock. Clean the larger fish and cut into chunks. Put the onion into a heavy-bottomed stainless steel pan, then the fish chunks, vegetables, wine and liquidized stock. Bring to the boil and simmer for 30–40 minutes. Sprinkle with paprika and salt and serve. Traditionally a little *paprikás* liquid is served as a sauce with home-made noodles, followed by the fish and vegetables. This dish is so highly prized that competitions are held for the best concoction, modelled on the original fishermen's freshly caught brew cooked in a cauldron over an open fire.

To attempt an equivalent to fish *paprikás* in Britain, you may have to take up river fishing. Try roach for the small fish and a mixture of pike and perch or any other good, firm, white freshwater fish for the large, even carp if you can tolerate the bones. The basic recipe admits of many variations, such as the addition of potato, a lacing of sour cream before serving or extra fiery peppers, and one or all of these may be tried.

George Lang attributes to the Hungarian city Szeged, across the border but not far north of Apatin, a fish broth that seems to be a near relative of the basic recipe above. A typical carp *paprikás* from central and western Hungary, that is, from around Budapest, or on the Great Hungarian Plain, or in the area west of the Danube (Transdanubia), may be much richer than the one from Apatin. The fish may be fried, and the paprika-flavoured whole thickened with flour, sweet peppers and tomatoes and finally cream. Real cooks like the Danube fishermen use what they have. Without stock, and baked, I have seen the same combination of flavours called 'devilled fish'.

Halpaprikás

1 kg (2 lb) fish, boned and skinned (monkfish, conger eel and shark are suitable, as are cod steaks if care is taken not to overcook them)
salt
120 g (4 oz) onion, finely chopped
50 g (2 oz) butter
1 level tablespoon paprika
12 tablespoons sour cream

Chop the fish into chunks, salt lightly and leave in the refrigerator for 30 minutes. Soften the onion in the butter, remove from heat and sprinkle on paprika. Stir in the sour cream, add the fish and cook slowly, covered, for 20 minutes. This dish, because of its dryness, would benefit from being cooked in a non-stick or very heavy-bottomed pan. Add just a little water if it threatens to stick. It is traditionally served with light *galuskas* (see p. 317), but is equally presentable with boiled new potatoes.

Another attractive Danubian way of cooking fish simply, which probably originated in the open, is with bacon. A stuffing may be made for pike by combining diced fried bacon, mushrooms and onion with moistened breadcrumbs. Flavour is added with anchovies, parsley and pepper, and the fish stuffed with this mixture before being baked surrounded with butter, raw sliced onions and chopped garlic. The pan juices are used to make a serving sauce with sour cream, lemon juice and paprika. The same forcemeat may be used for boned trout or bream.

Fish on a spit

Magyar shish kebab recipes show another way of bringing together fish and bacon.

1 kg (2 lb) white fish – whiting, pike, perch, red mullet, halibut
150 g (6 oz) smoked bacon rashers, cut into 3–4 pieces each
a few tablespoons bacon fat
1–2 teaspoons paprika

Small whiting should be cleaned but left whole. Larger fish may be cleaned and cut into chunks. Thread the fish on four skewers, alternating with bacon slices. While the grill or spit is heating up, brush the fish with melted bacon fat and sprinkle with paprika. Cook over or under a medium heat, turning and basting often, until the fish is brown and crisp. Serve with a salad of tomatoes, green peppers and raw onion in wine vinegar, seasoned with salt and pepper and a little sugar.

Spit-roasted fish Bulgarian style

A Bulgarian recipe for spit-roasting chunks of white fish is to marinate them first in olive oil, lemon juice and paprika, then grill them on skewers with tomato, onion and green pepper. The fish and vegetables are served with a freshly made dressing of oil, lemon juice, parsley and seasoning.

Romanian barbecued fish

Romanian fishermen traditionally rest two crossed sticks between two large stones over a fire. The fish, perhaps carp, is gutted and the backbone removed so that it may be cooked flat by this method, *à la protzap*. A French traveller at the turn of the century, Paul Labbé, attributed the technique to the Danube port of Galati, close to the Delta. The fish was wrapped in leaves after cooking, probably to protect the hands of the eater.

Fish with vegetables

Those who dislike vegetables served with fish are likely to reject out of hand some recipes popular with the Danubian peoples. Into this category, however, falls *djuvec*, of Serbian and perhaps Turkish origin, which should be tried. Written *ghiveci* in Romanian and *gyuvech* in Bulgarian, it is often hailed as a national dish in all three countries. Many people like a faintly sweet taste (tomato ketchup, tinned green peas, most mayonnaise-based sauces) in conjunction with fish, especially when it is oily-fleshed or fried. These recipes provide a similar balance of flavours. I shall not give the Serbian recipe, because it is very heavy, combining a fish such as mackerel with all the vegetables of a *ratatouille*, plus potatoes *and* rice. The Bulgarian and Romanian versions are much nicer. It is from Central Europe that the habit of fish with vegetables spread to North America.

Fish gyuvech

500 g (1 lb) carrots, sliced
500 g (1 lb) tomatoes, chopped
3 onions, chopped
2 cloves garlic, chopped

6 sticks celery, chopped
salt, pepper
1 kg (2 lb) fish fillets
½ cup of water or white wine

2 bay leaves	1 cup oil
fresh breadcrumbs	$\frac{1}{2}$ lemon, sliced

Put the carrots, tomatoes, onions, garlic and celery in a heavy pan or casserole to go on top of the stove. Season them, lay the fish fillets on top, with the wine and the bay leaves, and follow these with the breadcrumbs, the oil and the lemon slices. Simmer gently without stirring for 20–30 minutes, or until the vegetables are well-blended and tender but not disintegrating.

Cold ghiveci with tuna

The Romanians have fish recipes of great style and charm. I have adapted this one so that the essential ingredient comes out of a tin, because fresh tuna in good condition takes some searching for. The vegetables *must* be fresh.

2 large onions, chopped	12 stoned green olives
2 large carrots, diced	1 tablespoon capers
4 sticks of celery, chopped	2–3 slices of lemon
half a fresh cucumber, cut in small chunks	a few peppercorns, a bay leaf
8 tablespoons olive oil	salt
1 cup red wine	2 200 g (7 oz) tins of tuna
2 tablespoons tomato purée	fish

Lightly fry the vegetables in half the oil, add the wine and 1 cup water and all other ingredients except the fish. Simmer gently for 10 minutes. When quite cold, stir in the rest of the oil and pour this vegetable mixture over the flaked tuna in a serving dish. An excellent accompaniment to cold *ghiveci*, as a pre- or after-theatre light supper, or summer lunch, would be garlic bread. My second choice would be baked potatoes with butter or cream cheese and herbs to make up in calories for the lightness of the fish. A third is warm haricot beans in a sauce made by liquidizing $\frac{1}{6}$ of their quantity in some of the cooking liquid.

Ghiveci means the earthenware pot in which this dish is traditionally cooked. The Serbian/Romanian/Bulgarian word derives from the Turkish *guvec*.

With Western taste in fish opposed to the bulk and acidity of vegetables, sauerkraut may seem an even worse choice of partner. Not only is it cabbage, upon which many people accept the medieval judgement that it is the lowest form of vegetable life, but it is also pickled. Yet where are the gourmets who have not stuck a pickled onion or two into the fish-and-chip bag and sprinkled all with vinegar? Fish with sauerkraut is liked in Romania and Bulgaria as well as in Central Europe, and I give the recipe for the record.

Fish with sauerkraut

1 kg (2 lb) sauerkraut
½ cup oil or bacon fat
1 kg (2 lb) fish, preferably mackerel or fresh tuna
1–2 teaspoons paprika

Squeeze any excess liquid from the sauerkraut and keep for a sour soup. (See pp. 126–30.) Set the sauerkraut to cook gently in 1 cup water and half the oil for about 15 minutes, then turn it out with its juice into a greased baking dish. Lay the fish fillets across it, sprinkle them with paprika, pour over the rest of the oil and bake for about 20 minutes in a medium oven or until the fish is tender. This is a very hefty dish and the only possible accompaniment is a little potato purée.

In passing, let me say that there is a terrible Czech version of fish with sauerkraut, using dried fish, likewise a Polish fish *bigos*. If you are going to try it, do opt for the Balkan version. Poland and Czechoslovakia are better consulted for their meat cookery.

Trout with rice

This is another composite recipe, including rice and spring onions. It is wholly savoury, from Romania, and has delightful colours: white, pink and bright green.

1 kg (2 lb) trout	a large bunch of spring
salt	onions
2 teaspoons mild paprika	2 teaspoons curry powder
100 g (3½ oz) rice	1 cup water or stock
80 g (3 oz) butter	parsley

Clean and fillet the fish, removing the head. Sprinkle with salt and paprika and leave for 30 minutes. Brown the rice in a third of the butter, add water and cook until half-done, about 10 minutes. Clean the spring onions, but leave them whole. Sauté them in a little more butter, add the fish and seasoning, stock and rice and cook until the rice is tender and very little liquid remains. Melt the remaining butter over the fish and garnish with parsley.

Travellers through the ages have recorded the extreme delicacy of trout in various corners of Central and south-east Europe. According to Sacheverell Sitwell, the ancient Cozia monastery in central Romania, one of the country's great architectural monuments, was renowned for a fine red-spotted variety which when salted was carried in tribute to the Turkish Bey. The *bastrovus* sounds to be in the same class as the famous varieties in Ohrid and Balaton.

Other Hungarian Fish
𝕾𝕰

Lake Balaton, Balatonfuered, is two hours' drive south-west of Budapest. It is the largest lake in Central Europe, seventy-seven kilometres long and between two and fourteen kilometres wide. Its least glamorous aspect is that its name means mud. In the

Hungarian fishermen. Engraving by Valerio, 1859, Victoria and Albert Museum

early nineteenth century it developed into a charming health resort, with parks, trees and romantic little foot-bridges. It reached its heyday before the last war, when it thrived as a place to eat the freshest fish and to drink the excellent local wine whilst taking the air, enjoying the scenery and good company and listening to gypsy music.

The most celebrated fish was and still is the fogas. This is a species of pike-perch unique to Balaton and regarded as a great delicacy when it is poached very fresh in a court bouillon. The flesh is pure white and often compared to exquisitely fed young chicken. Moreover, it has almost no bones. 'The most Hungarian fish, the king of the sweet-water fishes,' declared the patriot István Széchenyi, campaigning to defend Balaton against an early nineteenth-century plan to drain it. A small fogas, called a süllö, is almost equally prized, and served grilled.

Joseph Wechsberg, a connoisseur of Central European food, recalls the Hungarian master-chef Károly Gundel improvising on the theme of this fish, *lucioperca sandra*:

'. . . just the fillet of fish, boiled in a court bouillon made with white wine, then covered with *sauce hollandaise* and topped off with a crayfish porkolt, I mean a ragout in a thick paprika sauce.' He made a circle with thumb and forefinger, closed his eyes, and shook his head slowly, and for a moment there was an expression of ethereal delight on his face.

Physiologically both Gundel, who was a very fat man until the siege of Budapest in 1944, and the fogas, were made for luxury. The fish derives its extra whiteness from living a calm, easy, privileged existence away from the turbulent river.

Apart from the fogas there may be as many as fifty other varieties of fish in the state-protected deep waters of Balaton. Today the state keeps a watchful eye on the stock. The most frequently caught is carp. The best inextravagant dish is a stew.

Balaton hálaszlé

3 onions	1½ kg (3 lb) mixed fish –
1 heaped tablespoon paprika or more	catfish, sturgeon, carp
	salt
1 chilli	1–2 red peppers
	1 tomato

Slice the onions and simmer for 15 minutes in 2½ litres (4–4½ pints) water with the paprika and chilli. Small fish for flavour can be included in the cooking, in which case cover the pan and continue cooking for 30 minutes. The firmer fish should be cut into chunks, salted and chilled until the final soup is ready to be assembled. Strain the broth, pour it over the fish chunks, together with the chopped red pepper and tomatoes, and cook gently for 10–15 minutes, shaking the pan occasionally. Allow to stand 5 minutes, still covered, before serving alone or with good rough bread.

To achieve the broth's traditional bright red, purists demand the deeply coloured peppers grown near Szeged, which bring with them plenty of fire. (This is now a state-protected paprika-growing area.)

Traditionally this stew was, made in the Hungarian fisherman's cooking pot, the round-bottomed *bogrács* which has been used in the Danube basin for centuries. The *bogrács* is a cast-iron kettle slightly shallower than a bucket, which can be suspended over an open fire or slung from a saddle. In the modern kitchen use an enamel, earthenware or stainless-steel pan, never aluminium for fish.

Other Romanian and Bulgarian fish recipes

The Danube Delta is more of a way of life than a distinctive region for fish dishes. Where the river divides into three branches the land becomes a spread of marshy waterways, canals, dense undergrowth, forest and reeds. Half of it is river, half flooded land, and it is a mecca for bird life, drawing 300 resident species to its luxuriant vegetation, not to mention millions of sheltering migrants. The fishermen make their greatest captures after the ferocious storms of early spring. When the flood waters recede, bream, carp, pike and pike-perch are left in pools and tanks. The fishing industry is most lucrative when devoted to catching sturgeon and processing grey Romanian caviare, but all the Danube fish are caught in the Delta, along with shad, swordfish, mackerel and sardine. The town of Tulcea is one of the most important centres for freezing, canning and manufacturing the Delta's produce. Travellers used to report armies of frogs on the pavements.

The haunting quality of the natural water-maze is enhanced by the mists that regularly descend and by the adherents of strange sects who in the past have made their lives there as fishermen. The Lipovani were Russians who fled the empire of Peter the Great when he modernized the Orthodox Church and ordered the faithful to shave their beards off. The Lipovani, whose icons were painted on wood from the *lipa* or linden tree, were close to the dissenting Old Believers, but took their protest further. They could not live in damnation on Russian soil. In 1938 Sacheverell Sitwell described these 'frequently red-bearded' men as 'a kind of Sea Cossack' living in the Bukovina and Galizia. Their Russian ways showed in their dress, their stature and their food. They drank tea and ate a commendable soup one Englishman transcribed as *aha*, containing about a dozen kinds of fish. This must have been the Russian *ukha*. Jack Lindsay and Maurice Cornforth hoped the arrival of Communism would help these fishermen, who eked out their diet by making flour from waterweed seeds and by boiling the stems. 'Now they have excellent motor boats, with the "Red October" life-boat close at hand in stormy weather,' they wrote in 1953. However, instead of flourishing they have virtually died out, their ability to endure daily hardship not helped by inbreeding. In 1963 only a few members of the sect that 300 years before numbered 25,000 were in evidence. At the turn of the century, though, every visitor noticed them as the red-clad cab-drivers of Bucharest, nicknamed *Muscal*, meaning Muscovite. Another Russian sect in the Delta were the Shkoptsy, a mainly vegetarian and sober-living community who castrated their men at twenty-five. They, it seems, are already extinct.

The Delta and its culture have rarely failed to impress. Sitwell described his journey:

It would be easy to lose direction in this wilderness of waters. There was no point for which to steer. But the long, pampas water grass now hid even the lagoon from sight. We came through it again, into the willow trees and landing for a moment saw hammocks hung up to the boughs. This was a summer camp of fishermen. The hammocks had occupants. Rough mosquito netting, and a tarpaulin and a bed of straw, made their shelter. This was their resting time, for they fished by night, but the curtain of one hammock was lifted by its corner and the fisherman looked out, a dark, bearded Russian, or Bessarabian, in a black Phrygian cap. An open fire, the fishing nets and some wooden boxes were the only other furniture in this encampment. And then in the distance we could see a swineherd and his pigs, the steam from the train was visible, and a lorry came along a road. This was the highway from Braila to Galati; and the waste of waters became more mysterious from its proximity to man.

Galați, on the river at the head of the Delta, is now an industrial town with the largest shipyards in Romania. At its height in the mid nineteenth century it was a thriving cosmopolitan port that daily exported fish and caviare, from the Delta and the Black Sea 120 miles away, up-river to Budapest, Vienna and beyond. The trick among restaurateurs was to pass off the catfish they bought as sturgeon. Galati coffee-houses took Viennese newspapers so that the Greek and Bulgarian fish traders could check news and prices. The local population also included immigrant Germans, Serbs, Turks, Tartars and Georgians.

The Albanian-born Romanian poet Victor Eftimiu (1889–1972) watched the activities of the fishermen landing their nets of silver zander, pink carp and sevruga (salmon); their catch of 'moustachioed catfish, seemingly in prayer' and of 'sturgeon, slant-eyed like a Tartar girl'; and he wrote admiringly of Romania's great riches piled high under grey March skies. It is well-known that in the dark, still waters of the Delta the fish, especially carp, grow to gargantuan size. They thrive almost unnaturally, hiding under the myriad tiny island clumps of reeds, the *plaur*, that clog up the waterways and change the lie of the land as often as a kaleidoscope. One half wishes Romanian tourism and gastronomy would wake up to the potential of this extraordinary heritage, but then it might be lost for ever.

Cold fish with garlic (1) – a recipe from the Danube Delta

2 tablespoons wine vinegar
1 onion, finely chopped
1 carrot, finely diced
1 tablespoon each fresh
    parsley, thyme and
    chervil, or ½ teaspoon
    each dried

10 peppercorns, 2 bay leaves
3 bulbs garlic
1 kg (2 lb) fish, originally
    catfish, but try shark or
    sea bass, turbot or halibut

Make a court bouillon by simmering 1 litre (scant 2 pints) water, 1 tablespoon vinegar, the vegetables, herbs, seasonings and one bulb of garlic for 30 minutes. Add the remaining vinegar and place the fish fillets in the hot stock. Cook it very gently for 10 minutes, cover, remove from heat and leave to cool in the liquid. Serve the fish in a cold sauce consisting of 1 cup of the cooking liquid mixed with 2 bulbs of garlic pounded with a little salt. You may also include the vegetables from the bouillon. Serve with slices of *mamaliga*, which is the Romanian name for polenta, fried in butter and either sharp green peppers or tinned red pimientos as a colourful garnish and a complementary taste. I have made this dish most successfully with shark steaks, which have the colour and texture of veal when cooked.

The name of the sauce used in this recipe is *mujdei*, and since it is ferociously strong you may wish to moderate the amount of fresh garlic going into it at the last minute. There is, however, nothing unattractive or unhealthy about the full-strength version, provided you borrow an Indian trick and have cardamom or fennel seeds to chew on and sweeten the breath afterwards. *Mujdei* is also excellent with spit-roasted chicken or any grilled or, especially, barbecued meat. The simplest Romanian combination is to pour this very garlicky stock over *mamaliga* as a snack in itself.

Here is a slightly different version, using cod or salmon.

Cold fish with garlic (2)

1 kg (2 lb) cod, salmon or salmon trout
5–6 cloves garlic
juice of 1–2 lemons, and extra wedges for decoration
salt
plenty of freshly ground black pepper
hot green chilli peppers

Poach the fish gently in 1 cup water, until tender. Pound the garlic, mix with the lemon juice, and stir this into the fish stock along with a pinch of salt. Grind in the black pepper and leave the fish to stand covered for an hour. Serve it just warm, garnished with parsley, lemon and a chilli pepper, and a little of the cooking liquid, reduced if necessary and allowed to cool. An ideal accompaniment would be small, sweet new potatoes boiled in their skins.

Caviare rissoles

An impossible thought, this! But where it is plentiful, the cheaper caviare abounding in the Danube Delta, from carp or grey mullet, is shaped into rissoles, dipped in egg and breadcrumbs and fried.

Fish à la grecque

A Romanian friend in London, asking what recipes I was planning to include, had as her first thought fish à la grecque. Romanian sauce à la grecque is an emulsion of lemon juice, oil, parsley and seasoning, diluted with water. It is used to dress cooked fresh mackerel, herring or tuna, cooked mushrooms or leeks, and also as the cooking liquid for raw fish. Bake carp, cod, hake or salmon with a few spoonfuls, together with some minced garlic and sliced green olives. Slices of onion and lemon usually lie on the bottom of the dish, especially when the fish is cooked whole. With fish fillets add a little more lemon juice instead, a little finely chopped onion, fine breadcrumbs and a little extra oil on top. Many Balkan recipes use whole slices of lemon in cooking fish.

Skordolea

This thick walnut sauce, eaten in Romania and Bulgaria with fish and large shellfish such as prawns and crayfish, is another speciality Romania shares with Greece. Walnuts are traditional, but almonds or mixed nuts may be substituted. The recipe was sufficiently highly regarded to appear on the menus of good Bucharest hotels seventy years ago.

50 g (2 oz) fresh bread without crusts
4 cloves garlic, crushed
50 g (2 oz) crushed walnuts
3–4 tablespoons olive oil
salt, pepper, lemon juice or wine vinegar

Moisten the bread and squeeze dry, combine with the garlic and nuts to make a smooth paste. Add the oil slowly, as if for mayonnaise, and finish with salt and vinegar or lemon juice to taste. A little water may be added if the paste is too thick.

This is an economical sauce where walnuts are plentiful, as in the Balkans. In Britain, where nuts are relatively expensive, it is more a low-cholesterol, high-fibre alternative to egg-based mayonnaise.

At the time of writing Romanians cannot get lemons or walnuts. Food and fuel shortages lead them to feel acutely the severity of their winters. Life when I visited Bucharest in 1986 was rather grim. They are a cultivated, fashionable, sociable Latin people, and their lot is a great burden. The winters when they cannot buy fresh food have plunged them back into a state of need that historically has often been Romania's lot, particularly in its most barren eastern region, the Dobrudja. When Ovid was exiled from fashionable, affluent, mild Rome to Tomis (modern Constanta) on the Romanian Black Sea, he called his new home 'the midst of barbarism'. In the savage winter he observed the Dobrudjans fending off aching cold with furs and skins as the frost settled on their beards; and he saw the fish freeze in the Black Sea, then miraculously thaw in spring and swim away.

The Black Sea freezes more easily than most salt seas, because of the high proportion of fresh water flowing into it. In summer the highly oxygenated water attracts an astonishing density of fish: the catch is four times greater than in the adjoining Mediterranean. Species found include grey mullet, shad, scad, sturgeon, shrimps, crabs and crayfish. The winter is brutal but summer brings months of mild sunny weather in which fruit trees and vines thrive. Tourism has developed in the last thirty years, although there are large canning industries and oil installations in the more built-up areas. The smaller resorts on the Bulgarian Dobrudja coast, the untouched fishing ports and the seascape are idyllic. A few years ago we left the night train from Sofia to Varna at five a.m., just as the sun came up over the water, and we were struck by the immense, sublime calm. Much of the coastline is still lined with dense woodland. Forty years ago some areas were still snake-infested marshes. The hand of Dionysus, the ancient god of the Thracian vines, is still evident.

But Dionysus is not Neptune and, sadly, one wouldn't recognize the Black Sea as a fish-eating region from the hotel restaurant menus. The single piece of fried pike I managed to order was far from divine. We had a taste of the fuller flavour of local life when we took the motor cruiser from Varna to the small port of Balcic. The now-Bulgarian town baking at the foot of steep, arid hills is where Queen Victoria's granddaughter, Queen Marie of Romania, planted her favourite lilies from the Isle of Wight and had her heart buried – while it was still a Romanian town. At lunchtime the outdoor beer-and-fish tavern near the waterfront was crowded with the swarthy, Byzantine figures, many with Tartar or Caucasian features, to whom my five-year-old daughter instantly allotted a place in the Bible. We ate tiny scad, rather like whitebait, which had been fried whole and were served in a huge mound, with wine or beer and doorsteps of rough bread. The long wooden refectory tables underneath a canopy of trees were crammed and animated. Dionysus's temple once stood in Balcic, and the little town was once called Dionysopolis.

Plakia

This is one of the best-known Bulgarian fish dishes, usually made with carp, but adaptable to shark, trout, salmon trout or cod. Like the Romanian dishes on p. 169–70, which are often given the same name, *glachi*, it is served cold. *Glachi* was considered suitable for an aristocratic midday breakfast, followed by a rice pilaf. The same succession of courses is recommended with this recipe. *Plakia* is also an Armenian fish dish.

1 kg (2 lb) cod	1–2 teaspoons paprika
salt	1 teaspoon sugar
350 g (12 oz) onion, sliced	1 tablespoon tomato paste
6 tablespoons oil	flour
2 cloves garlic, crushed	½ lemon, sliced or squeezed
black pepper	

Sprinkle the fish with salt and chill 30 minutes. Sauté the onion in oil, adding the garlic, salt, pepper, paprika, sugar, 2–3 tablespoons water and tomato paste. Dip the fish in flour, lay it on the onion mixture, which you have put in a baking dish, cover with slices of lemon and bake for 30–40 minutes in a medium oven. Though it is traditional to use lemon slices, I find it more convenient and tastier to squeeze lemon juice over the fish and to cook it tightly covered with foil to prevent drying. Serve at room temperature or cold.

Cold trout with walnut stuffing

Plakia may also be made with trout, rubbed with lemon inside and out, stuffed with crushed walnuts, and sandwiched between two layers of vegetables. For these, the onion is first sautéed in oil and then stewed with garlic and diced carrots. Use about ½ cup water and 6 tablespoons olive oil for 1 kg (2 lb) fish, and bake 30–40 minutes.

Black Sea fish sauce

This is a modern Bulgarian recipe, removed from the romance of Dionysopolis, and if I say it is good with fish fingers, I may further detract from its image. But try it with baked, grilled or fried coley. It brings new life to the blandest fish.

1 onion, chopped
3 tablespoons butter or oil
2 tablespoons flour
salt, cayenne pepper
3 medium tomatoes, fresh
    or tinned, chopped

1 cup white wine
1 cup fish stock
½ cup each cooked peas and
    cooked diced carrots
½ teaspoon dried basil

Sauté the onion in the fat and stir in the flour and seasoning. Cook for a minute, then add the tomatoes and cook, stirring, until soft. Add the wine and stock, bring to the boil and simmer for 5 minutes, stirring often. Add the peas, carrots and basil and cook for a minute. Serve hot or warm with cooked white fish. The aniseed taste of the basil is a particularly vitalizing ingredient here; don't be tempted to replace it with another herb. The quantities make ample sauce for 1 kg (2 lb) fish, and any left over can be frozen. You may also find you want to use it with cooked vegetables.

Bulgarian stuffed fish

The Bulgarians are fond of stuffing fish with onions, tomatoes and peppers, lightly pre-cooked, and with a mixture of cooked rice, fried onions, currants, nuts and cinnamon. A good forcemeat made at Christmas and used for carp, sea bass or pike combines cooked rice with a sautéd onion, coarsely ground hazelnuts, basil and rosemary, with plenty of olive oil and lemon juice around the fish to keep it moist and mix with the juices to provide a sauce. This sauce can also be used for trout.

Fish in Germany, Poland and Czechoslovakia

Soused herrings in wine

The herring industry with its facilities for drying, pickling and smoking small oily fish from the sea grew up around the Baltic ports of Rostock, Szczeczin (Stettin) and Gdańsk (Danzig), the ancient Hanseatic port at the mouth of the Vistula. This German recipe is eaten with boiled potatoes.

6 medium herrings, with roes if possible
$\frac{1}{2}$ teaspoon peppercorns
salt, pinch of cayenne
2 tablespoons dry white wine
mustard

Clean the fish, removing the heads, and divide into fillets and roll up in a shallow ovenproof dish. Season, pour over the wine and 2 tablespoons water and bake covered for about 35 minutes in a medium oven. Serve cold, with mustard mixed to a thin cream with the same wine as used for cooking.

Herrings in breadcrumbs

To make another main course, salt herrings are soaked in milk for an hour, dried, soaked in red wine another hour, then dipped in flour, egg and breadcrumbs and fried in butter. Serve with hot potato salad and sauerkraut.

Smoked sprats are a delicacy from the Baltic coast, and great thirst-inducers. Other popular Baltic fish are eels and flounder.

Freshwater fish

Pomerania and Mecklenburg have a sea coast. Brandenburg lies further inland. All three are dotted with small lakes, and in a happier age they would be known for their holiday potential. Until 1870 this was the Prussian countryside, with a strong Slav element attaching to its people from the Elbe to the Oder. The lakes stock pike, pike-perch, tench, roach and eel, and fish breeding is an industry. At the heart of old Brandenburg, Berlin, capital of the first united Germany, Bismarck's Reich, was once famous for its freshwater fish dishes. Newnham Davies, who compiled the *Gourmet's Guide to Europe* in 1908, reported that the pike, carp, perch, salmon and trout were of a far higher quality than the meat. Still commonly seen in German restaurants are the large glass tanks in which freshwater fish swim until the diner makes his decision. Eventually it comes back, on a plate, 'schöner Müllerin Art', poached and served with melted butter, i.e. *au bleu*. Crabs, though, were also a Berlin speciality of the summer months, with crab fricassee a favourite at civic banquets, and crab in parsley sauce served with new potatoes. The original Hotel Kempinski (which has bequeathed its name to a plush hotel chain today) had a chef who specialized in presenting lobster with butter and fresh truffles. Eels with cucumber salad was another recommended, though equally seasonal, dish.

Neither in Poland nor Czechoslovakia has fish-eating ever reached this standard.

The evening was coming on when they left the coffee house. They passed the prison at the corner of Nalevki and Dluga and went along Rymarska Street and the Platz Bankovy. On the Iron Gate Square the street lamps were already burning. A cold wind came from the direction of the Saxon Gardens. Tramcars rolled along. Crowds of people thronged the market stalls. Hadassah held Asa Heshel's arm tightly as though afraid she might lose him. Farther along, at the bazaars, stall keepers presided over mounds of butter, huge Swiss cheeses, bundles of mushrooms, troughs of oysters and fish. The torchlights were already ablaze. They passed a slaughterhouse. Floodlights blazed in the building. Porters with hoses were swishing water on the stone floor. Slaughterers

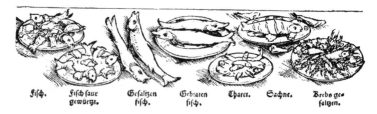

Fifch. Fifch faur Gefalizen Gebraten Tharet. Sachne, Brebs ge=
         gewürgt.   fifch.   fifch.   falgen.

From Hans Wegener, Küchenmeisterei, *facsimile, Leipzig 1939*

stood near blood-filled granite vats, slitting the necks of ducks, geese and hens. Fowl cackled deafeningly. The wings of a rooster, its throat just slit, fluttered violently. Hadassah pulled on Asa Heshel's sleeve, her face deathly white. A little farther on, in the fish market, stood tubs, barrels, and troughs. In the stale-smelling water carp, pike and tench swam about . . .

Isaac Bashevis Singer, The Family Moskat

At the turn of this century the fish Polish merchants bought in the Danube Delta and had sent up river to Warsaw took six days to arrive. It came packed in ice, in coffin-like boxes with insulating layers of straw and linden bark, and it must have been well and truly dead after making the journey in warm weather.

Fish ragoût

For eating purposes in Germany today, most fish comes from the sea. While travelling in Mecklenburg, a flat, untouched, slow-moving region, I had one of my best fish meals at the railway buffet in Güstrow: halibut in a buttery sauce. This is a similar, fairly bland recipe.

1 onion, chopped	1 kg (2 lb) white fish
1 tablespoon oil	2 eggs
salt, pinch of cayenne, pinch of ginger	1 tablespoon flour
	juice of 3 lemons

Fry the onion lightly in the oil with the seasonings. Put the fish, cut in small fillets, in a shallow oven dish and pour over the onion mixture, into which you have stirred 3–4 tablespoons water. Cover the dish and cook for 25 minutes in a medium oven 350°F (180°C, Gas Mark 4). Beat the eggs, add the flour and lemon juice and mix to a paste. Add some liquid from the fish, stir, and pour into the dish. Return to the oven for 10 minutes to cook the sauce. Serve with plain boiled potatoes and a cucumber side salad (p. 284).

Mackerel with gingerbread

Older German books always include recipes for carp 'in the Polish style', which is sweet and sour. This is a distant relation and a much finer recipe. I wrestled with the idea of fish and so much vinegar, plus cake, but the result was a stroke of genius on the part of the inventor. Genuine German or Polish gingerbread (see p. 371) is essential.

2 onions, thinly sliced
4 large mackerel, about 1 kg (2 lb) before cleaning
2 small slices gingerbread
½ cup wine vinegar
1 tablespoon golden syrup
lemon wedges, chopped parsley

Simmer the onions in about 1 cup water, until very soft. Put the cleaned, gutted fish, heads removed, into an oven dish, pour over the onion and water and bake in a hot oven for 20 minutes. Leave to cool. Allow the gingerbread crumbs to soak up the vinegar and syrup and spread them on a serving dish. Remove the bones and skin from the mackerel and arrange on top, decorated with lemon wedges and parsley.

This is a very potent mixture to which there is no suitable accompaniment except perhaps a few crisp, raw leaves of endive, to garnish.

German sea-fish eating thrives way inland, and nowhere better than in the historic green-belt of the south with its favourable sunny climate and rolling hills, Saxe-Thüringen. The historic county town of Weimar, hardly imaginable today as a one-time seat of national government, is a clean, residential spot, like Cheltenham or Tunbridge Wells, but with more parkland and statelier buildings. The streets are lined with bourgeois cafés and the memories of past German writers and musicians. Punks with transistors come and go. The names of Goethe and Schiller rub shoulders with those of early Socialist agitators, tokens of the fall of the Weimar Republic, the rise of the Third Reich and the arrival of Communism.

The Gaststätte des Meeres, on the unspoilt eighteenth-century Herderplatz, is Weimar's most popular spot for a modest fish lunch. It stands opposite the church where Pastor Herder, better known for his writings about nationality and the growth of national character, used to preach 200 years ago, and the queues last as long as the opening hours. The decor is plain, a large room like anyone's kitchen in the Formica era, packed to capacity with square tables covered with plastic cloths, painted pale blue and with a few fish on the wall. The fish on the menu are pike, plaice, herring, mackerel, halibut. They come with potato purée or chips and a side salad. The soup available the day of my visit was a spicy, sweet-sour Russian fish *solyanka* with prawn crackers from Vietnam. The only things amiss were those crackers, which I had seen going cheap on a Czech railway station six months earlier.

Carp recipes from Central Europe

One can be very rude about Polish fish and still not deny Poland is famous for its carp. In the thirteenth century it bred one of the best varieties, Polish 'royal carp'. Nowadays and in neighbouring Czechoslovakia the breeding continues. In Warsaw we queued for a carp which took forty minutes to buy. We baked it and it tasted sweet and good *au bleu*. If you can get a carp of this quality, try the Albanian recipe on p. 153. My London fishmonger, however, whenever I inquire about carp, begins with: 'Of course you would do better with . . .'

When the carp were bred on Polish country manors, they were cultivated as pets, like the big goldfish they are.

They were fed malt and potter's clay baked with oil, yeast, or bread, and they swam over at the sound of the bell, coming up to the surface when the owner and his daughter, who had a fondness for this, rang the bell on the gallery, bringing their favourite food and throwing it with her white hand.

This virtual fairytale was related by the eighteenth-century chronicler Lukasz Golebiowski and has led me to believe the carp's place in Central European culture is beyond the table more than on it. At Christmas it was brought into the house to spend its last days swimming in the bath, in the hope it would shed its muddy taste with frequent changes of water. In Hungary, Károly Gundel used to buy carp from the lakes and lower them in cages into the Danube for two weeks with the same purpose in mind. Nothing, though, would take away the bones. Central European children grow up with this problem, which makes a misery of the special occasions when carp is served. I believe the classic recipes are apologies for its shortcomings, which is why I shall not reproduce them here. Polish/Jewish recipes disguise the natural taste of carp with a 'grey sauce', or 'black sauce' rich in ginger, beer, sugar and vinegar, and with horseradish and strong marinades. Jewish *gefilte fisch*, combining carp with pike, was a blessed way of removing all the bones before mincing and cooking.

Pike-perch

Poles ate fish for the Church's sake. Herring followed carp as the fish of the Lenten winter. Often it made a meal, accompanied by a bowl of *zur* (see p. 102) and potatoes. The sour taste was everywhere. Sweeter and blander was pike-perch, usually boiled. Again Polish Jews were inspired to take the raw flesh out of the whole fish, chop and season it, then return it to the fish for cooking. What had finally become a good fish meal was washed down with Polish plum brandy.

A modern squid stew

Alas, poor Poland! Alan Davidson in *North Atlantic Seafood* noted a curious turn in the contemporary fashion of making do ten years ago, when he recorded the substitution of frozen squid for tripe in one of Poland's old and treasured meat recipes. Tripe had become difficult to obtain. All one can add is that now squid too is rare. Even the Anglers' Union restaurant makes some of its meals out of a tin, and the cavernous fish shops of Warsaw are unnecessarily large and cold for the small volume of packets and cans they contain.

Stockfisch and other remedies

Czechoslovakia has no coast except in Shakespeare. Its traditions in fish rate even lower than Poland's, and many of the same habits prevail. Carp is eaten as a festive dish at Christmas, and is sometimes served cold, in aspic. Herring is also eaten. The nineteenth-century standby was dried white fish, in German *Stockfisch*, in Czech *treska*. This was wind-dried and rehydrated when needed. Possibly it was good when carefully prepared and served with lashings of butter. The German poet Heinrich Heine, looking at it from his national point of view, certainly thought so. But good fish in Bohemia defeated even the national pride of Mrs Rettigova, who mainly listed dishes for pike or perch with sour cream. One or two were helped by the addition of sausage, but that was to invoke the Czech national salvation.

Trout from the Danube

I ordered and enjoyed this a few years ago in an extremely unfriendly establishment I would recommend to no one, set in the centre of Bratislava. Obsessed with the pretension of serving the West a mere sixty miles away, in Vienna, it was a smart, soulless, fragile place. Its only redeeming local touch was to sprinkle the grilled trout with caraway.

MEAT

꧁✿꧂

Beef

꧂✿

The Poles have long been known for their fondness for eating meat. In the reign of Sigismund Augustus (1548–72), the ostentatious Polish court had a passion for it. The king was the son of the Italian princess, Bona Sforza, whose marriage had brought many of her compatriots to Poland, particularly to the royal seat in Cracow. These Italians observed the strange Polish habits first-hand, gasping at the quantity of meat Poles ate, while Poles mocked the Italian love of vegetables.

Hussar roast is a noted, centuries-old Polish dish, comprising a sour pot-roast in which the half-cooked meat is sliced through in one-inch wide pieces, then each slice slit to make a pocket for stuffing with cooked onion, breadcrumbs and egg. The roast is re-shaped, tied together and the cooking finished. The 'joint' is then served with any sauce or accompaniment to roast beef.

A transformation like this made a piece of sirloin more interesting and more economical. It was also an advertisement for what could be achieved by time-consuming labour in the kitchen. (A Hungarian dish, Stefania roast beef, takes a similar though simpler form, a single opening being cut in the joint to take a chopped-egg stuffing.) These were the household habits the Polish middle classes received from the gentry and turned into virtues when their cooking established itself in the eighteenth century, and the dish continues today.

A modern source suggests the following accompaniment to Hussar roast. It may be used for any boiled or roast beef:

Polish sauce for roast beef

2 onions, finely chopped
1 small carrot, finely
   chopped
1 tablespoon parsley, finely
   chopped
1 clove garlic, finely
   chopped
4 tablespoons butter
small bay leaf
$\frac{1}{4}$ teaspoon dried basil

4 tablespoons flour
1 cup stock
1 cup red wine
juice of $\frac{1}{2}$ lemon
50 g (2 oz) ham
1 tomato
2 tablespoons horseradish,
   freshly grated or creamed
salt
1 teaspoon sugar (optional)

Sauté the chopped vegetables and herbs in the butter, together with the bay leaf and basil. Stir in the flour, cook for a few minutes, then dilute with stock. Simmer for 20 minutes. For a fine texture, sieve the sauce at this stage, or remove the bay leaf and liquidize. Return to the pan, add the wine and lemon juice, the ham cut into strips, the tomato, chopped, and the horse-radish. Heat through, season with salt and sugar and serve hot. The sugar may not be necessary if creamed horseradish is used.

This sauce is a model of Polish middle-class cooking as it was perfected in the nineteenth century. The technique and texture are French while the sweet-sourness is home-developed under Italian influence. The strips of ham, the basil, the bay leaf, tomato and wine and lemon juice or vinegar form the basis of Italian *agrodolce* sauces, while the sharp, bitter addition of horseradish belongs to Central Europe.

As a trading and diplomatic power during the centuries of the First Republic, Poland was influenced from many foreign quarters and was anxious to show off its broad contacts and wealth. Mikolai Rej complained in *The Life of an Honest Man* (1568) of 'these strange dishes and these indecent inventions of today's world'. He felt the threat of insanity brought on by the festivities of lighter-minded men and women in Carnival week and saw it as his duty to praise simple peasant concoctions. After Rej there were numerous intellectual objections to the eating habits of the Polish rich: that they lacked morality, manners, and national pride. As the cuisine expanded, a sense of what was properly Polish about it grew. Jerzy Ossolinski, ambassador to Italy in the early seventeenth century, gave banquets using only Polish products. The equivalents he established show where Polish and much of Central European food stands when it is not modified by outside influence:

Instead of wine in sauces, cherry juice
Instead of almonds, various home-grown nuts
Instead of raisins, dried cherries and/or fruit candied in honey
Instead of lemons to sour food, tart apples
Instead of pepper, horseradish
Instead of ginger, mustard
Instead of sugar, which was expensive, honey
Instead of olives and capers, fresh and dried mushrooms
Instead of wine vinegar, vinegar from honey
Instead of wine, beer and mead.

The noblest genealogy of any Polish meat dish is probably claimed by *zrazy*, mentioned by Mickiewicz in his national epic *Pan Tadeusz*. These are slices of cooked beef usually rolled around a filling such as sauerkraut, or horseradish, or sour pickles, though they may be arranged in layers spread with the same filling. As in Hussar roast, the idea of glorifying roast beef with a stuffing and a sauce underlies their popularity. They were first mentioned in the fourteenth century as a favourite dish of King Wladyslaw Jagiello, since when they have been connected with both Napoleon and Admiral Nelson.

Zrazy with buckwheat stuffing

500 g (1 lb) rump steak, cut into four thin slices	50 g (2 oz) mushrooms
	1 egg
salt, black pepper, mustard	½ cup wine
1 medium onion, chopped	bay leaf
4 tablespoons buckwheat	1 heaped teaspoon flour
50 g (2 oz) butter	½ cup cream

Beat the steaks flat, season with salt and pepper and spread with a little mustard on one side. Brown the onion and the buckwheat in half the butter, add the mushrooms and then break in the egg, stirring all the time until the egg firms. Season, divide into four portions, place one on each steak, roll the steaks up and fasten with a toothpick. Fry the rolls in the remaining butter, add the wine and bay leaf and simmer covered about 20 minutes, or until tender. Place the rolls in a dish and keep warm, first removing the skewers. Then thicken the cooking juices by stirring the flour into the cream and adding it to the pan. Bring to the boil and cook, stirring, for a few minutes before pouring the sauce over the steaks. Serve with boiled vegetables and potatoes or pasta.

Zrazy à la Napoléon are layers of beef and vegetables covered with white wine and sealed in dough.

In *Zrazy à la Nelson* the sauce is made with dried mushrooms, onions and cream, garnished with potato.

Military victories have provided good excuses for feasting. Serge Ganjou hazards a guess that in Poland so many dishes are named after Nelson (the same sour cream sauce over different meats, fish and mushrooms) because the Poles delighted in the outcome at Trafalgar. Bonaparte gave them little to celebrate. The diminished duchy courted him and provided legions of soldiers, a royal palace in Warsaw and a mistress, the Countess Maria Walewska. As a result Polish troops perished far away, while Walewska, ignored by her lover when he passed through Warsaw on the retreat from Moscow, was left to find her own way to Elba.

Other *zrazy* recipes are for pounded steaks, formed of a hamburger mixture, and either rolled and filled or cooked flat, coated with a brown gravy or a tomato sauce. Similar 'beef rolls' are found in Czechoslovakia (*ptachky*), Germany (*Rouladen*), Romania, Hungary (*rostelyos*) and parts of Yugoslavia. A rather interesting Yugoslav recipe rolls the beef around a thin red and green pepper omelette, then, after quickly frying it on the outside, cooks it in a stock flavoured with mustard. The whole is served with a dollop of sour cream on top and a garnish of green peas, boiled potatoes and whole baked tomatoes. George Lang includes what to my mind is a typically excessive Hungarian recipe, in which equal-sized slices of beef, veal and lean pork are rolled one inside the other and cooked in stock, onion and vinegar, with plenty of hot pepper, and finished with cream.

Polish beef *sztufada* is a good dish. The meat is marinated for one or two days in a mixture of raw soup vegetables, crushed spices, oil and sugar, the vegetables also being lightly crushed to force out their juice on to the surface of the meat. The joint is then larded and braised with stock, the marinade vegetables, a little paprika and marjoram, and served with its own juices enriched with garlic, tomato paste and wine, accompanied by potatoes or dumplings. The term comes from the Italian for a braised dish (*stufato*), also used by the Romanians (*stufat*). Spicy and vinegar marinades, which tenderize and enrich meat not of the first quality, have long been popular in Poland.

Otherwise, beef might be braised with a stock enriched with dried mushrooms and finished with sour cream, or it might be boiled and served with potato purée and a sauce of stock thickened with flour, sour cream and horseradish. If the beef were boiled as part of a soup, for instance for *barszcz*, it might be eaten as a separate course, with boiled vegetables.

Sauerbraten

German meat cookery places less accent on the sweet-sour element than Polish, but makes up for it with fruit and spices or rich marinades. The basic spiced and marinated pot-roast of beef has wide appeal.

1 cup red wine	6 peppercorns
1 tablespoon wine vinegar	1 teaspoon dry mustard
1 carrot, sliced	1½ kg (3 lb) topside of beef
1 onion, sliced	50 g (2 oz) lard
3 cloves	2 tablespoons flour
1 bay leaf	1 cup sour cream
¼ teaspoon dried thyme	½ cup stock
salt	

Combine the wine, vinegar, carrot, onion, cloves, bay leaf, thyme, salt, peppercorns and mustard in a large bowl and marinate the meat in it for 24 hours, turning 3–4 times. Drain, brown in the lard on all sides, pour over the marinade and bake slowly, tightly covered, for two hours. Strain the sauce and thicken it with the flour and cream, adding stock as necessary. Slice the meat, pour over the sauce and serve with noodles.

Beef is traditionally boiled to make staple one-dish meals (*Eintöpfe*). In 'Leipzig soup pot' the beef is cooked slowly with root vegetables, a bay leaf and salt and pepper (no herbs or garlic), then the whole served with separately cooked semolina dumplings. Dumplings instead of potatoes are a hallmark of south German cooking.

Another way to employ the *Eintopf* is to enlarge it into a soup and entrée by thickening the stock with flour and egg, or egg noodles (see p. 117 for *Kraftbrühe*), and to serve the meat separately, after the soup, with a fruit compote. This could be of plums or whortleberries preserved in a light syrup or cooked from fresh with sugar, or mashed apples (*Apfelmus*). Like the English, the Germans like to eat jams and jellies and sweet fruit with their meat.

Roast beef *garniert* (roast beef with a garnish) was a German restaurant speciality at the turn of the century, a dish borrowed from one empire to boost the self-image of another. The name brings legions of Prussian soldiers marching out of Daumier cartoons to mind. The Germanization of this dish is almost as helpful in understanding the German aspect of Central European food as was Ossolinski's Polish banquet. Roast beef *garniert* was served on a large dish with compartments for apricot jam, plum jam, stewed cherries, cauliflower, peas, lettuce, rice and spinach. Newnham Davies, no great enthusiast for German carnivorous habits, complained that this was what he didn't like about German meats, they were accompanied by too many sauces.

The distinction between vegetables and sauces seemed and still does seem very slight, given the way tinned vegetables are served in Germany, sweet and liquid, as if they were a vegetable compote. Vegetables tend to equal sauce and sauce tends to equal relish and there is a good etymological explanation for this, the word for vegetables having once been connected with the word for purée. The real vegetables come in the salad as a side dish.

But the most interesting feature of roast beef *garniert*, with its central dish surrounded by many relishes, is the design. This recalls the two distinctive cuisines to which German is closely related, Oriental and North American, and points up the Oriental thread running through Central European cuisine, thanks to the ancient spice-trade routes. It is a complicated business, but for those who like detail, the idea is taken up most stimulatingly by Paul Kovi in *Transylvanian Cuisine*.

The Czechs favour boiled beef with a tasty sauce. Mrs Rettigova lists twenty-four possibilities, based on intensifying the flavour of the reduced stock with onion, garlic, gherkins, mixed chopped fresh green herbs, sardines and freshly grated horseradish with or without sour cream. One of her cold sauces uses a little stock to dilute a dressing of wine vinegar and hard-boiled egg yolks. One attractive warm sauce is with dill. Joseph Wechsberg emphasizes the delicacy boiled meat was considered in his native country before the war.

Mrs Rettigova's dill sauce for beef

Bring to the boil one cup of beef stock, add two tablespoons wine vinegar and a few tablespoons of fresh chopped dill. Make a roux with 30 g (1 oz) each of butter and flour and dilute with the stock, stirring until smooth. Beat one or two egg yolks with a few tablespoons of sour cream, dilute with the sauce and return all to the pan, stirring until the whole is heated through.

Boiled beef with egg yolk and cheese sauce

A modern Czech book includes the following hearty winter treatment for boiled beef.

750 g (1½ lb) boiled beef
   shin or brisket
2 tablespoons butter
½ onion
2 tablespoons flour
1 cup beef stock

2 egg yolks
1 tablespoon lemon juice
butter and breadcrumbs to
   grease serving dish
20 g (¾ oz) grated cheese

After boiling, slice the meat and fry the slices on both sides in butter. Remove from pan and keep warm. Fry the chopped onion in the remaining fat, add the flour, cook for a few minutes and dilute, stirring, with stock. Beat the yolks together with lemon juice, dilute with a little stock and return to the pan. Stir constantly while heating through. Lay the meat in a greased dish sprinkled with breadcrumbs, pour over the sauce, sprinkle grated cheese and more breadcrumbs on top. Bake for a few minutes in a hot oven or under the grill until sizzling, and serve with potatoes or rice.

The modern preference, though, seems to be for braised or roast meat. A braise associated with Znojmo, and sometimes wrongly called a goulash, relies on pickled cucumbers to flavour the thickened cooking juices after the meat has been browned in bacon fat and gently stewed with plenty of onion.

A 'candle roast' or *Svickova* is a braise of beef with a little bacon for flavour, chopped root vegetables and onion, and a good pinch each of black pepper, juniper and allspice berries, crushed and added to the braising stock. When the meat is tender the stock is thickened with flour, sieved, then enriched with a generous amount of cream, a little sugar and lemon juice or vinegar to taste. Optional extras are a dash of mustard and madeira wine. Serve with dumplings (see p. 116) or potatoes.

Swineherds in a Hungarian wood, 1855. Bibliothèque Nationale, Paris (photo: J.-L. Charmet)

Preferred flavours with beef, to make quick dishes, include mushrooms, beer (the Czechs make a beef carbonnade as the Belgians do) and anchovy (to make a stuffing for beef rolls or to enhance the taste of beefburgers).

Hortobágy-style herdsman's stew

Hungary is inevitably associated with *gulyás* (see p. 120), but beef is generally less widely cooked than pork. I had always associated the romance of the *puszta* with beef and cowboys, only to prove myself wrong at the first inquiry. What the cowboys were doing was frying bacon. This excellent dish combines the two.

75 g (3 oz) smoked bacon, chopped	350 g (12 oz) potatoes, chipped
2 tablespoons lard	150 g (6 oz) *tarhonya* (see p.
2 onions, chopped	310), or small pasta
500 g (1 lb) braising beef, cubed	120 g (4 oz) *lecsó* (see p. 280)
salt, paprika	

Fry the bacon, add the lard if needed, brown the onions and the meat. Sprinkle over the salt and paprika, pour in water to cover and simmer till tender. When nearly done, add enough water for the remaining ingredients to cook in and cover the pot until the potatoes and pasta are done.

Beef pörkölt

Besides *gulyás*, this is the best-known Hungarian beef dish, one that is almost dry.

3 tablespoons fat	600 g (1¼ lb) lean stewing or braising beef, cubed
1 onion, chopped	salt
½–1 teaspoon paprika	

Soften the onion in the fat, sprinkle with paprika and add the meat. Stir so that the meat browns on all sides. Season with salt, add enough water not quite to cover the meat, and cook slowly, under a tight-fitting lid, for two hours, adding just a little water if necessary. Optional extras to the sauce include caraway seeds, a half-teaspoon of chilli or a few spoonfuls of red wine, but try the basic recipe first, not giving in to the temptation to season it with pepper. The traditional accompaniment is home-made pasta *galuska* (see p. 317).

To complete the traditional Hungarian meat-and-paprika trio a *paprikás* is also made with beef and sour cream, but more commonly with chicken.

Rostelyos

In Hungary this standard dish means a steak braised whole in sauce with a macedoine of root vegetables, onion and cream and served with noodles. In Germany and Austria, when restaurants offer Zigeuner schnitzel or Jäger schnitzel, this is the technique they have in mind, using veal or pork. The formula is similar to some Polish *zrazy* recipes. In the mid-eighteenth century the chef of Miklos Esterházy at the Esterházy estate created a well-known version.

Beef in disguise

Where does the desire to make one good thing taste like another come from? The ancient Romans did it, but they didn't directly pass it on. It is one thing for gluttonous priests to disguise meat to look like fish during Lent, or try to make their fish taste like meat, but nowadays, with the stress on authenticity on the plate, who wants beef masquerading as venison? The answer in the past was a combination of poor or limited ingredients and fashion. Metropolitan cooks wanted to bring the rural chic of the hunting lodge to their busy city tables. The Budapest National Casino, the most exclusive place to eat a hundred years ago, marinated best beef in red wine, wine vinegar, spices and root vegetables for several days to make it taste like game, then cooked it and served it in a sweetish sauce with dumplings. Pork was disguised as wild boar.

Beef in grape juice

This is a genuine country recipe, originally to use up some of the grape must left at the time of the wine-harvest. It is included in the first Hungarian-language cookery book of 1826.

850 g (1¾ lb) rump steak in a piece	1 large onion, chopped
3 tablespoons bacon fat or 2 slices bacon, rendered	1 cup beef stock
	2 hot peppers or ½ teaspoon chilli powder
1 carrot, chopped	1½ cups white grape juice
2 sticks celery, chopped	salt
1 parsnip, chopped	1 teaspoon arrowroot

Brown the meat in the hot fat, add the vegetables and stir until they are well coated. Add the stock, hot pepper and grape juice. Cover tightly and braise for an hour on top of the stove. When the beef is tender, strain off the liquid, adjust the seasoning, dissolve the arrowroot in a little of it, return to the pan and bring to the boil, stirring. Serve the abundant sauce with the meat, and perhaps pasta.

In Romania, Hungarian influence has brought in goulash-style stews of beef, and Saxon German hotpots have come in via Transylvania. Composite dishes made with boiled beef cooked in a sourish liquid, like *ciorba* with meatballs (p. 128) and *bors* (p. 129), partly under Russian influence, provide a rich soup followed by a plain meat course, and this habit is still widely practised in private homes. Good Bucharest restaurants, though, were thoroughly cosmopolitan before the war and would always have offered a French-style *filet de boeuf*, perhaps also *biftecks saignants à l'anglais*. The common people's food was far removed from this, and often Oriental in its flavours. Wind-dried beef, *pastrama*, of Armenian origin, was observed to be a much-loved food among the poor. A nineteenth-century traveller described it as 'thin, black, leather-like pieces of meat dried and browned in the sun, and with salt and squashed flies'. A traditional, more familiar dish served at peasant country-wedding feasts, but one that was no more appetizing, was jellied beef. The best native Romanian meat cookery is grilled, ideally over charcoal. It is the cooking of an Oriental street culture, and of the whole of Romania in the very hot summer.

In the air waft the aromas of hot oil, pepper, cooked tomatoes, and fried onions. The whole spicy gamut of the cooking of the Orient penetrates your nostrils, for all the shops are open to the street. You see your bread baking, your meat roasting, your peppers grilling, or your fish. This spectacle does not always excite the appetite, but the sight gives a strange animation to the city [Constanta].

Eugène Pittard, *La Roumanie*, 1917

Fleica la gratar

Use fillet steak. Keep the steaks in the refrigerator for 3 days before using. Leave them at room temperature for about 5 hours before cooking. Rub them with garlic on both sides and cook under a hot grill, turning once. The steaks can be anything from rare to well done, but just before the grilling is finished pour over them a couple of tablespoons each of garlic crushed in lemon juice or wine vinegar. Serve hot, sprinkled with parsley, on warm plates, and accompany with sour salads (see p. 81).

A Romanian sauce with quinces for boiled meat sounds chic today, perhaps, because of the rarity of this sour fruit except when home-grown, but Maude Parkinson, a university-educated Irishwoman who went to Bucharest in 1889 to teach languages, felt sorry for her charges having to eat a midday school meal consisting of 'meat and stewed quinces' followed by a wodge of *mamaliga* sprinkled with cheese. At home, where the children ate dinner at six p.m., the fare was not much better: thin soup, made from the meat which followed as the over-stewed, 'perfectly white' main course, with vegetables. Stewed fruit or a light pudding followed. The governess had thin red wine and occasionally a *bifteck*.

Biftec ala Sinaia

This is a recipe of Anisoara Stan, a Romanian who emigrated to the United States in 1922.

Ask your butcher to cut and trim a very tender piece of beef steak. Cut crosswise into slices 1½ inches thick and flatten a little. Dip each slice in hot butter, pile one on top of the other and let stand for one hour. While you are warming up a pan containing 3 tablespoonsful of butter (or lard), drench [*sic*] the slices of meat in flour and fry quickly on both sides over a high flame to a red brown colour. Add a little beef stock and some salt to taste, cover very tightly and heat for about 5 to 6 minutes. When done serve on a very hot serving plate. Place the meat in the centre, pour on the sauce and garnish all round with fried red cabbage, mushrooms, green beans, red beets, fried brains and peas. On top of the meat place some eggs sunny side up. Prepare the garnishing before you finish the meat.

The dish is typical of what Mrs Stan's equals among the well-to-do middle class would have eaten, at a great distance from peasant traditions, and some distance from Maude Parkinson. The middle classes went to the Carpathian mountain resort of Sinaia because it was the chic thing to do after the king, Alexander, took refuge there from the heat. The most famous restaurant in Bucharest, Capşa, opened a country branch there, and the beauty spot became known for its gastronomic delicacies along with its clean, bracing air and mountain scenery.

Pasticada

A speciality from Dalmatia; beef does not figure as prominently in Yugoslav cooking as lamb, mutton, pork and poultry. It is more often included in mixed meat stews, minced rissoles and sausages.

50–75 g (2–3 oz) bacon, preferably in a thick piece	rosemary
a joint of beef about 1 kg (1¾ lb)	bay leaf
	peppercorns
2–3 tablespoons oil or bacon fat	2 tablespoons flour
	scant ½ cup white wine
250 g (8 oz) vegetables – carrot, parsnip, celery, leek, onion	1 cup stock
	25–50 g (1–2 oz) stoned olives
	lemon juice, salt

Cut the bacon into matchsticks, make incisions in the beef, lard it, then brown it in the oil on all sides. Remove. Fry the chopped vegetables lightly in the same oil, add seasoning, place the meat on top and stew it covered, adding a little water or stock if necessary, until tender. Remove the meat, dust the vegetables with the flour, cook for a few minutes, then pour on the wine and 1 cup stock. Simmer for 10 minutes, add the halved olives and enrich with lemon juice and possibly a little salt. Slice the meat, pour over the sauce and serve with boiled chard and boiled potatoes. This dish is considered a staple of the people of Dalmatia, who have been poor and limited to using local produce for centuries. It employs the rosemary that grows freely in the region, though garlic may be included or substituted as a variation. On the coast it is more usual to eat fish with the chard and potatoes. The beef comes from further up the mountainside.

In Bulgaria there is only a slight history of eating beef, except in combination with other meats and with vegetables. The Bulgarians eat less meat generally than most Europeans, which might be another reason, apart from their yoghurt, for their legendary longevity. Their best recipes are for lamb.

Veal

🙚

The only 'legal' Wiener schnitzel is made with veal. The distinction was of religious importance in Joseph Wechsberg's home town of Ostrawa in Moravia, where it divided the Sunday menu: the Jews had Wiener schnitzel, the Gentiles had roast pork with sauerkraut and dumplings. In the Austrian style, as Julie Andrews sings, schnitzel often goes with noodles, while the Czechs prefer dumplings, potatoes or rice. All over Central Europe many recipes for veal echo the tastes of the Italian dishes that fathered them.

An excellent quick Czech dish with a hint of Italy is veal escalopes with anchovy, made by frying escalopes and coating each with a heaped spoonful of fresh breadcrumbs fried in butter and a lightly fried anchovy. For neat presentation curl the fish, and serve the escalopes overlapping each other, garnished with lemon wedges and slices of endive.

Similarly, Prague veal escalopes are coated in seasoned flour and quickly fried on both sides, then kept warm while a topping of chopped ham, peas and boiled egg is heated through in the pan. The escalopes are served with a slice of lemon, mashed potato and a green salad.

Veal mince with currants

The German and Czech tastes for eating meat with a sharp fruit compote or dried fruit add a dimension to veal cookery, however, that is not related to Italy. This is a very quick German recipe for ready-cooked veal.

50 g (2 oz) butter
30 g (1 oz) fresh
   breadcrumbs
50 g (2 oz) currants
2 cups white stock

$\frac{1}{2}$ cup white wine
500 g (1 lb) cold roast veal,
   diced
white pepper, salt if liked

Melt the butter in a pan, brown the breadcrumbs, add the currants, stock and wine. Simmer gently until the currants are plump, add the veal, heat through and season to taste. Serve with plain boiled potatoes and a cucumber side salad. This would make a very pleasant summer supper. The simplicity lends itself to an evening meal out-of-doors.

Veal, being light, is considered suitable for a rare hot dish in the German evening. In a restaurant an escalope might be offered just fried, with compote as a relish. In Berlin a particular escalope, simple to prepare, but lavish to look at and a strong image-builder with its conspicuously expensive ingredients, is said to have been created for a rushed local councillor, Baron Friedrich von Holstein. A Holstein schnitzel was dipped in seasoned flour, fried in butter on both sides and kept warm, while for each person the chef broke an egg into the pan and toasted half a slice of bread. The toast was cut in neat triangles, garnished with lettuce or endive leaves and a fillet of anchovy, a teaspoon of caviare and a sliver of smoked salmon placed on top. The meat was arranged on the serving plate with the egg on top and the toast triangles arranged decoratively around it. With it might come sliced fried potatoes and a green salad. The style might be called Berlin vulgar. The Berlin of the turn of the century was packed with large new brasseries to cater for the suddenly booming Prussian capital. One even had the Wagnerian name of *Das Rheingold*.

Prague veal escalopes with pancakes

300 g (10 oz) mushrooms, sliced
75 g (3 oz) butter
salt, black pepper
½ teaspoon dried marjoram
1 tablespoon fresh chopped parsley
2 teaspoons flour

300 g (10 oz) flour
2 eggs
good pinch of baking powder
milk and water as needed, or whey
4 slices of veal
slices of lemon

Sauté the mushrooms in a quarter of the butter, add salt, pepper, marjoram, parsley, sprinkle 2 teaspoons of flour on top, cover and set aside. Prepare a thick pancake batter from the flour, egg yolks, baking powder, salt, milk-and-water and beaten egg whites, and fry 8 small pancakes in half the remaining butter. Slide these onto a warm serving plate, stir the mushroom filling and divide it among the pancakes. Fold each pancake in half to enclose the filling. Beat the veal, season, and fry quickly on both sides in the last of the butter. On each slice of veal lay a pancake topped with a wedge of lemon. Serve with a green salad.

Veal paprikás

This is a nineteenth-century classic Hungarian treatment for veal escalopes.

Marinate four thin slices of veal in lemon juice for an hour. Meanwhile, slice the same weight of onions, sauté in butter and sprinkle with paprika. Dip the meat in seasoned flour and in a separate pan fry it on both sides. Place the meat on top of the onions, cover, simmer for a few minutes, then pour over two parts sour cream to one part stock (about 1½ cups in all), into which you have stirred two teaspoons of flour. Season, cook for another five minutes and serve very hot, with small dumplings or pasta.

Quick escalope of veal with garlic

Yugoslavia broadens the veal repertoire further by bringing in plenty of garlic. Coat the pieces of veal in seasoned flour, fry quickly on both sides, then place on a hot dish, with chopped garlic sprinkled on top. For each escalope bring a few tablespoons of water to the boil in the frying pan and pour over. The whole is served with salad. This recipe may be compared with those for meaty fish steaks on p. 169. The results are very similar, so much so that, according to Waverley

Root, in the sixteenth century in Italy the now celebrated cold veal dish *vitello tonnato* was created to circumvent a shortage of tuna. Veal was also referred to in those days as 'counterfeit sturgeon'.

Apart from schnitzels, veal is boiled, roasted, stuffed and stewed. Being lean and bland it is a good vehicle for rich sauces and forcemeats, and also nicely complements the southern vegetables. In the Balkans it combines with *djuvec* (see p. 282), and in Hungary with *lecsó*. Both of these are a kind of *ratatouille*. Some veal preparations are expressly made to be eaten cold, with the meat being used as a vehicle, like bread, for a delicious filling or spread or cold sauce.

Karlsbad stuffed breast of veal

Eggs and bacon, used to make a Prague schnitzel, make this Karlsbad speciality.

1¼ kg (2½ lb) boned breast of veal	100 g approx. (4 oz) smoked ham, or sausage
salt	2 pickled cucumbers
3 eggs	water or stock
1½ tablespoons butter	1 tablespoon flour
100 g (3½ oz) bacon	

Salt the meat. Beat the eggs, season and stir over heat in a little of the butter until thick. Combine this with the bacon cut in thin strips, the chopped ham or sausage and the chopped cucumbers, fill the meat with it and sew up. Brown the stuffed joint on all sides in the remaining butter, pour over a cup of stock or water, cover and simmer slowly for 1– 1½ hours, until tender. Melt a knob of butter in a separate pan, cook the flour for a few minutes, then dilute gradually with the juices from the pan and stir over heat until thickened. Serve the meat sliced, with rice, salad and fruit compote.

A Czech veal stew is flavoured with lemon and mace and served with cauliflower and dumplings. Czech roasts of veal are cooked with sour cream, or with bacon and vegetables and white wine, or with anchovies.

Braised veal

This *Kalbsnierenbraten* (the name refers to the inclusion of kidney, considered a delicacy) is a plain, charming and impressive dish from Germany to offer guests.

1¼ kg (2½ lb) (approx. weight) boned loin of veal, with fat and kidney removed	butter as needed
	1 sliced carrot
	1 bay leaf
any stuffing suitable for veal (optional)	1 cup sour cream
	2 tablespoons capers
	salt and pepper

If the joint is to be stuffed, lay the boned meat flat, spread over the stuffing, roll up and tie the joint securely with string. Slice the kidney and brown it along with the joint in about 55 g (2 oz) butter. Add the sliced carrot and bay leaf and enough warm water to come half way up the side of the meat. Cover and simmer for 1–1½ hours. Remove the meat, strain the stock and skim off the fat. Add the cream and capers, mix well and season. Bring this sauce to the boil and pour a little over the meat. Serve the rest separately, with spinach and boiled potatoes.

Veal with spinach and green pepper

At a blindfold testing I would have said this dish, which is as rich in vegetables as meat, was Bulgarian, but I came across it classified as Yugoslav. A compromise is to call it Balkan.

500 g (1 lb) pie veal
500 g (1 lb) spinach
salt
2 onions, chopped
2 tablespoons oil
1 tablespoon flour

1 green pepper, chopped in
  strips
salt and pepper
1 cup sour milk, or
  buttermilk, or pouring
  yoghurt

Simmer the veal in just enough water, covered, till tender. Wash the spinach, chop it finely, sprinkle with salt and leave in a strainer for the liquid to drain off. In a frying pan sauté the onions in the hot oil till golden, add the flour, then the spinach, stir and fry for a few minutes, then add the meat with its stock, stirring. Add the pepper slices, season and simmer until nearly all the liquid has evaporated. Serve on warm plates with sour milk at room temperature.

Veal with tomatoes and onions and peppers, the basis of the Austrian *Zigeuner* schnitzel, is another Balkan-style dish. The name means 'gypsy schnitzel', which in a nutshell expressed the imperial attitude towards the distant provinces of south-east Europe.

Veal tocana

Romanian cuisine has many recipes for veal stew, or *tocana*. All the *tocanas* are very oniony, in the manner of a Hungarian *pörkölt*, but with more liquid and cream. In restaurants a tomato sauce is common. This recipe with garlic and fennel is still simple, but more unusual.

1 clove garlic
3 tablespoons oil
1 kg (2 lb) onions, chopped
hot dried peppers
1 kg (2 lb) stewing veal, in
  chunks

salt
1 good tablespoon fresh
  fennel or dill, chopped,
  or 1 teaspoon dried dill
2 tablespoons sour cream

Wipe a heavy casserole with garlic, heat the oil, and sauté the onions until golden. Add the crushed peppers to taste and the meat with a little salt and the fennel, which ought to be fresh, or dill. Stir once, cover tightly and cook for 10 minutes. Add the sour cream, cook for 5 minutes, then add enough water to cover the meat and cook slowly for an hour. Serve hot, sprinkled with fresh parsley, dill or fennel, and rice or semolina dumplings.

Anisoara Stan's 'own veal' is a braise of veal cutlets filled with veal mince on a macédoine of root vegetables and bacon, with a little clove, chives and lemon peel. A sauce is made by diluting the pan juices and vegetables with stock, thickening them with flour and sour cream, and finishing with lemon juice. It is the presentation that makes this dish truly Romanian: the veal rolls in their sauce are topped with stuffed hard-boiled eggs and served with a fruit compote, perhaps apricot or cherry. Stan's book contains several instances of whole-egg garnish for mutton, beef and veal, and I suspect this is a habit of German/Transylvanian origin. She was born in Cluj (Kolosvar in Hungarian, Klausenburg in German) before she emigrated to the United States. The Saxon German influence on her Romanian cookery also shows through in her many recommendations to serve meat with a fruit compote.

Okra with veal

Another Balkan combination of veal with vegetables.

1 clove garlic	1 cup stock or water
2 tablespoons olive oil or bacon fat	2–3 tomatoes or 1 200 g (7 oz) tin
375 g (12 oz) onions	juice of 1 lemon
500 g (1 lb) veal, diced	salt, pepper
500 g (1 lb) okra	parsley, thyme, dill

Rub the bottom of the frying pan with garlic, add the oil or bacon fat and fry the onions until very soft. Add the meat and simmer until half-done. Top and tail the okra, cut it into chunks and add to the meat with the stock or water. Cook for 15 minutes, add the tomatoes, lemon juice, seasoning and fresh herbs, and more oil if a heavier dish is required. Cover and cook for another 10 minutes on top of the stove, or bake in the oven, until all the ingredients have blended. Serve with home-made semolina dumplings sprinkled with butter and parmesan cheese.

Veal generally gets a chic Franco-Austrian treatment in Hungary, where recipes range from escalopes cooked with cheese (an Italian idea passed on to Austria), to breast of veal *bourgeoise*, with a bread, egg, milk and onion forcemeat. Károly Gundel created for a Budapest restaurant a dish built up in layers, starting with spinach, then breaded veal cutlets, mushrooms, a cheese and nutmeg flavoured béchamel, grated cheese and breadcrumbs and a piping of mashed potato. It was laborious, but the result somehow not as vulgar as the efforts of a Berlin restaurateur. With less effort, lean veal in Hungary is sautéed with paprika and finished with sour cream, as in the veal *paprikas* above, or made into stuffed rolls. As an economical dish in the past, veal knuckles would have been boiled and the stripped meat then coated in breadcrumbs, fried and served with tartar sauce, a favourite Hungarian garnish when it is sweet. The boiling liquid would have made soup.

To represent an aspect of Hungary, however, I most like this down-to-earth recipe for veal chops of Fred Macnicol's, from his excellent, neglected *Hungarian Cookery*. He points out that nowadays, veal being hard to obtain, it is often replaced by pork, but this is the original.

Hungarian veal steaks

At its best the dish glistens with pure pork dripping and cooks like to waive restraint here when it comes to chillis. The meat is fried very quickly in abundant dripping and then removed from the pan. A chopped onion and thinly sliced raw potatoes are fried in the same fat, with a liberal sprinkling of paprika powder and chilli powder. To serve, this glowing mixture is heaped over the meat: accompany with thick chunks of strong bread, and a light wine.

Hortobágy pancakes

This is a famous Hungarian dish and very filling. The Gay Hussar restaurant in London, renowned for its vast portions of excellent solid food and the affluent leftish political conversation of its diners (at least some years ago), serves two of these as a main course. It is a dish that doesn't excite me, though there are many enthusiasts. George Lang is so negative he styles it a recipe for using up leftovers. Minced veal should be sautéd with chopped onions for a few minutes, covered and cooked for a further 5 minutes, then the pan is drained of its juices. Two tablespoons of sour cream should be added for each pound of meat, and the mixture cooked for half an hour. Plain white French-style pancakes are then filled with this mixture and coated with a sauce made of the reserved pan juices, a good cup of sour cream mixed with a heaped tablespoon of flour and a tablespoon of paprika. The leftover alternative Lang has in mind is chicken.

The *puszta* town of Hortobágy – at the centre of a region famed for its many varieties of bacon which therefore has given its name to several prominent Hungarian dishes – is now a tourist mecca: a place to buy Hungarian schnaps (called *barack* and pronounced 'barask') and hand-made leather boots. The name is pronounced 'Hawtobodj'.

Roast shin of veal

This a recipe from Tito's chef, Olga Novac-Markovic, who says it is a very popular dish for home entertaining in Yugoslavia, where it is presented on a wooden platter and carved by the guests themselves. Suggested accompaniments are jacket new potatoes, courgettes or rice with peas.

Kellemes karácsonyt!

Hungarian Christmas

1 leg of veal, about 1 kg (2 lb)
salt
mustard
50 g (2 oz) butter
scant ½ cup white wine

Salt the veal, coat it with mustard, place it in a baking tray and pour over melted butter. Add the wine and roast in a medium oven 1 hour, basting periodically and adding a little stock or water if needed. Turn up the temperature to 425°F (220°C, Gas Mark 7) for the last 10 minutes, to brown the joint.

Lamb
🐑

Lamb is an Easter treat in most countries, but the strongest traditions are to be found where it is eaten all year round: in north Germany and in the Balkans.

A joint of roast lamb studded with garlic opens the selection of recipes in Günter Grass's *The Flounder*. This exuberant and extravagant novel celebrating the evolution and fertility of German/Polish life in Kashubia, the area around Danzig, should be read by anyone with imagination and an interest in food. Roast a leg of lamb with garlic and serve it with green beans lightly steamed and mixed with stewed, unsweetened pears, seasoned with black pepper.

The Albanians eat young spring lamb with chard for Easter. They braise it, like the Romanians and the south Yugoslavs, with okra, or with onions and tomatoes; or they make it into rissoles flavoured with mint. Everywhere in the Balkans it is the meat most commonly used to stuff vegetables.

Lamb charlotte with peaches

1 shoulder of lamb	4 tablespoons parsley
salt, pepper	1 tablespoon ready-made
175 g (6 oz) coarse rye	mustard
bread	500 g (1 lb) tinned peach
1 onion, finely chopped	halves
15 g ($\frac{1}{2}$ oz) butter	

Season the meat and roast in a preheated medium oven for 20 minutes per pound. Rub the bread to crumbs, fry the onion till soft, mix these two with all other ingredients except the peaches. Remove the lamb and spread with the bread and mustard paste. Surround with peach halves, cut side down. Bake in a hot oven for 10 minutes, till the outside is brown and crisp. This is a modern West German recipe from Judy Ridgeway's *The German Food Book*, but one which continues the old tradition of meat, spices and fruit. The colour photographs in Ridgeway are the best guide to the different German sausages and cold meats, cheese and fine bakery.

Mutton in cream, and other Polish and Czech dishes

In the heart of Poland lamb is treated as a mainly foreign dish in modern books, and the recipes collected by Zofia Czerny in 1975 are either British or Romanian or Turkish, or obviously a borrowing from France. Lamb with garlic, or braised with caraway seeds, or in a pot with Savoy cabbage, are the dishes closest to native taste. Poland's last king, Stanislas, who at the end of the eighteenth century used to hold banquets for artists and enlightened men, liked on those busy, talkative, not wholly productive occasions to eat mutton in cream. It was generally thought the artists were taking their sovereign for a ride, though it gave everyone the excuse to eat well.

Of the few Czech recipes for lamb and mutton, mutton in

cream has stood the test of time. The mutton is marinated in
spices and vinegar, then larded and roasted with a generous
baste of sour cream. The whole is served with dumplings.
Another Czech way with lamb/mutton is to braise it in wine
and serve it with potato purée and cranberry compote, though
with good lamb this is heavy treatment.

Charcoal-grilled lamb steaks

The best lamb recipes come from the Balkans. For Romanian
or Transylvanian *flekken*, fry pieces of the finest lean young
lamb in a little bacon fat over a high heat, so that they are crisp
outside, but slightly underdone inside. Serve and eat immediately off warm plates, with a selection of seasonings:
mustard, ground ginger, dried, crushed herbs, salt, paprika,
pepper.

Shish kebab

Lamb on a spit is served throughout the Balkans, though
minced rissoles are generally more common. In Bulgaria cubed
lamb is marinated, preferably overnight, in oil and lemon juice,
with garlic and hot paprika to taste, and a pinch of salt. It is
grilled over charcoal on skewers with slices of onion, green
pepper and tomato in between.

Bulgarian lamb stew with vegetables

Like veal, lamb is often combined with vegetables in a stew, or
roasted and eaten with plenty of vegetables. This recipe,
comparable with a lamb *gyuvech*, combines a Bulgarian love of
vegetables with the influence of more northerly cooking.
German and Austrian tastes, thanks to trade and politics, have
left their mark.

3 onions, chopped
50 g (2 oz) mushrooms,
   sliced
cooking oil or fat as
   necessary
paprika
600 g (1¼ lb) braising lamb,
   cubed
4 peppercorns
2 bay leaves
a piece of root ginger

350 g (12 oz) white cabbage,
   chopped
100 g (4 oz) cauliflower,
   divided into florets
100 g (4 oz) tomatoes,
   quartered
100 g (4 oz) potatoes,
   chipped
2 cloves garlic, crushed with
   salt

Braise the onions and mushrooms in a little oil, sprinkle with paprika, pour in a little boiling water and add the meat. Season with pepper and add the bay leaves and ginger. Cover and simmer until half-done. Add all the remaining ingredients except the garlic, which should be introduced when cooking is complete. Reduce the sauce if necessary to make a rich brown gravy before serving.

Romanian lamb tocana with okra and white wine

250 g (8 oz) onion, chopped
2 cloves garlic, crushed with
   salt
3 tablespoons oil or bacon
   fat
1 kg (2 lb) lamb, cubed
250 g (8 oz) okra, topped
   and tailed, and cut in
   chunks

2–3 sticks celery, chopped
1 tablespoon each fresh
   parsley and chives,
   chopped fine
1 glass white wine
2 cups tomato juice
1 teaspoon dried thyme
3 tablespoons sour cream

Fry the onions and crushed garlic in the oil, taking care not to let them burn. Add the meat, brown on all sides and simmer for a few minutes, covered. Add the okra, the celery and fresh herbs, pour on the wine and simmer for 5 minutes. Add the tomato juice, thyme and sour cream and cook for a final $\frac{1}{2}$ hour. Serve hot with slices of *mamaliga* (p. 330) or new potatoes.

Bulgarian mutton pilaf

Rice pilafs of Turkish origin are common in all the Balkan countries and, in the last century, as rice became more widely available further north, dishes based upon them were quickly co-opted into the economical repertoire of Czech and Polish kitchens.

500 g (1 lb) shoulder of mutton, cubed	paprika
	salt
oil or cooking fat, as required	ground pepper
	160 g (6½ oz) rice
4 onions, chopped	250 g (8 oz) tomatoes

Brown the meat in its own fat or with added oil, add the onions and seasonings, pour in 1 litre (1⅓ pints) water and cook covered for 40 minutes. Add the rice and tomatoes and cook until the rice is just tender, adding a little more water if necessary.

In Hungary a similar, ancient dish was made with millet. These are plain, wholesome, filling, if not particularly interesting, dishes for a cold day.

Romanian lamb ciorba as a main dish

Boiled lamb is a great delicacy. The best recipes for it are those that fall between being a soup and a stew.

lean lamb on the bone	1 onion, chopped
salt, pepper	2–3 tomatoes, chopped
3 carrots, chopped	2 sticks celery, chopped

1 tablespoon each fresh
  tarragon and dill, also
  thyme, lovage and fennel,
  as available
2 tablespoons uncooked rice
1–2 eggs

3 tablespoons lemon juice,
  or to taste
sour cream (optional)

Bring the meat to the boil in plenty of cold water, seasoned with salt and pepper. Skim the scum from the surface and simmer slowly for about 40 minutes, or until nearly tender. Add the vegetables, ⅔ of the herbs, and the rice and cook until tender. Cover the soup tightly and leave it to stand. To serve, remove the meat, slice it and place it in a serving dish deep enough to hold the ample sauce. Beat the egg with the lemon juice, dilute it with a cup of stock and return to the pan. Adjust seasoning and add the remaining fresh herbs, also the sour cream, diluted with a little stock, if liked. Serve with crusty bread to soak up the soup, or with boiled potatoes or boiled white beans, which can be added to the soup.

Similar sour stews of lamb are found in Yugoslavia, like the traditional *Sar Planina* hot pot, from the mountains of western Macedonia, near Skopje. This is made with a lamb's head, liver and lights. After cooking in water with garlic, onion and parsley the meat is stripped from the bone and returned to the strained stock, together with rice. The soup is finished with lemon juice and a beaten egg, and served with fresh celery leaves.

The egg or egg-and-sour finish particularly complements lamb. Three of Paul Kovi's five Transylvanian recipes for lamb and mutton combine it with eggs, as do recipes from Czechoslovakia.

Romanian lamb with an egg-and-pickle garnish

Using eggs a different way, Anisoara Stan recommends serving mutton braised in red wine with stuffed eggs or stuffed tomatoes and a sour salad. Braise a leg of lamb or mutton with plenty of diced soup vegetables and bacon, two fresh red peppers, and some peppercorns and fennel. Add parsley, chives and thyme, and red wine, water and a little wine vinegar. Cook slowly, covered, for two hours. Slice the meat, purée the sauce and finish it with cream and a dash of lemon juice. Garnish with *muraturi* (p. 81) or gherkins or a salad of pickled peppers (p. 76). Any recipe for stuffed eggs or stuffed tomatoes is appropriate, including those on p. 78, 96, and 280.

Lamb baked with yoghurt

In south Yugoslavia the equivalent to egg-and-sour is yoghurt thickened with eggs.

This delicacy is called yoghurt *tava*. Season a leg of lamb with salt, pepper and paprika and marinate it in oil for several hours. Transfer all to a pan with a little water and stew, covered, until tender. When the water evaporates, stir in $\frac{1}{2}$ litre (1 pint) yoghurt or buttermilk mixed with a tablespoon of flour and two beaten eggs. Sprinkle the dish with parsley and bake for 15–20 minutes.

For another dish, *kapama*, lamb is braised with onions and spinach, with yoghurt as a pouring sauce.

Pot-roast leg of lamb

Another Yugoslav tradition, from Dalmatia, is to use a *sac*, which works like a hay box or a modern slo-cooker, to roast meat. The *sac* (pronounced 'satch') is a flat earthenware or iron dish with a tight-fitting, dome-shaped lid, the whole being placed in the embers of the fire. If a slo-cooker is not available, use foil, baking parchment or a chicken brick and bake in a conventional oven.

1 leg of lamb weighing about 1½ kg (2½–3 lb), sprinkled with salt	1 kg (2 lb) potatoes
a little cooking oil	2 green peppers, sliced lengthways in 1 cm (½ inch) wide strips
1 teaspoon rosemary, fresh or dried	2 tomatoes, halved
1 lemon	

Brown the salted lamb quickly in a pan with a little oil over a high heat, turning to seal the juices on all sides. Put it in the slo-cooker or on the foil in a baking tray, sprinkle with the rosemary, wedges of lemon and the vegetables. If using a slo-cooker, quarter and parboil the potatoes before baking. Cover the slo-cooker, and cook for 3–4 hours on high. If using foil, seal the parcel and bake for 1 hour in a preheated hot oven.

Macedonian lamb stew

1 kg (2 lb) lamb off the bone, or 1¼ kg (2½ lb) lamb shoulder on the bone	salt, pepper
a little cooking oil (optional)	140 g (5 oz) fresh tomatoes
140 g (5 oz) onion	140 g (5 oz) spring onions or leeks, including green parts
hot dried or fresh peppers to taste (try 2–3 dried chillies to begin)	2 cups white wine

Preheat a heavy-bottomed pan and brown the meat, using a little oil if it is very lean. Remove the meat and soften the onion in the remaining fat in the pan, then return the meat with the hot peppers and a little salt and pepper, cover the pan and stew gently until the meat is almost tender. Meat on the bone will shrink and, at this stage, can be easily removed, chopped into cubes and returned to the pan. Add the tomatoes and leeks, stew for a further 15 minutes, covered. Pour in the wine and heat through.

For a colourful combination of items on the plate, serve with corn bread (see p. 355) or *mamaliga*, though rice or boiled potatoes in their skins would do equally well. This recipe will make a cheaper cut of lamb succulent and tender and is highly recommended.

Lamb with tarragon

This classic combination of flavours in Romanian and Hungarian cooking combines to produce a soup (see p. 125) or, as here, a simple and quite luxurious stew, suitable for a dinner party.

1 kg (2 lb) lean lamb fillet, roughly diced	2–3 bunches spring onions
a few tablespoons sunflower oil	3 15 cm (6 inch) sprigs fresh tarragon, or 1–2 teaspoons dried
salt	1 cup water or stock
3 level teaspoons flour	

Braise the meat in a little oil, sprinkle with salt, then flour, and mix well. Add the chopped onions, including the green parts, and the leaves of tarragon. (The dried herb may be used instead, but it is a very second-class substitute.) Add the liquid gradually, stirring. Simmer, covered, until the meat is tender and the sauce has reduced by a third.

Pork and bacon

֍

After these came rows of tables sheltered under canvas roofs, displaying enormous coils of russet-hued sausages, as thick as a ship's mooring-rope; and piles of yellow fat and grease, brown flitches of smoked bacon, whole sides of fat salt pork, and hams by scores, rose in multitudinous tiers; while at other stalls entire carcasses of hogs were hooked up, wide-opened, gaping, and so dripping with blood that the dogs gathered round, and had to be driven away.

Wladislaw Reymont, *The Peasants*

Vienna has boiled beef and strudel, Prague has roast pork and dumplings. Joseph Wechsberg calls these the two prongs of Austro-Hungarian imperial cuisine. The French estimation of beef as superior underlines the different Czech attitude: people of all classes eat pork, and top restaurants feature a great variety of pork dishes. Poland has a similar reverence and fondness for pork, and it is also the most widely cooked meat in Hungary, Slovenia and Romania. The Germans eat pork schnitzel nowadays as often as veal. Pork fat is used for cooking in Hungary and Romania. The bacon and sausage industries therefore flourish right across Eastern Europe. Bacon is an ingredient, but even more so a flavour and a garnish for many otherwise meatless dishes. Germany has *Speck*, which is mildly cured and smoked pork fat, for cooking, and *Katerspeck*, including a few seams of lean meat, for garnishing and pot roasting. George Lang records over twenty categories of bacon in Hungary and, within each category, several variations. Smoked bacon can be cured with or without paprika. Another kind of Hungarian bacon is cured in saline heavily flavoured with garlic. Bacon from Transylvania comes German-style in big slabs.

The tradition on the Great Hungarian Plain was to roast a chunk of meaty bacon weighing about 250 g ($\frac{1}{2}$ lb) over an open fire. Incisions were made on all sides in a crisscross pattern and giant elongated slices of bread were toasted beside it. These were used to manoeuvre the bacon and to catch the drippings. The roasting was considered an art, with once again the pejorative description 'gypsy' reserved for any bacon burned black through carelessness.

Pork in Pilsen beer with dumplings

Many of the prized Czech recipes for fresh and cured pork are best accompanied by Czech beer, and some of them incorporate it, which produces succulent hefty dishes.

600 g (1¼ lb) pork shoulder, cubed	salt, black pepper, caraway seeds
paprika	500 ml (scant 1 pint) light beer, ideally Pilsen lager
375 g (12 oz) onions, chopped	3 tablespoons breadcrumbs
oil or fat for frying	

Roll the cubed pork in paprika. Fry the onions in the oil till soft, then add the meat and cook for 5 minutes. Add the seasonings and half the beer. Cover and simmer for 45 minutes. Add the breadcrumbs and the rest of the beer, and cook for another 15 minutes. Recommended with this dish are salty fried potatoes or dumplings. Given the chance, I would reach for a tomato or fresh cucumber salad.

Variations This northern Bohemian dish may be compared with a softer recipe attributed to Bratislava, the long-time Hungarian capital of Slovakia. There the pork is rolled in paprika and flour, fried in butter and then simmered in buttermilk with an apple, some caraway and a pinch of sugar. The quantities of meat and liquid are the same.

The important thing about Czech, Polish and much Hungarian pork cookery, whether it is a steak or a roast, is that it should be piquant. If beer isn't the medium, then the recipe will employ some other fermented liquid. Mustard and caraway are never far away, nor sugar nor fruit jelly, particularly in Poland. The partnership with caraway is a long-standing tradition in both countries, leaving marriages with tomato to look distinctly new-fangled and unoriginal. Pork is sometimes combined with mushrooms, but neither pork nor mushrooms are at their best when they are together.

Boiled pork with sweet and sour sauce

The sweetness or sweet-and-sour accent of much Central European pork cookery makes one think of the East. This Czech recipe is the closest I have come to an Oriental pork dish in Central Europe.

750 g (1½ lb) pork shoulder
salt
3 tablespoons butter
3 tablespoons flour
2 tablespoons vinegar
3 allspice corns
2 cubes sugar
2 tablespoons grated
   gingerbread (see p. 371)

3 tablespoons raisins
4–6 dried prunes, or
   1 tablespoon plum jam,
   or damson cheese

Boil the pork in 1 litre (1¾ pints) salted water until tender, bone it and cut it into cubes. Make a roux from the butter and flour, dilute it with ½ litre (1 pint) of the skimmed stock, then add the vinegar, spices, sugar and gingerbread. Use ginger cake or 2 ginger biscuits if home-made gingerbread is not available. Boil the sauce well and put it through a sieve. Add the raisins, stoned and chopped prunes and the meat, and serve with dumplings.

Pork offal and innards

Every scrap of the slaughtered pig was made use of in Central European pork cooking, with the head regarded as a prize. Every Yugoslav schoolchild knows a famous story about the boy Josef Broz, who became President Tito. He was brought up in a large Croatian peasant family, where food was always scarce and the larder was kept locked. The children learned the trick of asking for bread when strangers were present and their mother couldn't refuse. Afterwards, they had their ears soundly boxed. Tito was about ten when he led his brothers and sisters in cooking the pig's head his mother had been saving for the New Year. The children made themselves ill overeating the underdone meat and, worse, they were caught. Their mother had in mind for the forthcoming festivities *šara*, the traditional pork soup with root vegetables, potatoes, herbs and vinegar.

Scrapple

In Bohemia it was similarly the practice at Carnival time to boil a pork head with vegetables and a dash of vinegar, and to serve the meat with mustard or horseradish, and the soup separately as a second course. Pork, however, though it yields calories, doesn't make for a very rich-tasting stock, and the soft flesh was what was worth waiting for. This Czech recipe for the pork-head flesh, or pork leftovers, was one taken to America by thrifty Bohemian emigrants. It is a kind of head cheese.

Use almost any pork, even leftovers, but the best is a boiled pork head, liver, heart etc. Place all in a kettle with water, salt, pepper, garlic and marjoram. When tender, strain [the liquid] and add enough cornmeal to make as much mush as meat. Boil this for half an hour. Chop the meat fine and add it to the cornmeal. Pour the hot mixture into shallow pans to cool. This can be sliced cold and fried golden brown.

Paul Kovi quotes a similar recipe as being a Hungarian (*Szekler*) Transylvanian dish.

Pork crackling

The favourite use for pork skin and fat is to make crackling. In Slovenia it is used to dress salads and vegetables and pasta, and various forms of Hungarian and Yugoslav savoury baking incorporate it, which, after my testing, I don't recommend. The crackling goes soggy and gristly and loses its taste when buried in dough.

A pork and smoked ham pie

The Czechs eat pork to celebrate New Year, christenings and Easter. One of the traditional Easter dishes is made with a mixture of pork, beef and smoked ham with boiled eggs, like a continuous Scotch egg or the inside of a gala pie. It is served hot with potato purée and compote or cabbage salad, or cold with potato salad.

Czech food often reminds me of English pub food: it comprises a lot of solid, unspicy, usually wholesome preparations all on one plate. You either like it or hate it.

Sweet Polish roast pork

The Poles like to add a strong sweet element to slow-cooked pork, either by making a pot-roast with Madeira wine or, as in this recipe, by encrusting a roast with sugar and spice.

For 1–1¼ kg (2–2½ lb) pork loin:

1 tablespoon flour
½ teaspoon salt
½ teaspoon dry mustard or caraway seed

pinch each of sugar and ground sage
black pepper

For the topping:

¾ cup apple purée
2 tablespoons brown sugar
⅛ teaspoon each cinnamon or allspice, mace and salt

Mix the first set of ingredients and coat the surface of the meat.

Set it to roast, fat side upwards, in a medium oven for $1\frac{1}{4}$ hours. Mix all the ingredients for the topping, spread this over the meat and continue roasting until tender. Serve with noodles or barley and a lightly boiled green vegetable. Fresh cabbage cooked with apple or tomato is suitably astringent. The same treatment could be given to pork chops. A casual accompaniment would be pickled cucumbers and rye bread.

Sweet-and-sour pork

The other common Polish way with pork is 'sour', by combining it with sauerkraut, apple, barley and spices (allspice, caraway). For special occasions such as Easter, sucking pig might be roasted stuffed with buckwheat or breadcrumbs. Nor is it unusual at different times of the year to find wild boar, a favourite throughout East Europe, on the menu in a good restaurant. At the Basilisk restaurant in the Old Town in Warsaw it comes in a sweetish sauce. According to one elaborate and tempting recipe, the young meat is marinated in buttermilk, brandy and onion, then browned in fat and braised in beer and stock. A serving sauce is derived from some of the marinade mixed with redcurrant jelly and thickened. The same treatment could be given to a joint of tender pork.

I used to enjoy meat more than I do now, which perhaps makes me a victim of fashion. I had a mixed initiation into good food, partly in France, partly in Germany and the rest in my own kitchen. The French were my mentors where boldness with new tastes was concerned. But in my teens the straightforward high quality of the German cold table, centred on pork, had more appeal and seemed comfortingly close to home. *Kasseler Rippen*, a well remembered treat, is loin of pork, lightly salted, pickled in brine, flavoured with juniper and then smoked. It must count amongst the finest German delicacies. The name derives not from the West German town of Kassel, but from the Berlin butcher who perfected it. In one south German household where I stayed, we ate slices of it for breakfast, with strong black coffee. Yet when the whole ménage transferred to the south Tyrol, our breakfast became fresh peaches, white bread and *dolcelatte* cheese so new it was wet. My hosts had a taste for all good things in their place, German or otherwise.

Kasseler Rippen, eaten with green sauce (p. 74), would make a delightful cold lunch or supper. The sauce, often quoted as being Goethe's favourite, is French, but the combination shows just what the cold German kitchen can do. The green and pink also have great charm for the eye. Amongst the many varieties of Central European *charcuterie* I would also point out Polish smoked ham as a singular delight.

Pork with fruit

As with other meat, the Germans when they cook fresh pork also like to combine it with fruit. A typical recipe, the 'Cobbler's frying pan', simmers pork with pears, carrots and potatoes. But the dishes that have remained most popular this century are those involving long, sourish cooking of the cheaper cuts of meat.

Eisbein

Eisbein is a dish, said to have originated in Berlin, of smoked pig's trotters or knuckle, usually eaten with sauerkraut and potato purée. The name comes from the old practice of making ice skates from the bones in pigs' feet. Even today it is as popular in Germany and Bohemia as sausages and onions are in Britain, and less hard to find. I last ate it in the cavernous but excellent restaurant at Prague railway station, where the menu is typically Central European and the typicality even extends to the hardly legible, purple-ink carbon copy of the bill of fare. Menus in Eastern Europe are often in at least two languages, and anyone who has tried to order will know the difficulties: the German is abbreviated, and crucial additions have been made in handwriting that makes every letter look like a w or an n. To stick to schnitzel, however, is a certain indication of defeat.

Boldog ijévet!

Hungarian pig-killing

Braised pig's ears

I have not seen this old delicacy on a menu, but I do have written recipes. It has earned literary immortality by being eaten by the workers in Alfred Döblin's novel of German metropolitan street life in the 1920s, *Berlin Alexanderplatz*. The ears are boiled until very tender, with water, onion, apple and marjoram. The sauce is thickened with a roux, seasoned and spiced with mustard, meat extract (Maggi) and vinegar. The ears are served in the sauce with slices of hard-boiled egg and buttered rye toast.

Kebabs

The culinary and geographical opposite of slow-cooked German offal dishes with fruit must be kebabs, which dominate pork cookery further south and return to East German tables as exotic Ukrainian shashlik.

Yugoslav *raznjici* are pieces of tender lean pork marinated in oil, then charcoal-grilled on a skewer with rings of onion. They can be flavoured with paprika or garlic before cooking. As with all Yugoslavia's many kebab dishes made in different parts of the country with pork, lamb, beef, mixed meats, game, poultry and fish, they should be served with a salad of tomatoes and peppers, and *ajvar* relish (see p. 82), and eaten with the fingers.

Gammon with boiled potatoes and dandelion salad

The pork and bacon dishes of Yugoslavia are generally less heavy and less time-consuming to prepare. Serve this Slovenian salad with thick slices of grilled gammon or eggs. The salad proportions are for two people.

40 g (1½ oz) rindless bacon, cut in matchsticks
vinegar or red wine
salt, finely chopped garlic
150 g (6 oz) dandelion leaves, or watercress, or other mixed
crisp salad greens, washed and torn
100 g (3–4 oz) potatoes

Brown the bacon lightly in its own fat, add vinegar or red wine to taste, salt the salad lightly and pour over the bacon mixture with the garlic. Mix in the boiled potatoes and serve immediately. Pork crackling is sometimes used instead of bacon, but see my remarks on p. 221–2. This is the kind of instant meal one could expect in the countryside anywhere in Europe where the bacon was home-cured. The French equivalent of the salad has become very fashionable in Britain.

Pork paprikás

This Hungarian/Yugoslav dish in Croatia is nicknamed 'bachelor's pepper stew', because it generates thirst. To quote my Croatian au-pair: 'Boys like spicy food because it makes them drink.'

30 g (1 oz) bacon	200 g (7 oz) fresh green
600 g (1¼ lb) pork, in large cubes	peppers
	bay leaf
300 g (11 oz) onion, chopped	1–2 tablespoons tomato purée
2 teaspoons flour	1 chilli pepper
2 cloves garlic	50 g (2 oz) gherkins
salt	100 g (3½ oz) cooked
pinch of chilli, or more if liked	sausage
	2–3 tablespoons sour cream

Brown the bacon, meat and onion in their own fat or extra oil, cover and stew for 10 minutes. Add the flour, crushed garlic, salt, chilli and quartered peppers, bay leaf, tomato sauce and stir

once. Add the sliced chilli pepper, the gherkins and the sausage.
Bring to the boil, add the cream, stir and serve.

Pork chops flambéd in slivovica

This sounds like one the bachelors might try on their girlfriends;
or a way of using up the fiery contents of that bottle which has
been in the cupboard since last year's holiday. Soak a few prunes
per person and stone them. Brown the chops in butter with a
good teaspoon of caraway seeds, then add the prunes. A good
tablespoon of *slivovica* or other plum eau-de-vie should be
warmed before it is poured into the pan at the end of cooking
and lighted with a match. When the flames die down add the
same quantity of water or stock and serve immediately on
home-made *tarana* (see p. 310) or small pasta.

Pork, bean and barley casserole

For 500 g (1 lb) smoked pork and bacon, mixed or as available,
use 50 g (2 oz) beans, 350 g (12 oz) barley grits and 250 g (8 oz)
potatoes. Cook together in plenty of water. After an hour add
root vegetables, garlic, tomato and green pepper. Add cubed
potatoes in the last half-hour. Beware of adding salt until the last
minute, since most of it will come from the meat. Serve with
pickled cucumbers or pickled cabbage or sauerkraut. This is
Yugoslav *ričet*, but similar bean dishes are found in Romania,
Hungary and Transylvania.

Pork in Tokai

Hungary has many recipes for pork: in sour cream, with green
peppers, with green beans, with tomatoes, with garlic. The grand

Hungarian answer to the modest dash of *slivovica* in the pork frying pan across the border in Yugoslavia is half a bottle of sweet Tokai. Together with two pounds of lean pork, a large red cabbage, a large cooking apple and some bacon and tomato purée for added flavour, this makes a typically powerful, rather overwhelming dish.

Roast sucking pig

Sucking pig is roasted whole on New Year's Eve, basted crisp with bacon fat and beer. A curious tip is offered in a contemporary recipe book: 'Put an empty champagne bottle under the pig's belly, which will help it maintain its shape and prevent it from collapsing during the cooking.' The single necessary accompaniment to this festive dish, as to virtually all Hungarian pork dishes, is braised cabbage.

Romanian mixed grill

The Romanians, like their neighbours, enjoy sucking pig on festive occasions, but the supreme pork dish is a mixed grill. Eaten in a restaurant, this is an excuse for a long, vinous evening out. *Mititei* (p. 94) are arranged at the centre of a large hot plate, surrounded by grilled pig's kidney and liver, pork chops, pork loin, fresh sausage, pig's brains and pork ribs. The accompaniments are french fries, sour cabbage, pickled cucumbers and hot peppers.

Pork tocana

As with beef so with pork. One finds the Romanians cooking in beer under German influence, German breweries having been built as far east as the Danube Delta in the nineteenth century, but the true Balkan styles are nicer.

1–1½ kg (2–3 lb) onions,
  chopped
garlic
3 tablespoons oil or fat
dried hot peppers to taste
1 kg (2 lb) pork, cubed
2 glasses white wine

salt, pepper
stock
2 tomatoes
thyme
1 small glass brandy
3 tablespoons sour cream

Soften the onion and garlic pounded with salt in fat from the meat or extra oil, add the hot peppers when they are golden and add the meat. Cover tightly and stew, taking care not to let the mixture burn. When the liquid is absorbed, add 1 glass wine, season with black pepper and continue to cook slowly, covered, with a few spoonfuls of stock, tomatoes and thyme. Add more stock as necessary until the meat is tender. Add the second glass of wine for the last 10 minutes of cooking. With about 10 tablespoons of sauce left in the pan, pour on the brandy and sour cream. Serve the dish very hot, with potatoes and sour pickles or sour vegetables.

Pork tocana with sauerkraut

1 kg (2 lb) onions, chopped
1 kg (2 lb) pork, cubed
garlic
750 g (1½ lb) sauerkraut
½ teaspoon dried thyme, 1
  tablespoon fresh dill

½ teaspoon caraway seeds
salt, pepper
1 tablespoon paprika
a few tablespoons sour
  cream

Soften the onions and brown the meat in the pork's own fat, together with the crushed garlic. Add the sauerkraut, squeezed free of juice (keep this for a soup), and stir over heat for several minutes. Then add the thyme and dill, caraway seeds, seasoning and enough water to cover. Cook slowly until the meat is tender, adding the paprika and cream about 15 minutes before the end of cooking. Serve with *mamaliga* or fresh dark rye bread on a warm plate, with a blob of extra cream if the effect is to be decorative as well as highly aromatic. Drink lager with this *tocana*, which improves with age and can be reheated in a double boiler.

Bulgarian pork pizza

Bulgarian pork cooking is mainly either German-style with cabbage or Balkan with *gyuvech* (see p. 282), or grilled on a skewer over charcoal. This more unusual modern recipe probably developed out of the Middle Eastern tradition of folded pastry.

1 teaspoon flour
750 g (1½ lb) pork
salt, pepper
2 teaspoons or more melted bacon fat or olive oil

For the dough:
½ teaspoon dried yeast
750 g (1½ lb) white or brown bread flour
1 teaspoon salt

Sprinkle the yeast on a little warm water and when it foams combine with the sifted flour and salt and more warm water to make a soft dough. Knead well, cover with an oiled plastic bag and leave in a warm place. Heat the oven to 375°F (190°C, Gas Mark 5) allowing about 40 minutes for the pizzas to cook. Form the dough into four flat rounds about 20 cm (8 inches) in diameter and thicker at the edges. Brush them with water and flour, divide the meat among them, season well with salt and black pepper and pour over bacon fat. Bake immediately and serve hot. Be careful not to overcook the pizzas as the dough will become very hard. The amount of bacon fat or oil will depend on the leanness of the meat.

Sausages

All the Central Europeans – Czechs, Slovaks, Germans, Austrians, Poles, Hungarians, Slovenes – are legendary sausage-fanciers, and every region of every country enjoys its specialities and customs. I have in mind those shop and factory products in casings, often smoked, intended either for boiling or frying whole, as well as some small *saucissons secs*, which are cooked with vegetables and in stews. The recipes below mostly assume the sausage will be bought ready-made.

In Prague before the war, Joseph Wechsberg claimed, sausages were an essential part of a man's public image. Eating them was mainly done away from home:

Prague's *uzenarny* – the word can be translated only inadequately as 'smoked sausage shops' – were a unique institution. Some were combined with a butcher's shop; sausages, hams and smoked meats were sold in the front room, fresh meat in the back room. But the best sausage shops would not lower themselves to selling fresh pork, to say nothing of beef or veal.

In happier pre-war days . . . the social standing of a man was often determined by the sausage shop he patronized and the kind of sausage he ate there. A sausage eater never switched allegiance.

Sausages were part of the street culture and their origin and relative merits provided a recurrent topic for conversation. They were kept steaming all day in special shops and, when required, were served with a wooden fork by girls in white coats. With them went sauerkraut or potato salad, though orthodox consumers would take only mustard or horseradish, plus a slice of bread or a roll. The sausage shops were not licensed to sell beer, but were located near beer parlours so that the girls in white coats did not have far to go to ferry glasses back and forth. Trade began at eight a.m. with a rush at 10.30 (second-breakfast time) and again at noon.

Writing in 1953, at a time of acute meat shortages, Wechsberg was wrongly convinced Communism had obliterated a great culinary tradition and pleasure. The habit, though it has shed some of its *belle époque* trappings, lives on. The two main varieties of hot sausage are slim *parky*, which look like frankfurters and come in pairs, and fat, short sausages called variously *vursty*, *klobasy* and *taliany* ('Italians'). They are sold in strings. *Taliany* are white and very fat, with visible chunks of bacon and garlic, while *klobasy* are bigger, fatter and thicker-skinned. Most popular are *vursty*, juicy, less fat and with an edible skin. The juice should spout out when they are prodded with a fork.

Vursty-eaters recognized one another by the fat stains on their ties and lapels. They wore them proudly, like campaign ribbons,

enthused Wechsberg, declaring them the 'feminine' species of the hot sausage family. Femininity took him back to the white-coated sausage girls. My woman's eye didn't notice them more recently in Prague.

At home Czech habits today are simple: the sausage comes sliced in soup, cooked with sauerkraut or pulses, or sliced cold in a piquant sour salad. These are all post-war recipes.

Chatarsky salat

150 g (6 oz) onion, chopped
salt, pepper (optional)
500 g (1 lb) mushrooms
3 tablespoons vinegar
1 teaspoon sugar
8 frankfurters

Boil the onions in a little hot salted water for 2–3 minutes, drain and put in a serving dish. Boil the mushrooms similarly, slice them and add to the dish. Dress with the vinegar mixed with the sugar and 9 tablespoons of the cooking liquid, plus salt and black pepper as required. Mix in the thinly sliced sausage and chill. Serve with bread. This recipe originally called for 500 g

(1 lb) dried mushrooms, but at nearly £1 for 25 g (1 oz), authenticity would prove needlessly expensive.

Sausages in beer batter

This is both a Czech and a German recipe.

250 g (8 oz) plain flour	1 teaspoon baking powder
2 eggs	1 level teaspoon salt
½ cup brown ale	slices of any smoked sausage
1 tablespoon melted lard	oil, for frying

Mix all the ingredients except the last two to a smooth batter. Coat thick slices of smoked sausage, and fry them golden brown in plenty of hot oil. A Czech cookery book – for Czechs – by Fialova and Styblikova, in its 1987 edition recommends serving these fritters with a purée of dried green or chick peas and sour cucumbers.

Lentils with sausage

350 g (12 oz) lentils	30 g (1 oz) butter
80 g (3 oz) onion	50 g (2 oz) bacon
1 bay leaf	½ cup stock
salt	
250 g (8 oz) smoked boiling sausage	

Soak the lentils for three hours, then cook in plenty of water with half the onion and the bay leaf until the beans are soft. Remove the onion and bay leaf, add a little salt and mix with the cubed sausage and the rest of the onion, which has been chopped. Grease a baking dish with butter, fill with the lentils and sausage, dot with butter and thinly cut pieces of bacon, add the stock and bake for 30 minutes in a medium oven. Serve with sauerkraut salad (see p. 291).

Potato goulash with sausages

This is a very homely and quick modern recipe, which also shows how widely the term 'goulash' is used in practice across Central Europe. Here it denotes the flavouring of the potatoes with paprika.

750 g (1½ lb) potatoes	¼ teaspoon caraway seed
1 large onion	¼ teaspoon marjoram
80 g (3 oz) lard, butter or margarine	150 g (6 oz) boiling sausage stock or water
2 cloves garlic	2 tablespoons flour
salt, pepper	1 tablespoon tomato purée
½ teaspoon paprika	(optional)

Peel and cube the potatoes. Chop the onion, fry it in half the fat, add the crushed garlic with salt, pepper, paprika, caraway and marjoram. Add the sliced sausage to the pan, then the potatoes, stirring. Pour on just enough water or stock to cover and simmer until tender. Prepare a roux with the remaining fat and the flour, dilute with water or stock from the pan, cook for a few minutes and return to the sausage mixture with the tomato purée, which is suggested to improve the colour of the dish. Heat through and serve with bread.

It is hard to say who would win between Germany and Czechoslovakia in a cult-of-the-sausage competition. Towns all over the Germanies are famous for their specialities, like Zerbst, near Magdeburg, which produced both a brains sausage and Catherine the Great of Russia. A modern estimate for West and East Germany together suggests 1,500 different varieties of sausage. Sausages are eaten hot as a second breakfast or lunchtime snack away from home, or in the evening hot or cold. Amongst the best known and most popular are 'white sausages', about 15 cm (6 inches) long, usually served fried. Eat them with a roll and mustard for a snack, or with potato salad, or red cabbage and hot potato purée, or cucumber salad.

Sausages in beer

750 g (1½ lb) pork sausages
50 g (2 oz) fat (optional)
1 finely chopped onion
1 tablespoon flour

1 cup brown ale
mashed potatoes
sliced carrots

Fry the sausages in their own or extra fat with the onion. Remove them from the pan and keep warm. Stir the flour into the fat, cook for a few minutes, then dilute with the beer, stirring to make a smooth sauce. Arrange the sausages on a mound of mashed potatoes with a border of sliced carrots. Strain the sauce and pour over the carrots.

A classic accompaniment to sausages in Germany is apple sauce, *Apfelmus*, and for an instant meal this can be served neat from a jar. In this recipe, though, apples are incorporated in the cooking. Use *Bratwürste* or any good pork sausages in the English style. Ready-made pork and turkey sausages if available are excellent.

Sausages with apples

50 g (2 oz) currants
1 kg (2 lb) cooking apples
good pinch of cinnamon
sugar (optional)

2 tablespoons butter
750 g (1½ lb) pork sausages
½ cup red wine

Soak the currants in warm water, peel, core and quarter the apples and sprinkle them with cinnamon and a teaspoon of sugar if liked. Heat the butter in a saucepan, put in the pricked sausages, then the apples and any juice that has formed on top, plus the currants. Cover the pan and cook gently. As the pieces of apple become tender, remove them from the pan and keep them warm. Turn the sausages so they are evenly cooked. Remove the sausages, add the wine to the fat, boil it up, then strain it over the sausages and apples. Serve with potato purée.

The risk with this recipe, depending on the sausages, is that it will be swimming in fat. If excessive richness and thousands of superfluous calories are undesirable, avoid them by gently sweating the sausages without butter. To avoid burning, choose a heavy-bottomed pan and after adding the wine employ the ice cube trick. Put a few cubes in the pan off the heat and the fat will quickly solidify on the cubes. Remove them, boil up the remaining stock, reduce it a little and finally pour it over the sausages and apples.

Some facts about German sausages

Frankfurter Würstchen are made of lean and fat pork very finely ground, flavoured with nutmeg, black pepper and coriander and moistened with red wine. They are then lightly smoked.

Schwäbische Würste are made of pork and garlic, either smoked or unsmoked.

Leberwürste are liver sausages made by combining pig's liver and cooked pork with plenty of bacon fat, seasoned with allspice. To distinguish between these and German liver pâté, the latter is called *Streichleberwurst*.

Schwarzwürste are black sausages made with pork, pork fat, pig's blood and breadcrumbs, seasoned with garlic and cloves. They may be smoked or unsmoked.

The Poles with their strong peasant tradition and vast repertoire of pork dishes love sausage. *Kielbasa* is a pork-and-veal sausage like the German *Bratwurst*, but flavoured with garlic and mustard seed. Fry and serve with braised red cabbage or Savoy cabbage. Another traditional way of serving *kielbasa* offsets the rich meat with a sweet-and-sour sauce. Red wine and gingerbread and beer and sugar are variants. These sweet-sour Old Polish sauces, also used for boiled meat and carp, are typical of what foreign critics have sometimes called 'the concentrated quality' of Polish food.

A dish which has been a mainstay of the Polish-burgher cuisine since the eighteenth century is blood sausage or *kiszka*. A modern recipe given by Zofia Czerny thickens the blood with two and a half times its volume of buckwheat groats and adds cooked pork, ground offal meat, allspice and marjoram. Czerny, last republished in 1975, also includes a recipe for Polish pork-head cheese and gives full details of how to deal with jowls, abdomen, pork head, kidney, lungs and heart, knuckles and feet, to produce enough cooked meat to make it, mixed with bacon fat, garlic, allspice and nutmeg. The resulting haslet is served with grated horseradish moistened with vinegar, with 'home-made tomato paste', and mustard and bread.

All Polish *charcuterie* is bought in a *wedlina* or 'smoked pork-meat' shop.

Polish haslet

Ready-made haslet might be served in this attractive Polish way. Slice the meat on a serving plate and surround with three ramekins containing the relishes. For the mustard use whole-grain variety and have good rye bread to hand. Make the tomato purée by liquidizing a tin of tomatoes, reducing it over heat by about a third and adding a heaped tablespoon of tomato paste and a good teaspoon of sugar. Thyme, basil and tarragon may all be added in small quantities to enrich the taste.

For the most famous Polish dish including sausage with sauerkraut, see *bigos* (p. 244).

In Yugoslavia, particularly in Slovenia and Croatia, German, Polish and Czech-style pork sausages, blood sausages and salamis are enduringly popular. *Würstchen* are on sale in the streets and the stand-up snack bars of Ljubljana, served with rolls and mustard. But for the Slovene language you might believe yourself in Austria. The *Bratwürste* may contain raisins; products from other northern regions incorporate millet, buckwheat and barley. Blood sausage is a Slovenian country speciality, made along the same lines as the Polish recipe above, but thickened with millet and rice and flavoured with dried mint, marjoram and sometimes paprika and garlic. Yugoslav salamis are made mainly of pork and bacon in varying degrees of fine/coarse dice. After the skins are stuffed, the sausages are dried in smoke for five to six days, then boiled, cooled and served in thin slices. The equivalent of white sausages are called *Budelj*, made with cream and bread and cooked smoked meat.

A traditional Croatian way of storing small smoked sausages is in a *zaseka* of chopped raw bacon fat and garlic pounded together and well salted. It is said greatly to enhance their flavour. The pork sausages are embedded in the mixture in a tub, which is then sealed with lard. This is the French *confit* principle and George Lang has observed that it was long ago assimilated into the cuisine of the Hungarians who live close to the Croatian border.

Where the practical table is concerned, any sausages, including ready-made English varieties, can be given a Yugoslav flavour with the right accompaniments:

  with salami: chilli peppers, olives, pickled mushrooms
  with any fried, boiled or grilled sausages: *ajvar*; raw chopped
    onion, radishes; horseradish

Further south and south-east Yugoslav traditions become more markedly Middle Eastern. The sausages are often padded with cornmeal in Serbia, Macedonia and Montenegro and are generally hotter and spicier. Lamb and beef are used as well as pork, with plenty of garlic and red pepper. Try serving very hotly spiced sausages with chopped raw onion, or a mixture of raw onion, tomato and green pepper, or spring onions or radishes.

The south Yugoslav traditions continue into Albania, where much is made of the *basturma* individual sausage, made with cured beef and paprika, originally from Armenia. It has a curry-like aroma and is available from Balkan and Middle Eastern delicatessens. Distinguish though between the individual sausage and the dried beef with a spicy crust, sold in slices, with the same name.

Basturma sausage and bean stew

250 g (8 oz) haricot, pinto
  or broad beans
120–250 g (4–8 oz) *basturma*
  sausage, or other spicy
  sausage
1 medium onion
500 g (1 lb) fresh tomatoes
  or 1 large tin

1 large carrot
250 g (8 oz) leeks
salt, pepper, bay leaf, fresh
  parsley
optional if the sausage is not
  basturma: 1 teaspoon
  paprika and ½ teaspoon
  chilli powder

Soak the beans overnight and cook in 1½ litres (2½ pints) fresh, unsalted water until almost tender. Add all the other ingredients, chopped, and simmer for another 20–30 minutes, adding more water if the stew is too thick. Adjust seasoning and serve as a meal in itself.

Hungary has sausage-making rituals built into the domestic calendar which are reflected in provincial restaurant menus offering 'pig-killing grill'. The slaughter takes place in December or January and George Lang says it is still an important event in the provinces. *Kolbasz* and liver sausages are made by the women, along with dishes of pork offal in aspic and fried pig's ears. The products are sampled as the ritual proceeds over two or three days. This is Lang's simplified recipe for home-made sausages from the winter pig-killing.

Hungarian kolbasz

600 g (1¼ lb) lean pork
2 cloves garlic
2 teaspoons salt
¼ teaspoon black pepper

1 heaped teaspoon paprika
pinch of ground cloves
grated rind of a lemon
  (optional)

Put the meat through the large holes of a meat grinder, crush the garlic with the salt and add to the meat with the remaining ingredients, mixing well. Form the mixture into plump sausages

2–3 inches long and grill, turning once, either on a rack or a baking tray. Better still, fry the sausages in an iron frying pan. Even if the meat is lean they should cook in their own fat and emerge crisp and piquant after 10–15 minutes. Serve with a wedge of lemon and a garnish of fresh dill.

To accompany these, try a green salad with fresh dill, and perhaps some millet, which is full of nutrients. Vary the sausage by including a little bacon in the total weight of meat, and ½ teaspoon of crushed coriander seeds. In Transylvania the sausages might be flavoured with caraway seeds.

Hungary is famous for its widely exported salami made of beef and pork and pork fat, finely minced and flavoured with paprika and garlic. Elizabeth David however points out that 'Hungarian' salami has become a description of style rather than of origin and often comes nowadays from Italy. Watch the label!

Fresh sausages, meat loaves and rissoles

These are also sausage mixtures, but they are always, by tradition, fresh. Highly flavoured, they are strong points of Balkan cuisine, shaped into balls or fingers and sometimes served on a skewer. The classic Romanian dish is *mititei*, skinless spicy sausages often served as appetizers (see p. 94). 'Good hamburgers,' said the recipient of my most careful effort when given *mititei* for a main course. Serving them as part of a tray of various *meze* or a mixed grill (see p. 229) can make them seem more distinguished.

Yugoslav *cevapcici* are almost identical to *mititei* from over the border but include no baking powder. An interesting variation, however, is to eat *cevapcici* not only with the usual assortment of raw Balkan salad vegetables, or with *ajvar* (see p. 82), but with thick *kaimak*. This cream, somewhere between clotted cream and a strong cream cheese, depending on its age, threatens in a deliciously original way to turn *cevapcici* with soft white bread into the original cheeseburger. Try a blend of curd cheese and cream cheese, or just a high-fat curd cheese as a substitute. *Kaimak* is also sometimes incorporated as a creamy layer in the middle of grilled minced-meat rissoles and it is poured over grilled veal sweetbreads.

Sour-milk sauce for meat rissoles

This is also from Yugoslavia, designed to complement rissoles of minced mixed meats, onion and bread.

2 tablespoons flour
2 tablespoons butter or oil
½ litre (1 pint) sour milk or buttermilk
bouquet of fresh fennel
salt, pepper

Brown the flour lightly in the oil, cook for a few minutes, then slowly, stirring, pour in the sour milk. Heat through with the fennel and seasoning until thick. Pour over the cooked rissoles and bake in a preheated oven for 10–15 minutes, or until well heated through.

Pleskavica is another Yugoslav term for minced-meat steaks with onion, very similar to *cevapcici*. *Ustipci* are meatballs that include bacon as well as fresh pork and/or beef, but their distinguishing ingredient, blended in with the meat, is the strong, fatty ewe's-milk cheese called *kackavalj*. 50 g (2 oz) cheese per pound of meat, plus two cloves of garlic and a good ½ teaspoon of cayenne pepper are the requirements for these walnut-sized balls, which are then grilled.

Kavurma is a Yugoslav meat terrine for which less tender cuts of mutton, beef, veal and goat are used. The meat (off the bone) is chopped, just covered with water and brought to the boil. Garlic and crushed hot peppers are added, along with 50–75 g (2–3 oz) butter per 500 g (1 lb) of meat. Cover and simmer gently, or bake, until the meat is tender. Pour all into a terrine and chill. If it is to be kept, pour lard over the surface to seal. Serve as a cold snack with spring onions, peppers, tomatoes and bread.

Meatballs flavoured with mint

These meatballs with a Middle Eastern flavour come from Albania.

500 g (1 lb) minced lamb
2 beaten eggs
2 cups soft breadcrumbs
3 tablespoons chopped fresh
  mint
2 teaspoons flour

1 teaspoon cinnamon
1 teaspoon salt
1–2 cloves garlic, crushed
pepper
oil, for deep frying

Mix all the ingredients except the oil, knead and leave to stand for 1 hour or more. Shape with wet hands into smooth balls, and fry in deep oil until brown. Serve with rice or a pilaf. The mint is characteristic of Albanian cuisine.

The same glamour does not attach to German and Czech meatballs and rissoles, but they form an important part of the Central European diet, especially where economy is a factor. The main ingredients are *Hackfleisch* (mince), herbs and seasonings and bread. *Goethe's Grandmother's Cook Book*, a classic of eighteenth-century culinary and household literature, contains a high proportion of recipes for *Hackfleisch* amongst the few included for red meat. Only beware too much bread.

Classic mixed meat dishes
🐝
Bigos

This dish of mixed meats and sauerkraut has been described as a precious jewel in the treasury of the Old Polish kitchen. Mickiewicz referred to it in his patriotic epic *Pan Tadeusz* and it has remained popular at every level of society. It was stored in wooden casks or stoneware pots, reheated many times, and taken hunting and travelling. During Lent, which was a time of feasting for the gentry in the seventeenth century, *bigos* was always served among more elegant dishes offered to the sleigh-loads of revellers who visited each other's homes to test the kitchen and the cellar. It could either be a relatively frugal dish or be prepared with greater lavishness for Christmas and Easter. Modern restaurant and hotel menus feature it both as a standard dish and as a speciality. In all these respects *bigos* functions like *cassoulet* in French cookery and makes similar use of possibly leftover meats rich in fat – pork, duck, ham, bacon, various sausages and occasionally beef. Like *cassoulet* too, reheating improves it.

1 kg (2 lb) various meats off the bone, cooked or raw, including plenty of spicy cooking sausage

1½ kg (3 lb) sauerkraut or fresh cabbage plus 3 tablespoons vinegar

350 g (12 oz) onions, chopped and sautéd in butter or bacon fat

3 dried mushrooms, cooked in water and sliced (optional)

20 prunes, cooked in water and stoned (optional)

black pepper

1 tablespoon sugar, or more or less to taste

water to cover plus the cooking liquid from the mushrooms and any leftover juices from roast meat

½–⅔ cup red wine or madeira (optional)

200 g (8 oz) cooking apples, peeled, cored and sliced (optional)

60 g (2 oz) flour (optional)

1 tablespoon thick tomato purée (optional)

The various meats should be browned before adding to the sauerkraut if they have not been previously cooked. The onion may be sautéd in the pan in which the *bigos* is to be made. Add the sauerkraut to it, the mushrooms and the prunes, season with black pepper, cover with water and other liquids and simmer for 15 minutes. Add the various meats and sausages cut into chunks and continue to cook slowly for at least 1 hour, where possible a day in advance, so that the dish may be reheated. Very little liquid should remain when the *bigos* is ready. Serve very hot with black or rye bread and chilled vodka to improve digestion of the fats and the cabbage, both of which can prove troublesome.

Variations Of the various possible variations, many Poles may disagree with me, but I have found the addition of alcohol serves little good purpose, and particularly not red or white wine, which makes the *bigos* sour. Apples, which also add sourness, have an important role to play if fresh cabbage is used, and may be added at the same time as the prunes, otherwise they are dispensable. The prunes and the sugar balance the sourness of the sauerkraut.

The recipe needs no salt, since the sauerkraut is already preserved in it. Also, though many recipes call for bay leaves and allspice, these too seem to me a distraction from the overall *bigos* flavour. The dish can be thickened with 60 g (2 oz) flour when the onions are sautéd, but this was not a habit in Old Poland. (Nor indeed was the wine.)

A stimulating modern addition to *bigos*, however, is tomato concentrate. It can be stirred in to the mixture in the last stages of cooking, but far more exciting and good-looking, to my mind, would be a thick purée made with a tin of tomatoes, reduced and thickened with a tablespoon of tomato purée, and sweetened with a teaspoon of sugar. Heat this separately and spread it over the top of the *bigos* before serving. The idea for this topping is one I have borrowed from *cassoulet*. It adds an essential brightness to the dish and offsets perfectly the remaining hint of sourness.

Czech sausage and sauerkraut bake

A very simple Czech sauerkraut-and-sausage dish can be compared to *bigos*. Written down by Bohemian emigrants to America at the turn of the century, it is neither as pleasing nor as elaborate, but it remains tasty and quick. Mix together 1 kg (2 lb) sauerkraut with 500 g (1 lb) pork sausage-meat, season as necessary with salt and pepper (best to err on the side of caution with bought sausage-meat), and bake in a covered dish for 1 hour in a medium oven. Pour over 1 cup of sour cream and, without stirring, bake the dish a further 15 minutes. It should be brown on top when served.

Stuffed cabbage leaves

After sauerkraut, the classic East European combination of cabbage and minced meat is stuffed cabbage leaves. There is no country where these are not found pleasing under their various names – Polish *golabki*, Serbian *dolma*, Hungarian *töltött kaposzta*. In Romania, where the tradition has evolved under German, Greek and Russian influence, they are called *sarmale* and the meat mixture is the same as for *mititei*. Follow the recipe on p. 94, substituting the meat mixture for rice. As if to emphasize that this dish benefits from being made in advance, Hungarians traditionally prepare it for the day after Christmas Day.

Mixed meat stews

Bosanski ionac, traditionally served in earthenware pots, is best-known in Yugoslavia. Pork, beef and lamb are stewed very slowly in tomato juice with garlic, tomatoes, parsley, paprika and up to half a dozen different vegetables, as well as potatoes. The result resembles a *djuvec*, but is meatier. It is sometimes cooked partly with white wine, which makes it very rich. Mixed meats without the vegetables but stewed in red wine with tomato and garlic, are common across the border in Transylvania. One from Brasov with pork, beef and bacon in wine looks like the Central European equivalent of *boeuf en daube*.

Miscellaneous recipes

I am omitting many traditional recipes for such ingredients as tripe and brains and tongue. These are increasingly rarely cooked in their countries of origin. Poland, though, prided itself on its preparation of tripe according to centuries-old recipes.

Tripe à la Warsaw

This was one of the classic dishes of the middle gentry and the burghers from the late eighteenth century. It is Zofia Czerny's recipe, which I haven't tried.

1 kg (2 lb) beef tripe
1 cup mixed raw vegetables, diced (no cabbage)
250 g (8 oz) each beef bones (joints) and marrow bones with marrow

3 tablespoons flour
3½ tablespoons butter
3¾ cups strong beef stock
allspice, ginger, nutmeg, pepper, marjoram, salt
3 tablespoons parmesan cheese
2 tablespoons breadcrumbs
fresh parsley

Clean the tripe thoroughly, scraping with a knife. Wash and rinse several times in warm water. Bring water to the boil and parboil the tripe. Drain, rinse and drain again and squeeze dry with the hands. Place again in plenty of boiling water and cook about 4 hours, until almost tender. Divide the vegetables in two. Make a stock of one half plus the bones and, when the tripe water has almost boiled away, pour over the strained broth. Cook the tripe till tender. Cook the other vegetables separately in some broth. Drain the tripe, cut into thin strips, reduce stock to 3–4 cups, remove marrow from bones, chop and add to tripe. Make a roux with the flour and butter, add the stock, thicken, then add the vegetables, tripe and all seasonings. Cook a little. There should be plenty of sauce. Turn into an ovenproof dish, cover top with cheese then breadcrumbs browned in butter and bake for 15 minutes. Garnish with parsley and serve with potatoes or suet balls.

Poland is also known for its boiled tongue in that medieval 'grey sauce' used for carp (see p. 181). Bickel also lists a second *polonaise* sauce: a 'demi-glace with a reduction of red wine, seasoned with sugar and vinegar, garnished with blanched slivered almonds and raisins'. It is the French way to bring this sauce out of the Middle Ages.

Calve's liver with apple and onion

This is a German speciality, particularly associated with Berlin, but also popular in Poland and Czechoslovakia.

3 tablespoons oil	2 teaspoons butter
4 slices calve's liver, 100 g ($3\frac{1}{2}$ oz) each	2 onions, sliced in rings
salt, pepper	about 250 g (8 oz) cooking apples, sliced in rings
flour for dusting	

Heat the oil in a heavy frying-pan. Dip the liver in the seasoned flour and cook it quickly, 3 minutes on each side. Remove and keep warm. Add the butter to the pan and then the onion and the apple rings and cook for 5 minutes. Arrange these around the slices of liver and serve with potato purée.

Braised chicken livers

In Romania, especially under today's economic conditions, chicken livers are amongst the most easily come by meat dishes in hotels and restaurants. They are usually served fried with chips. This recipe, using all the ingredients it would take to make a chicken-liver pâté, does not take much longer to produce, but the result is exquisite.

500 g (1 lb) chicken livers	3 tablespoons butter
salt	1 glass brandy
1 tablespoon each chopped chives, parsley, fresh fennel, plus extra parsley for garnishing	1 glass sherry
	3 tablespoons sour cream

Clean the livers, rinse in cold water, sprinkle with salt and chill until needed. Sauté the fresh herbs in the butter, cover and continue cooking for a few minutes to release the flavours. Remove the lid, increase the heat and add the livers, cooking them for a couple of minutes on each side, stirring. Add the warmed brandy, set it alight in the pan, cover for a few seconds, then add the sherry, stir, then finally add the cream and a little more parsley. Heat through but do not boil. Serve immediately on hot plates with plenty of fresh crusty or rye bread.

POULTRY AND GAME

❧❧❧

Chicken

❧❧

Germany has few elaborate recipes for chicken. A plain, crisply grilled half-bird is most popular. An old favourite though, for fowl, when young tender birds were less easily available, was a dish of 'sour chicken'. The young Goethe living in Frankfurt remembered the pleasurable Sunday lunches of fish or game or chicken he ate with his grandparents. Grandmother Anna Margarethe Justina Lindheimerin was a good cook and careful housewife. Among her housekeeping and family health notes, written partly in alchemists' symbols and chemists' Latin, is this recipe.

Goethe's grandmother's chicken fricassée

1 medium chicken about
   1½ kg (3 lb)
50 g (2 oz) butter
salt, pepper
½ teaspoon ground ginger
good pinch of nutmeg
1 medium onion
1–2 tablespoons chopped
   parsley

2 tablespoons chopped
   chives, spring onion or
   leek
½ teaspoon dried marjoram
1 cup white stock or water
2–3 tablespoons lemon juice
2 egg yolks
1 teaspoon mild vinegar

Dalmatian seller of fowl. Engraving after Valerio, 1864,
Victoria and Albert Museum

Joint the chicken, brown the pieces in butter, season them with salt, pepper, ginger and nutmeg. Add the onion, parsley, chives and marjoram, cover the pan and simmer for 15 minutes, shaking the pan occasionally. Add the stock and lemon juice and stew until tender. Set the chicken pieces in a warm dish, mix the egg yolks with the vinegar, dilute with a little stock and return to the sauce in the pan, stirring. Heat through without boiling and pour over the chicken.

I have modernized Frau Lindheimerin's recipe by including quantities. Serve it with rice and green beans and/or red cabbage. A friend astutely remarked of the sourish chicken and sweetish red cabbage that the combination was 'rather Chinese'.

A modern recipe for sour chicken stews the meat in one part vinegar to two parts water, spiced with an onion, bay leaf, nutmeg and cloves. Remove the bay leaf and cloves when the chicken is tender, add a small (140 g/5 oz) carton of sour cream and cook for a further 10 minutes. The recommended accompaniment is green peas.

In other parts of Central Europe a sweet-sour effect with chicken is also liked. It comes from cooking chicken with fruit, which may be sweetened, or from stuffing it with dried or fresh fruit, or from serving it with a fruit compote. George Lang quotes a Hungarian chicken and apple casserole in which sugar, cream and soup vegetables soften the tartness of the fruit. I have cooked a Polish dish of chicken with gooseberries, though this proved to be less distinguished than it sounded. More attractive is a Berlin roast chicken stuffed with rice and grapes, very like the classic Polish chicken with a forcemeat of rice and raisins. A Polish plain roast chicken or guinea fowl served with boiled potatoes, Polish fresh cucumber salad (p. 284) and a sharp fruit compote is also highly recommended. To vary the sweet stuffings you can include nuts with bread and dried fruit, as in Albania, or make a stuffing of chestnuts, which introduce a sweet element to many poultry dishes in southern Europe.

Chicken with apricots

A recipe from Romania.

400 g (12 oz) dried apricots
1 medium roasting chicken,
  1½–1¾ kg (3½ lb)
oil
1 heaped tablespoon flour
scant 1 litre (1½ pints) liquid
  from apricots

1 chopped onion
salt and plenty of black
  pepper
1 teaspoon sugar (optional)

Soak the apricots overnight. Joint the chicken and brown the pieces in oil. Set aside to keep warm. Pour off most of the oil and brown the flour in what remains. Stirring, add the liquid from the apricots, then the onion, cook till soft and strain or liquidize. Return the chicken pieces, add the fruit, seasoning and sugar. Cover and simmer gently until very tender. Serve immediately or, better still, cool and reheat the following day. The colour of this luscious dish calls for green things – leeks, green beans – and its unctuous texture, the grittiness of perfectly dry rice to accompany it.

Guinea-fowl Polish style

The unusual sour-fruit element here comes from the rosehips, which should be picked in late autumn, after they have been softened by the first frost.

Chop the wings, neck and upper part of the back of the guinea-fowl and brown them in butter with about 200 g (8 oz) mixed vegetables and a large onion. Add about ¼ litre (½ pint) water and 20 g (1 oz) of rosehips which have been soaked for a few hours in cold water. Brown the halves of guinea-fowl separately in butter and add them to the pan, cover and simmer until tender. To serve, remove the two halves and set on a dish. Sieve the remaining sauce, add a pinch of sugar, a pinch of ground cloves, salt, black pepper and lemon juice to taste. Pour over the guinea-fowl and serve with new potatoes and a cucumber or lettuce salad.

Chicken with rosemary, mushrooms and cranberries

This recipe from the south of Czechoslovakia marries sharp semi-sweet fruit with white wine to create a distant relative of *coq au vin*. The wine, light and flowery in the neighbouring Austrian style, comes from the Slovakian slopes, and a Riesling from Yugoslavia would be a good substitute. The rosemary with chicken recalls some similar Yugoslav and Hungarian cooking.

1 chicken, about 1¾ kg (3½ lb)	1 teaspoon rosemary
	1 glass white wine
½ teaspoon salt	250 g (8 oz) mushrooms
1½ teaspoons paprika	4 tablespoons cream, fresh
3 tablespoons butter or	or sour
sunflower oil (optional)	fresh, frozen or preserved
1 large onion	cranberries
3–4 cloves garlic	

For a low-fat dish skin the chicken first, otherwise cut it into serving pieces, rub with salt, dust with paprika and brown on all sides in a frying pan in butter or oil or on its own. (Unskinned chicken has enough fat of its own, I think, not to need the addition of butter or lard to a heavy pan, and even when it is skinned the inevitable small amount of skin left should be enough to turn the flesh golden without burning it. But the pan must be heavy, preferably cast-iron.) Add the chopped onion, crushed garlic, rosemary, wine and the same amount of water. Cover and braise until tender, or turn into a casserole dish and bake, covered, in a medium oven for an hour, basting the meat occasionally. Simmer the sliced mushrooms separately in their own juice. Just before serving, drain off the sauce, add the

mushrooms and the cream to it and reheat gently. Pour the
sauce over the chicken pieces. Serve with plain boiled rice or
potatoes, hot or cold stewed and slightly sweetened cranberries
and Brussels sprouts or a green salad to follow.

Many German, Polish and Czech recipes for poultry, game,
ham and smoked sausage call for cranberries, in a way most British/
North American tastes can easily respond to. (For cranberry read
also bilberry, whortleberry and blueberry.) The very high acidity
of these berries helps to neutralize fat, and even with sugar the
taste is never cloying. Czechoslovakia exports under the Nova
brand label an excellent product, 'cranberries in syrup', which
contains only fruit, water and sugar.

A very different style of chicken dish is produced by introducing other meats, most often bacon. In the Hungarian wine
region of Eger they casserole chicken with bacon and sauerkraut
and sour cream. In Poland and Czechoslovakia, older-style recipes
advocate larding a roast chicken with anchovies or herring as a
Lenten substitute for bacon.
    Chicken in Hungary can be stuffed with liver or sausage or
pork or veal, though the result tends to be hefty. George Lang's
Oroshaza chicken and pasta casserole, combining a large chicken
in a braise with a pound of quickly fried chopped chicken livers,
soup vegetables, stock and a pound of home-made egg-barley,
seasoned liberally with paprika, is one of the more eye-catching
examples of this body-building genre.

Polish roast chicken with dill

Polish savoury ways with chicken are more refreshing. Apart
from the rice and raisin stuffing already observed, chicken, in a
typical style, is given a very mild forcemeat. When this is served
with a cucumber side salad (p. 284) or lettuce dressed with sour
cream, plus new potatoes garnished with fresh dill, it provides a
charming balance of flavours.

1 roasting chicken, about
$1\frac{3}{4}$ kg ($3\frac{1}{2}$ lb)
3 slices stale white bread, or
two rolls
milk for soaking
3 tablespoons butter
3 eggs

3 heaped tablespoons
chopped fresh dill
salt, freshly ground black
pepper
extra breadcrumbs as
needed

To make the stuffing:
Soak the rolls, squeeze out, chop or mince finely. Cream the
butter and egg yolks, add the rolls, the dill and season to taste.
Fold in the beaten egg whites and extra breadcrumbs as needed
to give the consistency of sponge-cake batter. Fill about three-
quarters of the cavity, and sew up with a needle and thread
before roasting in the usual way.

A second serving suggestion makes this dish reminiscent of a
British Christmas dinner: eat it with Brussels sprouts and cranberry compote.

Another excellent stuffing for chicken is buckwheat (see p.
267).

I associate dill, which is so evocative ot cool, bright, new spring
grass, with summer cooking. The winter equivalent is paprika,
with its obvious associations with fire. From Hungary to Serbia,
Poland and Czechoslovakia paprika with sour cream makes the
very popular chicken *paprikás*. On what 'popular' might mean
here, however, note what a Hungarian in Britain, Kato Frank,
wrote some years ago: 'I always go for paprika chicken when I
have some guests whose tastes might be conservative and yet
who expect a Hungarian meal in my house.'

Chicken paprikás

Brown a chopped onion, a small green pepper and a tomato in
some oil, then add a jointed chicken, browning the pieces on
both sides. Season with salt and a good half tablespoon of sweet

paprika powder. Add half a cup of water, cover and simmer till tender. Mix together a teaspoon of flour and 2–3 tablespoons sour cream, dilute with liquid from the chicken and heat through to thicken. To serve, pour the sauce over the chicken and garnish with rings or, better, matchsticks of green pepper. (Rings of green pepper look ungainly because of their irregularity. I also find them difficult to eat – not a test one wants to set conservative guests.) Serve the *paprikás* with *galuska* (see p. 317), or rice.

A few years ago the *Observer* gave a prize to the reader who sent in the 'typical' reaction of a British couple to the offer of goulash: 'Oh, no! We wouldn't want anything like that. We're from Bognor!'

Chicken dishes from Romania

Apart from the Polish roast chicken with dill, I would look to Romania, where chicken, poussin and turkey are all greatly favoured, for new ways of cooking poultry. Romanian cuisine and culture stand at the confluence of many styles. At a difficult time of food shortages I was able to walk into a very ordinary café and order a spit-roasted very tiny baby chicken with a sour salad. The traditional combination of flavours, simply prepared, was delightful and goes back hundreds of years. A splendidly modest-living, enlightened Moldavian prince of the seventeenth century, Dmitri Kantemir, a Romanian Montaigne, considered chicken with a sour accompaniment of cooked sorrel his favourite dish. He had the instinctively modest taste of a natural Epicurean, though unfortunately he left no recipes.

Chicken with garlic and butter sauce

1 medium chicken, jointed	fresh dill
4 tablespoons butter	1 tablespoon flour
1 bunch spring onions	6 cloves garlic

| 3 potatoes, cooked and peeled | 1 tablespoon sour cream |

Brown the chicken in a third of the butter in a casserole and keep warm. Warm the rest of the butter in a small pan, add the chopped spring onions, the dill, the flour, the crushed garlic, the potatoes in pieces and a little water. Stir well and cook for 5–10 minutes. Add the sauce to the chicken in the casserole with about a cup of water and cook slowly, covered, or bake, till tender. Add the cream towards the end. Serve garnished with parsley, with dumplings or *mamaliga*, and a green salad with lemon juice.

The Romanians, unlike the Hungarians, love to cook in butter, and its absence from the shops is one of the present-day laments in the Communist kitchen.

Chicken with walnuts

In parts of the Balkans where walnuts are widely used in cooking, for instance Albania and parts of Yugoslavia, to make a very garlicky dish the jointed chicken of the previous recipe can be baked covered with a little water and seasoning until nearly tender. Use the pan juices to dilute a flour and butter roux, and add 50 g (2 oz) ground walnuts and as much crushed garlic as desired. Pour the sauce over the chicken and return it to the oven for 10 minutes.

Chicken with tarragon

Like lamb, chicken is also cooked with tarragon in Romania. The idea seems to be original rather than a conscious French borrowing. Chicken sautéd with tarragon, white wine, root vegetables, green pepper, and finished with sour cream is one of 'the true flavours of Transylvania', according to Paul Kovi.

Chicken with wine and olives

garlic	2 cups white wine
1 medium chicken, jointed	½ cup sour cream
2 tablespoons olive oil	½ cup olives
1 tablespoon flour	salt, pepper
1 tablespoon each chives,	
fennel, parsley	

Rub the frying pan with garlic, brown the chicken pieces in oil and set them aside. With 2 tablespoons of hot oil in the pan, add the flour, cook a minute or two, then add the fresh herbs, stirring. Dilute gradually with the wine, cook for 5 minutes, add the cream and the olives and, finally, the chicken. Season, cover and simmer, or bake, until tender.

The influence of Greece shows up in many Romanian recipes like this. Another well-known one is chicken with an egg and lemon sauce.

The limits of the various Romanian styles become clear as one moves away. They do not go so far west into Yugoslavia that the chicken might be eaten with buckwheat, as in Slovenia.

Chicken obara

Brown a jointed chicken, any of the giblets you may want to use, a chopped onion and some soup vegetables. Sprinkle over one or two tablespoons of flour, cook for a little while, then dilute with water to cover. Add a twist of lemon peel, some fresh or dried marjoram and a few fresh or tinned tomatoes. Cook until tender and before serving check the seasoning and add a tablespoon of wine vinegar. Serve in soup bowls with cooked buckwheat, or to meet Western expectations, buckwheat bread. Another traditional accompaniment is *zganci* (see p. 319).

Chicken with summer vegetables

Chicken stews with green pepper, tomato and onion, flavoured with bacon, are very acceptable in Hungary and the Balkans. A quick way, prescribed in a Hungarian book, is to stir into plain braised chicken a few tablespoons of tinned *lecsó*. The instant equivalent in Britain would be to use tinned *ratatouille*. Otherwise, sauté onions, green peppers and tomatoes in plentiful equal quantities with a jointed chicken, pour in stock and flavour with paprika and garlic. Thicken the sauce with flour and sour cream as desired. For a more unusual touch, use okra instead of green pepper and omit the flour and cream.

Bulgarian chicken with tomatoes

The most genuine Bulgarian recipes are as usual very simple. Roast the chicken rubbed with salt and oil in a medium oven, with two pounds of halved fresh tomatoes arranged around it. Season with salt and plenty of black pepper and serve with rice.

Bulgarian chicken with chestnuts

Chicken may also be braised in tomato juice with plenty of lightly fried onions – three to a medium bird – and 400–500 g (about 1 lb) of shelled uncooked chestnuts.

Chicken pilaf

Fry chicken pieces, preferably legs, in some good oil with a large chopped onion. Add salt, pour over stock and add, coarsely chopped, a stick of celery, two small carrots, two tomatoes and a bay leaf, also two fresh green peppers if liked. Add, according to generous Yugoslav proportions, 100 g (3½ oz) rice per person and twice its volume of boiling water. Cover tightly and bake for half an hour. In Bulgaria and Serbia this pilaf is served with sour milk or yoghurt. The amount of chicken can vary. The original recipe is generous in suggesting two chicken legs per person.

Romanian cold chicken

Season a chicken and roast it. Grate a small celeriac and two eating apples, chop fine two pickled cucumbers and two pickled hot peppers or one pickled sweet pepper. Combine these with two tablespoons of oil and lemon juice and freshly grated black pepper to taste. Serve the chicken carved into joints, each piece on top of a generous portion of salad. This would make an excellent buffet or picnic dish as well as a summer supper, with crusty bread. If celeriac is unavailable, a different but equally good salad can be made by substituting half a dozen chopped celery sticks with leaves.

Dalmatian cold chicken

In Dalmatia, across the Adriatic from Italy, cold roast chicken is dressed Italian-style with a sauce of anchovies, capers, grated onion, parsley, oil, vinegar and lemon juice. My instinct, sitting in London, would be to serve this for lunch with baked potatoes and the sweetest tomatoes to be found.

Turkey

🖤

Poland was once greatly admired for its turkeys. They probably entered Polish cooking in the fifteenth century, when they were eaten stuffed and roasted. The stuffing bound turkey liver, eggs and raisins with bread. Sometimes almonds were also included and nutmeg, ginger and cloves used for seasoning. In more recent times another stuffing, favoured in Poland and Czechoslovakia, is chestnuts. About the same time as they did in Poland, turkeys arrived in Hungary on command from Italy. The sovereign was King Matthias, prepared to have his preference for roast peacock challenged by his wife Beatrice, who brought with her the gastronomic tastes of Naples.

Turkey with yoghurt and ratatouille

This light Bulgarian turkey *gyuvech* is ideal for small boneless cuts of turkey, or legs.

400 g (12 oz) turkey, off the bone	2 leeks
1–2 cloves garlic	4 green peppers
salt, pepper	1 large fresh cucumber
1 teaspoon paprika	2 tomatoes
4 tablespoons oil	parsley
	1 cup yoghurt

Chop the turkey meat into 2 cm (1 inch) cubes, mix with the crushed garlic, salt, pepper, paprika and half the oil. Cut the leeks into pieces 2 cm (1 inch) long and sauté in the rest of the oil with the chopped peppers. Add the turkey, fry a few minutes, stirring, then add a little water and cook gently, covered, for 10 minutes. Add the peeled cucumber in chunks, the tomatoes, quartered, and the parsley. Cook for another 10 minutes or until tender, correct seasoning and serve, with yoghurt, in *guvec* (i.e. earthenware bowls; this Turkish word has given its name to a whole style of Balkan cooking).

To cook turkey *ghiveci* 'Bucharest style', substitute aubergines or courgettes or a mixture of both for the cucumber and simmer in white wine. No yoghurt is called for when the dish has an alcohol base.

Stuffed turkey breast

Mince together 150 g (6 oz) garlic sausage, a small slice of bread soaked in water and squeezed dry and two hard-boiled eggs. Skin the turkey breasts, keeping the skin in one piece. Lard the breasts with matchsticks of bacon, spread over the mixture, then cover with the skins and fasten with skewers. Season and braise covered in white wine in a slow oven for two hours.

The recipe is from Hungary.

Duck and goose

Duck and goose will always seem luxurious to me, partly because we ate them only on festive occasions when I was a child. On my first visit to Erfurt, East Germany, the medieval city where Martin Luther preached, I was astonished to see butchers' windows crammed with neatly prepared duck and goose breasts among other delicacies. I had seen no opulence to compare with it in the rest of Eastern Europe, not even in Hungary; those select poultry cuts were the crowning touch. Nowadays I have another reason for holding goose and duck a little in awe: I know they involve their weight in kitchen work if fat and flesh are to be used equally judiciously. Duck and goose cuisine belong to the great days of provincial cooking, when the bourgeoisie refined its culinary techniques based on the ways of the countryside, and had time to spare.

The country model was outstanding in East Europe too. The day the family goose was slaughtered not only meant a special meal, but also a red-letter day for the winter larder. Slaughter-days were close to the feasts of St Martin's Day, 11 November (or sometimes on the eve, 10 November) and Christmas. On those occasions the people of the former north German states of Mecklenburg and Pomerania would cook this fat bird with dried fruit, either local prunes or imported raisins.

Mecklenburg roast goose

1–1½ kg (2–3 lb) cooking apples
350 g (12 oz) currants and sultanas mixed
120 g (4 oz) fresh bread-crumbs
a good pinch of cinnamon
2 beaten eggs

salt, pepper
1 goose, cleaned and trussed
butter for basting
red cabbage
stock
6 small frankfurter sausages
3 tablespoons vinegar

Peel and core the apples and cut into eight pieces each. Mix with the dried fruit, breadcrumbs, cinnamon and beaten eggs, lightly seasoned. Stuff the goose, seal the opening, rub the outside with butter if liked and place in a baking tin with 1 cup water. Roast 2 hours in a hot oven, basting frequently. Meanwhile, simmer the chopped cabbage in stock till tender, add the sausages and, at the end of cooking, the vinegar. Serve with the goose, with boiled potatoes. To make a sauce, strain off the fat and juices from the goose by floating ice cubes in it to which the fat will stick, remove the ice cubes, combine with the juices from the cabbage, boil up, strain, check seasoning and serve.

To preserve something of this combination of flavours for modern use, roast or grill portions of goose with smaller quantities of the stuffing and the cabbage mixture cooked separately.

Another recipe for Christmas roast goose from north Germany called for a stuffing of onion and mugwort. The stuffed goose would be served with baked apples with cranberries and dumplings, red cabbage or potato purée. I am changing the tenses

A banquet of German princes in the seventeenth century, from Hans Wegener, Küchenmeisterei, *facsimile, Leipzig 1939*

misleadingly here, for the mugwort stuffing is still given in a modern recipe published in West Germany in 1972. Mugwort (*artemisia vulgaris*), an aromatic herb of the wormwood and tarragon family which grows wild, neutralizes fat, making it more easily digestible. It is the traditional herb for goose in Germany because of these properties. The English name mugwort possibly comes from its use in making tea and beer.

Like mugwort, caraway also eases the digestion of fat and it is with this that the Czechs roast goose and duck. Another simple Czech way with goose breast is to rub it all over with garlic, then roast it crisp in its own fat in the oven.

In Romania duck is appreciated, though many recipes appear to have foreign and mixed origins such as one – also for goose – roasted with marjoram and sour cucumbers and another with olives and beer. The preferred native way is to prepare duck with cabbage. This is Anisoara Stan's sophisticated version.

Duck à la roumaine

1 large duck	flour
1 orange	sauerkraut juice
100 g (3½ oz) bacon	garlic, peppercorns
1 small onion	1 small cabbage or 500 g
1 tablespoon fresh fennel	(1 lb) sauerkraut
½ teaspoon each dried	1 glass sherry, madeira or
thyme, marjoram, sage	similar

Put the cleaned duck on a wire rack over a baking pan in a very hot oven. Prick with a skewer in several places and roast, basting, for 15–20 minutes to brown and release some of the abundant fat. Remove, cool somewhat, and, having poured off the fat, pour over the orange juice. Meanwhile fry the chopped bacon, onion, fennel and thyme, stir in 1 tablespoon of flour, cook and thin with sauerkraut juice. Rub a casserole with garlic, add the duck in pieces with the orange juice. Brown a head of cabbage or the drained sauerkraut with the sage and dried marjoram in a little duck fat and add to the casserole. Pour over the sauce and bake slowly for 2 hours, uncovered for the last 20 minutes. Pour over a glass of sherry before serving.

This recipe is also suitable for goose.

The Poles associate their *duck à l'orange*, made sweet with orange liqueur and fresh orange, with the Baltic port of Gdańsk, for a reason I haven't been able to fathom, unless it was there that imported oranges were unloaded.

Duck djuvec with peppers, tomatoes, potatoes and rice

Roast the duck for 20 minutes, covered in its own fat and a little water. Joint it and arrange in a well-greased casserole on top of 200 g (7 oz) parboiled rice, an onion in rings, 2–3 green peppers, 500 g (1 lb) each sliced tomatoes and potatoes, arranged in ascending layers. Season each layer with salt and pepper and pour over the juices, skimmed of fat, from the duck. Bake until golden brown, adding a little water if necessary. This is a Serbian dish that makes good use of the duck fat to moisten the *djuvec* cooking with it.

The most famous Hungarian goose dish is *cholent*, a kind of cassoulet with barley and beans. See p. 302.

Goose, duck or chicken stuffed with buckwheat

In Slovenia and also in Poland, buckwheat is used for stuffing all kinds of poultry. This is one of my all-time favourite combinations, which I first discovered in conjunction with Russian food. The stuffing can be plain boiled buckwheat, or made more elaborately, as follows.

20 g (¾ oz) dried mushrooms	100 g (3½ oz) onion
200 g (7 oz) mixed vegetables	40 g (1¼ oz) dripping
300 g (10 oz) buckwheat groats	2 eggs
	salt, pepper
	parsley, fresh dill

Cook the dried mushrooms in water, add the mixed vegetables and continue till tender. Strain, chop the mushrooms, and use the liquid, plus enough water, to cook the buckwheat and leave it dry. Fry the chopped onion in the dripping. Combine all the cooked ingredients with the egg yolks, seasoning, herbs and beaten egg whites. Use to stuff the cavity of chicken, duck or goose and sew up before roasting.

Wild goose peasant style

Braise a goose in its own fat in a covered pan with a glass of water and seasoning. Boil in water with raw ham (the original calls for *prsut*, see p. 55) about 500 g (1 lb) green or brown lentils until soft. Joint the goose, lay it in a greased casserole, cover with slices of ham, then pour over the lentils, puréed, and the juices, skimmed of fat, in which the goose was cooked. Sprinkle the top of the dish with 50 g (2 oz) parmesan cheese and put in the oven to heat through and melt cheese. The recipe comes from Yugoslavia, probably from Dalmatia.

Using up the giblets

This is a declining art, though one can be sure the food industry returns everything edible to our modern tables in some form or other. One of the best-known old Central European and Jewish giblet delicacies is stuffed goose neck. The neck, lined with its own fat, is filled with a forcemeat made from the liver of the goose with eggs, spices, butter, vegetables, milk, minced veal and bread.

In Czechoslovakia goose liver is cooked in its own fat and eaten sliced with potatoes, or cold with more fat spread on bread. In Romania it might be dipped in egg and breadcrumbs and fried, or even stuffed with mushrooms, baked surrounded by strips of bacon, then removed, sliced and allowed to cool in aspic. In Hungary it might be potted with its fat and a good flavouring of garlic paprika.

Old ways of dealing with less valuable leftovers can be confined to history with fewer qualms. In the interests of economy the meat from a goose or duck neck would be simmered along with the gizzard, wings, and feet, boned and served in a white sauce with soup vegetables and sour cream. With this Poles might offer cooked barley, the Hungarians of the Great Plains millet and Czechs rice or noodles and boiled cauliflower. The Romanians call a similar giblet dish Dragomiroff and the East Germans appear to have something similar today. This is a little preparation of meat scraps in a well-flavoured béchamel sauce, served as a hot starter in small oven-proof pots like Russian mushroom dishes and given the name *Würzfleisch*, 'piquant meat'. It is a very common item on restaurant, hotel and tavern menus. The Yugoslavs have a related recipe for chicken innards with prunes, *tingulet*, prescribed as a sauce for pasta. Prunes also turn up with giblets in Poland and Hungary. I have tried some of these and would give them a wide berth in future. The best way to use up scraps of flesh and liver is in sausages, pâté or dumplings. The Czechs and Hungarians cherish liver dumplings, albeit most often with calves' or ox liver, but sometimes with chicken.

Game

There is hardly a region in Eastern Europe which has not been called a huntsman's paradise. 'Toute la Pologne est le plus beau pays de chasses que j'aie jamais vu,' reported Molière's successor in the French theatre, the exuberant poet and traveller Jean-François Regnard, towards the end of the seventeenth century. Two hundred years later a British sportsman, Randolph L. L. Hodgson, was having the time of his life as a gun in Bohemia:

Picture a vast plain, sweltering beneath an August sun. Stiff rows of plum trees, affording but the smallest minimum of shade, line the dusty roads and here and there intersect the fields. The country – its surface chequered by the various crops like a patchwork counterpane – lies dull, flat and uninteresting. One village resembles another – a collection of low-rooved, whitewashed houses, one-storied and built of wood many of them; a white-washed church with a single bell hanging in the turret; a public house – possibly two or three – or *hostinez*, as it is called in Bohemia, and a dirty pond, form the regular characteristics. Dirty, half-clothed children play in the dust; flocks of geese occupy the roadway and fly cackling from beneath the horse's feet as one drives along; and a troop of mongrel curs pursue every vehicle with angry barking. The landscape is monotonous, to say the least of it. The tall chimneys of an occasional sugar *fabrik* are the only landmarks to meet the eye. Such is the country over which one shoots the partridge.

Hodgson found hunting rituals and manners rather formal among the Czechs. He also wished to record that the men and sometimes the women propped themselves up with frequent nips of *slivovica* carried in small bottles about the person. But the sport was undoubtedly good. In Austro-Hungary in one year of Hodgson's lifetime, nearly 4 million creatures were shot, including 210 bears. Many foreigners came to pursue red deer, wild boar, capercailzie, blackcock – which frequented the birch trees – pheasant, hare, partridge and roebuck. The last from the gastronomic point of view was a particular delicacy, and modern Czech cookbooks still abound with recipes for venison.

Saddle of venison braised with cream

1 kg (2 lb) venison
60 g (2 oz) bacon
salt
100 g (3½ oz) onion
80 g (2½ oz) lard
150 g (5 oz) root vegetables
¼ litre (½ pint) stock

3 peppercorns, 3 allspice
   corns, 1 bay leaf
60 g (2 oz) flour
½ litre (1 pint) sour cream
½ lemon
either: 2 small pickled
   gherkins, 30 g (1 oz)

| capers and a few pickled | tablespoons cranberry |
| mushrooms, *or*: 3–4 | preserves or apple sauce |

Lard the meat with bacon and rub in salt. Fry the chopped onion in fat and add the chopped root vegetables, the meat, stock and spices and braise, covered, until tender. Remove the meat, thicken the gravy with flour and cream to make a thick sauce. Simmer and strain, flavour with lemon juice and pickles and serve poured over the sliced meat, with dumplings. If using fruit, spread this over the meat first and then cover with sauce.

Another very popular albeit more routine dish in Central Europe has long been hare stewed in red wine with dumplings, though I cannot say I much enjoyed this in a restaurant filled with smoke and Czech-speaking African students in the centre of Brno. It was rather tough and heavy, which is always the threat with both hare and venison. We fell to drinking Moravian Pils to pass the evening and make up for the meal. Ideally, the hare should become tender during several days of marinating.

Hare marinated in buttermilk

The marinade for hare is generally red wine, though this good Polish recipe for either hare or wild boar uses buttermilk. Clean two hind-parts of hare plus legs, lard them with bacon, season and place in buttermilk with a few cloves, bay leaves and a raw onion cut into rings. Leave 2–3 days, then wipe the meat dry, braise it in butter with two chopped onions and a pickled cucumber and a little of the marinade and simmer until tender. Add one grated pickled beetroot before serving. The effect of this, of course, is to give this dish the colour of *barszcz*, to whet Polish appetites.

Rabbit with blackcurrants

Simple, lighter dishes for rabbit avoid the need for advance preparations, compared with hare. Rub the rabbit with salt, pepper and paprika, brown on all sides in a pan, then roast in the oven for 30 minutes, basting occasionally. Towards the end pour over $\frac{1}{4}$ litre ($\frac{1}{2}$ pint) single cream. Baste with this sauce, roast another 5 minutes, then serve with cooked pears and a compote of blackcurrants.

This is a German recipe.

Braised rabbit, Prague style

1 rabbit boned	1 small celeriac
bay leaves	1 cup tinned peas
100 g (3½ oz) smoked bacon	2 green peppers
1 onion	flour
salt, paprika	100 ml (¼ pint) cream
2 tablespoons tomato paste	parsley

Make a stock with the rabbit head and bones and bay leaves. Melt the bacon in a pan, fry the onion in it, then brown the cubed rabbit meat, seasoning it with salt and paprika. Add the tomato paste and stock and cook covered. When almost tender add the chopped or grated celeriac, the peas and the chopped peppers and finish cooking. Thicken Hungarian style by mixing 2 teaspoons flour with the cream to make a paste, and diluting it with stock from the pan before combining all. Garnish with parsley and serve with dumplings. This is a very homely, unpretentious style of cooking, just the sort of thing served in a Prague tavern.

Gastronomically the staples of Central European cooking – sauerkraut, pickled cucumbers, cranberries, bacon, sour cream, gingerbread, plums, prunes and apples – cannot but fit well with game. Polish gingerbread, *piernik*, comes into its own as a means of thickening, darkening and spicing, all in one go, sauces for venison and hare. The combination bears out the common view of a robust, strong-flavoured, meaty cuisine.

The eating of game, though, has always seemed to me more enjoyed by men than women, because the hunting of it appears to be half the pleasure and the taste is very strong. I find myself sticking to the lighter, quicker recipes in preference to the hearty old plodders. Modern sensibilities, directed against hunting and against any pleasure being exclusive to one class or sex, have tended to thrust the whole institution into the past, along with the politics of empires and colonies, albeit with a certain nostalgia. The great game dishes of Central Europe, with red wine, with sauerkraut, with bacon, belong to the cosmopolitan epoch and milieu of men in green loden collarless jackets and women organizing large family meals at home on fine porcelain and silver. They also belong to those pre-war restaurants where fish swam in tanks, and the self-same German establishments were renowned for their game dishes. In Dresden customers at the Englischer Garten praised the partridge and woodcock, and in season pheasant was another common dish, cooked with sauerkraut. The Romanians could be relied upon even in those days to be more extravagant than solid. In Bucharest a recommended delicacy was bear's paws.

A connection still exists between game-hunting/game-eating and the Central European game of political appearances, though that too is old-fashioned. George Lang says of the internationally prestigious face of hunting in Hungary: 'Be it a Russian premier or an English prime minister, you'll find his picture on the pages of international magazines when he is posing with the tusk of a huge wild boar, with the imposing mountains of the Borzsony patiently providing the background.' I'm not so sure about the English prime minister. A man who *was* inextricably associated with both hunting and a hopeless last attempt to hang on to nineteenth-century landed grandeur was Mussolini, a dyspeptic who could digest little more than bread and milk, but who liked to place his shots in the Albanian hinterland. His example certainly belongs to the past.

Suffice to say there hasn't been much modernization and minceur leavening of the game recipes of yesteryear. An exception is the contribution of Olga Novak-Markovic, who prepared a sophisticated cosmopolitan table for President Tito.

Medallions of venison with fresh fruit

Bone well-hung meat and, if liked, marinate it overnight in vinegar and spices. Dry it, season with salt and pepper and spread with mustard. Leave to stand in a cold place for a few hours if possible before cutting into medallions and frying in oil or bacon fat. Fry some mushrooms separately in butter, then add the venison and half a cup of red wine with some chopped parsley. Serve on fried bread or rice, surrounded by rings of orange warmed in wine and topped with mushrooms. Garnish with fresh herbs and serve with potato croquettes. The various pan juices can be combined with cream and stock to make a sauce.

Markovic knew Tito's taste for game. Born of a large peasant family in Croatia, he spent many days with his grandparents in Slovenia, where he acquired an early love of hunting, fishing and riding, and an outdoor appetite. Her repertoire included a traditional roast venison with bacon and juniper, and she generally recommended sage or rosemary to flavour game dishes, balm (*melissa*) to garnish them and dumplings or baked cornmeal to go alongside. A game pâté was *de rigueur* for special occasions.

VEGETABLES, RICE AND PULSES

It is very pleasant to stroll through the market on a fine summer morning. On all sides there is a wild riot of colour which delights the eye. There are the fruit stalls piled high with oranges, pomegranates, dates, green grapes of the native variety, and grapes of light amber hue from Constantinople. Scarcely less effective are the vegetable stalls with their bright-red tomatoes affording a brilliant contrast to the fresh greens of cauliflower and cabbage. Here too are radishes and piments. Then there are stalls with mushrooms of all varieties, stalls with cheeses, stalls with golden butter and white and brown eggs, and every here and there are mounds of melons.

Maude Parkinson, *Twenty Years in Roumania,* 1921

Stuffed vegetables

This tradition, prominent in Oriental, Middle Eastern and Balkan cooking, has been independently pursued in Central Europe and Russia for centuries.

Stuffed cabbage leaves

Unquestionably delicious are stuffed cabbage leaves from a Savoy cabbage, either fresh, blanched in boiling water or pickled. Shave off the thickest part of the stem of the leaf, so

Polish peasants from Stryj, 1840. Bibliothèque des Arts Décoratifs,
Paris (photo: J.-L. Charmet)

that it is the same thickness as the rest. Place about 2 tablespoons of filling in the centre, turn the right and left edges towards the centre but not so far that they touch, then roll the leaf loosely and tuck in the sides.

Variations Polish *golabki* are usually filled with pork or pork and rice and cooked in a tomato sauce. Yugoslav *sarma* are similar but spicier, with cayenne pepper and garlic in the stuffing.

For a deluxe version, lay pork-and-rice-stuffed cabbage parcels in a large, deep earthenware dish lined with sauerkraut, and place pork spare-ribs over the top of the *sarma*. Add a little water or stock and stew till half-cooked, then add a spicy tomato sauce and stock as needed and finish cooking slowly, till tender. *Sarma* are served with yoghurt or sour cream.

Romanian *sarmale* can be filled with the same mixture of pork and beef as for *mititei* (p. 94), plus a little rice.

In Lent *sarmale* are made without meat. The following stuffing is suitable for vegetarians.

1 onion	salt, pepper
7–8 tablespoons oil	1 cup uncooked rice
1 teaspoon each dried thyme and dill, or 1 tablespoon fresh	120 g (4 oz) sauerkraut wine, or tomato juice (optional)
1 tablespoon chopped chives, or spring onion	

Chop and fry the onion in 2 tablespoons oil, add most of the herbs, the seasoning and the rice. Stir and cook for a few minutes. Fill the leaves and arrange in a deep pan between layers of sauerkraut. Sprinkle each layer with the remaining herbs and cover the rolls with sauerkraut juice, water or wine or tomato juice plus 5–6 tablespoons of oil. Leave to stand a few hours or overnight. Begin cooking on top of the stove uncovered, shaking the pan occasionally, then cover and simmer very slowly for 2 hours. Place for a third hour in a slow oven, after which only a cup of liquid should remain. Serve, or, better still, allow to cool then reheat next day. The accompaniments are sour cream or yoghurt and baked *mamaliga* (p. 330).

The Polish Lenten version of stuffed cabbage leaves is with barley.

Peppers stuffed with curd cheese

Mix together 350 g (12 oz) curd cheese with two eggs and plenty of parsley or other fresh herbs. Curd cheese is a marvellous vehicle for any fresh herb. A good combination is tarragon and basil. Savory, known as *chubritza*, is most prized in Bulgaria. Stuff the cheese into the cleaned, cored and seeded green peppers, dip them in flour and beaten egg, then fry them in good oil. Drain on absorbent paper, cool and slice to serve. Ideally the peppers should be skinned before filling, by charring them in the oven or under the grill till the skins can be peeled off easily. This makes them less indigestible, though I find the task a chore. Tinned Spanish peppers, which have an excellent flavour, turn this recipe into fast food.

Stuffed aubergines with garlic

For stuffed aubergines either a minced-meat or vegetable filling is usual, with the aubergines cooked in tomato sauce or stock or white wine. Both ways are very popular in Bulgaria and in Romania, whence this recipe comes.

4 aubergines, 200–250 g (about 8 oz) each	2–3 tablespoons chopped parsley
250 g (9 oz) onion	4 tomatoes
12 tablespoons oil	tomato purée or tomato juice
2 cups diced mixed vegetables: celery, carrot, turnip, leek	garlic salt, pepper

Wash the aubergines, cut lengthwise in half and scoop out pulp. Soften the onions in the oil in a covered pan, then add the mixed vegetables, parsley and aubergine pulp. Cook for 10 minutes, then fill the aubergine shells and place them in a greased baking dish. Slice the tomatoes and lay them over the top and sprinkle with olive oil. Add a cup of tomato juice or purée diluted with water, with plenty of garlic crushed with a little salt. Bake in a moderate oven for 45–50 minutes or until tender. Serve hot or cold, garnished with fresh parsley. The Romanian accompaniment is sharp peppers and *mamaliga*.

This dish is most eye-catching. The pale yellow-green of the filled aubergines is picked out by the red of the tomatoes and carrots, and the green garnish is a refreshing contrast to the hot colours. Tinned tomatoes may be used for the topping and cooking liquid, but the visual result is less attractive.

Stuffed courgettes

Cut six medium-sized courgettes in half lengthwise, score inside like a melon and scoop out most of the pulp with a small pointed spoon. Blanch the courgette shells in boiling water while the pulp simmers in butter. Add to the filling a tablespoon of breadcrumbs, 250 g (8 oz) curd cheese and salt to taste. Off the heat stir in a good tablespoon of fresh dill, two tablespoons of cream and two egg yolks. Stuff the courgette shells and bake side by side in a buttered dish with a little water. Sprinkle the tops with a little parmesan. This Romanian recipe, from an *émigré* living in Paris, Doina Dor, is very good if also very Western. It would go well with a buttery, baked *mamaliga*.

Stuffed onions

In Yugoslavia (where they are called *grne*) and Bulgaria these are filled with minced meat and rice, well seasoned with garlic and baked in stock. The onions should be boiled peeled but whole for 10 minutes before being scooped out and filled. The scooped out middles are braised in oil with the rest of the filling.

Stuffed tomatoes

These are very popular everywhere served cold as hors d'oeuvres. This for variety's sake is a Bulgarian recipe, to be eaten hot. It is a bland and honest display of foods that are plentiful in that country.

8 medium-sized tomatoes	150 g (6 oz) rice
salt, pepper	30 g (1 oz) raisins
1–2 teaspoons sugar	1½ cups yoghurt
200 g (7 oz) onions	2 egg yolks
3 tablespoons oil	

Cut the tops off the tomatoes, scoop out the insides, sprinkle the cavities with salt and 1 teaspoon of sugar. Sauté the onions in oil, add the rice, raisins and tomato pulp, seasoning, remaining sugar and a little water and cook until the rice is tender. Stuff the tomatoes and surround them with any remaining mixture in a baking dish. Pour over the yoghurt mixed with the egg yolks and bake in a moderate oven for 30 minutes.

Fruit too can be stuffed – most commonly apples and quinces – with minced meat flavoured with cinnamon and cooked in stock, thickened with an egg yolk to finish.

Vegetable stews
Lecsó

1 large onion
3 tablespoons oil
500 g (1 lb) green peppers
250 g (8 oz) tomatoes
salt, pepper

This is a simple and satisfying version of a well-known Hungarian vegetable stew to be eaten on its own or with meat or sausages. Braise the onion in thin rings, add the peppers in rings, then the quartered tomatoes, season to taste, cover and stew till tender. Serve hot.

Lenten ghiveci

Like Hungarian *lecsó*, this Balkan relative of Provençal *ratatouille* will go with anything, including roast meat. It is excellent with garlic bread. This recipe is Romanian.

250 g ($\frac{1}{2}$ lb) each of
carrots, parsnips,
mushrooms, green
peppers, onions, green
beans
350 g ($\frac{3}{4}$ lb) potatoes
6 sticks celery
120 g (4 oz) peas
$\frac{1}{2}$ cup sunflower oil
1 bay leaf
2 tablespoons chopped
parsley

1–2 teaspoons sweet paprika
$\frac{1}{4}$ cup white wine
1 cup tomato juice, or
water mixed with 2
tablespoons tomato paste
salt, black pepper
$\frac{1}{2}$ teaspoon dried thyme or 2
tablespoons chopped fresh
chervil

Wash the vegetables, chop them into cubes and place all except the onion in a large bowl, adding the oil with each layer and stirring, so that all the vegetables are coated. Sweat the sliced onions in a heavy casserole, covered, in a few tablespoons of the oil, until soft. Add all the other ingredients except the chervil, which should go in at the last minute, season lightly and cook the mixture gently, occasionally shaking the pot or lightly stirring, until it becomes a rich, unctuous stew. In *ghiveci* the flavours should be well blended but the different vegetables still recognizable. Other vegetables – swede, cauliflower, turnip, uncooked beetroot, sprouts, sweet corn, courgettes, etc. – and also fruit – apples, pears and grapes – may be used according to availability, the liquid may be stock and one of the flavours garlic. You may also add warmed grapes at the last minute as a garnish.

The Bulgarians make the same vegetable casserole and call it *gyuvech*. It can include meat, or mushrooms, and potatoes, and be eaten hot or cold. The Serbian version is *djuvec*. It is said each family has its own *ghiveci* recipe and all good cooks know instinctively what is the right combination of vegetables in the right proportion.

I have read a suggestion that the happy blending together of so many different vegetables in harmony suggests similar human success, but this does not seem wholly apt given the bloody history of the Balkans and centuries of national squabbling in Central Europe.

More attractive and no doubt truer is the association of dishes like this with the Balkan monasteries. One version is called 'monastery garden casserole'. The monasteries maintained richly productive kitchen gardens and wherever they existed they were the centre of local life. As a young scrumper, the Romanian story-teller Ion Creanga always had his eye on the monastery orchard in his native Humuleşti, south-west Moldavia, though he described with a single word, '*dentage*', the resentment his father and other small-holders felt in the 1850s towards the priests and their privileged existence. *Dentage* was the fee the peasants would pay a young man when he became a priest. It evoked the entire unjust feudal order. To add insult to injury, *dentage* was the sum one paid the Turkish overlord to sit at one's table at Christmas and wear out his teeth.

Privilege meant the priests were well-fed and led a gentler life. There is an expression in Romanian for one who eats too much, taken from the irreverent Latin for a priest. On the other hand, the men of God distributed food to the poor and gave shelter and generous hospitality to travellers. More than anyone, before the advent of professional chefs and food writers, they made their local cuisines memorable to foreigners. Despite the antagonisms they provoked among the poor classes in their own country, they generally supported the native cause against the alien ruler. In Romania and Bulgaria the monasteries became the keepers of native traditions, repositories of simple wisdom. The priests lived close to the soil and their lives appeared nationally 'true'. In Ivan Vazoff's panoramic novel chronicling the beginning of the Bulgarian uprising against the Turks, *Under the Yoke*, much of the action takes place in a monastery where the nationalist protagonists hide.

In the 1930s the legacy of the monasteries was plain to see. Sacheverell Sitwell described the alms-giving at the nunnery of Hurez near the Romanian town of Piteşti:

In one corner of the courtyard, under shadow of the church, trestle tables were set up and the peasant women and children were at their dinner. Great cauldrons of soup were carried up, huge hunks of white bread and bunches of white grapes. It was a scene of a thousand years ago: the monks, or nuns, and their serfs lived in this manner in any great Byzantine convent of the tenth century.

Sitwell found the monasteries to be timeless, silent oases, radiating a deep feeling for the locality, even through their food:

The other feature . . . in this delightful place [the monastery at Cozia] . . . is the apartment of their abbess or prioress. It consists of a set of whitewashed rooms furnished with divans on which to rest while helping yourself to the glass of water and spoonful of jam which is the traditional hospitality of the nuns . . . Nothing could be more spotlessly clean than these rooms. Their pastel shades – for the colour gives the effect of gouache – have exactly the tone of the bright sunlight coming through green shutters and are the entire equivalents of the carafe of crystal water and the saucer of cherry jam.

It is probably fair to say the inspiration of the monasteries is the spiritual shadow of the wonderful vegetable and fruit cultivation and cooking all over the Balkans.

Vegetable, fruit and salad side dishes

❦

Fresh cucumber side salad (1)

This is called *mizeria*, 'misery', in Polish, for no explicable reason. Fresh cucumbers are peeled, sliced, salted, drained and then dressed with vinegar and sour cream, garnished with fresh dill or freshly grated pepper.

Fresh cucumber side salad (2)

The dressing is made with sugar and water so that this salad functions as a fruit compote, a refreshing contrast in flavour and texture to rich, cooked, concentrated food. This recipe is Hungarian, though I have eaten salads like this in Poland, Czechoslovakia and Germany on a number of occasions. The predominant, cross-border influence is surely Jewish.

Peel, slice, salt and drain the cucumber as above, then dress in a mixture of one teaspoon of wine vinegar to 3–4 table-spoons of water, and a good pinch of sugar. The cucumbers should be almost covered, or almost floating. They can be garnished with chopped onion or spring onion and seasoned with black or white pepper, and/or paprika, the choice of seasoning depending on the blandness or otherwise of the accompanying dish.

Lettuce salad with bacon

This is another water-dressed salad, this time from Moravia. Toss a washed and dried lettuce in a mixture of 4 tablespoons water, 1 tablespoon vinegar, 1 teaspoon sugar, with a pinch of salt. Chill to crisp and garnish with sliced hard-boiled egg and warm bacon. The tossed lettuce may also be served plain.

Green beans with pears

The sharp, sweet element in accompanying salads persists in the preparation of cooked vegetables as a garnish to rich food in the German/Czech/Polish style. The Germans particularly like to combine green vegetables with fruit or to use root vegetables to sweeten others less sweet, or to preserve them with sugar.

Top and tail the beans and cook them lightly in salted water. Peel, core and stew the sliced pears separately in very little water. Drain the beans, combine with the pears and sprinkle with plenty of freshly ground black pepper. Serve with roast lamb. In Germany, yellow 'wax' beans would often be used, but French or 'bobby' beans will do nicely. They are also often served garnished with fried bacon.

Leipziger Allerlei

250 g (8 oz) each green
    peas, carrots, French
    beans
1 cauliflower
120 g (4 oz) mushrooms
120 g (4 oz) butter

1 tablespoon flour
½ litre (1 pint) vegetable
    stock
salt, paprika
small bread dumplings, or
    shrimps to garnish

Cook the vegetables separately to the degree of tenderness liked. Drain them, reserving the liquid, toss them in butter and keep warm. Sauté the mushrooms in butter, remove them and use the butter to make a roux with the flour. Cook for a minute or so, then dilute with the vegetable stock. Thicken over heat, season with salt and paprika. Pour over the vegetables on a plate with the cauliflower in the centre. Garnish with the dumplings or shrimps. Other vegetables may be used in season, even potato chips.

A Hungarian cauliflower seller from the Tisza region
(photo: J.-L. Charmet)

Stewed chestnuts

In Austria chestnuts are cooked with poultry and with sour vegetables to add a touch of sweetness. Yugoslavia probably assimilated from there the following idea as an accompaniment to game.

1 kg (2 lb) chestnuts
1 tablespoon sugar
50 g (2 oz) butter
2 tablespoons honey

1 cup wine
salt
lemon juice (optional)

Peel outer and inner skins from the chestnuts by plunging them in cold water, bringing to the boil and removing them to handle one or two at a time. Then simmer the chestnuts in water until almost tender. Brown the sugar lightly in the butter and add the honey and drained chestnuts. Stir until glazed, add wine, and salt and sugar to taste. Simmer until the flavours are well blended and the chestnuts soft. A little lemon juice may also be added. This dish may also be eaten alone as a pudding, or served with other vegetables such as red cabbage and stuffed onions to make a meatless meal.

A German asparagus feast

Peel, trim, wash and bind 1–1½ kg (2–3 lb) asparagus and cook in boiling salted water. While they are cooking make small pancakes, browned on both sides, from 350 g (12 oz) flour, 3 eggs and about ⅜ litre (⅓ pint) milk. Fold each pancake twice and lay them on a large serving plate with the asparagus on top and a plate of mixed raw and cooked ham alongside. A small jug of melted butter should be available to pour over the asparagus and pancakes.

Beetroot in yoghurt

Bulgarian cuisine stands out for its healthy emphasis on yoghurt rather than oil or eggs as a dressing.

1 small carton plain yoghurt
1 tablespoon vinegar
2 tablespoons fresh dill

salt, pepper, cayenne
500 g (1 lb) cooked beetroot, fresh or bottled, drained

Combine all the ingredients except the beetroot and chill. Chill the beetroot. Dress the beetroot just before serving.

Sauerkraut and peas

A classic of a frugal kind, served at a Polish Christmas Eve dinner and in Czechoslovakia.

1 cup dried split peas, green or yellow
1 kg (2 lb) sauerkraut
120 g (4 oz) mushrooms, sliced
salt, pepper
50 g (2 oz) small tin anchovies, drained

Pour plenty of boiling water over the peas in a saucepan, bring to the boil and cook for 2 minutes. Remove from the heat, cover and leave to stand 30 minutes, bring to the boil again and simmer for 20 minutes. Meanwhile, cover the sauerkraut and mushrooms with 3 cups water, cover and cook gently for an hour. Mix the peas and sauerkraut together well, season with salt and pepper, turn into a buttered baking dish and garnish with anchovies. Bake covered in a slow to moderate oven for 20–30 minutes.

Variations A non-Lenten version of this dish, also non-vegetarian, blends two tablespoons of flour with a cup of the sauerkraut cooking liquid and returns it to the mixture with a chopped fried onion and half a pound of lightly fried salt pork, bacon or sausage.

Anyone who has dipped into the volume on spring in Reymont's graphic 1,200-page account of nineteenth-century rural Polish life, *The Peasants*, will feel as well as understand what a relief from hunger the return of bacon to favourite dishes meant after the starving winter months.

Cauliflower

In north Germany and Czechoslovakia, where cauliflower is a favourite, it is usually served in familiar ways: in a white sauce, with cheese, or boiled and served plain, or with buttered breadcrumbs. In Poland the crumb garnish can become *polonaise* sauce with the addition of plenty of butter, chopped hard-boiled egg and fresh dill. But cauliflower is firm enough and sufficiently adaptable to lend itself to main courses as well. Deep-fried cauliflower fritters, made with parboiled florets, are more than a side vegetable. Both of these recipes are for supper dishes, the first substantial, the second light and quick.

Cauliflower musaka

The common version of this recipe from Yugoslavia is with meat, but I have made a very successful vegetarian version with cooked white beans.

1 kg (2 lb) cauliflower, parboiled
flour and beaten egg for frying
oil for frying
250 g (8 oz) white beans, soaked and boiled until tender, *or* 600 g (1¼ lb) minced pork

or veal and 80 g (3 oz) fried onion
salt, pepper, garlic, nutmeg, fresh parsley
generous ½ litre (1 pt) white sauce

Drain the cauliflower florets, dip in flour and beaten egg and fry in oil. Line the base of a greased baking dish with these, add a layer of beans or meat with seasoning and alternate layers, ending with cauliflower. Pour over the sauce and bake till golden brown.

A traditional alternative sauce of sour cream or yoghurt and eggs instead of a flour-based béchamel sauce makes this recipe drier and sourer and is less recommended.

Cauliflower with scrambled eggs

This is a solid example of Czech provincial cooking. Parboil a large cauliflower and divide into florets. Braise a chopped onion in butter, add a good pinch of cumin, the cauliflower, and, after a few minutes covered, add five or six eggs, beaten and seasoned, with a little milk if liked. Cook gently, stirring, until just set. Serve with rye bread or potatoes and green salad.

Braised red cabbage

Many recipes exist for this excellent sweet-and-sour accompaniment to roast pork, chestnuts and to some chicken dishes. The cabbage is soured, usually with vinegar or sour apples, or both, and sweetened with fruit, sugar, or dried fruit. A little fat and extra taste comes from the use of bacon fat or a few tablespoons of strong meat or mushroom stock or Maggi liquid-meat extract. Cloves and a bay leaf may be added and an onion included. Some recipes include wine, but for the reasons I have suggested on p. 245, and the instant reaction of my palate, this seems to me to be an extraneous introduction and a waste. This is a rich, modern German recipe.

2 apples	2 cloves
1 onion	1 cup stock
1 small red cabbage	2 tablespoons liquid-meat
2 teaspoons butter or	extract/soy sauce
margarine	3–4 tablespoons each
1 bay leaf	vinegar and raspberry juice

Core and slice the apples, chop the onions and shred the cabbage. Melt the butter in a large, heavy saucepan, add the onions and apple, then the cabbage, and mix well. After a few minutes add all the ingredients except the vinegar, meat extract and fruit juice. Stew, covered, very slowly until soft. If the cabbage can rest a day or two, after cooking, it will improve. Whatever the time span, heat through and, just before serving, combine the last three ingredients and add them to the pan to be heated, mixing them in well.

Other recipes for cabbage and sauerkraut

Too much can be said on the subject of fresh and pickled cabbage in a book which, with the exception of the Chinese and the French, includes every people in the world which lays claim to owning sauerkraut as a unique national institution. What is true is that to ferment cabbage in brine as a means of preserving it for the winter was an idea developed in the East over 2,000 years ago, one that spread west and proved specially likeable to the various peoples of Central Europe and the Balkans. The Romanians liked its sourness, the Germans and Hungarians its susceptibility to sweet-sour treatment, the Poles and the Czechs the very harmonious marriage it made with all pork products. According to Bickel's international classifications, the German way is with white stock, onions, fat and bacon, while the Hungarians add white wine, onions, butter, tomato purée, red peppers, lean bacon and stock. The best dishes today are those in which sauerkraut uniquely enhances other contrasting flavours. *Bigos*, the Polish speciality (p. 244), and the vegetarian *sarmale* or stuffed cabbage leaves from Romania on p. 277 are showpieces. Otherwise sauerkraut may be prepared in the same manner as red cabbage or served as a salad.

Sauerkraut salad (1)

Combine one medium carrot, grated, with $2\frac{1}{2}$ cups chopped sauerkraut and a grated onion. Season well with sugar, black pepper and oil.

Sauerkraut salad (2)

Combine the same quantity of chopped sauerkraut with a grated onion, sugar, pepper, oil and caraway seeds.

Personally, though I know it helped build the Great Wall of China, I find a little sauerkraut goes a long way. It can be very unsettling on the stomach. Most East Europeans believe it has the opposite effect on the head, and recommend it for hangovers, the sharpness being enough to scale the most furred tongue.

Courgettes with dill and sour cream

750 g (1½ lb) courgettes
1 teaspoon salt
2 teaspoons butter
½ onion
1 tablespoon flour

1 tablespoon fresh dill
1 tablespoon white-wine
   vinegar or lemon juice
1 teaspoon sugar
2–3 tablespoons sour cream

It is essential to have fresh dill for this French-influenced recipe. Cut the courgettes into chunks about 1 cm (½ inch) thick and halve them if they are more than an inch across. Sprinkle with salt and leave to drain. Melt the butter in a pan, add the finely chopped onion and cook until soft. Stir in the flour, cook for 1–2 minutes, then add ½ cup water to make a smooth sauce. Add the courgettes and the dill, cover and cook for 10 minutes, taking care the sauce does not become too thick or stick to the bottom of the pan. Stir the mixture occasionally, if necessary adding a little water. When the vegetables are cooked but not mushy add half the vinegar or lemon juice and the sugar, bring to the boil and adjust the sweet/sourness to taste. Mix in the sour cream and serve. This dish is excellent alone hot or cold, with a bean salad and good bread, or with veal or chicken.

Courgettes with lemon

Brown an onion in 5 tablespoons of olive oil, add half a dozen sliced courgettes, 2–3 tablespoons fresh parsley, a little thyme, seasoning and a splash of water. Simmer gently and serve cold, garnished with lemon. This Romanian recipe is fine.

Radishes

No recipe here: eat them raw with black bread and butter or in a mixed side salad. Bernard Newman observed in the 1950s that 'radish' was used to describe the large number of people who had jumped on the Communist bandwagon: red outside, white when peeled.

Spinach Zagora-style

1 kg (2 lb) spinach, washed, cooked and drained
2 tablespoons butter
2 cloves garlic, minced
1½ cups sour cream
1 cup coarsely chopped walnuts
3 tablespoons parmesan cheese
1 tablespoon chopped onion
salt, pepper

Combine all the ingredients, well mixed, in a buttered baking dish, bake 30 minutes in a medium oven and serve immediately. The recipe is from Bulgaria.

Celeriac fritters

I have found recipes for these in Czechoslovakia, Hungary and Bulgaria, and they make a very tasty introduction to a vegetable little-known in Britain. So rare is demand for this large knobbly root, because of ignorance of what to do with it, that most greengrocers refuse to stock it. That's a pity, because it is easy to cook and difficult to abuse, and the flavour is always there. It keeps for weeks in a cool place, even when cut, and can be eaten raw or cooked, whole or made into soup. What more could one ask of a vegetable which is also very good value and would surely be cheaper if more of us would buy it more often?

Clean the celeriac, cut into rounds 2 cm (1 inch) thick, drop these into boiling water and leave for 3 minutes. Make a batter of an egg, 3 tablespoons flour and some water, seasoned with salt and pepper and fresh parsley. Dip the dried celeriac rounds in the batter and fry in deep hot oil, or a covered shallow pan. Serve with a slice of lemon and a bowl of sour cream.

Aubergine fritters are made the same way, prepared for frying by salting and squeezing dry. Omit the immersion in boiling water.

Raw celeriac and apple salad

A Czech recipe in the manner of the water dressings on p. 284.

2 tablespoons oil	1 small celeriac, about 400 g
1 tablespoon vinegar	($\frac{3}{4}$ lb)
salt	2 apples
$\frac{1}{2}$ teaspoon sugar	2 spring onions

Mix together $\frac{1}{2}$ cup water, the oil, vinegar, salt and sugar and pour over the peeled and grated celeriac. Grate the apples and add, together with the finely chopped onion. Don't omit the sugar here! It softens the character of this tangy salad to some advantage.

Kohlrabi is another root vegetable popular in Central Europe but obscure in Britain. Even in London's largest and most cosmopolitan supermarkets it lies neglected and unwanted, so much the worse for its prolonged shelf-life, and overpriced because demand is so low. As the name in German suggests, it has the qualities and partly the appearance of a root vegetable like turnip, though it is a member of the *brassica* (cabbage) family and sends out shoots from the root at every angle. It is best when small and tender, before it becomes woody. The taste is usually said to resemble young turnip, though it is neither so peppery nor so sharp and to my palate comes closest to the stalks of tender young cauliflower, a close relation. It is important to note that this flavour is only fully released when the *kohlrabi* is as tender as soft fruit, so there is no merit in undercooking it, and even less in following some Central European recipes for a raw grated salad.

Kohlrabi sauce for pasta

500 g (1 lb) kohlrabi	1 heaped tablespoon flour
6 tablespoons butter	2 tablespoons fresh fennel
120 g (4 oz) onion	1 teaspoon dried thyme
1 tablespoon each parsley	salt, white pepper
and dill	sour cream (optional)

After removing any woody parts from the kohlrabi slice them, cut the slices in quarters and brown them lightly in butter. Reserve while you brown the onion, then add the herbs, the flour and about 600 ml (1 pint) of water to the pan. The fresh fennel is particularly essential to this recipe, so don't be tempted to replace it when it is not to hand. Return the kohlrabi and cook slowly, covered, until they are very tender. Check seasoning, reduce the sauce if necessary, and add some sour cream or a nob of butter just before serving, if liked. Garnish with fresh fennel and eat with spaghetti, tagliatelle or noodles.

Kohlrabi are also stuffed with veal or chicken and baked with sour cream. In Hungary on a special occasion they might accompany the main meat course.

Corn

With the amount of maize grown in the Balkans, baked corn on the cob is widely eaten, though rarely remarked upon. In Hungary it used to be sold by gypsy women from baskets, freshly boiled. As a change from butter, try serving it Hungarian home-fashion, boiled or grilled with sour cream, as an accompaniment to chicken.

Mushrooms

From the noisy breakfast they had gone out to the solemn ceremony of mushroom-gathering ... Of mushrooms there were plenty: the lads gathered the fair-cheeked fox-mushrooms, so famous in the Lithuanian songs as the emblem of maidenhood, for the worms do not eat them, and, marvellous to say, no insect alights on them; the young ladies hunted for the slender pine-lover, which the song calls the colonel of the mushrooms. All were eager for the orange-agaric; this, though of more modest stature and less famous in song, is still the most delicious, whether fresh or salted, whether in autumn or in winter. But the Seneschal gathered the toadstool flybane.

The remainder of the mushroom family are despised because they are injurous or of poor flavour, but they are not useless; they give food to beasts and shelter to insects, and are an ornament to the groves. On the green cloth of the meadows they rise up like lines of table dishes: here the leaf-mushrooms with their rounded borders, silver, yellow and red, like glasses filled with various sorts of wine; the kozlak, like the bungling bottom of an upturned cup; the funnels, like slender champagne glasses; the round, white, broad, flat whities, like china coffee cups filled with milk; and the round puff-ball, filled with a blackish dust, like a pepper shaker. The names of the others are known only in the language of hares or wolves; by men they have not been christened, but they are innumerable.

Adam Mickiewicz, *Pan Tadeusz*

A mushroom gatherer (photo: Hulton Picture Library)

The supreme mushroom is the *boletus edulis*, closely followed by the chanterelle and the morel. These are found and prized growing wild in every country along the Danube, from south Germany to Bulgaria, as well as further north in Poland and Bohemia. Olga Novac-Markovic includes in her collection of recipes from her years as chef to President Tito two exquisite soups, one with fresh boletus, one with fresh chanterelles (see p. 111). She also notes the truffle particular to Istria, called the tartuffe, which is served with pasta or eggs or preserved in brine.

The champignons that came into Poland with French cooking in the eighteenth century do not have the same glamour or exquisite taste as these kings and queens of fungal life. Fred Macnicol, keen to preserve traditional standards, claims that they would be shunned in any discerning country and that anyway he has scarcely ever seen an anonymous cultured mushroom in Hungary.

The reality for most of us and for many people nowadays in Central Europe, however, is champignons or nothing. These forced creations do not invoke the same romance as the mushrooms picked in the Polish and Bohemian woods, in Alpine Slovenia or on the Buda Hills, but the taste is not negligible.

Fresh mushrooms in sour cream

This is a general recipe that might be found anywhere in Central Europe.

500 g (1 lb) mushrooms
1 bunch spring onions, sliced
2 tablespoons butter
1 tablespoon flour
1 small carton (5 fl. oz) sour cream

1 tablespoon lemon juice
2 tablespoons fresh dill or 1 tablespoon dried
salt, white pepper

Sauté the mushrooms and spring onions in butter, add the flour and cook for a few minutes before gradually stirring in the cream. Season with lemon juice, dill, salt and white pepper. Serve warm on small rounds of toast.

A variation on this recipe, omitting the butter, lemon juice and dill, and using instead an ordinary onion and paprika and bacon fat, produces a Hungarian mushroom *paprikas*.

Old Polish mushroom cutlets

Mushrooms with sour cream were eaten in Poland after the end of the Lent or Christmas fast. During Lent, when cream was proscribed, plainer dishes were served, made of dried mushrooms, such as these mushroom cutlets.

Clean and slice a pound of mushrooms and cook them in a little water till tender. Drain, reserving the cooking liquid for soup, and either chop the mushrooms very finely or put them through a mincer, together with 8 oz white bread that has been previously soaked in milk and squeezed dry. Add a finely chopped onion that has been fried in butter, 2 eggs and a little pepper. Knead by hand and form into small flat cutlets. Dip in flour, egg and breadcrumbs, or simply flour, and fry in butter or oil.

Serve with a potato sauce: Lightly brown an onion in 3 tablespoons butter, stir in 2 tablespoons flour, then slowly add 600 ml (1 pint) of light vegetable stock, a few grains of allspice and a bay leaf. Simmer for 10 minutes, strain through a sieve, return to the pan and add 6 oz finely diced raw potato. Cook until tender, season with the juice of $\frac{1}{2}$ lemon, salt to taste and $\frac{1}{2}$ teaspoon sugar if liked. Just before serving some chopped parsley can be added to the sauce.

Most British palates will find this dish plain but surprisingly exotic for a concoction of familiar ingredients. The mushroom cutlets are naturally sweet and the overall effect sweet-sour.

The dried *boletus* is so widely used in Polish cooking as to have become an emblem of its unique character. The presence of dried mushrooms in the national soups: *grochowka*, *kapusniak* and *barszcz* is indispensable to authenticity.

Mushrooms with pearl barley

This Polish country recipe is also plain, but good for adding interest to a dish of cooked barley, perhaps with roast chicken, or lamb, or a rich bake of tomato, cheese and vegetables. Boil an ounce of dried mushrooms or half a pound of fresh, chop finely, reserving the liquid. Cook 12 oz barley in salted water with an onion, crushed garlic, some lard or oil or butter, and marjoram. Drain, mix with the mushrooms, turn into a greased dish, sprinkle the top with oil or lard or butter, add the mushroom stock and bake slowly for 30 minutes. For vegetarians, interest can be added to this Christmas recipe by using a well-flavoured olive oil and plenty of garlic and marjoram.

Grilled mushrooms

Tastes closer to home are to be found in Yugoslavia, where champignon caps are grilled inverted, with their cavities filled with garlic, oil, parsley and breadcrumbs.

In Bulgaria they are sometimes cooked on a skewer, basted with oil and lemon juice, basil and black pepper. While grilling mushrooms this way, save the juices. Warm some brandy just before serving, ignite it and pour it over the mushrooms on a serving dish containing the juices beneath. Good white bread is the only accompaniment.

Mushrooms with olives

An astonishingly good combination from Bulgaria, and something different, despite the familiar sounding ingredients.

500 g (1 lb) mushrooms, sliced
2 cloves garlic, crushed
¼ cup olive oil
120 g (4 oz) stoned and

sliced black olives
2 tablespoons tomato paste made up to ½ cup purée with water
2 tablespoons white wine

½ teaspoon sugar	2 tablespoons spring onions,
juice of 1 lemon	chopped, including green
3 tablespoons parsley,	part
chopped	

Clean and slice the mushrooms, and cook with the garlic in the oil for 2–3 minutes. Add the olives, tomato purée and wine, heat through for a few minutes, then add the remaining ingredients and simmer another couple of minutes. Serve with crusty white bread.

Beans and other pulses
🐍

Haricot beans with apples and lemon

This is an unusual German recipe.

500 g (1 lb) haricot beans
1 kg (2 lb) cooking apples
50 g (2 oz) butter
1 lemon
salt, black pepper

Soak and cook the beans till tender. Peel and core the apples, cook them till just tender in a little water and half the butter. Combine the apples and beans, flavour with lemon juice, season and pour over the remaining butter, melted and browned. Fried bacon and fried onion may also be used to garnish this dish. Heaven and earth, from the Rhineland, is the name of a similar dish made with potato and apple.

Cholent

Dried beans, barley and meat cooked together very slowly become soft and succulent. This is a Jewish Sabbath dish, very popular in Central Europe, made mainly of beans, but with the meat when it could be afforded. Since the Sabbath forbids cooking, the *cholent* was made on the Friday and taken to the local baker's oven to cook for 24 hours. The fire was banked during the Sabbath and the pots stewed very slowly. Its hallmark, long, slow cooking, has given rise to various theories about the name of the dish. The idea was adopted by Transylvanian Christians and passed into the Hungarian repertoire under the name *solet*. The Transylvanian Sabbatarians, fundamentalist followers of Moses and a very ancient Jewish sect, made *solet* with goose meat, vegetables and oil. A non-kosher version with pork developed as well. Both of these meats and George Lang's addition of smoked beef and extra goose fat make *solet* strongly reminiscent of a French provincial *cassoulet*. According to Lang, the dish lost its beans and acquired more barley as it moved towards Vienna. This is a Jewish recipe with all its components intact.

2 cups dried white beans (navy, lima, pinto, haricot)	3 tablespoons oil or fat
	2 teapoons salt
	$\frac{1}{4}$ teaspoon pepper
stewing beef, or lamb, or smoked goose, up to $1\frac{1}{2}$ kg (3 lb)	$\frac{1}{4}$ teaspoon ginger
	1 cup pot barley
3 onions, chopped	2 tablespoons flour
	2 teaspoons paprika

Soak the beans overnight. Brown the meat and onions in the fat, sprinkle with seasoning and spice, add the beans and barley and sprinkle with flour and paprika. Stirring, add boiling water to 2 cm (1 inch) above the mixture. Cover tightly and bake as slowly as possible, up to 24 hours in a slow oven or slo-cooker. This quantity serves 8–10 and remainders can be frozen and will improve when reheated.

Bean purée

Considered 'a real man's dish' in Romania, these beans are good served with fresh white bread, garlic bread or *mamaliga*. Soak white beans, cook them till tender, then purée with some of their cooking liquid. Separately fry some bacon, a coarsely chopped onion, some parsley, spring onion and paprika. Pour the purée onto a heated dish, garnish with pieces of sausage and, just before serving, sprinkle over the mixture from the pan. In Romania some sauerkraut or sour pickles would also be considered desirable with these beans and *mamaliga*. The name for this dish is *iahnia*, meaning a purée – of potatoes or beans – garnished with onion.

Haricot beans, which grow in the shade of the maize, like melon, are a Romanian national dish, which the present-day food industry salutes with instant bean powder.

In Yugoslavia *matevz* is a mixture of equal parts of white bean and potato purée, with a sprinkling of fried onion, garlic, parsley and bacon. It is also served with sauerkraut and smoked meat or sausage.

Red bean or brown lentil salad

250 g (8 oz) red beans or brown lentils
1–2 tablespoons sugar
salt
6 tablespoons oil
2 tablespoons vinegar
1 small onion

Soak the beans or lentils and cook till tender in plenty of water. Drain, sprinkle with sugar, salt, oil and vinegar. Fry the onion, add this mixture and cook for 5 minutes, stirring. Cool before serving.

Tinned kidney beans may also be treated this way. Cook for 3 minutes. Usually there will be no need to add sugar, for the beans are already sweetened.

Potatoes
🎜

In Poland, Bohemia and north-eastern Germany the peasant table quickly came to depend on the potatoes that were introduced in the seventeenth century. Günter Grass, whose memories of his childhood in Kashubia, around Danzig, are swathed in the aroma of food, begins *The Tin Drum* in the potato fields. But potatoes were not immediately popular and took more than a hundred years to be wholly accepted. Goethe's grandmother, Anna Margarethe Justina Lindheimerin, included not a single recipe for potatoes in her collection of recipes, which reflected the enduring south German preference for dumplings and noodles. Frederick the Great, anxious to alleviate threatened famine, made them seem more desirable by having some grown behind a high fence. Thinking they were valuable, the story goes, the people stole them and made them their own. Once potatoes caught on, though, they were relished. On the Polish peasant table would appear huge dishes of plain boiled potatoes, garnished with bacon or bacon fat, and eaten with a thick warming soup like *barszcz*, or with herrings, or with sour milk. Any cooked leftover potato would then go in place of flour to make dumplings, pancakes, bread and cakes.

Potato casserole

In Bulgaria, with an abundance of wheat flour to ensure every-day needs, the potato regularly received deluxe treatment as a vegetable.

500 g (1 lb) potatoes, sliced	2 tablespoons chopped dill
oil for frying	or parsley
1 large onion, chopped	2–3 tablespoons fine dry
1 cup fresh tomato sauce	breadcrumbs
1 teaspoon dried oregano	3–4 tablespoons grated
salt, pepper	parmesan cheese

Fry the potatoes on both sides for a minute and drain them. Sauté the onion, add the tomato sauce, seasoning and herbs and simmer for a few minutes. Fill a buttered baking dish with alternate layers of potato and sauce and sprinkle the top with breadcrumbs and cheese. Bake for about 30 minutes in a medium oven or until the potatoes are very soft. It would be usual to serve a dish like this, which the Bulgarians call a *musaka*, with yoghurt. White wine can be mixed with tomato paste as a variation tomato sauce.

Krumpli with paprika

The potato's fate in Hungary was also rich. Fred Macnicol describes a dish of potatoes fried in bacon fat with paprika as so pleasingly earthy that it cannot fail to ignite the Hungarian soul.

1 large onion	750 g (1½ lb) potatoes
90 g (3 oz) bacon fat	½ teaspoon caraway seeds
1–2 tablespoons paprika	1 teaspoon salt
½ teaspoon chilli powder, or as desired	200 g (7 oz) smoked sausage

Soften the onion in the fat, mix in the paprika and chilli, stirring, and taking care they do not burn. Add the peeled, sliced potatoes, making sure they are well coated with the fat and powders, add the caraway seeds and salt and water to cover. Simmer covered 20–25 minutes or until soft. Add more water in cooking as necessary, though only a little should remain when the potatoes are tender. Add the sliced sausage, heat through and serve with chunks of bread.

Macnicol also passes on an excellent tip from Edith Rasko, by which sliced and parboiled potatoes are finished in a white sauce made with water, flour, fat and sage, to which an optional splash of vinegar may be added as well as plenty of sour cream before serving.

Rice dishes

Rice as a popular food crop has moved north over the past two centuries. In Hungary, Yugoslavia, Romania and Bulgaria, where it was already well established before World War Two, particularly in the Danube Delta, cultivation has been greatly expanded. Its cheapness and easiness to prepare have also led to its growing popularity in Poland and other parts of Central Europe where it has no historical background. Mainly it takes the place of local grains such as barley and buckwheat as an accompaniment to meat, an ingredient in stuffings, and an alternative to flour or pasta or buckwheat or breadcrumbs in sweet puddings. None of these uses quite does justice to the passion for rice the Turks brought with them when they swept into the Balkans and Central Europe. The best dishes are in the Ottoman style: milk puddings and pilaf, though Mrs Stelea – who on a brief visit to London had a flat overlooking the statue of Eros in Piccadilly and kindly cooked for me there – swears by a rice salad made with chopped olives, fresh dill and quartered tomatoes, dressed with oil and lemon juice.

Rice with olives

The proportions used for this Bulgarian recipe are plain and rich. Braise an onion in half a cup of oil, add one cup of rice, and stir for a minute or two, until the rice is well covered with oil. Then add three and half cups of water. After 8–10 minutes add a half to three-quarters of a cup of pitted olives, which have been soaking in warm water for a couple of hours. Finish cooking and allow to cool. Serve cold with freshly ground black pepper.

Rice with cabbage

The Bulgarians call this a *musaka* because it is arranged in layers. Shred a medium cabbage, bring it to the boil in salted water and drain. Braise half an onion and two chopped carrots in 5–6 tablespoons oil, add half a cup of rice, salt and pepper and two cups of water and cook as for pilaf (see p. 308). Mix the cooked rice with a cup of grated or crumbled feta (or Cheshire) cheese and plenty of finely chopped fresh parsley. Put half the cabbage in a greased baking dish, followed by the rice, then the rest of the cabbage. Pour over three to four tablespoons of oil and three eggs beaten with two cups of sour milk, buttermilk or yoghurt. Bake for 30 minutes in a moderate to hot oven.

Rice with spinach

Another Bulgarian *musaka*. Shred 1 kg (2 lb) spinach and cook in its own moisture with 3–4 tablespoons oil. When soft, stir in 1 cup dry breadcrumbs, remove from heat and add 2 eggs and 100 g ($3\frac{1}{2}$ oz) grated yellow cheese. (Parmesan or pecorino are closest to the Bulgarian kashkaval.) Meanwhile, add $\frac{1}{2}$ cup rice to $1\frac{1}{2}$ cups boiling water, together with 1 chopped onion, 1 tablespoon oil and salt to taste and cook covered till the liquid is absorbed. Arrange half the spinach in a buttered baking dish, then the rice, then the rest of the spinach. Pour over 2–3 tablespoons hot oil and 3 eggs beaten with a cup of sour milk, buttermilk or yoghurt. Bake in a hot oven and serve with a green salad.

Rice with fresh broad beans

Grate a large onion and in a pan soften it in half a cup of oil and a little water. Add plenty of fresh black pepper, a tablespoon of tomato purée and 2–$2\frac{1}{2}$ cups boiling water. Bring to the boil and add 500 g (1 lb) shelled new broad beans. Bring to the boil again and add a coffee cup of rice. Cover and simmer on a low heat. Turn off heat when nearly cooked, sprinkle with fresh dill and parsley, replace lid and leave to stand for 5 minutes before serving. The Bulgarians call this mixture a *yakhnya*, their general word for stew.

Pilaf

Like *moussaka*, the word *pilaf* or *pilau* has narrowed its meaning in English to suggest a particular dish rather than a way of cooking. In the Balkans plain rice with raisins or olives or mushrooms is just as much a *pilaf* as one with chicken. The only essential is that the rice should begin cooking in butter or oil, and then gradually absorb the liquid and flavours added to it.

Pilaf with raisins

An Albanian national dish. Heat the butter in a deep, heavy-bottomed pan, cook the rice till transparent, stirring, add stock slowly, cook for 10 minutes, then add the raisins, cover and lower heat or turn off altogether. The pilaf is ready when all the liquid has been absorbed and the rice grains are soft but not mushy. This will take about 10 minutes more. Don't lift the lid before this. To serve, mix together a little sugar and cinnamon and stir in. Serve with boiled chicken or alone with butter. For 120 g (4 oz) rice use 3–4 tablespoons butter, 375 ml ($\frac{2}{3}$ pint) chicken stock, 60 g (2–3 oz) raisins; 1 tablespoon sugar or to taste, with $\frac{1}{4}$ teaspoon cinnamon.

PASTA, PUDDINGS, KASHAS AND STRUDELS

%%%%

Let no one talk of times being hard, so long as he has wild marjoram cooked with bran.

Wladislaw Reymont, *The Peasants*

What the Austrians call *Mehlspeisen*, and which are eaten throughout their old empire, are those savoury or sweet dishes of dumplings, yeast pies, noodles, pancakes and other mixtures of grain with milk, sugar, cream and curds, which constitute more than a pudding and less than a meal. These dishes are deep tureens of nursery memories. As they literally translate, 'foods made with flour' can be sweet, semi-sweet or savoury, with more or less sugar and/or salt, depending on availability, or nowadays on taste. New dishes have evolved in every direction from the basic conjunction of coarse flour/meal and water.

In Hungary, Romania and parts of Yugoslavia it used to be traditional to use cornmeal rather than wheat flour to make dumplings, sponges and baked sweet or savoury puddings. Elsewhere buckwheat was popular. It made pancakes in Slovenia, Moldavia and Poland, and bread and pasta in Slovenia. When using wheat flour, Central European and Balkan cooks will often mix in a good proportion of wheat semolina for baking, dumplings and noodles, to get a stronger dough and taste.

The various doughs and pastes combine with vegetables or fruit or soft cheese, cream, butter, bacon, nuts, jam, poppy seed and honey. The *Mehlspeisen* are mostly very economical and generally suitable for vegetarians, having evolved as standbys for meatless Fridays and Lent. Leftovers, mainly cooked potato and stale bread, are often used.

In Central Europe flour and eggs are made into various forms of pasta, mainly under centuries-old Italian influence. Via Russia and Transylvania there is also the distant influence of the Orient to ponder. Characteristic of Hungary and Poland, as a result of early Italian presence at their royal courts, and predominant in those parts of Yugoslavia close to or occupied by Italy, are flat noodles. In Polish they have the Italian-sounding name *lazanki*, in Czech, *fleky*. They take their place in Central Europe alongside other home-made pasta, such as Hungarian egg barley, and are commonly also made into sweet dishes. Central Europe designates pasta as an accompaniment to meat dishes, but often makes it the substance of everyday meatless cooking, combined with cheese, eggs or vegetables. The Czechs have a great variety of these economical *nakupy*, some of them shared with the Poles and Hungarians. The Germans eat flat noodles called *Spätzle*. These are always savoury and usually served with meat, as an alternative to potatoes.

Home-made egg barley

This Hungarian *tarhonya* became popular in Vienna as an imported dish. The Polish *zacierki*, and the *tarana* popular in Kosovo and Bosnia, south Yugoslavia, are very similar.

325 g (11 oz) flour
2 eggs
1 teaspoon salt

Knead a stiff dough from all the ingredients mixed together with 4 tablespoons water and either grate it or break off into tiny pieces rubbed between the fingers to form the 'barley'. Leave these to dry spread out on a floured tea-towel and when perfectly dry store in an airtight jar or tin, to be served boiled with meat dishes or salad, or in soup. Egg barley is also very good in the following fashion: brown it in a little butter, then add a good tablespoon of tomato purée mixed with boiling water or stock and a handful of celery leaves. Simmer covered for 15 minutes or bake in a medium oven until *al dente* or tender, according to taste.

Mlinci is another kind of home-made pasta from Yugoslavia, using only half the eggs required for *tarana*. The flour, water and egg dough is rolled out and cut into flat pieces, which are then dried in a warm oven, traditionally after the bread has been removed and the heat switched off. Baking should leave the pasta pieces nicely browned on both sides. They are then broken into smaller fragments, 2–3 cm (about 1 inch) wide, soaked in boiling water for 10 minutes and drained. Toss the *mlinci* with cubed fried bacon and bacon fat (the *zaseka* used to preserve sausages, see p. 239, is traditional) and serve it with salad, or use it, tossed in the pan juices, to accompany roast meat. Vegetarian/Lenten preparations of *mlinci* are prepared with sour cream and cottage cheese, or in Slovenia with poppy seeds and honey.

Noodles with poppy seeds

Tell Yuzka to pound some more poppy seed. There is yet much work and the day is far spent.

Wladislaw Reymont

On Christmas Eve in Poland it is traditional at the meatless festive meal to serve *lazanki* with poppy seeds and butter. The seeds should be scalded first with boiling water, allowed to stand, then lightly crushed, well-drained and crushed again before mixing with butter. Dress the pasta in a warm bowl or on a warm plate, adding sugar or honey to taste, and make piping hot by heating the bowl over boiling water before serving.

The poppy-seed sweet dressing is common throughout Central Europe. Sometimes almonds are added.

A Hungarian pasta 'soup'

This is an ancient '*Lebbencs* soup' recipe from the Great Hungarian Plain, which I have restyled as a pasta dish.

500 g (1 lb) potatoes, peeled
  if liked, and diced
1¼ litres (2 pints) stock or
  water
4 rashers smoked bacon,
  diced

1 small onion, chopped
1 green pepper, thinly sliced
1 tablespoon paprika
salt
1 medium tomato, chopped
200 g (7 oz) fresh pasta

Cook the potatoes in the stock or water for about 10 minutes. Meanwhile fry the bacon gently, add the onion, and when soft the green pepper, potatoes and their liquid, the paprika, a little salt and tomato. Bring to the boil, add the pasta, cook until tender, adjust seasoning and serve.

Hungarian noodles with bacon and soft cheese

This is a light version of pasta *carbonara*. For every 250 g (8 oz) pasta uncooked weight take 180 g (6 oz) cottage or curd cheese, two rashers of bacon and a small carton (5 fl oz) of sour cream. Toss the cooked pasta in bacon fat or olive oil, mix with half the cheese, pile into a serving dish and put the rest of the cheese on top. Fry the diced bacon crisp, pour over the pasta, followed by the sour cream and heat through in a warm oven before serving. For a vegetarian version, replace the bacon with onion or with diced aubergine previously stewed in olive oil.

Pasta with sauerkraut or cabbage

In Czech cooking a traditional combination is pasta with braised sauerkraut or fresh cabbage and cream. The sauerkraut should be squeezed dry and braised in a little fat with an onion for about 20 minutes before being added to the cooked pasta and tossed. It is not the most inviting combination compared with the Western-style dishes of cooked noodles, eggs, cream and grated cheese which have found a place in Czech cooking.

Czech noodles with apples

A typically ambiguous semi-sweet pasta dish.

350 g (12 oz) noodles	120 g (4 oz) cottage cheese
salt	4 tablespoons thick cream
750 g (1½ lb) apples	2 eggs
3 tablespoons butter	a pinch of mustard/
sugar	cinnamon

Cook the noodles in salted water and drain. Peel and slice the apples, sprinkle with salt and melted butter and sugar to taste. Cream the cheese, cream and eggs. Add all the ingredients together, mix well and bake in a well-greased soufflé dish in a medium oven for about 40 minutes. Serve hot or cold.

Pierogi

Poland is well-known for its savoury pasta pockets, *pierogi* and *pierozki*. The recipe for these on p. 133 can be adapted to any filling, sweet or savoury. A famous old dish is Lithuanian *kolduny*, which are *pierogi* filled with meat. Savoury fillings include cabbage, sauerkraut and mushrooms and curd cheese, as well as meat, and the *pierogi* may be served with melted butter or cream or bacon fat and a garnish of fresh herbs, sugar or bacon crackling, as appropriate. Little savoury *pierozki* are often eaten with soup, though they may also be served as a dish or course in their own right. A more unusual dough is made with buckwheat, which has a smoky, almost bacony flavour of its own when combined with savoury foods.

Polish buckwheat pierogi with cheese

180 g (6 oz) buckwheat
   flour
250 g (8 oz) white flour
pinch of salt
1–2 tablespoons butter

For the filling:
120 g (4 oz) curd cheese
1 small egg yolk
salt
2 tablespoons sour cream

Make the filling by creaming the ingredients together. Pour $\frac{1}{4}$ cup boiling water over the buckwheat flour, add the white flour and salt and knead into a smooth dough. Roll out $\frac{1}{2}$ cm ($\frac{1}{4}$ inch) thick, cut out rounds 6 cm (2–3 inch) in diameter, fill, dot with butter and seal. Cook by dropping into boiling water. Serve well drained on a warm plate with more melted butter. Reheat the *pierozki* on the plate over water to offer them piping hot, with sour cream.

Variations In parts of Yugoslavia close to Hungary, where millet is eaten, ravioli made with white and buckwheat flour is filled with a mixture of boiled millet and curd cheese.

From another part of Yugoslavia comes an interesting, very heavy Adriatic ravioli or *zlikrofi*. The filling is mashed potato mixed with chopped fried bacon, fried onion, marjoram and chives.

Czech ravioli are sometimes called by their Austrian name, *Tascherln*, meaning little pockets, and sometimes by the Czech version of the word, *tasky*. The dough may be made with all white flour, water and egg, or a mixture of flour and boiled potato. The classic sweet filling is 'plum cheese' or *povidlo* (see p. 431).

In Slovenia the sweet ravioli is called *strukjli*. A pasta dough made with half buckwheat, half white flour, or two-thirds, one-third, plus a little egg, water and oil, is rolled around a mixture of curd cheese, raw eggs and sugar with vanilla or rum or lemon to flavour it, then boiled in water either whole or in small sections.

A creation close to pasta, but with a disproportionate reputation for excessive heaviness, is dumplings. The Czechs particularly are famous – and from a health point of view infamous – for their consumption of dumplings, large and small, sweet and savoury. These are made of all varieties of padding – fresh breadcrumbs, mashed potato, flour, cornflour, semolina – and raised with eggs, baking powder and/or yeast. Of the different Czech kinds, little dumplings or *knedliky* float in bowls of soup, arm's length dumplings are sliced to accompany the national dish, pork and sauerkraut, and steaming, plum-sized leavened dough balls are served as a dish in their own right, garnished with soft cheese and sugar and fruit.

In general, most dumpling recipes will respond to modern treatment, i.e. don't make the accompaniments to them too rich. I can find little to commend in the arm's length variety, however, neither as prepared by Czech chefs in Prague and London, nor home-made. Even after a long walk on a cold day they are the epitome of bland stodginess. By contrast, the little yeast-leavened dumplings prepared all over Central Europe are a delight. Quite apart from the taste they are amongst the easiest pasta to make at home without special equipment or a lot of time. They can be filled with a stoned plum or fresh berries and served as either sweet or savoury. Another common way is to serve them unfilled, with a layer of curd cheese or crumbly white cheese and butter over the top. If you are making them in Britain, a cheese to try is Wensleydale, which has its own hint of sweetness. A Czech idiosyncrasy for a semi-sweet dish is to sprinkle them with grated gingerbread.

Leavened dumplings with fresh fruit or cheese or other dressing

$\frac{1}{2}$ teaspoon dried yeast
$\frac{1}{4}$ litre ($\frac{1}{3}$ pint) milk

315

250 g (8 oz) flour
250 g (8 oz) fine semolina
½ teaspoon salt
1 egg

Dissolve the yeast in the warm milk and when it foams add to the sifted flour and semolina with the salt and the egg yolk. Beat the egg white stiff and fold it in. The dough may be a little sticky but it should be workable, so only add a little more flour if necessary, before leaving it to rise for 30 minutes. For fruit-filled dumplings, with floured hands tear off pieces of dough and wrap them around stoned soft fruit cut to the size of half a plum. Roll in a ball, sealing the dumpling carefully, place on a floured board and leave to rise 15 minutes if time permits. Cook in plenty of salted boiling water for about 8 minutes. Drain well and serve.

If fruit dumplings are given a savoury treatment don't forget the freshly-ground black pepper, otherwise pass round the castor sugar.

Any leftover dough can be rolled into little balls, eventually to reappear as a dish of *gnocchi* in a sauce or in soup. It can also be frozen or incorporated in your next loaf of bread.

I first ate the plum dumplings, which Czechs and Poles and Romanians praise to the skies, plain, without sugar. The next time I finished them in the oven with butter, black pepper and garlic. The softness and tartness of the fruit, the savoury solidity of the pepper pasta and the smoothness of the cheese together brought about a minor culinary experience. The idea also works – just – with a stuffing of fresh, slightly under-ripe pear. The taste is excellent though the fruit falls apart.

Like ravioli, another savoury topping for fruit or plain dumplings is crumbled crispy bacon. The filled Hungarian dumpling, *gombóc*, sweet or savoury, is very similar.

Bauernklösse

The south Germans call their dumplings *Klösse*, the Austrians call them *Knödeln*. Various *Klösse* are the German housewife's standard economical device.

4–5 rashers bacon, with
  plenty of fat
1 minced onion
2 cups milk
coarse oatmeal
cooked mashed potato

salt, pepper
chopped parsley
$\frac{1}{4}$ teaspoon dried sage
butter
brown gravy or other sauce

Dice and fry the bacon with the onion without allowing either of them to crisp. In the same pan bring the milk to the boil and add oatmeal and cooked potato in equal quantities to make a stiff paste. Season to taste, and add the herbs. With a spoon dipped in hot water cut out egg-shaped pieces and lay them in a buttered dish. Bake in a moderate oven till golden brown. Pour over a thick gravy or tomato sauce and serve with cooked vegetables.

Hungarian galuska

Galuska are the proper accompaniment to gulyás and other stews, but the poor would once have eaten them alone as a main dish.

1 tablespoon melted butter
1 egg
250 g (8 oz) flour
$\frac{1}{2}$ teaspoon salt

Beat the melted butter and egg, add $\frac{1}{2}$ cup water and the sieved flour and salt. Mix quickly and leave to stand in a cool place for 1 hour. When ready to cook, drop small pieces into boiling salted water with floured hands. The pasta is done when it rises to the surface and loses its floury appearance. If necessary, the amount of flour can be doubled and no fat added. For soup it is customary to add an extra egg to these proportions and reduce the amount of water. Use to accompany meat stews or in any dish requiring freshly cooked pasta.

Romanian semolina dumplings

Galuste are eaten in Romania, made in varying ratios of egg to flour. These semolina dumplings are somewhat lighter.

1½ tablespoons butter
2 eggs
salt
semolina

Beat the butter with the eggs, and add salt. Ideally, do not add the semolina until the salted water in which you will cook the dumplings is already simmering. Then add the semolina in a stream, mixing it in lightly with a fork in one direction, to make a soft mixture. Form small dumplings with a spoon dipped in hot water and drop into the pot. Don't boil too long or too hard or the dumplings will become heavy. Serve in soup, with stews or with cheese.

Raw potato dumplings

Throughout Central Europe a special place is reserved for dumplings made from raw grated potato. These are *pyzy à la Warsaw* with meat in Poland, and 'fluffy dumplings' in Bohemia.

750 g (1½ lb) potatoes
1 cup milk
salt
1 egg
180 g (6 oz) each flour and semolina, or as necessary
bacon fat

Grate the peeled potatoes, squeeze out the liquid and pour over boiling milk to stop them discolouring. Add salt to taste, the egg, and the flour and semolina to make a stiff dough. Drop by the large spoonful into boiling water and cook for 5 minutes.

Drain, toss in bacon fat and serve with roast pork and cabbage, or use as required.

A curious kind of dumpling or pasta made with a mixture of potato and flour, and usually dressed with bacon or, if not, then with butter or *kaimak* (see p. 63), is *zganci* from Croatia. A similar dish called *lemieszka* figures in Zofia Czerny's collection of modern Polish recipes, and both resemble the German *Bauernklösse*. Potatoes are peeled and boiled in salted water, and when they are nearly done about half their raw weight of flour is poured into the undrained pan where the still hot potatoes have been mashed in their own liquid. The whole is thoroughly mixed and cooked over heat and then left, covered, to thicken over a tiny heat. From the finished mass half-moons are gouged out with a spoon, dressed with butter, oil or bacon fat, and sprinkled with cheese.

The only countries where one can be sure of encountering no dumplings are Albania and Bulgaria. There the pasta/dumpling cuisine gives way to pastry and belongs firmly to Greece and the Middle Eastern tradition.

The pancake is a humble food that often counts as sophisticated in Central Europe because to fry it thinly demands finesse. It is a marvellous vehicle for sweet and savoury fillings of every description. Hungary and Romania, who had many a foreign chef and wealthy families in their capitals a hundred years ago, promoted to the front rank of their bourgeois and aristocratic cooking a French-style thin pancake made of refined wheat flour and a high proportion of eggs. It was an irresistible invitation to inventive, extravagant chefs like Károly Gundel, who featured triple-filled pancakes (with chestnuts, rum and chocolate) in an elaborate sauce on the dessert menu of his Budapest restaurant. Anisoara Stan, the only writer on Romanian cookery in English, favours as Romanian something close to crêpes Suzette. The simple model occurs with a solid meat or soft cheese or jam or fruit filling, made with instant pancake mix and chemical leavening. The greatest success story occurs in Poland, where small, sweet, curd-cheese pancakes called *nalesniki* are commonly assembled as a snack or a dessert.

A sweet-cheese filling for crêpe-style pancakes

This is one of the recipes Poles all over the world have taken with them into exile.

2 eggs	vanilla
1½ cups curd cheese	lemon rind
4 tablespoons butter	raisins
sugar	sour cream as necessary

Beat the egg whites stiff. Combine all the remaining ingredients except the sour cream and fold into the egg whites. Add a tablespoon or so of sour cream to give the filling a spreading consistency. Use to fill thin crêpes which have been re-browned on one side. Fold the pancakes into quarters and fry on both sides in butter till golden. Sprinkle with sugar and serve hot.

Other sweet pancake fillings include jam, ground almond paste and sweet or sour cream.

The same curd-cheese filling can be use to fill a baked strudel.

A simple walnut or other nut filling for sweet pancakes

½ cup cream
1–2 tablespoons castor sugar
vanilla essence, or vanilla sugar
120 g (4 oz) ground walnuts, or almonds, or mixed nuts
cinnamon and crushed cloves

Whip the cream stiff, add the sugar and vanilla and blend in the nuts. Season to taste. Spread the pancakes while still hot with the filling and roll or fold on a hot serving plate.

Savoury fillings for thin pancakes are the same as for *pierogi*. Fred Macnicol suggests a Hungarian habit of including raw grated cabbage in the pancake batter, which gives a rich taste like English bubble and squeak.

For Hungary's famous savoury *Hortobágy* pancakes filled with minced veal, see p. 207.

It is well that the foregoing fillings are highly flavoured, however, for the crêpe itself is tasteless. The original pancake was better. It was a flat cake cooked in a round pan, the pan itself being called by the Greeks and Romans a *placenta*. George Lang observes that primitive Hungarian pancakes were made by mixing cornmeal and water, and that in Transylvania cornmeal was mixed with wheat flour, egg, milk and honey and baked on a stone greased with bacon fat. One can see in these beginnings the germ of many a sweet/savoury cake and scone, as well as the ultra-thin crêpe.

Today the Romanian *placinta*, Hungarian *palacsinta*, Austrian *Palatschinken*, Czech *palacinky* and Yugoslav *palacinka* are crêpes. 'Pan cakes' of the thick, yeast-leavened kind like the Russian *blini* exist alongside them. The thin, foldable pancake has an affinity with strudel pies and with lasagne. Other close relationships are with the fritter and the doughnut. Stacked crêpes can be used to make a large kind of 'cake'. In Romania and Hungary, and especially in Transylvania, the speciality is many-layered 'pancake pies'. To create a pancake worthy of the name the only essential is that some form of paste should be cookable quickly over an open fire in a flat pan and emerge firm enough to build with.

The heavy pancake, the unfoldable anti-crêpe, the direct descendant of the *placenta*, has made its contrasting way in the world by using lower-gluten flours and meals, raised with yeast. It has come to resemble our muffins and crumpets. Not requiring long cooking, but needing a relatively high heat, it was traditionally baked in the oven after the bread was removed. *Nalesniki*, *rakuszki* or 'Polish *blini*' invite the traditional Russian accompaniments of sour cream and caviare or herring. In the area around Pilzen, western Bohemia, small leavened potato- or wheat-flour pancakes sprinkled with poppy or caraway seeds came with beef and sauce and beer. The Slovenians and the Moldavians of south-east Romania also make thick pancakes with various meals, flours or potato, or with buckwheat flour.

Buckwheat muffins

These are unleavened Polish buckwheat crumpets or griddle cakes, which can be served hot for breakfast with bacon or spread with curd cheese.

1½ cups buckwheat flour
1 cup sour cream
salt
melted butter or bacon fat

Beat the flour and cream together with enough water to make a thick batter, and season with salt. Drop by tablespoons into a frying pan with hot butter or oil, brown on both sides and serve very hot on hot plates. Small *rakuszki* made with 1 tablespoon of batter are most manoeuvrable and convenient.

Livance

1 teaspoon yeast
2 cups milk
350 g (12 oz) flour
1–2 eggs
salt

For the topping:
plum cheese
cottage cheese
yoghurt

Dissolve the yeast in a little milk and when it foams add to the sifted flour, beaten egg, salt and enough milk to make a thick batter. Fry small pancakes on both sides in hot butter and spread with plum cheese while still warm. Add a layer of cottage or curd cheese and a topping of yoghurt or thick sour cream.

Instead of jam, fresh soft fruit in season is delicious, in which case begin the layers with the cheese. The name *livance* for this Czech speciality also includes small sweet pancakes chemically raised. The muffins may also be fried with blueberries *in* the batter.

Baked cornmeal muffins

A Yugoslav recipe.

90 g (3 oz) cornmeal	2 tablespoons butter
180 g (6 oz) wheat flour	100 ml (⅓ pint) milk
salt	120 g (4 oz) yellow cheese,
1 teaspoon baking powder	grated
2 tablespoons lard	oil

Mix the dry ingredients well, add the fats, rub in, then add the milk to form a dough. Roll this out to 2–3 cm (1 inch) thick, cut in round cakes and place on a greased baking tray. Sprinkle the tops with grated cheese and oil and bake in a medium oven for 15 minutes. Serve hot as a snack, with salads, or with roast meat. Wrap the cakes in a cloth to help keep them warm.

The inclusion of cooked grain or potato or fruit in the batter can easily push the pancake towards being a fritter. Those made of grated raw potato, in the style of Jewish *latkes*, and served sweet or savoury, are prized in Poland and Czechoslovakia and considered a speciality of the south-east German region of Thuringia.

Svitek

In a refined mode, the sweet pancake sometimes gets a thickening of flour and is either fried or baked like a sponge, to be served with jam or fruit. This is a Czech recipe for a baked sweet batter.

50 g (2 oz) butter	lemon peel
1 tablespoon sugar	2 cups milk
4 eggs	180 g (6 oz) semolina
pinch of salt	stewed fruit

Cream together butter, sugar and eggs, add salt, lemon peel and, alternately, milk and semolina, to produce a thick batter. Keep a few tablespoons of the milk aside. Grease a baking tin and bake the pudding till golden, then pour over the extra milk and leave to absorb. Serve pulled apart with forks, with stewed fruit.

Omelette with strawberries

Try this dish without the vanilla and sugar first.

Make the omelette mixture with milk, eggs separated, with the whites stiffly beaten, salt and a few tablespoons of melted butter. Throw a good handful of washed strawberries into the mixture and bake in a buttered dish lined with fine breadcrumbs. The omelette may also be made in the ordinary way, in a pan, and the strawberries added just long enough to be warmed before the omelette is folded and slipped on to a warm plate. Add a little powdered sugar and vanilla to the basic mixture if a decidedly sweet dish is preferable.

Curd schmarren

This is a variation on the *Kaiserschmarren*, one of the best-known and most loved nursery dishes of the Austro-Hungarian Empire. The convention with the original, flour-thickened, sweet cream omelette (usually served with jam or vanilla sauce), and also with this curd-sponge variation and with the curd dumplings below, is that they should be pulled apart with two forks and then put back in the oven for a few minutes to firm.

70 g (2½ oz) butter or margarine, plus 2 tablespoons	3 eggs
	80 g (3 oz) sugar

324

vanilla essence
grated lemon peel

2 tablespoons cornflour
250 g (8 oz) curd cheese or
fromage frais

Cream together the 70 g (2½ oz) butter, egg yolks, sugar, vanilla and lemon, stir in the cornflour and cheese, then the stiffly beaten egg whites. Grease a deep cake tin or soufflé dish with the extra butter, pour in the mixture and bake till golden in a preheated medium oven. Loosen the sides and turn out on to a plate. Break into pieces with two forks, turn back into the baking tin, sprinkling with icing sugar if desired, and return to the oven for a few minutes. Serve with fruit sauce or fruit salad or jam.

Schmarren baked in Croatia and served with jam is made of cornmeal with eggs, cream and milk.

Czech nakup with soft white cheese

The Czechs and the Poles bake or boil curd cheese with everything from noodles to leftover bread, rather as we do milk, to make puddings.

80 g (3 oz) butter
sugar to taste and raisins for a sweet dish
4 eggs
350 g (12 oz) dry cottage or curd cheese, or half curd cheese,
half feta
3 tablespoons cornflour or potato flour

Cream the butter, sugar and egg yolks and add the cheese, grated if necessary, the beaten egg whites and the flour. Turn into a well-greased baking dish and bake in a medium oven for about 45 minutes.

The standard *nakup*, intended to be sweet, includes more than 250 g (8 oz) sugar as well as raisins and is served with stewed fruit. Try serving a savoury version. Add just a teaspoon of sugar and serve with buttermilk, or melted butter, or onion sauce.

Curd dumplings

Another nostalgic dish of the Habsburg Empire, these are curd *knedliky* in Czechoslovakia and either *Nockerln* or *Knödeln* in Vienna, depending on whether they are baked or simmered in boiling water. An optimum description of the pleasure they bring comes from Joseph Wechsberg:

My favourite dumplings . . . are of the bantamweight variety. They are made of butter, egg yolks, dry cottage cheese, salted and with a little flour to keep the dough from falling to pieces . . . it is about as light as a soufflé and much better . . . Our dumplings are the size of golf balls and are served on very hot plates. You separate them in small pieces – with a fork – and perform the ritual of sprinkling them with brown butter, cottage cheese and sugar, and the same ingredients again, with the sugar last. You may add more layers . . ad infinitum, until the dumplings have disappeared like a northern landscape under the snow. It's a dish for Lucullus.

Rich proportions are 70 g (2½ oz) butter and 3 eggs to 350 g (12 oz) cheese with two tablespoons each of white flour and semolina. With floured hands quickly drop little balls of the mixture into boiling salted water, remove them when they come to the surface and toss the dumplings in a little melted butter before serving.

Papanas

The Romanian favourite, eaten at home or in a restaurant, comprises the same little balls of curd cheese mixed with semolina, either boiled or fried, then served with butter or sour cream or sugar or jam. They are nicer and more distinctive fried.

3 tablespoons butter	250 g (9 oz) curd cheese
1–2 eggs	½ cup sour cream, plus extra
2 egg yolks	for serving

120 g (4 oz) flour   oil for deep frying
1 teaspoon salt

Cream the butter, add the 4 egg yolks, the cheese and the sour cream, the sifted flour and salt and finally the stiffly beaten egg whites. Work the ingredients well, leave to stand a little, then drop by the tablespoon into boiling oil until golden. They need only a couple of minutes. Drain on greaseproof paper and serve with sour cream and a sprinkling of icing sugar. Sugar and grated lemon or orange peel may also be added to the batter.

Try serving *papanas* to adults with a glass of Tokai or other sweet wine. Like many other *Mehlspeisen*, they don't obviously fit into the British meal pattern, but they would make an unusual late breakfast or, preceded by a plate of hors d'oeuvres in the Italian style, could make a light lunch. If they are served savoury, 4–6 make a light meal with a side salad. The uncooked batter can be frozen.

Curd-cheese pie with apples

Cheesecakes spread to America from Central and Eastern Europe, whence they have returned to us sweet and impure, lying on a base of damp, sugary biscuit crumbs, wobbly with gelatine and laced with jam and whipped cream. The domestic cheesecake in its native surroundings is a simpler and more wholesome semi-sweet preparation, suitable for lunch or a picnic, or preceded by a large mixed salad for a light summer supper involving no cooking.

Pastry: *Filling:*
80 g (3 oz) butter   500 g (1 lb) curd cheese
2 eggs   1 egg
200 g (7 oz) flour   a handful of raisins
2 teaspoons baking powder   vanilla essence, or vanilla
6–8 tablespoons milk   sugar
                                       sugar
                                       3 eating apples

Cream together the butter and egg yolks and add the sifted flour, baking powder and milk. Beat the egg whites stiff and fold in. Spread the dough to fit a well-greased flan tin, then cover with the filling. Cream the cheese, egg yolk, raisins, vanilla, sugar if liked and the egg white, stiffly beaten. Sprinkle the apples, peeled and grated, over the top, and bake for about 45 minutes in a medium oven, or until the filling is firm and the pastry golden. Serve warm or cold.

Cornmeal

Here is a dish of Turkish wheat,
Cooked with plenty of lard, for lean folk to eat.

So sing the cooks and bridesmen bringing in the cornmeal at a Polish village wedding. Cornmeal was not uncommon in various parts of Central Europe before the last war. Czech *livance* could be made this way, and *puliszka*, cornmeal dumplings, were eaten in northern Hungary, in Slovakia and Transylvania. But once wheat flour and semolina became more widely available, the inferior grain began to be pushed aside. In two trips to Romania, one to Hungary and two to Yugoslavia I didn't come across a crumb of cornmeal, which comes a poor second to wheat in gastronomic quality, nourishment value and versatility.

The cornmeal tradition reached its height in Romania half a century ago. Everywhere travellers went they found *mamaliga*. During the Habsburg Empire, after parts of Romania were annexed following the defeat of the Turks, *mamaliga* made its way to Vienna as an exotic new 'Austrian' dish. Across the world it was a Latin passion. The habit came from America in the sixteenth century, when cornmeal instantly pleased the Spanish, Portuguese, Italians and Romanians. Though labour-intensive and susceptible to lack of rain in spring, in south-east Europe it became so widely cultivated as to be the staple food crop. It provided not only corn and cornmeal, but also the shade necessary for growing watermelons and haricot beans. The name was taken from the earlier Romanian staple, millet, *malai*.

A decreasing amount of land was given over to millet, and a tiny proportion fell to oats and rye. The balance now remains with maize and wheat. It is an irony of taste that Romanians rate cornmeal so highly but disparage oatmeal. Oatmeal bread is considered a sign of famine-induced desperation in Romania and oatmeal porridge is unknown.

Northern travellers who would not have minded a bowl of porridge from the Highlands loathed their plates of *mamaliga*.

This yellow maize-flour porridge . . . is the staple food of the peasant, who will eat it hot or cold, in summer or in winter, if he be in good health or in sickness, always he is ready for it – laying down but one condition, that it shall be in abundance. It is also popular among the cultured classes, who are fond of taking it in place of bread, or they will have it as the fundamental item of a dish with eggs and milk and grated cheese and butter playing hide-and-seek within it. *Mamaliga*, you may have built up one of the most handsome nations of the world, but very little of you is enough for me.

Henry Baerlein, *In Old Romania*, 1940

They picked it out as a mark of Romanian poverty, especially in the parched region of Bessarabia, on the Russian border, and inland from the Black Sea. They failed to appreciate the rich traditions behind it. The truth was, *mamaliga* – and popcorn – had a cherished place at the heart of Romanian rural life, for richer for poorer.

In November the nights are the longest. In one homestead or another people gather as soon as candles are lit to do some quiet handwork together. A kettle of boiling maize or corn is simmering . . . At the back of the hearth the big oven sometimes contains some big pumpkin and potatoes baking, to be, with the maize and corn, the refreshment of the assembly, to which are added the sweet-tasting *cucuosei* or *cucurugi*, maize grains baked in a kettle with sand and some salt, by which process they split and spring into beautiful white flowers.

Tereza Stratilesco, *From Carpathian to Pindus*, 1906

In Romanian folk history the tools for making *mamaliga* – the iron kettle, the fire, the wooden stirring stick – are hallowed objects. A handmill would be used to grind the maize into meal, then it would be cooked with water in a *ciaun*, suspended over an open fire in the middle of the peasant's living quarters or in the open air. This would produce a yellow mass so thick that when it cooled it could be sliced like bread, but with a thread. According to Anisoara Stan, the cooking process was long. After three hours the *ciaun* would be removed from the fire, wrapped in towels so it could be taken between the knees, then the *mamaliga* would be stirred smooth for as long as the stirrer had time, before being returned to the fire for a few minutes to dry in the pot. The stick, the *facelet*, was often carved with the name of the family and with artistic patterns. It had many uses in ensuring harmony between spouses and between parents and children besides producing a well-mixed *mamaliga*.

Mamaliga was served at every meal in the peasant's day and almost as widely enjoyed by the middle classes, who ate it at home in place of bread, relishing it with their sour cabbage dishes. At a full meal in the country *mamaliga* might be the first course, preceding a roast chicken or some eggs. For a peasant's breakfast it might be flavoured with raw onion or melon, and it had the great advantage of being enjoyable cold and being easily transportable. A typical meal given to the local poor by the monks at Sinaia on their monastery's saint's day consisted, the year it was observed by Maude Parkinson, of *bors* and *mamaliga* with cheese and onions, and thin local red wine.

Mamaliga perfectly complemented the three or four flavours most prominent in Romanian cuisine: sour cabbage and pickles, bacon, sour cream and cheese. Boiling was just the first stage.

Basic mamaliga

For each cup of cornmeal, fine or coarse, add $2\frac{1}{2}$ cups salted water and cook for 12 minutes, stirring until it thickens and then covering and turning the heat down low. Use a heavy pan to prevent burning. This will make the firmest consistency, suitable for slicing with a thread or making 'bears' (see p. 331). For a pudding consistency, add an extra $\frac{1}{2}$ cup water.

Some possibilities for mamaliga:

Slice it thickly, fry it in butter and eat it with sour cream or creamy yoghurt, or with a fried egg on top.

Serve a small slice hot with mujdei sauce (p. 170) to accompany a meat dish like kebabs, or slip a fried slice into the bowl with fish *ciorba* (p. 127).

Serve it sliced like a loaf then heated through, with *ghiveci* (p. 281). The 'loaf' could be spread with garlic butter before heating, for extra flavour.

Oven-baked mamaliga with cheese topping

Prepare some *mamaliga* to pudding consistency, mashing in a little butter if desired. Pile into a greased flat baking tin to a thickness of about 2 cm (1 inch) and sprinkle liberally with grated cheese. If the *mamaliga* is already warm, put the dish under the grill until the cheese bubbles and begins to brown. If starting from cold, heat through in the oven before finishing under the grill, as necessary. Serve with any sour salad, sour cabbage dish, but above all with the bean casserole on p. 303. The combination will make a most unusual lunch, yet one full of familiar and welcome savoury flavours.

Mamaliga 'bears' or balmus

. . . what we called a bear was a ball made of mamaliga, nice and round and stuffed with cheese, and toasted on the hot embers, just the thing to put heart into your belly when you are hungry. The boys rushed to catch it . . .

Ion Creanga, *Recollections*

The bear looks like a Scotch egg. Into cooked, firm, still warm *mamaliga* mix butter and grated brine cheese or curd cheese to taste and form into large balls. In the centre of each ball make a hole and fill it with ham or mushrooms, or boiled egg, or more cheese. Close up and bake in a greased dish, and serve with sour cream or fry in butter and serve with a sour salad.

Cornmeal soufflé with cheese

The cornmeal is cooked before it is blended with the eggs, cheese and milk. This gives a lighter and more appetizing result than the rich cornmeal breads – *proja, razlevusa* – from Serbia, which add the cornmeal dry.

350 g (12 oz) coarse cornmeal
90 g (3 oz) butter
180 g (6 oz) feta, or well-flavoured Cheddar, or Cheshire
3 eggs
6 tablespoons milk
up to $\frac{1}{2}$ teaspoon salt, depending on the saltiness of the cheese

Cook the cornmeal in $1\frac{3}{4}$ litres ($2\frac{3}{4}$ pints) lightly salted water, until thick. In a greased baking dish arrange the cornmeal in layers, interspersed with the butter and cheese. The last layer should be cornmeal. Beat the eggs with the milk, add the salt and pour over. Sprinkle the top with a little grated cheese and bake for about 1 hour at 375°F (190°C, Gas Mark 5). Serve with a tangy mixed salad. This recipe goes down well with women and children, though the spear side are less impressed by the pervasive mildness.

Kasha is another fading category of *Mehlspeise*. It is one of those cherished, comforting old dishes disappearing from restaurant menus because of the old-fashioned image it conveys. The Slav word *kasha*, used in the appropriate spelling by the Czechs and Bulgarians and Poles, is usually associated in Britain with Russian cooking. It is a purée of cooked grain, though the Czechs also use the term for potato purée. Millet in its semi-liquid, spoonable form used to be the stable *kasha* in Hungary and was also widely eaten in other parts of Central Europe and Romania. Buckwheat similarly prepared provided bulk in

Slovenia and eastern Poland and barley did duty in other parts of Poland and north Germany, along with spelt. But when one comes across these grains cooked nowadays they are invariably served 'dry' with meat and sauce, or they have ceded their place to bread, potatoes and rice.

'A Pole will allow no one to blow on his *kasha*,' goes the saying. Serge Ganjou, longtime manager of Daquise restaurant in Kensington with its famous 'Russian and Polish specialities', surprised me when I asked him about Polish food by quoting the Russian refrain: '*Shchi da kasha pishcha nasha*' ('Our food is *kasha* and cabbage soup'). But Polish peasant food was often very similar to Russian in the east of the country, over territory that from time to time was or has been incorporated into Russia. Traditionally *kasha* is cooked with water or milk, or a mixture of the two, and enriched with lard or, nowadays, butter and/or soft cheese, then flavoured with sugar or salt, herbs or jam. Cornmeal is the exception because it cooks quickly, but most kashas need slow gentle cooking to acquire the right taste and a naturally rich consistency. That is another reason why they can seem so insipid and unappealing today, if they have been cooked in a hurry. Any latter-day *kasha*-lover would do well to invest in a slo-cooker, which will provide just the right amount of heat through the night to yield up the real thing in the morning.

Buckwheat kasha

Cook buckwheat groats in $1\frac{1}{2}$ times its volume of water with a pinch of salt until the liquid is absorbed and the groats are soft. Use as required, to accompany dishes with a rich sauce, or to stuff chicken. In Slovenia cooked dry buckwheat is served garnished with parsley, fried onion and shreds of bacon.

Variations For a sweet *kasha*, pour hot milk sweetened to taste over the buckwheat when it is nearly cooked and finish, or over wholly cooked dry groats. A third *kasha*, an old Polish recipe called *prazucha*, is a mixture of browned buckwheat flour and water, cooked thick and eaten with butter, soft cheese and sour milk.

Barley kasha

According to two Bohemian nineteenth-century recipes, the best way to prepare a sweet *kasha* is to cook the well-washed grits in a double boiler with water and milk and a little salt. Serve with melted butter, sugar and cinnamon. A savoury *kasha* is made with water and caraway seeds and served with melted butter and chopped smoked meat or sausage. The slo-cooker can be used instead of a double boiler in either of these recipes, as can a slow oven. The meat in the savoury recipe might well be replaced by cooked onion or mushrooms or parmesan cheese.

Millet kasha

A sweet *kasha* may be made by cooking the well-washed grains in milk with a good pinch of salt and serving the unctuous result with melted butter and grated *piernik*. Mary Rosicky wrote, by way of advice, to Bohemian settlers in America, lest they should forget their native cuisine: 'If you beat an egg with milk and add one tablespoon of flour and pour this over the mush while boiling, it will add very much to the flavour.'

The Hungarians cook a savoury millet *kasha* with water, salt and garlic. Allow a good three parts, by volume, of water, to millet and skim off any scum on the surface when the *kasha* first boils. Garnish with diced onion fried in bacon fat.

Kasha has never established a widespread presence in Bulgaria or Albania.

Strudel

From Germany in the north through Austria, Hungary and Yugoslavia, to Bulgaria, Turkey, Greece and Lebanon, half the world has a passion for dishes of intricately folded pastry. The strudels of thin pastry enriched with fat are sweet in Central Europe, and sweet or savoury by the time they reach the Balkans. *Rétes* is strudel in Hungary, *placinta* in Romania, *gibanica* in Yugoslavia, *banitsa* in Bulgaria. *Borek* or *burek* are also common names. The dough is *pita*, though we know it more commonly by its Greek name, *filo*.

The strudel paste

Each country has nourished what might seem to an outsider an excessive pride in the art of the strudel, with its dough which must be deftly handled and is paper-thin. The kitchen legends this dough has inspired reflect how pleasing it is to work with and what a transformation can be wrought. Flour and water become so smooth and elastic with long kneading and pulling that they expand into almost transparent sheets that behave and sound like rubber, breaking into stringy holes with fatigue when overstretched. Each layer is spread with oil before being coated with filling and topped with another pastry layer or rolled up. A strudel cook has to work quickly, the layers being so thin they soon dry up in the air. For the sensual experience it is worth first making this pastry at home, though excellent results can be obtained on subsequent occasions by buying ready-made filo or puff pastry. In the case of puff pastry, there is no need to oil each layer, since the fat is already in the pastry.

500 g (1 lb) flour
1 teaspoon salt
120 g (4 oz) butter, or 8 tablespoons oil

Mix the flour, salt, 1 cup of water and 2 tablespoons butter or oil to a smooth dough and knead for at least 10 minutes by hand, less with electronic help. Add more flour or water if necessary. Break off tennis-ball-sized pieces with floured hands and work them on a floured board until they stretch out in thin sheets. Whatever the pulling and tugging tradition, it really is easier to use a rolling pin. Make sure the dough isn't sticking to the surface below or you will have to start again. Use the sheets quickly, greasing them with the rest of the butter or oil, or divide them with wax paper and freeze them. Strudel paste recipes vary a little, including more or less oil or butter and perhaps an egg. Vinegar is sometimes added to Hungarian and Balkan strudel dough, or baking powder, to encourage elasticity.

Apple strudel

This is the German and Austrian favourite, which can be reliably bought from cake shops all over Central Europe and also from delicatessens in this country. Even the most ordinary examples I bought in Poland were moist, full of fruit and not excessively sweet. They came in a tin-foil tray and looked a little like very thin rolled pancakes in thick juice. It is the thinness of the pastry that keeps them from being 'cakes' in the English sense, though some drier, sweeter German recipes push the strudel in the cake direction. Roll out the pastry as thin as you can, therefore, spread it all over with butter, a thin layer of fresh breadcrumbs, peeled, sliced cooking apples and a few raisins, sugar if liked, and roll up. Brush with melted butter and bake 40 minutes in a medium oven. Serve warm or cold.

A cake that is very popular in Romania is one made of alternate layers of dough and a mixture of apples, currants and sugar. It must be made in a very cool place, and one requires a large table for the task. When the dough is ready, it is rolled out very thin, then placed on the table and drawn out over it at every side till it is scarcely thicker than paper. The mixture of apples, currants, raisins, sugar and spice stands ready, and a portion is spread over the paste, which is then doubled over and another layer of the mixture spread upon it. The process is repeated till the paste has assumed the form of a great sausage nearly a yard in length. It is then bent in the shape of a horseshoe, put into the oven and baked. When it is cooked, no better cake could be desired.

This was Maude Parkinson's description of an apple strudel in Bucharest. She had evidently not come across anything similar in her native Ireland, nor was it quite the same in Magdeburg, where she 'finished', nor in Vienna, where she lived prior to going to Romania to teach. But to a Central European, strudels are *Mehlspeisen* rather than cakes. They are distinct from both folded, Oriental-style sweetmeats and yeast-leavened cakes like the Polish *babka*, the Romanian *cozonac*, the German *Stollen* and the Bohemian *Gugelhupf*. It is interesting then to reflect that *baklava*, the sweetest of sweetmeats, still perpetuates the art of folding.

Cherry strudel

Of the fruit strudels, this Balkan and Hungarian favourite is a masterpiece.

1–1½ kg (2–3 lb) cherries
250 g (9 oz) strudel pastry in oiled sheets, or home-rolled
puff pastry
sugar
2 tablespoons fresh breadcrumbs
cinnamon, vanilla essence, lemon peel (optional)
2 teaspoons butter

Wash and stone the cherries and spread them over a third of the oiled pastry. Sprinkle them with sugar and breadcrumbs, and the other flavourings if liked, and dot with butter. Roll up the pastry, place on a well-greased baking tray, brush with oil and bake for 40 minutes in a medium oven.

On a health note, I have successfully used bran in place of breadcrumbs in this and other similar recipes. The amount of sugar required and additional flavouring depends on the quality and ripeness of the cherries.

Variations Other common sweet fillings for strudels in Central Europe are sweetened poppy seeds with sour cream, sweetened curd cheese and sour cream and occasionally (especially from Sopron, in Hungary) a paste of almonds and eggs with red jam. Further south, walnuts are popular. A time-consuming recipe for special occasions, from Prekmurje in Slovenia, combines all four, alternating the layers. To ring interesting changes, poppy seeds can also be combined with pumpkin, and sweetened cottage cheese with raisins and chopped fresh dill. George Lang even notes a potato filling, popular though solid, in Hungary.

Banitsa with milk

Bulgaria can be singled out for its excellent strudels, sometimes rolled, but more often cooked in layers. These can enclose a sweet or savoury filling, but often, in making a *banitsa*, the Bulgarians use the Turkish technique of pouring a rich semi-liquid coating over plain pastry during baking. It's a procedure that again shows the close relationship between layered pastry and the ultra-thin pancake. Also, if it is in Germany that the strudel comes closest to being a cake, it is in Bulgaria, where the preferred texture for any sweet preparation is soft and sticky, that the strudel comes closest to being a sweetmeat. The favourite sweet filling is milk or sour milk, with sugar.

Brush liberally with oil or butter 250 g (9 oz) strudel paste rolled into 5–6 sheets, or use puff pastry. Bake these one on top of each other in a greased tin for 10 minutes, then pour over a scant pint of milk mixed with 6 tablespoons sugar (more to taste) and a beaten egg. Bake for 10–15 minutes more, until the milk has been absorbed.

Wine strudel

This Hungarian recipe is of Oriental inspiration, while using wine in a way characteristic of the wine-growing areas of Central Europe and foreign to the Muslim world. It is guaranteed to mystify guests and keep costs to a minimum, provided you have plenty of leftover white wine. Try serving it for a late breakfast with plenty of strong coffee.

2 tablespoons butter
1 cup fresh breadcrumbs
2 cups white wine
½ cup sugar
250 g (9 oz) strudel pastry in sheets

Melt the butter in a pan, stir in the breadcrumbs, pour over half the wine, remove from the heat and add the sugar. Dot some extra butter over the strudel if liked, spread the wine filling over a third of the surface, roll up and bake on a greased tray in a medium oven for 15 minutes. Pour over the second cup of wine and continue baking until all the liquid is absorbed and the pastry starts to crisp.

Romanian placinta with cheese

The Balkan flaky-pastry pies with soft cheese are wonderful. As a rule of thumb, the weight of soft cheese should equal the weight of pastry. Unless it is very firm, the cheese will need binding with a tablespoon or two of semolina and one or two eggs for each pound, and any mixture can be enriched with butter as desired. If it is dry, add thick cream. A tasty, not too rich filling can be made by combining about 120 g (4 oz) crumbled Cheshire or feta cheese with 350 g (12 oz) curd cheese, flavoured with chopped fresh dill or fennel and bound with an egg. Serve warm or cold. A very light filling, which makes an excellent cold pie and uses more cheese, can also be made. Mix together 500 g (1 lb) curd cheese, 120 g (4 oz) cream cheese, 3 eggs, 2 tablespoons semolina, 2 tablespoons parmesan cheese. Spread either of these fillings over thin layers one on top of the other, brush with egg yolk or butter and bake in a medium oven for about half an hour. Alternatively, bake for 20 minutes in a hot oven and a further 20 with the heat reduced to 325°F (160°C, Gas Mark 3). Serve alone as a snack, in small portions as a starter, or as a light meal with salad. The best partner though is *tarator* sauce, from Yugoslavia (see p. 341).

Borek with minced beef

In Albania *borek* cafés are to be seen in every town, and they are the obvious place to go for a snack. To make the common meat *borek* use equal weights of pastry, minced beef and chopped onion. Fry the beef and onion in oil, season with salt and pepper and use to fill layers of pastry. End with a pastry layer well-coated with oil and bake as for other strudels. Eat with yoghurt or buttermilk, or serve as a snack/light meal with iced lager.

Cheese and spinach banitsa

For 500 g (1 lb) pastry take an equal weight of spinach, wash it, shake it dry and chop it fine. Add curd cheese, or curd cheese and feta or Cheshire mixed, to make a firm filling, plus seasoning and an egg yolk. The amount of salt added should take into account the saltiness of the cheese. With feta use less. Spread between pastry layers and bake as above.

If spinach is not available, an excellent alternative is an Albanian *borek* filling of leeks and cheese:

Use all the leeks, including the green part, up to 750 g (1½ lb) in weight. Clean them well, chop into small sections and soften in butter, under a lid, for about 5 minutes. Be careful they don't burn. Add 300 ml (½ pint) milk, simmer for 5 minutes, then set aside. Mix 250 g (8 oz) curd cheese with 2 beaten eggs, then combine with the leeks and milk. Spread over the pastry layers and bake. Serve with buttermilk or yoghurt or *tarator* sauce (see p. 341).

Macedonian cake

This is a quick recipe for when you have no pastry, no time to make it and no time to roll it. Mix together 150 g (5 oz) crumbled feta or Cheshire, salt, three eggs, a cup each of oil and sour milk or buttermilk or yoghurt, plus a teaspoon of baking powder and 15 tablespoons flour. Knead, place in a well-greased baking tray and bake until golden. Serve with buttermilk or *tarator* sauce (see below).

Small cheese pasties

Make a pastry with 500 g (1 lb) flour and two eggs, salt and enough warm water to bind. Divide it into 16 balls, flatten out each one into a thin circle about 12 cm (4 inches) in diameter and spread with crumbled cheese mixed with two beaten eggs. Curd cheese, feta or Cheshire are all suitable, either alone or mixed. Fold over, press edges together, brush with hot oil and bake till golden. Sprinkle with salt when done and a little hot oil. Cover with a cloth and leave to stand for 10 minutes. Serve as above.

Tarator sauce

For one large cucumber weighing about 600 g (1¼ lb), take 250 g (½ pint) yoghurt or buttermilk or sour cream diluted with mineral water. Peel and slice the cucumber, salt it and leave to drain. Pour the buttermilk or whatever liquid is used into a serving bowl, add the chopped cucumber squeezed dry, some finely chopped green pepper and spring onion and a minced clove of garlic.

Tarragon potica

In Central Europe besides strudel pastry other doughs are rolled or folded. From Slovenia, northern Yugoslavia, comes this rolled and filled leavened dough called *potica*, which makes a good semi-sweet pie.

½ teaspoon yeast	30 g (1 oz) sugar
250 g (8 oz) flour	a few drops vanilla essence
pinch of salt	6 teaspoons rum
2½ tablespoons butter	1 teaspoon lemon peel
2 egg yolks	140 ml (¼ pint) milk

Filling:

40 g (1½ oz) biscuit, plain crispbread or cake crumbs	½ cup sour cream or *fromage frais* (fermented skimmed milk)
50 g (2 oz) butter	2 egg yolks
6-8 good sprigs of tarragon	lemon peel
50 g (2 oz) sugar, or to taste	

Dissolve the yeast in a few tablespoons warm water and when foamy add to the sifted flour and salt. Melt the butter in a bowl over hot water, add the remaining ingredients for the dough and stir well. When just warm add to the flour and yeast and knead to a soft, unsticky dough, adding more flour or liquid as necessary. Leave to rise in a warm place.

Brown the crushed biscuit crumbs in the butter, remove from heat and stir in all other filling ingredients. Very little sugar will be needed, if any, if the crumbs are sweet. Roll out the dough into a rectangle 1 cm (½ inch) thick, spread with the filling and roll up. Place on a greased baking tray and leave to rise for an hour or so. Brush with beaten egg and bake in a medium oven for about 50 minutes, or until golden. Leave in the tray to cool, then turn out on to a plate and if desired sprinkle with icing sugar. The nicest way to eat this cake is just warm, with a dollop of sour cream or *fromage frais*.

Thanks to its many layers the inside of this *potica* will be moist and succulent and, quite without any extra skill on the cook's part, neat enough to photograph. It is also the only instance I have come across in any cuisine of tarragon, the doyenne of French savoury herbs, being used to make a sweet course, though dill in this capacity is common.

Carob filling for potica

Potica can be more decidedly sweet, with about the same range as the strudel. Other fillings include walnut – the nuts are ground and mixed with milk, butter, rum, cinnamon and lemon peel with a few coarsely chopped nuts for texture – and cream with hazelnuts. This is one of the most unusual I have come across.

350 g (12 oz) carob flour
1½ cups milk
100 g (3½ oz) honey
lemon peel

1 tablespoon butter
cinnamon, cloves
100 g (3½ oz) sliced figs
(optional)

Make a paste of the carob flour and milk and bring to the boil, stirring, adding the honey and other ingredients. When the paste has cooled to warm, spread over the *potica* dough, roll up and proceed as above.

Buckwheat struklji

A kind of *pasta asciutta* can also be rolled. The dough for *struklji* belongs with the pastas, but the product here is a boiled strudel.

300 g (11 oz) buckwheat
flour
200 g (7 oz) white flour
salt

For the filling:
2 eggs
50 g (2 oz) butter
25–50 g (1–2 oz) sugar
vanilla essence
lemon peel
few drops of rum
250 g (9 oz) dry cottage or
curd cheese

Make a dough by pouring ½ cup boiling water over the buckwheat flour and mixing with the white flour and salt. Roll out in a rectangle ½ cm (¼ inch) thick. Combine the filling ingredients by creaming the egg yolks, butter and sugar, vanilla, lemon peel and rum, then adding the cheese and beaten egg white. Spread over the dough and roll up. Wrap the *struklji* in foil and cook it in boiling water for 15–20 minutes. Unwrap, slice and sprinkle with sugar or melted butter.

Strukjli is typical of the ambiguity of *Mehlspeisen*. When tarragon and curd cheese are used to fill a boiled strudel the result is sweet if sugar is added, but savoury if served with melted butter.

Omitting all the sugar and the rum from the preparation, this strudel could even be served with parmesan cheese.

A recipe for folded bread dough will be found on p. 373.

BREAD, LARD DOUGH
AND PLAIN CAKES

The wholesomeness of bread from Erfurt to Constanta, from Gdańsk to Tirana, is much to be prized. Or is that almost all bread in the world seems closer to the ideal than British bread? Central Europe is the home of dark, pungent rye and wheat breads in various shades of grey, brown and black, which are almost sweet when newly baked but quickly sour. The Balkans bake robust white loaves more the colour of loofahs than snow. The bread industry seems closer to the peasant tradition and isn't encouraged to produce a softened, bleached, aerated pap. The preference from Germany eastwards is for sour dough and the consumer likes a relatively heavy bread, such as might be made by hand. In this sea of robustness Vienna, which refined its food under French influence, is an unexpected island, having given its name to long crusty white rolls. The taste for white bread is marked there and in Hungary.

The difference between our island bread and white or brown bread on the Continent, however, is not all lack of better judgement. Everywhere in east and south-east Europe, where the winters are very cold, and the summers hot, spring wheat is sown. This has a shorter growing period than the winter wheat grown in England, but produces a stronger flour, higher in gluten and protein. It is this fundamental difference that distinguishes Continental from British bread.

Wheat grows as far as the eye can see across the broad plains of Bulgaria, Hungary, Romania and Yugoslavia. In Bulgaria, where copious harvests have been enjoyed for centuries, bread is both the staple food and a national passion. The town of Stara Zagora near the Valley of the Roses is a famous wheat centre, as is Ruse on the Danube. In Hungary the wheat grows on the

Simelbrot.　Kleyenbrot.　Vngeböfelt brot.　Kyßbrot.　Ofenbrot.　Scherbenbrot.　Steynbrot.

Varieties of bread, from Hans Wegener, Küchenmeisterei, *facsimile
of the book printed in Nuremberg by Peter Wagner in 1490,
Leipzig 1939*

Alföld or Great Plain. This merges in the east with the
Pannonian Plain, the backbone of Yugoslavia. These vast
growing areas are sublime sights in their high season. The finest
month, when the wheat is at its height and the unnatural blues
and reds of the workers' overalls stand out like brilliant flowers
in the desert, is June, just before the harvest. In Romania the
wheat flourishes in the Banat, on the western plain adjacent to
Yugoslavia. It continues across the baked southern plain north of
the Danube and flourishes in Moldavia, where the fertile lands
of the Ukrainian 'bread-basket' extend down to the Black Sea.

As a child I took off my clothes and walked in a bath of wheat,
Up to my lips.
I relished it like a dream and felt the feeling on my shoulders like a
stream.
Even now, as I ripen in age, when I see seeds heaped on threshing
floors,
I strain not to lie down and caress them with my cheek.
What stops me is fear, that I will disturb
The flaming sun gods in their quiet, steady sleep.
Now and forever: praise the seeds of the empyrean.

Lucian Blaga (1895–1961), *The Miraculous Seed*

All devotees know bread is a romantic object. When I spent a
few days in Albania, the first thing I found myself doing in
Shkodra was buying a loaf. As the women deliberated amongst
themselves whether the last half-loaf of the day was fresh
enough to offer a foreigner, a young man in the queue called
out: 'If it's not good enough for her, I'll have it,' which restored

everyone's sense of value. The bread was greyish-golden, spongy and slightly sour, the kind of mixed rye and wheat bread to be found everywhere from Russia to Germany.

Romania when I was there was short of bread. Too much of the produce of the wheat plains was being exported. In the countryside one knocked on doors to find a 'bakery', in other words a family with its own flour. An Arab friend of ours who had acclimatized himself in the villages used to give local children lei and ask them to bring him a loaf. Typically, though there were no shops in sight, they would return with a hard, golden-white bun 45 cm (18 inches) in diameter, then give him the money back. In Bucharest in 1986 there were bread queues morning and evening, each time the bakers opened. I met a learned man in a train going *back* to the country. His briefcase was full of bread he had travelled to town to acquire.

When the first woman novelist of the Bohemian National Revival, Bozena Nemcova, wished to draw attention to the importance of native Czech ways in preference to assumed foreign habits she wrote about bread in *The Grandmother*, a classic account of rural life in the Sudeten mountains:

The first thing of which Grandmother assumed full charge was the baking of bread. She did not like to see the servants handling 'the gift of God' without any reverence or ceremony. They never signed it with the cross, either before or after taking it out of the oven; they handled it as if the loaves were so many bricks. When Grandmother set the sponge she blessed it, and this she repeated each time she handled it until the bread was placed on the table. While it was rising no gaping fellow dared come near it lest he should overlook it and make it fall; and even little Willie, when he came into the kitchen during baking time, never forgot to say: 'May God bless it!'

Whenever Grandmother baked bread, the children had a feast. For each one she baked a little loaf filled with plum or apple sauce; this had never been done before. They, however, had to learn to take care of the crumbs. 'The crumbs belong to the fire,' she used to say as she brushed them up and threw them into the stove. If one of the children dropped a bit of bread, she made him pick it up, saying: 'Don't you know that if one steps upon a crumb the souls in Purgatory weep?' She did not like to see the bread cut unevenly, for she used to say: 'Whoever does not come out even with this bread will not come out even with people.' One day Johnny begged her to

347

cut his slice from the side of the loaf, as he wanted the crust, but she said: 'When one cuts into the side of the loaf, one cuts off God's heels! But whether it be so or not, you must not get into the habit of being dainty about your food.' So Johnny could not indulge his appetite for crust.

For Nemcova the state of bread-making and bread-keeping was a marker of spiritual well-being in the rising Austrian-influenced middle-class household. The Polish poet Cyprian Norwid, writing from exile, used the same idea to praise the quality of life in an idealized Poland to which he could never return:

> For the land where a crumb of bread
> Is raised from the ground with reverence
> For the gifts of heaven . . . I yearn, O Lord.

Years ago the sacredness of bread was a fact of community life, because of being written directly into religious observance, folk wisdom and domestic ceremony. Part of the folk culture of Poland, Bohemia and parts of Romania and Yugoslavia was to offer bread and salt to welcome a guest and to salute a bride as she crossed the threshold. Nor, as the Grandmother taught, was the least crumb wasted, and any which fell on the floor had to be blessed. George Lang writes that as a child if he dropped a slice of bread he had to kiss it before eating it.

The art of nineteenth-century bread though was not the cult of fresh bread we practise today. The Grandmother baked a batch of very large loaves every two or three weeks. By the end of a fortnight the children found it was impossible to cut the bread, let alone pick off a piece in passing. Nearly all peasant breads were made of a mixture of flours, whatever was available. Paul Kovi points out that the poor sharecroppers of Transylvania eked out their dough in the hardest times with ground tree bark, acorns and forest plants. Otherwise fine cornmeal was often used, alone or with wheat, or a mixture of wheat and rye, or wheat and potato. The same variations were found right across the continent. In Bulgaria, where, as in Romania, the round 4 kg (8 lb) loaves in country parts are still as enormous as they were a hundred years ago, the dough used to be made of rye, wheat or cornmeal or a mixture of two.

Wheat, the privilege of certain regions – the Dobrudja Plain, Bessarabia, the Banat, the counties of Taurien and Cherson in Bulgaria – was the best.

Today's East European cookery books have few recipes for loaves of any kind because of the relative high quality of bread in the shops. Yet wherever there is a growing interest in food history, particularly in Poland, Hungary, Germany and Czechoslovakia, old ideas and techniques are being re-examined and there are a few signs of nostalgia.

I am no devotee of the school of thought 'brown is always best'. A true sense of gastronomic priority would reject many of the heavy breads we chase after in the name of health. They are too intrusive to accompany delicately flavoured food and much of the brown bread manufactured in this country is unsuitably acid. Everything depends on the balance of the meal, however, in which respect the complimentary piles of brown and white bread one finds on restaurant tables from Russia to Bohemia and south to Romania are ideal. (It is only a pity these are usually cut hours in advance.)

There is a Romanian saying, however: 'There must be something to go with the bread'; and an ancient Greek word for 'all that goes with bread or grain'. If a modern meal is to be classically bread-centred like this, then only a heavy, whole grain bread will do. The sour doughs accord particularly with 'sour' food like herrings, beetroot, cabbage, dishes dressed with sour cream and all the sour soups. The heavy breads, plain, cut in doorsteps, are also essential to serious wine and beer drinking.

But if richly flavoured protein foods and especially sauces are to play the most prominent role, as they tend to in the non-peasant, richer diet, the bread should be as light and unobtrusive as possible. This is the lesson the French, through the royal courts and the aristocracy, spread all over Eastern Europe as well as the West, so that to this day refined baking, with white flour and with chemical leavening, is still considered indicative of a higher standard of living and culture. The exceptions are Bulgaria, southern Yugoslavia and Albania, which have never been touched by French standards. The bread there, white or brown, is always robust but always good.

A quick guide to making bread at home

꽃

• Unless you love going through the motions and are prepared to knead exhaustively, use a food mixer or processor to do the work.

• Don't worry too much about exact quantities. More flour or liquid can always be added, but be cautious about the amount of salt.

• In my experience, loaves rarely rise in the 'two hours' suggested. Sometimes they haven't moved an inch after four hours. The most satisfactory results come from leaving them overnight.

• Most recipes advocate two rises, one before the bread is shaped and one in the tin. I have never seen the need for this.

• Once dried yeast has dissolved in the water or milk, a matter of a few minutes, you can proceed with the recipe. It's nice to see it 'foam', but not necessary.

• My preference with wheat flour is to use unbleached white flour, adding 2–3 tablespoons each of bran and wheat germ per pound for a wholemeal loaf. The result is lighter bread with proportionally more roughage and an excellent pale brown colour.

• Grease or oil the tins well. There's nothing more disappointing than well-made bread which has to be torn apart before it can be served.

• If a loaf fails to rise, or is baked with too much salt, seeds, etc., recycle it. Break it into rough pieces, pour over boiling water and leave it to cool. Breaking up any lumps which may remain, use this sponge as the liquid basis of two new loaves. Sprinkle over new yeast at room temperature and add flour and any necessary salt or seasoning to make an unsticky, elastic dough. By this method, however, for every one failed loaf you will make at least two new ones because of the extra water involved.

• Freeze any bread you cannot eat fresh and when it is required warm it slightly after defrosting.

Bread baked in cabbage leaves

The Polish food historian Maria Lemnis wrote in the early
1980s: 'The wheat-rye breads of long ago, baked in leaves of
cabbages or horseradish, the so-called peasant breads, are an
exquisite delicacy.'

The cabbage-leaf baking method, whereby the dough is
contained in oiled cabbage leaves, was practised as widely afield
as Transylvania and Romania. It produces a golden brown
crust. The technique can be applied to any firm white (or
brown) dough.

Place a large oiled leaf in the bottom of the baking tin, put
the dough in a ball on top and cover it with more oiled leaves
until it is completely covered. Leave to rise, then bake at the
usual temperature, still covered with the leaves.

Bread baked in *a* sac

A *sac*, pronounced 'satch', is a cast-iron or earthenware baking
sheet or shallow dish with a domed lid, like an iron cloche, the
whole of which is placed in the embers of the fire. This is a very
ancient means of baking bread, traceable as early as the Bronze
Age. Elizabeth David writes in *English Bread and Yeast Cookery*
of her rediscovery of 'under-cover breadbaking', which was still
practised in parts of England early this century and described in
cookery books of the 1930s. The ancient Athenians used a device
just like the *sac*, but made of clay. J. G. Kohl, the greatest
traveller in East Europe in the nineteenth century, found the
common people of Dalmatia baking bread in their chimney-less
huts by this method.

If you want to try, a slo-cooker will double as a *sac*. The only
drawback is that, with this crock not being as hot at the top as
the bottom, the bread forms a very thick bottom crust and
hardly any on top, where it is more like a steamed loaf. The
problem is alleviated by not putting the dough directly into the
pot, but in a tin that will fit inside the pot. Preheat the cooker
on 'high' and bake the bread for 3–4 hours. To have hot bread

for breakfast, begin cooking on 'high' but switch to 'low' before you go to sleep. A hot fresh loaf which it is impossible to overcook will be waiting in the morning.

Potato bread (1)

The most common mixture advocated today for making a good all-purpose loaf at home is wheat or a mixture of wheat and rye flour and cooked potato. The Czechs flavour this bread with fennel or caraway and bake it into golden round loaves. Elsewhere the same loaf is dusted with sesame or poppy seeds, or scored before baking and brushed with melted bacon fat or butter. In Transylvania it may be enriched with eggs, sugar and butter for Easter until it comes to resemble one of the classic yeast-leavened Easter 'cakes' on pp. 365–6. The potato is usually cooked, mashed and mixed into the dough while still warm. This produces a moist loaf that keeps well and is moreish eaten hot with butter, though less tempting cold. The proportions quoted in a contemporary Yugoslav book, two parts flour to one part potato, belong to a wartime economy, according to Elizabeth David, but do not dismiss them for that reason.

$\frac{1}{2}$ teaspoon dried yeast
$\frac{1}{2}$ cup milk and water
500 g (1 lb) potatoes, boiled, peeled and mashed while still warm
1–2 tablespoons fennel seeds
1 tablespoon salt
1 kg (2 lb) white bread flour

Dissolve the yeast in the milk and when it foams add to the warm potatoes, salt, seeds and flour. Knead thoroughly to make a firm, unsticky dough. Divide between 2 greased loaf tins and leave a few hours or overnight in a warm place to rise. Bake about 45 minutes in a medium to hot oven and serve warm. This bread may not show much of a rise till it gets into the oven, but once there it expands dramatically and acquires a lift-off golden crust. Do use fennel. I have not come across these liquorice-flavour seeds in any commercially produced bread, but they are the making of this recipe. They rival caraway as a bread-enhancer, particularly of rye.

Potato bread (2)

A high proportion of potato to white flour may be a sign of need by English standards, but an even higher proportion, combined with a flavouring of cumin or aniseed, according to a contemporary Slovene recipe, produced the best off-white bread I have ever made at home. This loaf is light and spongy, yet full of taste.

1 kg (2 lb) potatoes\
milk or water\
2 teaspoons yeast\
1½ kg (3 lb) flour\
salt\
cumin or aniseed

Make a warm batter with the freshly cooked mashed potatoes and some of their cooking water or hot milk. When just warm sprinkle over the yeast, leave to dissolve, then add the flour, salt and seeds to make an unsticky dough. Knead and leave to rise overnight before baking in tins in a medium to hot oven.

Buckwheat bread

This is another recipe from Slovenia, where buckwheat flour is widely used in traditional bread and cakes. Even the uncooked dough is a revelation: lustrous and silky like fine skin to touch, soothing as a mud pack and speckled like a bird's egg to look at. The result when baked, with a surprisingly light texture and greyish-black colour, is musky. It is the nearest thing imaginable to 'smoked bread'.

$\frac{1}{2}$ teaspoon dried yeast
about 1 cup warm water
500 g (1 lb) white bread flour
180–250 g (6–8 oz) buckwheat flour
1$\frac{1}{2}$ teaspoons salt
1 tablespoon oil

Dissolve the yeast in a few tablespoons of the water, add the flours, salt and oil, then knead to an unsticky dough with the remaining warm water, as needed. Form into loaves, leave to rise, preferably overnight, and bake as usual. I disagree with Waverley Root that buckwheat produces crumbly, tasteless bread. Quite the opposite.

Graham rolls

'Graham flour' and 'Graham meal', invented by Sylvester Graham, an American doctor of the last century, are wholewheat products, containing the whole content of the wheat grain. Zofia Czerny's *Polish Cookbook* uses 'ground wheat' and flour to make these rolls, and I have had excellent results interpreting her instructions to mean a mixture of bulgur wheat and unbleached white flour, with or without a little extra bran. Whole wheat berries could also be used, though they need long soaking and chopping compared with bulgur, which is ready to go.

4$\frac{1}{2}$ cups bulgur wheat
1 teaspoon dried yeast
1 tablespoon sugar
2$\frac{1}{2}$ cups flour plus a few tablespoons bran (optional)
salt

Soak the bulgur wheat in enough water just to cover it, if possible for a few hours. Dissolve the yeast with the sugar and a little more water. Combine the two, add the flour and salt and knead into a smooth, unsticky dough, adding more flour as necessary. Form into small, long rolls. Place them on a greased baking sheet, leaving plenty of space between them. Put the whole in a plastic bag and leave to rise. Brush with water and bake in a hot oven till firm and golden.

White or brown bread with cornmeal

This is a dense, golden, neutral bread from Slovenia that can be served on any occasion. It is best eaten very fresh. But the dough is hard to knead without a machine.

> 250 g ($\frac{1}{2}$ lb) cornmeal
> I teaspoon dried yeast
> 750 g ($1\frac{1}{2}$ lb) unbleached white flour ⎫
> 4 tablespoons bran ⎬ or wholemeal flour
> 4 tablespoons wheat germ ⎭
> I tablespoon oil
> $1\frac{1}{2}$ teaspoons salt

Pour $\frac{1}{2}$ cup boiling water over the cornmeal and mix. Dissolve the yeast in about I cup warm water and add to the flour. When the cornmeal is just warm add to the flour and yeast, together with the oil and salt. Knead to a smooth, elastic dough. Put into tins, leave to rise and cook for approx. 20–25 minutes in a hot oven.

Millet bread

Millet has faded from use both for *kasha* and for bread, but 300 years ago, before the spread and development of wheat, it was a staple grain in Central Europe, Hungary and Romania, and was still widely used in the nineteenth century. In one area, now divided between the Soviet Union and Romania, it grew particularly abundantly, without cultivation, alongside maize and barley. The area was lower Moldavia, where Prince Dmitri Kantemir (1673–1723) made a study of local nature and

355

customs. He was an enlightened man whom history and imperial power-mongering deprived of a military and political career. Sentenced to leisure, and an attractive figure for food historians to rely upon, he sang the praises of the territory around the River Dniester, which had been prized since antiquity for the fertility of its fields. He observed that a very good bread, to be eaten warm with butter, was made out of the millet. Millet *kasha* can replace some of the flour and liquid in any standard white bread recipe, or a little millet flour can be added. Since millet has next to no gluten, the proportion should not exceed 120 g (4 oz) to every 500 g (1 lb) of wheat flour. Kantemir's millet bread was probably made entirely of coarsely ground millet flour and unleavened. It would be good hot but would petrify as it grew cold.

Rye bread

A spongy light rye is one of those breads on sale in most of Eastern Europe. Rye is particularly common in bread in Germany, Poland and Czechoslovakia, where it grows well and can survive the cold. Since rye has little gluten, such loaves are inevitably mixtures of rye and wheat flour. It is often a disappointing loaf to buy in Britain because to keep it light, in line with public taste, the greater part of the flour used must be white. A real Polish rye is unmistakably heavy for its size compared with an English 'brown' bread and I always use that as the test of whether what is proposed is genuine. A home-made loaf will be more genuine, even if brick-like and hard to knead without a machine.

Either of the potato breads above may be made using rye for a third or a half of the flour. The usual flavouring is caraway, which has the additional function of countering the in-digestibility of this grain with a strong taste of its own. Bohemian housewives used to recommend using milk, whey or sour milk instead of water, to make rye easier on the stomach and to improve generally the quality of the dough. The liquid in the basic recipes for potato bread can be adjusted accordingly.

A genuine rye loaf is not a 'background' bread like a French stick, but one designed for the prominence of the hors d'oeuvre or evening cold table, or for eating on its own, East European style, perhaps with yoghurt or a glass of buttermilk.

Black bread

🙰

Black bread is rye bread, usually with some molasses added. A truly black bread is artificially coloured. The molasses which makes these loaves strong-tasting and quite sweet puts them in a category apart. Their deliciousness is beyond question for *aficionados*, but their gastronomic flexibility is limited. They are best with yellow cheese, soft cheese, smoked and other cured fish and salads dressed with sour cream. Discriminating bread-eaters all over Germany, Czechoslovakia, Poland and parts of Yugoslavia and Bulgaria keep the commercial product, which is far less sweet and obtrusive, in demand, but I have yet to find the equivalent in a shop in Britain. Too often the weight test alone suggests commercial black breads are 'debased' in favour of lightness.

German country rye bread

$\frac{1}{2}$ teaspoon dried yeast
2 cups rye flour
$4\frac{1}{2}$ tablespoons cocoa
1 teaspoon salt
4 tablespoons molasses, or
    more to taste

2 tablespoons caraway seeds
$2\frac{1}{2}$ tablespoons butter, or
    vegetable oil
approx. 3 cups white flour
    with 3–4 tablespoons bran

Dissolve the yeast in $1\frac{1}{2}$ cups warm water. Meanwhile, mix the rye flour and cocoa, and when the yeast foams add it to the flour, together with the remaining ingredients to make a firm, unsticky dough after kneading. Leave to rise, if possible overnight. Most recipes for this kind of bread made at home call for larger quantities of molasses than I have suggested, and they tend to be overwhelmingly treacly compared with similar shop-bought breads. The easiest way to handle molasses is to pour it from the jar straight into the mixing bowl, making the quantities approximate.

Grease two bread tins or a large baking sheet, dust with cornmeal and bake the loaves in a medium oven for 35–45 minutes.

Pumpernickel

Pumpernickel, which is an expensive delicatessen item in Britain today, was originally a way of minimizing waste by using the coarsest grains in the granary to make an unleavened bread – in other words it was made of coarse meal, usually rye, rather than flour. It is north German and Dutch in origin, of dubious etymology. The name is enough to bring a smile of otherness to English lips. It was at its most exploitable in the mid-nineteenth century when both *The Times* and Thackeray used it to characterize 'Their Impecunious Transparencies, the German Princelings'. This is the basic recipe for Baltic pumpernickel I included in *The Food and Cooking of Russia*.

100 g (3½ oz) butter	500 g (1 lb) rye flour, or
100 g (3½ oz) molasses sugar	finely milled rye crumbs
1 teaspoon cinnamon	50 g (2 oz) finely chopped
3 eggs	hazelnuts or wheat
pinch of baking powder	berries

Cream together the butter, sugar and cinnamon and add the eggs one at a time. Beat until very smooth and white. Add the baking powder mixed to a paste with a teaspoon of water, the flour and the nuts. Add a little water or milk if the dough is too dry to manage. Roll out to about half a finger's thickness, brush with egg and bake on a greased tray for about 25 minutes in a medium oven. Cut into squares or rounds while still hot, then allow to cool before serving.

Vary the recipe by replacing the nuts or wheat berries with up to 120 g (4 oz) soaked bulgar wheat, squeezing the grains dry before mixing them with the rye flour and other ingredients. The eggs, which would not have formed part of any original economical recipe, can be omitted by substituting a little milk, sour milk or sour cream, as in the related Czech recipe below.

Pumpernickel will stay moist for several days wrapped in foil or plastic film in a sandwich box, preferably in the refrigerator. Any leftovers can be used up in pumpernickel pudding (see p. 393).

Black cake bread

As a way of binding coarse grains and not relying on gluten and yeast to produce a rise, pumpernickel may have served as a model for the following 'brown bread' from Bohemia, *hnedy chleb*, which is so much more like a wonderful, soft-textured, rich malt cake that I have felt free to rename it. It is the richness more than the sweetness that demands it be eaten on its own, for its own sake. Try it for a healthy tea, with contrasting light items in weight and colour, like crustless cucumber sandwiches, fruit salad, curds and nuts.

1 kg (2 lb) coarse cornmeal
2 cups rye flour
8 tablespoons molasses
1 teaspoon baking soda, dissolved in hot water
sour milk
salt

Combine all the ingredients to make a thick batter and beat well. Pour into bread tins and bake slowly for at least an hour, until firm.

Dill bread

This is a German recipe for a home-made delight.

½ teaspoon dried yeast	1 tablespoon minced onion
2½–3 cups white flour	1 tablespoon melted butter
1 cup creamed cottage	1 egg
cheese, or curd cheese, at	1 teaspoon salt
room temperature	2 teaspoons dill seed
2 tablespoons sugar	

Dissolve the yeast in ¼ cup warm water and when it foams add to the flour and all other ingredients. Use more or less flour to make a smooth, unsticky dough after kneading. Leave to rise in a warm place and bake in a medium oven for about 40 minutes or until golden brown. Brush with melted butter and sprinkle with salt while still warm.

Leftovers

Stale bread was made into dumplings and savoury puddings in Germany and Bohemia. The Bulgarians make a pudding with cheese called *popara* (see p. 49). Dark bread was used to make spicy sauces and in Hungary, according to an old technique, the same function was performed for general sauces by white rolls instead of flour.

A piece of old dough would always be retained to make a new loaf. A piece of dark bread would act as the starter for home-made fermented beer, the basis for many soups.

Bohemian cornbread

Out of necessity in some parts of Central Europe and the Balkans, a cornbread is baked and used like wheat bread. A humble *proja* made with cornmeal, milk or water, and plenty of fat, but no eggs, has at times been a staple in the Serbian countryside, though it is not appetizing to reproduce. Czechoslovakia also has many old recipes for cornbread, some steamed, some baked, with cornmeal and egg yolks and sometimes flour, leavened with baking soda and sometimes stiffly beaten egg whites. With more eggs the 'bread' tends to become 'cake'.

Make this loaf, which is plainish, firm and very yellow, on a day when you want to rediscover the pleasure of eating butter. It is the perfect vehicle. The texture makes it most suitable for breakfast or tea.

1 egg	$\frac{3}{4}$ cup white flour
1–2 tablespoons sugar	$1\frac{3}{4}$ cups cornmeal
$\frac{1}{2}$ teaspoon salt	1 cup of sour milk
2 tablespoons melted butter	1 teaspoon baking powder

Mix all the ingredients together, knead well and bake for 45 minutes in a greased loaf tin in a medium oven. Serve warm.

Cornmeal preparations benefit greatly in taste from the addition of sugar and butter and the texture is improved by blending with white flour. The best recipe I have ever encountered is close to this Bohemian version, but not of East European origin. It uses $\frac{5}{8}$ white flour to $\frac{3}{8}$ cornmeal and adds 5 teaspoons of baking powder. Retain the other ingredients as given.

In Central Europe until the advent of refined white bread, the special occasion alternative to the coarse, sourish brown and black breads of everyday were plain, rich leavened cakes and buns. They were made with fine flour, yeast, butter, eggs, sugar and sometimes milk. Our present habits have contracted the range of bread, so that cake seems a distinct phenomenon, but it is properly a continuation of the line. When after twelve months of eating Russian black bread I rediscovered the taste and texture of English white bread, it seemed extraordinarily sweet and delicate; and I am told that loaves made with 100 per cent English wheat are strikingly 'cake-like' even to those who have not become excessively used to coarse bread. When I was in Romania during widespread bread shortages, I was given plain cake with my fish hors d'oeuvres at a private meal. This was not even a sweet yeast dough but a form of *Sandtorte* (see p. 368), a recipe popular throughout Germany and neighbouring countries. Out of necessity the function of plain cake to double as bread had been rediscovered and transferred to the chemically leavened plain cakes that were most easily available in the shops.

Recipes for 'cakes' in the modern English sense therefore will mainly be found in the chapters on 'Sweet Things', while what follow are for cakes that can double as bread. They are mostly the classic bread treats traditionally served at Christmas and Easter and other festive occasions. All are best made in Britain with what is marketed as 'bread flour'. This is blended with imported flours to achieve greater depth.

Stollen

This German Christmas offering was first mentioned in 1329. The shape is said to be symbolic of the Holy Child wrapped in a cloth. The traditional recipe is from Dresden and is baked on the first Sunday in Advent. All year round a plain *Stollen* is eaten for Sunday breakfasts, when the bakeries are closed. It is regarded as closer to bread than to layer cake or *Kuchen*.

1 teaspoon dried yeast	120 g (4 oz) blanched
$\frac{1}{8}$ litre ($\frac{1}{4}$ pint) milk	almonds
500 g (1 lb) strong white	150 g (5 oz) sugar
flour	a pinch of salt
200 g (7 oz) butter	125 g (4 oz) each raisins,
grated lemon peel	sultanas and candied peel
$\frac{1}{2}$ teaspoon powdered	200 g (7 oz) melted butter
cardamom	150 g (5 oz) icing sugar

Dissolve the yeast in the warm milk, add a little flour and leave to foam. Mix the rest of the flour with the butter, lemon peel, spices, nuts, sugar and salt, add the yeast mixture and knead till the dough is smooth. Leave to rise in a warm place. Add the dried fruit by flattening the dough, sprinkling with fruit,

Serbian Christmas celebrations. A German engraving after S. Kamtz, 1862 (photo: J.-L. Charmet)

folding together and repeating till all the fruit is used up. Form into a cylinder on a greased baking sheet, pour over melted butter and leave to rise. Paint with butter again and bake in a medium oven for about 40 minutes. Baste with butter half way through the cooking. When cooked, paint with any remaining butter and sprinkle with icing sugar. The cardamom can be replaced with a tablespoon of rose-water.

Vanochka

The Czech 'Christmas plait' is like Jewish egg bread or *challah*, but sweeter and richer.

1 teaspoon dried yeast
½ cup sugar
100 g (3½ oz) unsalted butter
1 teaspoon salt
1 cup milk
3 egg yolks
4½–5 cups strong white flour
⅛ teaspoon each crushed cardamom and anise seeds

1 teaspoon grated lemon peel
1 cup raisins, soaked in rum
½ cup chopped blanched almonds
2 egg yolks and 1 tablespoon milk, for brushing
sliced blanched almonds and sugar, to decorate

Dissolve the yeast in ½ cup warm water. Add sugar, butter and salt to hot milk in a large bowl. When the butter has melted add the egg yolks, yeast mixture and half the flour. Beat briefly with a mixer or a wooden spoon for a few minutes, then add all but ½ cup flour with the spices and peel. Knead until smooth and unsticky and leave to rise. Mix the drained raisins, nuts and remaining flour and add to the dough, making sure they are well distributed. Divide the dough into six long cylinders, three longer, three smaller. Pinch the long three together and plait them, then brush with egg and milk. Plait the smaller three and lay the small plait on top of the long one. Place on a well-buttered baking tray and leave to rise. Brush the whole with eggs and milk, sprinkle with almonds and bake in a preheated medium oven for 1–1¼ hours. The plait should be golden brown; a skewer should come out clean. Sprinkle with icing sugar while still hot and leave to cool. Cover and leave overnight before slicing.

The Czech Easter cake, *mazanec* or *bochanek*, is a loaf of sweet yeast dough, richer than the Christmas plait and the German *Stollen*, though the flavourings are the same. It is baked in a round shape with a cross on top. The idea is close to our hot cross buns.

The Czechs also twist their leavened Easter buns into plaits and spirals. One modern source suggests these symbolize the rope with which Judas hanged himself, while the holes left in the buns are marks of Christ's wounds.

In Austria-Hungary a plaited sweet loaf is served at weddings.

Babka

The Polish Easter and general festive cake has as its hallmark the use of saffron as the traditional spice. The recipe for it probably came to Poland from Italy in the sixteenth century via Queen Bona, as a transplant of the Milanese *panettone*. Since then much ritual has surrounded the baking of this fragile masterpiece. Precious pastrycooks declared it needed to rest on an eiderdown before it went into the oven, after which baking took place in an atmosphere of maternity. Men were forbidden to enter the kitchen and no one was allowed to speak above a whisper.

8 egg yolks	500 g (1 lb) strong white
120 g (4 oz) castor sugar	flour
1 teaspoon dried yeast	saffron
⅛ litre (¼ pint) milk	½ teaspoon salt
vanilla	120 g (4 oz) melted butter

Beat the eggs and sugar over hot water until white and thick. Dissolve the yeast in some warm milk. Add the two mixtures with all the ingredients except the butter. Beat, pour in the butter and beat again. Fill a greased baking tin, traditionally a

Turk's Head mould, to one-third. Cover and leave to rise. Bake in a medium oven for about 1 hour.

Varieties of *babka* were also prepared for weddings.

Other rich breads

The basic Romanian yeast-leavened cake is *cozonac*, and this is the dough used to make the Easter cake of the Romanian Orthodox Church, *pasca*, which is baked with a bottom layer of sweetened, spiced curd cheese. In neighbouring Russia, stemming from the traditions of Russian Orthodoxy, the cheese (*paskha*) is served separately under the same name, moulded and marked with a cross, with the cake (*kulich*) baked separately to accompany it.

In Catholic and Orthodox parts of Yugoslavia, mostly in the north, the holy 'breads' of Germany, Czechoslovakia, Poland and Romania have counterparts. *Turo polje* bread is a yeast dough, like *Stollen*, flavoured with rose-water.

Nussbeugeln/Beigli

The Austrian-Hungarian nut roll is traditional at Christmas. George Lang attributes it specifically to Bratislava, which has been Austrian (Pressburg), Hungarian (Pozsony) and is now the capital of Slovakia.

180 g (6 oz) butter	*For the filling:*
300 g (10 oz) strong white flour	200 g (7 oz) sugar
1 teaspoon dried yeast	5 tablespoons milk
4 tablespoons milk	300–350 g (10–12 oz) ground walnuts
2 egg yolks	50 g (2 oz) butter
1 tablespoon castor sugar	4 tablespoons sultanas
pinch of salt	

Rub the butter into the flour. Dissolve the yeast in the milk. Add together with remaining ingredients and knead to a smooth dough.

For the filling, heat the sugar and milk, add the nuts and cook over a low heat for a few minutes. Remove from heat and beat in butter and sultanas. Leave to cool. Roll out the pastry thinly into two rectangles, spread the filling over half the area of each, roll up and place on a greased baking tray. Leave to rise, then brush with egg white and bake for 30–40 minutes in a medium to hot oven. Leave to cool. Serve in slices.

In Poland the Christmas *makowiec* is rolled around poppy seeds. Similar festive baked goods are found in Slovenia, Serbia and Croatia. In Romania the *cozonac* can be folded around a paste of either ground nuts or poppy seeds. Everyday equivalents – various sweet-filled roulades – are common. It is only in the old Turkish-occupied parts of southern and south-east Europe, notably the south of Yugoslavia, Albania and Bulgaria, that these semi-sweet cake-making traditions fall away and are only known as foreign ideas.

Gugelhupf

A number of the yeast-leavened round 'cakes' share the Slav word *kolac*, originally signifying dough baked in a ring. The Polish *babka*, baked in a Turk's Head mould, and the *Gugelhupf* come closest to the original meaning. The *Gugelhupf* or *Kugelhupf* is a dryish cake, which the Czechs classify among the *babovkas*, and is one of the best-known food products of Central Europe. The Austrian Emperor Franz Joseph who had a pronounced taste for plain, well-made food, was known to prefer it, and many chemically leavened recipes have been developed in the last hundred years, with French encouragement, to provide a quick version. The French say this cake was much liked by Marie Antoinette, daughter of Maria Theresa of Austria and wife of Louis XVI, who set a fashion for yeast-raised sweet pastry in eighteenth-century Paris. Others say the master pastrycook and chef to many European courts and rich dignitaries, Marie-Antoine Carême, learned how to make it from the chief chef to the Austrian ambassador at the beginning of the nineteenth century. The name (which the French sometimes scramble into 'kougloff') seems to come from the Jewish *kugel*, a kind of firm sweet or savoury pudding, baked with eggs, potatoes or grain and some savoury or sweet addition. The only similarity is the round shape and the fact that when the *kugel* is cold it is sliced. There are many varieties of *Gugelhupf*, a number with dried fruit and nuts, as in the foregoing recipes. I've chosen this Czech recipe with cocoa for the sake of variety.

1 teaspoon dried yeast	1 egg yolk
200 ml (⅓ pint) milk	70 g (2½ oz) melted butter
350 g (12 oz) strong white flour	
	For the filling:
pinch of salt	30 g (1 oz) cocoa
50 g (2 oz) sugar	30 g (1 oz) sugar
lemon peel	3 tablespoons milk

Dissolve the yeast in the milk. Add this and all the remaining ingredients to the flour and work to a smooth dough. Leave to rise while you mix the cocoa and sugar with the warm milk to a stiff mixture. Knead the dough again, flatten, spread with the cocoa mixture, fold over and place in a well-greased tin, traditionally a Turk's Head mould, to rise again. Sprinkle the top with melted butter and bake in a preheated medium oven for about 45 minutes. A skewer inserted should come out clean. Turn out and dust with icing sugar. Leave to cool before serving.

Sandtorte

250 g (8 oz) butter	4 beaten whites
250 g (8 oz) sugar	1 liqueur glass rum
4 egg yolks	a good pinch of salt
250 g (8 oz) semolina	

Cream the butter and sugar together, add the yolks one by one, then add the rest of the ingredients while continuing to beat, and end by folding in the egg whites. Bake in a well-greased, deep round tin for 1 hour in a medium oven.

Bishop's bread

This Austro-Hungarian recipe is what we might call fruit bread. It is neither to us nor to the Central Europeans quite a cake, though it is fairly sweet. Bishop's bread can include preserved fruit, orange peel and sometimes chocolate chips, and is often made with whole eggs. Kato Frank, however, who wrote a good, homely book on Hungarian food twenty-five years ago, declared the following recipe with egg whites only to be her mother's favourite.

6 egg whites
180 g (6 oz) castor sugar
180 g (6 oz) chopped candied fruit, or equivalent in fresh apple
1 tablespoon rum
grated rind of 1 orange
juice of ½ orange
150 g (5 oz) flour
120 g (4 oz) chopped walnuts

Beat the egg whites stiff, whip in the sugar, fold in the remaining ingredients. The fruit can be raisins and sultanas, cherries, candied peel, even finely chopped tinned fruit. Bake in a greased bread tin in a medium oven for 30–40 minutes. Cool and cut into 1 cm (½ inch) slices.

Gingerbread

Here is the nearest cake relative of black bread, but again in a category of its own. Gingerbread (honey cake, pepper cake) is the old-fashioned sweet festive bread of Central Europe, a celebration of imported spices. As the Polish saying goes: 'more expensive the seasoning than the food'. A nobleman showed his generosity by putting in as much as he could in the way of cloves, cinnamon and so on. The resulting gingerbread is the confection Saint Nicholas hands out to children at Advent, on 6 December, along with honey biscuits, holy pictures and big red apples, and it has special connections with the first cities to make it, notably Torun in Poland and Nuremberg in Germany. The connection to bread in our sense is easiest to make via pumpernickel, of which this is a kind of sweet, spicy version. Both were once made with a coarse rye meal.

Torun, connected by the Vistula to the Baltic Sea and thus on the spice route, pioneered the idea of embellishing the traditional Slavonic honey cake with the aromatics brought by traders from the Orient. Nuns at St Catherine's Convent in the town baked choice *pierniki* that were named *katarzynki*, 'little Catherines'. They used finely carved hardwood moulds to shape the long-lasting, dark and pungent dough. The exotic spices helped generate a myth that *pierniki* had magic powers, such as encouraging children to learn to read, and the aristocracy, who kept the sweet, medicinal, aromatic powders of Eastern origin locked up in caskets like jewels, also coveted those spices in the form of gingerbread. Lovers exchanged gingerbread hearts, pilgrims bought *pierniki* bearing the images of saints and hung them in their homes, and gingerbread cakes became such popular talismen that eventually inedible versions were baked. The *piernik* was also valued for its aromatic properties, like a pomander.

The gingerbread cake was a popular art form, and the Renaissance marked a watershed in its figurative development. From confinement to the saints and the Bible, the subjects depicted broadened to include scenes from court life: knights and their ladies and their favourite animals – horses, deer, bears, hares, cows. A *piernik* embossed with a rooster wished the recipient success and fertility. Torun factories turned out cakes with likenesses of Polish kings. In modern times the artistic dimension has been lost, but a large collection of old wooden *piernik* moulds can be seen in the Ethnographic Museum in Cracow. Necessarily it is a celebration of imagination compared with the modern industrial output of St Nicholas and reindeer gingerbread. But a glance in any Central European delicatessen around Christmas will confirm the continuing demand for sentimentally shaped, thoroughly pagan sugar and spice.

Torun piernik

Gingerbread can be very easily and very successfully baked at home. I have based my recipe on the one from Torun, with only optional additions, but equally famous recipes and decorative traditions can be found for German *Lebkuchen*, Bohemian *pernik*, Hungarian *mézekálacs* or *duluciariorum* and Russian *pryanik*. It is a cake considered ideal for nibbling with vodka and other spirits.

140 g (5 oz) butter	1 teaspoon each ground
250 g (8 oz) honey	cinnamon, crushed
500 g (1 lb) white flour	cloves, ground ginger,
$\frac{1}{4}$ teaspoon salt	ground or crushed
2 small eggs	cardamom seeds
2 tablespoons baking	4 tablespoons bran
powder, dissolved in 4	2 tablespoons wheat germ
tablespoons milk	

Heat the butter and honey in a pan to near boiling, then allow to cool before gradually adding the remaining ingredients. Knead thoroughly, shape into a ball, place in a greased plastic bag and keep in a cool place until ready to bake. Crushed nuts and/or candied peel can be added to the dough if liked, also a cup of sugar, and wholemeal flour may be used instead of the white flour, bran and wheat germ with which I have replaced the old rye meal. The dough should be firm and unsticky once kneaded. Add more milk if it is dry or more flour and an extra pinch of spices if it is too wet.

The gingerbread dough was traditionally assembled on All Saints' Day and baked four weeks later, at Advent. It was then left to mature for eating at Christmas. This timing is largely a matter of ritual, but for practical purposes it is advisable to allow at least a day for the dough to stand and absorb the spices.

To bake, roll out the dough about 1 cm ($\frac{1}{2}$ inch) thick and cut in decorative shapes with a cutter or a knife. Bake on a greased baking tray in a medium oven for about 40 minutes, or until firm. Allow to cool thoroughly on a wire rack before storing in an airtight jar or tin. The cakes may be covered with chocolate icing or sandwiched together with plum cheese or marzipan, but are best left alone.

Some Polish families who believed in the spiritual power of *piernik* sprinkled crumbs of it in the pans in which all other Christmas delicacies were baked. This habit perhaps, combined with the fact it will keep almost indefinitely and would always have been in the winter store cupboard, has led to the inclusion of gingerbread in a number of classic Polish sweet-and-sour recipes, for instance carp in grey sauce (p. 181) and similar sauces for tongue and game. There is also the astonishingly good German recipe for mackerel and gingerbread on p. 179, for which it is worth making a little *piernik* specially.

Lard dough

Pogácsa in Hungarian, *pogaca* in neighbouring parts of Yugoslavia, are yeast doughs folded and baked around a semi-sweet or savoury filling. They differ from bread in being rich in fat, which is nearly always lard, not butter. They have a faint family resemblance to lardy cake. The *pogácsa* in fact is like a strudel, oiled between the layers, but made of leavened dough. It may be plain and fat, like a croissant, or flavoured when the fat used is pork crackling. Sometimes cream is added as a filling, and in the dough some of the flour may be replaced by cooked potato. The 'bread' is leavened but baked flat and eaten in strips. My first *pogaca* in Yugoslavia instantly reminded me of the salty, oily leavened flat bread sold in Tuscany as *schiacciata*, elsewhere as *focaccia*, and the Central European lard doughs do indeed belong in the middle of an unexpectedly large tradition that includes these spongy savoury breads and pizza. The art of folded, lard-enriched bread dough probably came to Central Europe via the Turks, who have a *borek* made with bread dough. The idea though probably arose when out of leftover bread dough something quick and cheap was made, as Elizabeth David speculates in *English Bread and Yeast Cookery*, 'for children, for the poor, the hungry'.

Plain pogácsa

$\frac{1}{4}$ teaspoon dried yeast
$\frac{1}{2}$ teaspoon sugar
500 g (1 lb) bread flour
$\frac{1}{2}$ teaspoon salt
1 egg yolk (optional)
300 g (10 oz) lard, or
    dripping, or a mixture
    of the two

1 tablespoon sour cream,
    sour milk, or water
beaten egg and coarse salt
    to glaze

Dissolve the yeast and sugar in 6 tablespoons warm water. Mix together the sifted flour, salt, egg yolk, a quarter of the fat and a tablespoon of liquid, and combine the two to make a soft dough, adding extra water or flour as necessary. Knead well and set aside in a warm place while you beat the lard creamy, then roll out the dough thinly, spread over a third of the remaining lard, fold up, and leave to rest. Repeat the process till all the lard is used. Finally roll the dough to finger thickness.

The Hungarian way is to cut the dough into rounds before baking. The Italian and Yugoslav way is to score the dough lightly in strips so that it may be broken off when cooked, and this seems to me more suited to savoury presentation. Whatever the shape, brush the dough with egg and bake in a greased tin in a hot oven for about 20 minutes. One use immediately suggests itself for this recipe: sprinkle the *pogacsa* with coarse salt before baking and serve it as an appetizer with beer or wine.

For a plainer version omit the egg yolk.

Rich bread with cream and bacon

This Yugoslav recipe doesn't bear the name *pogaca*, but is a close relative. It is the composite bacon sandwich of the Balkans. The original calls for 750 g (1½ lb) pork scratchings to go inside. Not only is this a huge quantity of crackling to make or get hold of, let alone eat, but also in my hands the result has proved most unappealing. The crackling goes soggy and has little flavour. A better idea is to use lean bacon or ham. Raw smoked ham would be ideal if it were not so expensive. Try the bacon *pogaca* alone or take it out of context and serve it in strips with fish kebabs or a bowl of creamy mussels.

½ teaspoon dried yeast	2 eggs
½ cup milk	250 g (8 oz) lightly fried
1 kg (2 lb) white bread	bacon, or ready-cooked
flour	ham, in small squares
salt, pepper	egg for brushing
1 cup sour milk or cream	paprika

Dissolve the yeast in the milk. When it foams, beat in the eggs and add to the seasoned sifted flour with as much sour milk or cream as needed to make a soft, unsticky dough after kneading. Leave to rise, then spread out the dough to ½ cm (¼ inch) thickness, place the bacon or ham over half of it and fold over the other half. Fold the dough a few times into a square, roll it and refold it, then leave it to rise again. Before baking, roll it finally to a thickness of two fingers, and to fit a greased baking tray, using extra flour if the dough threatens to stick. Brush with egg yolk, sprinkle with paprika and bake for about 30 minutes in a preheated medium to hot oven.

Saxon pie

Another relative of the *pogacsa*/pizza is a Saxon pie or, in German, *Hanglich*, described by Paul Kovi as a vital element in Transylvanian cooking:

. . . the most famous Saxon specialty, Hangklich, [is] customarily made out of leftover bread dough or scrapings. Its name supposedly comes from '*eine Hand gleich*' and refers to its literal meaning: a handful of dough. With its numerous versions it has since grown in rank, prestige, fame and popularity to become an important dish on its own: a kind of Saxon pizza. Its virtue is forged from necessity.

Kovi compares the Saxon pie, which can have a sweet topping of sour cream and cherries, with the original sweet (fruit) or savoury quiche Lorraine. Elizabeth David makes the same comparison between the varieties of quiche and the sweet or savoury pizzas in their early days. The Transylvanian yeast dough is enriched with an egg and 2 tablespoons of butter for each 250 g (8 oz) flour, and the dense filling is made with a fat-laden mixture of beaten egg and lard. The missing piece in the jigsaw may be the emigration of German farmers from Alsace and Lorraine to Transylvania in the eighteenth century.

Crisp cabbage pogácsa

Hungarians have difficulty conveying the idea of a *pogácsa* to English speakers because the term – as well as something soft and leavened – also conveys a hardish biscuit. George Lang has a *pogácsa* recipe for a 'crackling biscuit' that is the 'snack cracker' version of the rich bread with cream and bacon. Another Lang idea is to serve a cabbage *pogácsa* 'as the English serve Yorkshire pudding', which is interesting, because it places the *pogácsa* back alongside lard dough, Neapolitan pizza and lardy cake.

salt	1 tablespoon sour cream
1 small head of cabbage, shredded	½ teaspoon salt
10 tablespoons butter	½ tablespoon granulated sugar
1¼ cups flour	½ teaspoon freshly ground pepper
1 teaspoon baking powder	1 whole egg
1 egg yolk	

Salt the cabbage and leave to stand. Mix together 8 tablespoons butter with the flour, baking powder, egg yolk, cream and ½ teaspoon salt. Keep the pastry cool while you squeeze the water from the cabbage and soften it very gently in the remaining butter and sugar over a low heat. Cover the pan and beware of burning. Mix in the pepper when the cabbage is done and leave to cool. Blend the cabbage mixture and dough, roll out to 1 cm (½ inch) thickness, cut out with a biscuit cutter, score the surface, brush with a beaten egg and water and bake about 30 minutes in a preheated medium oven, until golden.

Pretzels

All visitors to Germany know these salty chestnut-coloured figure-of-eight savouries, which are easily made at home. They are also found in Poland and Czechoslovakia. Roughly, they imitate the hygienic shape of Arab/Turkish bread, with a handle in the middle of the circle to be eaten.

50 g (2 oz) butter
2 eggs, separated
250 g (8 oz) flour
salt, pepper
milk
coarse salt

Work the creamed butter, beaten whites and yolks into the flour with seasoning, roll out on a floured board and shape. Brush with milk, sprinkle with coarse salt and bake in a hot oven for 10 minutes. Serve with lager beer. These may also be strewn with caraway.

Turkish crescents

The croissant we associate with the French began life, according to one legend, in Budapest in 1686, when Christian soldiers from all over Europe joined forces to oust the Turks from the city they had held for 145 years. The siege lasted seventy-four days and victory was marked by having bakers make a special pastry in the form of a crescent, in memory of the emblem on the Ottoman flag. A very similar story, however, commemorating the unsuccessful Turkish siege of Vienna three years earlier, is also told to explain the origins of a kind of hard roll called in Hungarian *császárzemle* (emperor's roll). This was baked with a cross on top, the sign of the victors. There is probably some truth in both stories, for both sieges, which resulted in defeat for the Turks, were great events in Europe, and both forms of baking still exist. *Larousse gastronomique*, however, confuses the dates and details in describing the origin of the croissant. It seems more likely to have come into being in Vienna in 1683, not Budapest three years later. If it is true that bakers working through the night gave the alarm when they heard the invader tunnelling underground to reach the centre of the town, then certainly the town must have been Vienna, not Budapest. The bakers may have been rewarded, as Larousse says, or simply asked to sell a special victory pastry called in Austrian-German *Kipfel*, in Hungarian *kifli*.

Kiflis

300 g (10 oz) butter or margarine	scant ½ cup milk
500 g (1 lb) plain flour	40 g (1½ oz) sugar
½ teaspoon yeast	1 egg plus 1 yolk
	salt

Cut the butter into 80 g (3 oz) flour, shape into a brick and chill. Dissolve the yeast in the warm milk, add the sugar, creamed with the egg and yolk, the rest of the flour, sifted, and a pinch of salt. Work together to make a smooth, soft dough, leave to rise in the warm for an hour, then let cool for 20 minutes. Put the soft dough on a floured board, put the 'brick' in the middle and fold and roll as for puff pastry. For basic 'crescents', roll thinly the final time and cut into triangles with a 15 cm (6 inch) base and 8 cm (3 inch) tail. Roll up, starting from the base and curl into crescent form. Place on a greased baking sheet two fingers' distance from each other. Brush with milk, leave to stand for 15 minutes, then bake in a medium oven till golden, about 25 minutes.

The *kiflis* can be filled with curd cheese or nuts and sugar, or with chocolate. Sophisticated Hungarians used to fill them with ham, sour cream and tarragon and served them as a French-style 'starter'. George Lang observes of a 200-year-old recipe for 'water-dragging kiflis' that the old practice in draughty houses was probably to place the dough in warm water to rise. The crescent shape ultimately inspired both savoury and a wide range of sweet pastries (see p. 423).

In some languages the word *Kipfel* came to mean the same as *csaszarzsemle*. Maude Parkinson when she was teaching in Romania observed that the children of a well-to-do family began the day with coffee and a *Kipfel*, which she described as 'a small roll'. The Austrian word, as well as still meaning croissant, is now used generally to describe rolls of soft *white* bread, as is *kifle* in Bulgaria. It remains a croissant in Hungary.

A melon stall, from Antoine Ignace Melling, Voyage Pittoresque de Constantinople, Paris 1819

SWEET THINGS

'Pudding'

The first stop for a sweet tooth in Czechoslovakia and Poland is the milk-bar, a café of bright, often childlike decor, selling coffee, cakes, chocolate, ice-cream, milk, and milk and fruit jelly puddings. Before the advent of instant packet mixes various forms of thickened and sweetened starch, with the flavour or addition of fruit, or spices, or chocolate, were popular in Central Europe. It's not what we mean by the word, but the Germans call them '*Pudding*'. Likewise the Czechs speak of *pudink*. The word has been carried over to the modern quick mixes, all of which may also be eaten at home as the sweet course to end the main meal.

Rote Grütze

This cold dessert of thickened soft fruit is the German and Scandinavian equivalent and probably forebear of the better-known Russian *kisel*, Polish *kisiel* and Bulgarian *kissel*, which are thickened with potato starch. It uses as a thickening agent the rather more attractive semolina or buckwheat.

1 kg (2 lb) raspberries, or redcurrants, or a mixture of both
2 cups sweet red wine
120 g (4 oz) sugar, or to taste
120 g (4 oz) buckwheat or semolina

Cook the fruit gently, purée it, add the wine and sugar and bring to the boil, combining it with the semolina or buckwheat, until the mixture thickens. Pour into a wetted mould and when cold turn out and serve with fresh raspberries and cream.

Potato pudding

Once the Prussians, encouraged by their king, took to the New World of potatoes, they devised ways of using them everywhere possible when flour was short. Potato bread, potato scones, potato dumplings, potato pancakes and sweetened potato pasties all established themselves. The treatment of potatoes in this recipe is thoroughly sweet.

3 eggs
50 g (2 oz) castor sugar
grated rind of 1 orange or lemon
1 cup cream
cold cooked potato

Beat the eggs and sugar till frothy, then add the peel and cream. Dilute 2 tablespoons of cold mashed potato with the mixture, stirring all the time to keep it smooth. Use this mixture to dilute a little more potato, until you have a very thick batter. Pour this into a buttered mould and bake it in a slow to medium oven for about 45 minutes. This is traditionally served with sugar or a fruit sauce. Try a purée of fresh soft fruit or a splash of liqueur to attract adult interest.

Bulgarian scented ground rice

Rice puddings are popular in Bulgaria and known in all the Central European countries. The rice is generally cooked first in water or milk, drained and enriched with sour cream and sugar and served with a sweet preserve like rose-petal jam. The effect is not much different from our own creamed rice, despite the more unusual ingredients. Bulgarian *malebi*, however, a preparation of ground rice and aromatic spices known throughout the Middle East, is more subtle and won't remind anyone of school.

1–2 tablespoons ground rice	50 g (2 oz) ground almonds
1 tablespoon cornflour	1½ tablespoons rose-water
2 cups milk	chopped or slivered nuts, or
sugar	cinnamon, to decorate

Mix the ground rice and cornflour to a paste with a little of the cold milk, while the rest of the milk is heated. Combine the two, with sugar to taste, and bring to the boil gently, stirring, until the pudding thickens. Off the heat stir in the almonds and rose-water. Turn out the pudding into a heatproof dish and finish for 10–15 minutes in a warm oven. Serve hot or cold, decorated. The pudding may be more or less firm, according to taste. It is sometimes served with fruit syrup or jam.

Cracow buckwheat pudding

The western Polish city of enlightenment has given its name to a fine grade of buckwheat groats, used to make both savoury and sweet dishes. This recipe with a rich earthy taste has a long history, and has survived keen competition from potato and rice puddings.

120 g (4 oz) buckwheat groats	¼ teaspoon salt
2 cups cream, or creamy milk, or half and half	vanilla essence
	rum and lemon peel (optional)
1½ tablespoons butter (optional) for extra richness	icing sugar and cherries, or whipped cream, to decorate

Put all the ingredients except the last into a well-greased baking dish and cook slowly for 2 hours. Breadcrumbs rubbed into the buttered sides of the dish will help stop the pudding sticking, and it further helps to wait a few minutes after removing it from the oven before running a knife around the edges to loosen it. Turn out on to a plate, decorate and serve hot.

Semolina jelly

A light recipe from Yugoslavia and Hungary, useful for using up egg whites.

2 cups milk
100 g (3½ oz) semolina
1 packet gelatine
4 egg whites

2 tablespoons sugar or more,
    to taste
lemon peel
juice of ½ lemon

Bring three-quarters of the milk slowly to the boil, adding the semolina gradually and stirring until it thickens. Dissolve the gelatine in the remaining milk, which has been warmed, and add to the semolina mixture off the heat. Whip the egg whites with the sugar, fold into the mixture, together with the lemon peel and juice. Blend well, divide between serving dishes or glasses and chill. Serve decorated with whipped cream and fruit.

Almond jelly

This Polish sweet most probably came from the Orient.

30 g (1 oz) gelatine
3 cups milk
½ cup ground almonds
3 bitter almonds, scalded,
    peeled and ground, or
    bitter almond essence

½ cup sugar
vanilla essence, or vanilla
    pod
2 egg yolks
fresh fruit or angelica leaves,
    to decorate

Dissolve the gelatine in 3 tablespoons hot water, following the instructions on the packet. Bring the milk to the boil and add the almonds and the almond essence, stirring for a few minutes, then the sugar and vanilla, then the gelatine. Allow to cool slightly, then beat in the egg yolks. Pour into a serving dish and leave to set. Garnish with fresh fruit and angelica leaves.

Chestnut cream

Chestnuts are a most ancient food, easy to harvest and store and adaptable in cooking. They have an unusual dual identity in being loved by the rich, who created *marrons glacés*, and needed by the poor, who in France spoke of their – in English – bread-and-water existence as living on 'water and chestnuts'. The fruits of the sweet chestnut tree were popular with the Romans, who are credited with spreading the taste through Europe. Chestnut cream is popular in Yugoslavia, Hungary, Romania and Bulgaria.

Either buy 500 g (1 lb) of chestnut purée or boil, peel and purée 1 lb shelled nuts and add sugar to taste. Spoon into glasses and pour over a sauce of sugar and water heated till they spin a thread, blended with 100–120 g (3–4 oz) chocolate melted with a tablespoon of butter, scant ½ cup rum and a few drops of vanilla.

Chestnut purée may also be combined with or served alongside apple purée (see below, 'witches' cream', p. 391) or whipped up with fresh cream.

Sweet bean or mock chestnut cream

Chestnuts have long been associated with holiday feasts, but they are also one of those poor foods which have now become expensive, being seriously cultivated only in certain parts of south-east Europe, France and Italy. The need for a cheap substitute has given rise to this sweet purée of beans.

250 g (8 oz) kidney beans
120 g (4 oz) castor sugar, or to taste

6 tablespoons milk, or fresh cream
2 tablespoons rum

50 g (2 oz) ground walnuts grated chocolate, to
vanilla essence decorate
½ cup whipping cream

Soak and cook the beans until they are very soft, purée them, then beat in the sugar, milk, rum, walnuts and vanilla essence. Whip the cream stiff and fold in. Serve in glasses decorated with grated chocolate.

Hazelnut ice-cream

A recipe from Yugoslavia.

4 eggs
120 g (4 oz) icing sugar
1 cup fresh cream
1 teaspoon maraschino
vanilla
150–180 g (5–6 oz) ground hazelnuts

Beat the yolks and sugar, and separately whip the egg whites stiff. Whip the cream and blend in the liqueur, vanilla and hazelnuts. Combine all the ingredients and freeze for 6–8 hours. Serve in slices.

In Albania this ice-cream is served very sweet, without liqueur, but flavoured with cinnamon.

Twelve-fruit compote

Compotes of dried fruit are popular everywhere, served alone or with dry biscuits. A classic Polish recipe combines prunes and figs and plays an important part in the meatless Christmas Eve meal, *Wigilia*, when it forms the first of two sweet courses in a seven- or nine-course meal, or the first of four sweet dishes in an eleven-course meal. Generally it is served after the main fish course and is followed by pastries and other confections with nuts and poppy seeds. The most magnificent festive recipe combines twelve different fruits and sounds Chinese. Try it as an original alternative to English Christmas pudding.

500 g (1 lb) mixed dried
  fruit – pears, figs,
  apricots, peaches
1 cup stoned prunes
½ cup raisins
1 cup fresh or tinned stoned
  cherries
2 fresh eating apples, peeled
  and sliced, or 6 oz dried
  apple
½ cup cranberries

1 lemon, sliced
6 cloves
2 small cinnamon sticks
1 cup sugar (optional)
1 orange, plus its grated
  peel
½ cup grapes, or stoned
  fresh plums
½ cup fruit-flavoured
  brandy or fruit juice

Bring the washed dried fruit and 3 cups water to the boil and simmer gently until plump and tender. Add the cherries, apples, cranberries, lemon, spices, and sugar if liked. Cover and simmer 5 minutes more. Add the orange, peeled and cut into half or quarter segments, the grapes and the brandy or juice. Bring to boiling point then remove from heat. Add the grated peel of the orange, cover and leave to stand 15 minutes. This quantity will serve about 12 people.

The fruits most commonly used in compotes, which may be a purée but are most often a fruit salad in which the fruit is cooked or simply plunged whole into hot syrup, covered, and removed from the heat, are apples, pears, cherries, plums and greengages, together with blueberries, bilberries, strawberries, blackcurrants, redcurrants and gooseberries. The pan used must not alter the taste or colour of the compote.

Serbian apricot dessert

Combine 500 g (1 lb) dried apricots, cooked and puréed, with 3 tablespoons maraschino, 2 tablespoons of ground nuts and about 150 g (5 oz) each of curd cheese and ice-cream. Whip together and pour over fresh raspberries in a glass. Serve chilled.

In Hungary the dry apricot brandy *barack* is incorporated into a rich apricot cream that takes its name from the town of Kecskemet on the Great Plain, home of the best of Hungary's various fruit brandies.

Fruit with wines and liqueurs

Compotes of fresh cherries, raspberries and apricot are popular in Bulgaria, served with or over sponge fingers and chilled. Fresh fruit salads are liberally laced with local sweet white wine, which is of a very good dessert quality and a bargain alternative to Sauternes. Yugoslavia serves peaches and strawberries with their best complement, wine, white or red.

Mainly in Hungary and parts of Yugoslavia wine and fruit liqueurs are used to turn fresh or dried fruit, and many cream-, flour- and milk-based sweet dishes into faultless desserts. The most famous liqueur dessert dressing, from the *maraska* cherry, comes from Zadar, the capital of Dalmatia. Zadar, having been Austrian before 1918, became the Italian town of Zara between the wars, which is why internationally we know its brandy by the Italian name *maraschino*. Another cherry brandy, less famous but equally liked locally, is also manufactured in Zadar. This or maraschino mixed with rum and lemon juice makes an excellent dressing for fresh fruit salad.

Liqueurs are also poured on ice-cream. In Bulgaria the rose liqueur and sweet cherry liqueur which are widely available could be similarly used, though the Italianate habit does not come as readily to mind as it does closer to the Adriatic seaboard.

Fresh fruit

The best fruit is fresh. Wild strawberries, raspberries and blueberries are amongst the fruits growing in Czech mountains and forests, picked to make compotes to accompany dumplings, meat, poultry and game, or eaten alone with sugar as a dessert, or puréed to make a cold fruit soup with cream and cinnamon. The same berries are found in the more temperate parts of Yugoslavia, and from among the cultivated fruits strawberry soup and cherry soup are well-known on Polish and Hungarian menus. For the wild berries to be found in the Carpathians, Romanian bears are said to risk their lives and some Western gourmets in the East Bloc tell me they feel the same way when they see wild berries on the menu.

Meanwhile in the long, burning Balkan summers on the plains sweet melons, watermelons, grapes, peaches, plums and apricots abound. Sweet melon and watermelon are scooped out in balls and served together, sometimes with ice-cream. In these countries fresh fruit is a summer way of life.

The Apricot Tree

Today I woke in morning's early light –
he knocked impatiently at my window
with the frail fingers of his twigs
the apricot, which blossomed overnight.

I did not recognise him from the first . . .
The wealth of white and rose close to my house
was such that I could think a mission'd angel
had hurt his wings when passing through his boughs.

Perhaps it's not the apricot, I thought,
and angry that I did not want to see,
he struck me with the blossoms in the face
and then I understood that it was he,

my childhood friend, my dear apricot tree.

Magda Isanos, translated by Leon Levitchi

Maude Parkinson tells a wonderful tale of the growing of watermelons in Romania, where Serbian gardeners came every year, rented plots of ground, raised excellent fruit and vegetables to sell and returned home in winter with the proceeds.

When the melons were ripening they even took it in turn to sit up and watch all night, so that would-be thieves might have no opportunity of helping themselves. Very often through the night we were startled by a rifle-shot. It was only the Servian on guard who fired from time to time to advertise his wakefulness. Two or three times a week a big waggon was loaded with produce and driven for miles round the country, even to Sinaia and beyond. Their produce was eagerly bought, as vegetables are not too abundant, especially in the summer resorts. When the market gardeners were quite sold out they retired to Servia with their profits, where they remained till next season. It must have been a profitable enterprise, as 15 Servians were engaged in it at the place I speak of [near Piteşti, when this was still a small country town] . . .

But perhaps no country deserves to be more celebrated for its Garden of Eden fruit harvest than Bulgaria, where the gardening has always been done first-hand and with a passionate sense of national identity attached to it. In May, the month I was in Varna, we ate huge bags of cherries by the Black Sea. Before World War Two the fruit- and vegetable-growing industries were famed for their exports all over Europe. Since then they have been boosted by new investment and Bulgaria suffers few if any shortages. Like the Serbians in the nineteenth century, the Bulgarians rank as the natural market gardeners and orchard-men of Eastern Europe in the century of COMECON. A famous centre for fruit-harvesting is Kustendil, on the central plain. There, for both domestic consumption and massive export, the Bulgarian fruit-canning and jam-making industries process some of the best produce in the world from an abundance of temperate and tropical produce: apples, pears, plums, cherries, quinces, medlars, peaches, strawberries, raspberries, figs, almonds and melons. Bulgarian brand names are to be found on supermarket shelves from Prague to Moscow.

As for home benefits, Kustendil is only one of the many Roman spas in Bulgaria so rich in local produce as to be able to offer visitors a fruit cure alongside the familiar balneological regime. Along the southernmost part of Bulgaria's Black Sea coast tangerines, oranges and lemons now grow where they have been introduced from the Caucasus, and the whole coast abounds in fruit trees. The only fruits that conceivably are absent are coconuts, mangoes and bananas.

Baked quinces or apples

There are few recipes for fruit, because most is eaten raw in its season. This one might be saved for late autumn or winter. Core and bake with a filling of mixed nuts, cinnamon, sugar and butter. Serve the fruit cold, in its own rich sauce. Use plenty of sugar with quinces, little for apples.

Baked peaches

Save this for the last, less sound peaches or for a glut. After cooking, the fruit can be frozen. In Albania and Bulgaria it is common in the long summer to have two peach harvests, so that new ripe fruit is to be seen on the trees in September.

Halve the peaches, stick each with a clove and bake in a buttered dish skin-side down, sprinkled with sugar. After 15 minutes add a few tablespoons of brandy and a little water and bake for another 30 minutes, until very soft. Add more liquid during the cooking as necessary, to end up with a good half cup of sauce to pour over the fruit while it chills. Serve with whipped cream and coarsely crushed nuts.

Fresh fruit 'fools'

These are made in Romania by stirring puréed fresh fruit such as raspberries into a şatou sauce of egg yolks, sugar and white wine (p. 394). Serve with sponge fingers.

For a delicious Romanian use of fresh strawberries in an omelette see p. 324.

Citrus fruits have to be imported. Even in Bulgaria, where some have been transplanted, oranges historically have the foreign name 'portugals', and recipes using them are mostly modern. Lemon is used more often, having been a standard import for hundreds of years, though not to peasant households. A cold lemon mousse Paul Kovi describes as a Saxon favourite in Transylvania would have been the privilege of wealthy households. Fugger's lemon cake (see p. 406) – a gastronomic monument to one of the richest families in medieval Europe, bankers to kings and sinners to sober-minded chroniclers – falls into the same category. It was a measure of Romania's extreme national poverty in the late 1980s that lemons disappeared from the shops.

Apples in dressing-gowns

After the short Central European season of fresh berries come plums, then apples and pears. There are many ways of baking apples, but this seems to be a favourite with the children of what was once Maria Theresa's vast empire, stretching from Vienna to Belgrade and, nearly, to the Black Sea. The peeled and cored apples are filled with red jam, then wrapped in an envelope of puff pastry, brushed with egg, sprinkled with chopped nuts and baked for 15–20 minutes in a preheated medium oven. Sprinkle them with vanilla sugar if desired before serving.

The Czechs also bake their apples sliced in a soft pudding, (*zemlovka*) with bread and milk and raisins.

Witches' cream

This is another widespread dish, found in Hungary, Yugoslavia and Bulgaria, and a good way to use up leftover egg whites.

1 kg (2 lb) apples
150 g (5 oz) sugar, or to taste
1 egg white
1 tablespoon rum

Bake the apple or stew it in a little water, purée the cooked flesh and add the sugar while still warm. Mix in the egg white and

THE FOOD AND COOKING OF EASTERN EUROPE

beat together till the mixture thickens. Whisk in the rum and serve in glasses with dry sponge fingers.

Variations One variation is to include an equal part of chestnut purée with the apple, another to arrange the two purées in alternating layers and top them with whipped cream. For the apple-only version, George Lang uses Calvados instead of rum, with an extra dash of lemon juice.

For fresh plum dumplings, see p. 315.

Curd cheese cream

Curd cheese forms the basis of some quick desserts. The Czechs make a 'cheese cream' of soft cheese with melted butter, sugar, vanilla and a few spoons of whipped cream, rum, egg yolk and stiffly beaten egg white. It is served with fresh fruit salad and more whipped cream. The result is nourishing and filling to a degree most adults would not find desirable at the end of a meal.

Orange cheese cream

Quarkspeise, beloved of German children, is a naturally good alternative to packet 'whips' and 'delights'. (Can they really have these names?) Mix together 250 g (½ lb) curd cheese, 1 tablespoon sugar, a few drops of vanilla, 150 g (6 oz) peeled, chopped orange segments and juice, 1 small egg and 2 tablespoons sour cream. Decorate with orange segments and maraschino cherries.

Blackcurrant cheese cream with pumpernickel

For adults this lighter cream, served in small quantities with a dessert wine, would be a delight in summer.

Wash and drain 250 g (8 oz) blackcurrants, scatter with sugar to taste and leave a while for the sugar to soak in. Crumble or finely grate a slice of pumpernickel and mix with a little vanilla sugar. Grate 30 g (1 oz) chocolate. Mix 180–200 g (6–7 oz) curd cheese with 2 teaspoons lemon juice, a pinch of salt and sugar to taste and fold in half a cup (a small carton) of whipped cream. Arrange the dessert in cocktail glasses in layers of cheese, fruit, cheese, pumpernickel, and finish with a layer of cheese garnished with grated chocolate and a few berries.

Albanian pasca

The Albanians for a festival dessert at Easter eat a sweet cheese that closely resembles the Russian and Romanian sweet cheese pastes eaten with cake. The Bulgarian equivalent is *patcha*, which I have also seen called 'Boyar cream', alluding to the obvious Russian influence, and the same dish is made in Greece.

Şatou

'Wine soup for the ladies' say the older Polish cookery books. The tradition of specifying a sweet and delicate, yet nevertheless alcoholic pick-me-up for feminine use is one for which we should be grateful, whether it is described as pudding or soup or tonic, or, in English, egg-nog. The mixture of wine, egg yolks and spices and sugar served the Polish way, in a tea-cup with sponge fingers, is certainly revivifying, though I would be less keen to substitute tea for the wine as an old Czech recipe suggests. Since it is probably least likely to be taken at the start of a meal, more likely in between or instead of, it is not best called 'soup'. In emerging middle-class Poland it was probably taken in mid-morning by ladies of leisure, to relieve their boredom.

The French for several centuries have had a similar restorative, *chaudeau*, with eggs, milk, cinnamon and spices, but no alcohol, from which come all the East European terms: *chateau* (Austria), *satou* (Romania), *sodo* (Hungary), *sato* (Bulgaria). All these, served as desserts, are the equivalent of the *zabaglione/sabayon* mixtures that occur in Italy and France. The Romanians under the heading *satou* make a range of gorgeous custards based upon white wine, egg yolks, sugar and some extra flavouring, which may be fresh lemon or orange juice, fresh soft fruit purée, vanilla or chocolate. I think champagne *satou*, while well-suited to extravagant restaurants like Capşa, must be an error of taste, not to say a waste. *Sodo* probably came to Hungary in the fifteenth century as part of the culinary dowry of Queen Beatrice, though the name is French. The Germans and Austrians when they whip up their egg and wine mixtures call them a *Weinschaum*.

Şatou de vin

This is the basic Romanian recipe.

1 lemon
1 orange
250 g (½ lb) sugar
10 egg yolks
½ litre (1 pint) white wine

Grate the rinds of the fruit, add to the sugar, mix well, cover and leave as long as possible for the flavours to permeate. Stir the sugar and egg yolks together, bring the wine nearly to the boil and slowly pour it into the egg mixture, stirring constantly. Stir the mixture in a bowl over hot water until thick. Continue stirring while the *şatou* cools to warm, then pour over cakes and puddings or eat by itself in tiny quantities.

Bird milk or floating island

This is a vanilla-flavoured egg custard made with milk and served with stiff egg whites previously cooked in the sweet milk. The childish impression this Hungarian and Romanian dish makes on the eye fortunately doesn't impair the taste of the custard. On the other hand the little white nests don't appeal to any children I know, so they are hardly worth the extra work.

Custard cake from Dalmatia

In Dalmatia a thick, sweet egg custard, *ražata*, is considered a speciality of Dubrovnik. The proportions are six eggs to a ½ litre (scant 1 pint) of milk, with six tablespoons of sugar. Further afield the recipe develops into a 'custard cake'. The technique of pouring over a syrup is in the Oriental sweetmeat style, though there is also a strong affinity with the more northerly idea of serving a plain cake like a *babka* or a sweet soufflé pudding with a fruit or alcohol-based sauce. The custard itself is half-way between being a *crème pâtissière* and a home-made semolina *halva*.

4 cups milk	1 cup coarsely crushed
⅔ cup semolina	walnuts
½ teaspoon salt	
¼ cup butter	*For the optional syrup:*
6 eggs	½ cup sugar
1 cup sugar, or to taste	juice and grated peel of 1
1 teaspoon vanilla	lemon
⅔ cup raisins, soaked in ½	cinnamon stick
cup rum	3 tablespoons rum

Bring the milk to the boil, add the semolina in a stream and stir until thick, adding the salt and butter. Beat the eggs, sugar, and vanilla and add to the semolina, stirring slowly off the heat. Finally add the raisins, about a tablespoon of the rum and the walnuts. Spread the mixture in a well-buttered soufflé dish and bake in a medium oven for about 45 minutes, or until firm.

Boil with 1 cup water all the syrup ingredients except the rum, which should be added off the heat after 10 minutes, when the syrup is thick.

Alternatively, bathe the custard cake in young white wine, as is the tradition in Dalmatia at Christmas.

Berliner Pfannkuchen

Fritters and doughnuts belong to the same family and are still popular in Central Europe, though I think hardly at all in Britain and certainly not home-made. Apple fritters are traditional in Bohemia, but for most of us it would be more exciting to be further south, in Yugoslavia, and find a whole fresh fig inside golden batter. In theory rose petals too are made into fritters in Bulgaria, the land of the Valley of the Roses, though in practice these may be as hard to come by as deep-fried courgette flowers. As for doughnuts, the lightest and best known in Yugoslavia are said to come from Dalmatia, where they are made of a yeast batter with eggs, milk, rum and raisins. They resemble Polish *paczki*, which are associated with Carnival week and New Year's Eve and are ideally filled for the occasion with a mixture of rosehip preserves mixed with ground almonds. Berlin is similarly known for its leavened *Berliner Pfannkuchen*, filled with jam and dusted with sugar and cinnamon.

1 teaspoon dried yeast	2 tablespoons oil
$\frac{1}{2}$–1 cup milk	2 tablespoons rum
2 tablespoons sugar	plum jam, or other jam
500 g (1 lb) flour	powdered sugar
1 teaspoon salt	cinnamon
2 egg yolks	

Dissolve the yeast in a little warm milk and sugar, then combine with the flour, salt and the rest of the milk. Add the eggs, oil and rum and beat until the mixture is smooth and comes away from the side of the bowl. Leave to rise on a floured board.

Form into rounds 6 cm (3½ inches) in diameter and about 1½ cm (1 inch) thick with a well in the centres. Place on a greased baking tray and leave to rise again. Deep-fry in a covered pan for 2½–3 minutes on each side. Drain on greaseproof paper, fill with jam and roll in the sugar and cinnamon. Serve warm with coffee. These would be attractive for a late breakfast, made ready to fry the night before.

Lamance

This is a delicious and most unusual poppy-seed dessert, which Poles eat on Christmas Eve. The pastry triangles are dipped into sweet poppy seeds and cream.

3½ tablespoons butter	1 egg yolk
2½ cups flour	salt
½ cup icing sugar, or to taste	about ½ cup sour cream

For the dip:

2 cups poppy seeds	3 tablespoons ground
honey or sugar, to taste	almonds
½ cup cream	lemon peel

Rub in the butter with the flour, add the other ingredients with enough cream to make a workable dough. Knead, roll out about 3 mm (⅛ inch) thick and cut into triangles. Bake on a greased sheet until golden. Scald the poppy seeds with boiling water, drain well, then grind until smooth and moist. Add remaining ingredients with enough cream to make a thick sauce. Arrange in a dish with triangles added around it just before serving. Offer the remaining triangles separately.

Creamed wheat

🙊

The savoury Lebanese salad, *tabbouleh*, of soaked cracked wheat, a well-known example in Britain of a common Middle Eastern preparation, has as its Balkan counterpart the Serbian sweet dish *zito*, served on saints' days. In Bulgaria the equivalent is *asure*. For all the Slavs, creamed wheat is almost always a sweet festive dish. It was *zito* that the ancient Slavs offered to the gods and which they continue to use to pray for well-being for house and family. The Bulgarians, Greeks and Romanians all associate this food, shaped into a cake-like *kolivo/koliva/coliva*, with death. They eat it at funerals, either in church or at the graveside after the grave is closed. More is left at the graveside. Following the belief that Christ took meals with the disciples for forty days after the Resurrection, the human soul was supposed to need food for this length of time after burial. More *kolivo* was offered on the fortieth day.

One of Saul Bellow's novels describes an American meeting this custom at a Bucharest funeral:

Now came the traditional cake, white and creamy, huge, swimming loosely and quivering on its platter. The beggars went for it. This was their main course. Dincutza politely offered Corde a taste but he wanted no part of the death sweet. Anyway the beggars were helping themselves with their hands.

Saul Bellow, *The Dean's December*

It was more than his fastidious heart could take.

In Russia a similar dish is found, *kutya*, also eaten on Christmas Eve with a purée of cooked dried fruit. This same *kutia* is served in central and eastern Poland that evening and at the *stypa* after the funeral. The Polish recipe combines whole wheat kernels with poppy seeds, honey, cream and nuts to make a thick dessert.

The following Romanian recipe, using either whole wheat kernels ('wheat berries') or pot barley, makes a soft, nutty confection with a taste similar to muesli. It has no obvious place in modern Western eating habits, but try a small piece, like cake, with coffee. The original recipe calls for 1 kg (2 lb) wheat, but I have reduced it to trial proportions.

Coliva

120 g (4 oz) whole wheat
  kernels or pot barley,
  boiled until tender in ½
  litre (1 pint) salted water
120 g (4 oz) ground mixed
  nuts
1 teaspoon vanilla sugar

1 tablespoon rum
grated peel of ½ lemon
a good pinch of cinnamon
1 teaspoon breadcrumbs
2 teaspoons powdered sugar
cake decorations

When the grain is tender and nearly all the water absorbed, leave it to cool in the pan covered with a damp cloth to stop a crust forming. Next day, mix in the nuts, vanilla sugar, rum, peel and spice and with wet hands form the mixture into a cake shape on a plate. For testing purposes the *coliva* is complete at this point, to my taste, though the convention is to sprinkle the top with breadcrumbs and a layer of powdered sugar, and then to decorate it.

The Romanian country tradition used to be to hand out the *coliva* to passing strangers who would say in response '*bogdaproste*' – asking God's mercy for the deceased.

Plum cake with crumble

The Poles and the Czechs have long prided themselves on being expert pastry cooks. The reputation of Bohemian *Küchenmeister* stood so high in the Habsburg Empire that they were in constant demand in Vienna, where they inspired attachment to a host of sweet Czech delicacies. Crumble-topped cakes (*Streuselkuchen*) may be an Austrian favourite popular in Czechoslovakia and Poland, or they may have been introduced in Austria from further east.

The basic mixture of butter, sugar and flour rubbed together to make fine crumbs was the original topping for cheesecake, and is far better than the soggy biscuit crumbs that have become a substitute in the West. The crumble topping is used on a plainish biscuit cake designed to show it off, and it also adds the friable finishing touch to old-fashioned yeast bakery. Zofia Czerny writes that the Easter cake in Silesia is a yeast dough with eggs and milk such as might be used to make a not-so-rich *babka*. This is baked in a flat pan sprinkled with crumble and served cut into squares.

Following is a good, simple recipe from Bohemia.

For the dough:	1 egg
½ teaspoon dried yeast	500 g (1 lb) plums
½ cup milk	
300 g (10 oz) flour	*For the crumble:*
30 g (1 oz) sugar (optional)	50 g (2 oz) butter
lemon peel	120 g (4 oz) flour
a pinch of salt	2 tablespoons sugar, or to
40 g (1½ oz) butter	taste

Dissolve the yeast in the milk. Sieve the flour and mix with the sugar if liked, lemon peel and salt, then add the liquid, the butter, melted, and the egg yolk. Knead a smooth dough, spread with wet hands on a greased baking sheet and leave to rise. This quantity of dough will make a rectangle about 25 cm × 16 cm (11 inches × 27 inches). Halve and stone the plums and place on the dough. Rub together the crumble ingredients and scatter over the plums. Brush the edges of the pie with egg white and bake in a moderate oven till golden. When cold, cut into squares.

Variations The same dough may be formed into 'Moravian buns'. These are filled twice, once with a mixture of curd cheese and egg yolk, some lemon peel and juice and a little butter, then closed and left to rise, the second time (make a new indentation and brush with egg white) with plum cheese (see p. 431). Sprinkle the jam with the crumble before baking for about 30 minutes.

The rise of the Czech sugar industry was part of its early prosperity in Central Europe. Beet was refined in record quantities while wheat flourished in the Danube Basin. Rapid industrialization in Bohemia and Moravia meant that the machinery for grinding, brewing, canning, distilling and baking foodstuffs was on hand.

Festive Czech tart

The fillings most popular for *Mehlspeisen* are also those for cakes. Poppy seeds, curd cheese and plum jam occur over and over again with every variety of dough and topping. This open pie from Czechoslovakia combines all three and looks marvellous without much effort. It is served at weddings and on other festive occasions.

dough made with 500 g
    (1 lb) flour, as for plum
    cake with crumble (see
    p. 400)

Filling (1):
250 g (8 oz) curd cheese
30 g (1 oz) butter
1 egg yolk
vanilla essence
1–2 tablespoons raisins
3 tablespoons sugar
    (optional)

Filling (2):
120 g (4 oz) plum cheese or
    thick prune purée
1 teaspoon rum
a pinch of cinnamon

Filling (3):
100 g (3½ oz) ground
    poppy seeds
½ cup milk
1 tablespoon sugar, or more
    to taste
1 dessertspoon butter

After making the dough and leaving it to rise, divide it to form two round pies. Place each one on a greased baking sheet, then fill with the three mixtures in a pattern. Concentric rings are very effective, or a large cross of cheese across a background of jam and poppy seeds in alternate triangles. The cheese can be further decorated with raisins or circles of poppy seed or plum cheese, and the dark fillings are usually highlighted with whole peeled almonds.

Cheese crumble pie

150 g (6 oz) butter
1 tablespoon sugar
1 egg yolk

200 g (7 oz) flour
1 tablespoon milk
500 g (1 lb) curd cheese

2 egg yolks	50 g (2 oz) butter
1 teaspoon sugar	50 g (2 oz) sugar
lemon peel	*or*
handful of raisins	50 g (2 oz) flour
2 stiffly beaten egg whites	100 g (3½ oz) ground almonds
	50 g (2 oz) sugar
Crumble:	
100 g (3½ oz) flour	

Cream the butter, sugar and egg yolk, add the flour and milk. Knead the dough lightly, line a greased flan tin with it and fill with the cheese creamed with the egg yolks, sugar and lemon peel. Sprinkle with raisins, smooth over the egg whites and sprinkle with crumble. Bake for half an hour in a moderate oven.

Walnut tart

Walnuts are widely used in the Balkans and Hungary to fill sweet cakes and as the basis of sweetmeats. Paul Kovi writes that in Transylvania, where religion sanctioned them as symbols of purity, nuts were also considered to be aphrodisiacs, which made them particularly popular as Carnival week approached. This recipe comes from Romania, where many centuries of subjugation to the Ottoman Empire have resulted in some splendid *pâtisserie* to eat with Turkish coffee or to crown a rich meal.

For the pastry:
120 g (4 oz) plain flour
½ teaspoon baking powder
a pinch of salt
50 g (2 oz) butter
1 tablespoon sugar
1 egg yolk
milk

For the filling:
100 g (3–4 oz) sugar
2 egg yolks
150 g (5 oz) ground walnuts
3 egg whites, stiffly beaten
6 tablespoons apricot jam
3 tablespoons lemon juice

Sieve together flour, baking powder and salt and rub in butter. Add the sugar and egg yolk and bind into a pliable dough, adding a little milk if necessary. Knead for a few minutes, then leave to stand for 20 minutes in a cool place.

For the filling beat together sugar and egg yolks, add the ground walnuts and fold in the beaten egg whites.

Roll out the dough to line a 22 cm (9 inch) flan dish. Spread the jam mixed with lemon juice evenly over the surface and top with the walnut mixture.

Bake in a medium oven for 35–40 minutes and serve warm or cold.

Linzer slices

These Austrian cakes are popular throughout Central Europe.

175 g (6 oz) flour	grated rind of 1 lemon
120 g (4 oz) butter	a pinch of cinnamon
175 g (4 oz) sugar	few drops lemon juice
50 g (2 oz) ground walnuts	2 tablespoons redcurrant
2 egg yolks	jam

Make a soft pastry with all the ingredients except the jam. Roll out ⅔ of the pastry 1 cm (½ inch) thick and spread in a greased baking tin. Spread the jam evenly over the surface and with the remaining pastry make a lattice of strips across it. Bake for 25–30 minutes in a moderate oven, cool and cut into diamonds.

Rigo Jancsi chocolate cream slices

A Hungarian confection named after a gypsy fiddler at the centre of a society scandal in the 1920s.

Cake:	Filling:
3 eggs	30 g (1 oz) cocoa
3 tablespoons sugar	50 g (2 oz) sugar
30 g (1 oz) grated chocolate	vanilla essence
2 tablespoons flour	
soft chocolate icing	1 cup double cream

Cream the yolks and sugar, then gradually add, alternately, the grated chocolate, flour and whipped egg white. Bake in a well-greased oblong baking tin for about 15 minutes. When the sponge is cool, divide in two crossways. Cover one piece with chocolate icing and cut into 1 cm (½ inch) squares. Cover the other with a mixture made by adding all the other ingredients to the stiffly whipped cream. Place the chocolate-iced squares on top and cut into serving portions with a warm knife. Chill slightly before serving. According to George Lang, a layer of apricot jam originally came between the cake base and the cream covering.

Tree cakes

Using a piece of a tree as a cake mould seems so obvious as to be immediately eccentric. In Hungary yeast dough used to be rolled around a log and baked like a spit roast and the hollow tubes filled. In 1988 we were served unfilled tree cakes nine inches tall and three inches in diameter. Dried greased corncobs could also be used for the purpose of making what the Hungarians call these chimney-cakes, which are rolled in chopped walnuts and eaten with jam. Transylvania caps both these ideas with its 'bridal-cake tree' which used also to be made in other parts of Hungary, in a small version, for Christmas. The idea is to cover with sweet dough a thick branch that has as many offshoots as possible. The bark is first removed and the bough sanded smooth. The dough tree is baked, then decorated with edible decorations made of gingerbread, marzipan and various biscuits, also ribbons and baubles. The stem is rooted in a pot of earth like a Christmas tree. During Christmas children can break off branches, gnaw at the pastry and eat the decorations.

With the traditional German *Baumkuchen* ('tree-cake') from Berlin, layers of dough are spread on a continuously turning plate with a pole in the centre. When one layer is browned the next is poured on, and so the cake rises to a grand height. The finished cake is covered with a sugar glaze. It cannot be made properly at home.

Bublanina

This is a Czech sponge with the fruit baked into it. It is very good with cherries.

6 eggs
150 g (5 oz) sugar
50 g (2 oz) butter
180 g (6 oz) flour
180 g (6 oz) semolina
500 g (1 lb) fruit

Beat the yolks with half the sugar, add the melted butter gradually, then the stiffly beaten egg whites, flour and semolina. Grease a sandwich tin, pour in the mixture, then add the fruit, dipped in flour to prevent it sinking to the bottom of the cake. Bake in a preheated slow oven for about 30 minutes, or until golden.

Indianky

These 'Indians' are as widely loved across the lands of the Habsburg Empire as is *Sachertorte*, especially by children. They resemble profiteroles.

4 egg whites	(optional)
50 g (2 oz) castor sugar	3 egg yolks

90 g (3 oz) plain flour

Filling:
1 small carton (5 fl. oz)
cream, whipped

Icing:
1 tablespoon cornflour
1 tablespoon milk
90 g (3 oz) butter
90 g (3 oz) icing sugar
15 g ($\frac{1}{2}$ oz) cocoa

Whip the egg whites, add sugar to taste. Beat the yolks, add the flour and add this to the whites. Grease a baking tin, flour it, then spoon in the mixture in blobs. Bake for 8–10 minutes in a hot oven. Cut the sponges in half, place the bottoms in paper cups, and sandwich the halves together with the whipped cream. Ice the tops by mixing the cornflour and milk over heat till thick, then adding the creamed butter, sugar and cocoa. The tops of these cakes are usually set at an angle, to look like faces, possibly those of Indian squaws.

Fugger's lemon cake

As if to prove the Fuggers' wealth long after their day, this is the lemoniest cake I have ever encountered. The Fuggers came from Augsburg in south Germany and made their money as merchants, which the aristocracy found upsetting. This is really what disturbed the chroniclers. Apart from this cake, the only other surviving earnest of their estate I have come across is Fukier's Wine Cellar in the Old Town in Warsaw. The 'cake' is more of a pie and best made on a pie plate or a flat, ovenproof dish.

60 g ($2\frac{1}{2}$ oz) butter or
margarine
250 g (8 oz) plain flour
$\frac{1}{8}$ teaspoon salt
1 egg
1 egg yolk

For the filling:
180 g (6 oz) ground
almonds, or 90 g (3 oz)
fresh brown breadcrumbs
plus 50 g (2 oz) butter
$\frac{1}{2}$ cup sugar
grated rind of 1 lemon
juice of 2 lemons

For the topping:
2 tablespoons milk
50 g (2 oz) slivered almonds

To make the filling, mix all the ingredients together thoroughly. If using bread and butter, mix over a bowl of hot water to make a smooth paste. The alternative filling is my invention for the moment you find you have no ground almonds in the cupboard or they have become too expensive.

To make the dough, rub the fat into the flour and salt, add the eggs and 1–2 tablespoons water, and chill. Roll out half the dough in a circle to fit an approximately 26 cm (10 inch) tin. Prick the surface, spoon in the filling, cover with the remaining dough and pinch the edges together. Prick a pattern with a fork over the top, brush with milk and sprinkle over the almonds. Bake in a preheated medium oven for 40 minutes and cool on a rack.

Strudels and jam rolls

Strudels will always be found on the menu of Central European coffee- and tea-houses and milk-bars. Their popularity is as widespread at home as it is abroad. The cafés are less likely to have leavened sweet pastry nowadays, but a modern unleavened version of the sweet roll is common, with a traditional filling of curd cheese, nuts, chestnuts, poppy seed or apple, or a more modern one of coffee, chocolate, jam or wild strawberries and fresh cream. The last are listed by Zofia Czerny among her extensive collection of Polish contemporary recipes. The fillings are wrapped in a dough very rich in eggs and sugar. In Yugoslavia, Bulgaria and Hungary, where chestnuts are carefully cultivated for food, and in Austria, where they are much favoured in *pâtisserie*, a chestnut roll is another interesting possibility and one of the oldest, made long before coffee or chocolate rolls.

Chestnut roll

4 eggs
90 g (3 oz) sugar
vanilla sugar
90 g (3 oz) flour
a pinch of baking powder
100 g (3½ oz) chestnut
  purée

Filling:
160 g (5½ oz) each butter
  and sugar
40 g (1½ oz) chocolate
1 teaspoon rum
200 g (7 oz) chestnut purée

Mix the eggs, sugar and vanilla sugar and beat until mixture doubles in volume. Blend in the remaining ingredients to form a dough. Line a baking tray with greaseproof paper, grease well and spread the dough in a rectangle 1 cm (½ inch) thick. Bake it in a medium oven for 15 minutes. Rest on a sheet of sugared paper and spread with filling. Make this by creaming the butter and boiling the sugar in ½ cup water until it spins a thread. Pour the hot syrup into the butter, then stand the whole in cold water while adding the melted chocolate, rum and purée. Roll up the roulade. Spread remaining filling on sides. Decorate with whole glacé chestnuts and/or grated chocolate, or more purée mixed with whipped cream.

Coffee and cake

The Central European middle classes virtually came into being on the dietary supplement of coffee and cake. After coffee was introduced via Turkey at the end of the seventeenth century, the habit, though expensive, quickly became popular with most classes, including those who could not afford it. The café became a significant phenomenon of urban life, and one which brought strangers as well as friends together at leisure. In Vienna the coffee-houses may have been extensions of the office and the backdrop for financial decisions and therefore mainly male preserves, but elsewhere the business function and masculinity of cafés were less pronounced. They brought together men and women, women and women, and people in related professions, such as painters, poets and lawyers. Many unofficial beginnings of the larger-scale political and social groupings which shaped the life of the middle class and the emancipated proletariat were rooted in café life. The tea and coffee saloons played the role of trade guilds, literary salons and political clubs.

In Poland, where coffee was a passion, coffee-houses serving cakes multiplied; there were over ninety in Warsaw by 1822. An aura of luxury surrounded these exotic products of Araby and the New World, for, as well as the coffee and chocolate, only bankers and wealthy merchants were in a position to be tempted by the best sweet ingredients for cakes and *Torten* – imported apricots, peaches and oranges, hot-house pineapples, figs and lemon. Expectations of high standards were quickly formed amongst the middle classes when they realized refined eating and coffee-drinking were civilizing and implied a measure of gracious leisure. A certain gastronomic elegance has remained with Poland to this day.

The old coffee-houses and confectionery shops underlined the emerging bourgeois style by supplying Polish and foreign newspapers and periodicals to give a taste of a larger world. When many better-off Poles emigrated to western Europe in the nineteenth century to avoid living through the political obliteration of their country, they were well schooled in the ways of a café society. Whole cafés in Rome and Florence and Paris were colonized by Polish *émigrés*.

The German bourgeois style though was unique to Germany, because the *Café-Konditorei* quickly arose alongside the coffee-house and eventually took its place. German shopkeepers opened *Konditoreien* because of the instability of coffee, tea and chocolate on financial markets. They began offering clients cakes and sweetmeats, which were not subject to high taxes nor dependent on the quality of the harvest, to offset their losses. The *Konditorei* atmosphere had little to do with art or finance, but everything to do with family life. I can quite believe that before the war in Berlin the Sunday walk would be directed past a 'coffee garden', where some promenaders would lessen the expense of the drink by bringing their own cake. In the cheaper gardens they brought their own coffee too and the patron supplied the water for a modest charge. Town cafés followed the more orthodox

Turkish coffee, from Jacques Le Hay, Recueil de Cent Estampes
Representant Differentes Nations du Levant, *Paris 1714*

public reading-room pattern established in Vienna and further east.

Magdalena Rettigova, best-known for her authorship of the early nineteenth-century Czech bible of home cooking, *Domaci kucharka*, as well as for autobiography and fiction, published in 1843 a volume entitled *The Coffee House or Everything Sweet – One Hundred Recipes for the Preparation of all Kinds of Drinks and Things which will bring People together for Conversation and Society*. She believed the coffee get-together was the perfect vehicle for realizing and spreading contemporary social ideals of national vitality through more and better education. The appetite could be whetted for delicious sweetmeats and public affairs simultaneously.

Rettigova, not alone in her thoughts but a pioneer, provided many recipes for yeast bakery, *Mehlspeisen*, puddings, biscuits and *Torten*. But her advice, directed at the women of Bohemia, went deeper. If they understood their scope in the kitchen they might never be bored: food was to reflect the wit, curiosity and energy desirable to enhance society. As cook, writer, pedagogue and aesthetic theorist she made a unique contribution to the Czech National Revival.

Yet who were these dreadful people who wanted to show everyone else the cultural way forward by refining their aesthetic and moral outlook over tea or coffee and cake? In Berlin in the 1830s the sad and incisive Heinrich Heine had an idea:

> They sat and drank tea at tables
> And talked a lot about love.
> The gentlemen, well, they were aesthetic,
> And the ladies like soft little doves.

The hopes surrounding coffee and cake have come and gone.

The cafés, though, continue. In Prague and Cracow, Budapest and Bucharest, they do so despite the dulling effects of Communism. Many of the famous old cafés with attached histories and personalities have been spruced up for the tourist industry. The ambience, less malleable, is more private, inverted and parochial than an idealistic visitor from a non-café society like Britain might want to believe. The cafés are comfortable if no longer very stimulating places to sit and talk or write or reflect. I learned to ask the question in Polish a few years ago: 'Do you have coffee?' The answer was often, 'No', though the cakes were there. The *kawarka* in Czechoslovakia, the *kavarnia* in Poland, is a place to eat cake with coffee or tea, or eat a sandwich and some goulash soup, and get out of the winter cold. In Central Europe in less glamorous self-service establishments the names of the cakes are written by hand, but you need to be able to read, memorize and pronounce them in a hurry if your foreignness is not to hold up the mid-afternoon queue. Large, chic establishments perform a saving grace and wheel their cakes round by trolley; a separate waiter with a separate purse does cake duty. In a modern concession to health it is possible to buy low-sugar, 'diabetic' versions of favourite cakes and most Western visitors would probably jump at the chance. There are newspapers in some cafés and there is always tobacco smoke. Only the cakes are to be found in the milk-bars.

I have to say, though, that a high-class *Konditorei* is still a magical place, shiny with the machinery to make coffee, with mirrors, and ornate with many confections of translucent sugar and rows of elaborate cakes well-displayed behind glass. The magic works for politicians of all persuasions. It's curious to see how Communist Berlin has made the luxurious, revamped Berliner Kaffeehaus on the Alexanderplatz a veritable shrine to the bourgeois past. The newspapers aren't international any more, but they do come on sticks, while the pastries under large plastic domes and the several varieties of coffee, served by neat, efficient, black-and-white-uniformed waitresses, are excellent, and suitably expensive.

Layer cakes

It was particularly layer cakes which in the Habsburg and Prussian Empires accompanied and symbolized a new gentility of life. In this respect Poland's political fate was not at all destructive of its kitchen. The layer cake, which I call by its German name, *Torte*, reached a height of popularity in the western Polish territories under Austrian rule.

The same taste for Vienna's luscious layer cakes spread south into Slovenia and Croatia and as far east as parts of Romania and

Bulgaria when the Habsburgs reached the full extent of their power. The Hungarians were particularly inspired and in fifty years, from the poorest beginnings around 1830, rapidly developed a range of luxury cakes. Through trade the German influence was also widespread.

For people on holiday at the spas, layer cakes were inseparable from the rituals of the five o'clock *thé dansant*. On Lake Balaton in Hungary, where the dancing was to a gypsy orchestra, sweet delights like Rigo Jancsi slices perhaps originated. The intricate sandwich cakes that enhanced these occasions took a long time and a lot of professional patience to make, and the fine presentation demanded skill and invited whimsicality. Because the message these cakes bore was leisure, however, no one ever thought of imitating them at home. They are the cakes of the German and Hungarian afternoon, the delayed pudding, available only in the cafés, never the restaurants. The American passion for a pudding of cake with coffee grew out of these Central European habits.

The layers of the giant cakes you see in the *cukraszda*, the Hungarian cake shop, are of sponge sandwiched together with creams flavoured with lemon, chocolate, nuts, strawberries, chestnuts, coffee and caramel.

A very acceptable cream is also made of potato. This is boiled, puréed and mixed with sugar, vanilla and a good half its weight in butter, plus ground walnuts and rum. The layers are spread with raspberry jam, then a layer of the potato cream.

A chestnut cream, which the potato cream resembles in taste, is made by beating a chestnut purée with sugar to taste and a third of its weight in butter. A little rum may be added and also a tablespoon of milk or cream. The cake is chilled before serving to allow the cream, which may also be piled over the outside of the *torta*, to solidify a little.

To make a nut layer cake, ground walnuts or hazelnuts with a dash of rum are stirred into any basic cream of butter, sugar, vanilla and cream.

The basic sponge mixture is normally of flour and eggs and butter, though both a bean and a potato purée can be substituted for the flour.

Bean torta

This is not quite what you will find in a café but since the ingredients are unlavish, healthy and intriguing and it is a rare *torta* that can easily be made at home it is worth trying. The result is moist, robust and tastes of nuts. I have seen it rediscovered in contemporary, belt-tightening Czechoslovakia as an 'economy' cake.

250 g (8 oz) puréed dried beans (haricot, lima, black-eye, kidney or dried broad beans)
1 large slice bread, crumbled, or 40 g (1½ oz) fresh breadcrumbs
4 eggs
250 g (8 oz) castor sugar or to taste
vanilla essence
90 g (3 oz) ground walnuts, hazelnuts or pinenuts, or a mixture of the three
grated lemon rind
90–120 g (3–4 oz) blackcurrant or cherry jam, or whipped cream

For the topping:
juice of 2 lemons
300 g (10 oz) sugar or to taste
1 tablespoon water
1 teaspoon rum

Soak the beans overnight and set to cook in plenty of fresh water. When they are soft but not mushy, drain and use a mincer or food processor to grind them and the bread into a smooth dry mixture. Cream the egg yolks, sugar and vanilla together and add to the beans with the nuts and grated lemon rind and stiffly beaten egg whites. Mix well. If you grind the nuts at home the cake will have a gritty but rather pleasing texture. Turn into a greased and floured cake tin and bake for about 40 minutes in a medium oven. Allow to cool for 10 minutes before turning out on a wire rack. Slice the cake then and sandwich together with whipped cream or jam. Make the glaze by mixing the topping ingredients together over a low heat and pouring over when smooth.

Dobostorta

The Café Gerbaud in Central Budapest still has its comfortable upholstery, pastel decor and good manners, and older people continue to refer to it by its original name. When it was nationalized after World War Two it was renamed the Vorosmarty after the nineteenth-century poet of the Hungarian National Liberation Movement. Of the many famous layer cakes you might choose to help you recover after an afternoon's shopping, the *Dobostorta* is renowned. It is easily recognized by the caramel glaze across the top of its chocolate cream layers. From the first the *Dobostorta*, created by the owner of a Budapest delicatessen in 1887, transcended its food function to become a sentimental symbol of the joys of being Hungarian. The cake was exhibited at the Millennium exhibition of 1896 and the recipe published to swell the funds of the Budapest Bakers Guild in 1906. In 1962 Hungarian chefs gave the torte a seventy-fifth birthday party, parading a two metre (six foot) version through the streets; Vorosmarty's sold only Dobos' creations for two whole days. The rival *Stefanietorta*, which replaces the Dobos caramel with more chocolate cream and a top sprinkling of grated chocolate, holds up under the weight of competition.

For anyone who is curious about such differences and has the time and patience to assemble the cakes at home, George Lang in *The Cuisine of Hungary* has compiled a virtual catalogue of the Hungarian nineteenth-century layer cakes, with sixteen rich recipes verified by the Budapest Bakers Guild and other authorities. The most I can do here is give the instructions for the most famous chocolate layer cake in the Habsburg Empire.

Sachertorte

This is probably also the most famous chocolate cake in the world. It originated in Vienna at the Hotel Sacher and became an outstanding treat and consolation to cake-lovers across the Empire. It is unusual in having no cream and being less rich compared with the usual Viennese gâteaux. One story has it that

Prince Metternich, architect of reaction in the empire after the defeat of Napoleon, asked *Mr* Sacher to create 'a plainer and more masculine gâteau, since the others in existence were only for sweet-toothed women'. The result was a great success, hailed as the epitome of lightness and fineness in cake-making. So fine was it, indeed, that another recipe-collector refused to connect the cake with *Mrs* Sacher, 'a rather tough, jovial, cigar-smoking lady whom one would certainly not associate with anything as delicate as the *Sacher Torte*'. The origins sound apocryphal, but the fan club is legendary. I gathered a Czech, a Romanian and a Pole to test this recipe, which is simple, and all three dissolved in reminiscences of childhood.

350 g (12 oz) butter	250 g (8 oz) plain chocolate
300 g (10 oz) castor sugar	2 tablespoons rum
5 eggs	raspberry jam
150 g (6 oz) flour	chocolate icing

Cream together the butter and sugar. Beat the egg whites stiff. Add the yolks to the butter, mix well, fold in the flour and the whites and mix well. Melt the chocolate with the rum and add when cool. Butter and flour two sponge tins, divide the mixture between them and bake in a medium oven about 45 minutes. Cool, spread the top of one with jam, and sandwich together. Cover with chocolate icing.

As a teenager, it seemed to me Germany gave much of its spare-time energy to ritual cake-eating. In the families where I stayed there was a short family walk after Sunday lunch, to stimulate the appetite, then the failed slimmers went to a café on the edge of the park or the forest or the cemetery and indulged in a huge piece of *Torte* topped with whipped cream. On another occasion I lodged with a Protestant pastor and his wife who smiled kindly on my being family-less in Germany. Every religious holiday they presented me with a piece of *Torte* from the *Konditorei*. I gratefully lost count of how many high days there were between Easter and Whitsun.

Karlsbad layer cake

The Central Europeans are poor slimmers. That perhaps is why they so much enjoy the ritual of an annual spa visit, and why their fellow men and women fill the pastry-shop windows of the health town with delicious temptations to weaken the will of 'cure guests'. Joseph Wechsberg recalled the arduous three weeks his family and his class spent every year at the spa of Karlsbad or Karlovy Vary, in western Bohemia, recovering from eleven months of over-indulgence:

There was a theatre, there were concerts and always Karl Bayer's *Oblaten*, paper-thin pastries pressed together with almond and sugar filling, that were permitted between sips of water . . . the glorious day when you had lost five kilos . . . you would go to Pupp's [hotel restaurant] and order everything à la carte, from foie gras to fish to roast duck to dessert, and maybe another dessert. When you got up you felt like a human being again . . . not like a cure guest.

Some elaborate compensatory trick lies behind the invention of the Karlsbad layer cake out of these *Oblaten*. It is not the *minceur* version with sugar and almonds, but an elaborate confection made by sandwiching a rich cream between these thin, potentially slimming wafers that has been passed on from generation to generation in celebration of the enjoyment of Karlsbad cafés. (The *Oblaten* themselves though must be one of the first manufactured, patented food products designed to help weight loss.) The grandest recipe for a Karlsbad layer cake plasters these nineteenth-century round crispbreads with layers of creamed butter, cocoa and cream and tops the lot with thick chocolate icing and almonds. Plainer versions bind the wafers with blancmange, *crème pâtissière* or a mixture of ground almonds, dates and chocolate. They are pressed under a weight before final decoration and serving. A pastry layer cake similar to that of Karlsbad, but made with pastry layers, is attributed to Cracow, in Poland. It's the sweet compressed filling that ap-peals.

Carlsbad, from J. Baker, Pictures from Bohemia, London 1894

Chrust-faworki

Like my student self in Germany, ordinary people in the nineteenth century could only afford cakes on high days and holidays. Amongst those high days was Carnival week, when *faworki*, fried strips of pastry with icing sugar, were eaten. They also took the name 'God's mercy'.

350 g (12 oz) flour	lemon peel
1 tablespoon sugar	a little milk
50 g (2 oz) butter	oil for frying
1 egg yolk	vanilla sugar for dusting
1 tablespoon rum	

Mix together all the ingredients except the last two and work into a dough with some milk. Leave to rest for an hour in a cool place. Roll the dough out very thinly. Cut into squares, diamonds or strips and fry in hot oil till golden brown. Drain on greaseproof paper and roll in powdered sugar while still hot.

Royal mazurek

At Easter, alongside the twenty-egg *babka*, the favourite Polish small pastry is *mazurek*. These are flat cakes, covered with a paste of nuts, almonds, sweetened cheese or dried fruit, and may also be eaten at Christmas and Carnival week and other special occasions. The local priest used to come and bless these famous biscuits after midnight on Easter Saturday as a sign that Lent was over and feasting could begin. As he went about his duties he would expect to be given food to end his own fast at each house; the priest's gluttony barely concealed under a mantle of holiness was often a butt for jokes.

1 cup butter or margarine	¼ cup finely chopped or
1½ cups white flour	ground almonds
1 cup sugar	1 teaspoon grated orange or
¼ teaspoon salt	lemon peel
6 egg yolks	

Cream the butter, mix the flour, sugar and salt, then beat each egg yolk individually, together with a portion of the flour mixture, into the butter until well combined. Stir in the nuts and peel. Grease a baking tin or tins, and press or roll the dough into an oblong, approx. 35 cm × 25 cm (15 inches × 10 inches), or two oblongs. Bake for 35–40 minutes until just golden. Cool for 10 minutes then cut into oblongs. The recipe makes about 36 biscuits.

The *mazureks* most clearly show the Turkish influence on Polish sweet bakery, which arrived in the eighteenth century. Poland had in its own way excelled in *friandises* since the Middle Ages. The monasteries, which in southern Europe produced some of the best wine and vegetables from their lands, in the north were qualified in the baking of elegant pastries. This sweet bakery was made in great quantities on the holiday of each monastery's patron saint, and was known as 'monastery bread'. The leavened cakes, spiced and sweetened with honey, had fillings which have remained characteristic: poppy seed, dried fruit, apple, plum, soft cheese. Wladislaw Reymont also suggested that in later centuries Jewish pastry cooks produced some of the daintiest delicacies. Working with yeast dough, honey, nuts and poppy seeds they made fritters and strudels and crumble cake and many of the favourite *Mehlspeisen*. But the Orient and France brought the modern touch. A visit by a Turkish emissary in 1778 turned into a festival of sweetmeats and left a permanent mark on Polish confectionery, according to the modern food historian Maria Lemnis. The adoption of Oriental techniques in cake-making coincided with the arrival of chocolate, coffee and sugar and together these two events inspired a minor revolution in Polish eating habits and social manners.

Other festive biscuits

German Advent and Christmas biscuits were baked in the oven after the *Stollen* (see p. 362). Some were eaten on 6 December, others kept until later in the month. Typically they were spiced, glazed, thin honey biscuits made in various shapes and moulds and highly decorated. The most common are *Spekulatius*, which go equally well with coffee and with a white wine from the Mosel. Nowadays they are usually bought.

Altogether biscuits on the Continent have a more festive and decorative function than our own. In Yugoslavia, under the names *drazgose* and *skofja loka*, highly ornamental glazed biscuits are made of a dry mixture of rye flour, honey and spices, akin to gingerbread. Some of the honey is retained to make a syrup and the biscuits are glazed with this before baking so that they appear lacquered when removed from the oven. Thin threads of the cake mixture are fashioned into patterns, whirls, wheat sheaves, birds and flowers, and the biscuits themselves are shaped into hearts, stars and diamonds. They look like examples of fine wood carving.

Such bakery is a reliable bearer of history. *Goethe's Grandmother's Cookbook*, compiled in the early eighteenth century, which contains a predominant number of recipes for sweet goods, reflects the preference of the day for using all manner of moulds, dyes and decorations to bring these to the table. The same habit is reflected in the Polish Christmas Eve wafers, nowadays made of rice paper embossed with religious motifs.

Black almond tart

The unknown first compiler of the book handed to Goethe's grandmother, the newly wed thirteen-year-old Anna Margarethe Lindheimerin, insists that sweet cooking is the way to win love. The good housewife should make efforts to provide cakes, *Torten*, gingerbread, sugar-bread, marzipan and biscuits. The following tart is recommended.

14 egg yolks
350 g (12 oz) sugar
500 g (1 lb) ground
    almonds
10 stiffly beaten egg whites

3 teaspoons cinnamon
1 teaspoon powdered cloves
the grated rind of 2 lemons
5 tablespoons hard fine
    breadcrumbs

Beat together the yolks and sugar, then stir in the remaining ingredients and bake in a moderate oven till firm. Presumably the blackness comes from the bread originally used.

Both the almonds and the lemons for this recipe would have been imported in Frau Lindheimerin's day, bought at the cheapest time of the year and stored. Other nuts and fruits such as cherries, raspberries and quinces she would have had in her garden, and she would have saved her rosebuds too for flavouring or making the rose-water for *Stollen*.

Almond tubes

More in the Oriental tradition are these small German cakes which are very light and good to look at if the cream filling is coloured green and flavoured with pistachio. The technique of rolling them round a wooden spoon is a small-scale version of the tree cakes described on p. 404.

2 egg whites, stiffly beaten
120 g (4 oz) sugar
120 g (4 oz) ground almonds
$\frac{1}{2}$ teaspoon cinnamon
whipped cream, colouring, pistachio flavouring

Mix together all the ingredients but the last, roll small pieces thinly and lay on greased tins. Bake in a slow oven till pale yellow, then, while still supple, wrap them around the stems of wooden spoons and cool on a wire rack. When cooled, slide off the spoons and fill with the coloured cream.

Sweet crescents

Two symbols have dominated the shape and decoration of a significant part of East European bakery for the past 300 years: the cross and the crescent. The cross was inscribed in Easter cakes and in Easter cheese and the crescent made into savoury pastries and bread rolls. The crescent has informed many sweet pastries and biscuits.

In Bulgaria sweet *kiflichki* made with *banitsa* pastry are filled with ground nuts moistened with milk and flavoured with cinnamon and handed round at New Year, and something similar, adapted to become an Oriental pastry in sugar syrup, is handed round by Romanians on All Saints' Day. The Austrians make *Kipfeln* of meringue and fill them with jam, while in Yugoslavia, Czechoslovakia and Poland various rich biscuits with nuts, sometimes iced, are made in the crescent shape. The Germans ahistorically call them 'horns'.

Miscellaneous confectionery

Besides bakery there have always been sweets. In Poland poppy seed and honey toffee was a confection which could be made at home. On the Baltic coast the town of Königsberg was famous for its marzipan, while everywhere local fruits such as apples, pears and quinces were boiled with honey and later with sugar to make fruit pastilles. Top of any child's list anywhere today, however, is chocolate. Yet chocolate is now, as cake was once, a sign of the political times. It needs to be imported, is good for high prices and taxes, and is therefore one of those few edible substances which enjoy a double existence along the lines of the East–West political divide. I am speaking here from experience, and as a carrier of English chocolate for presents. A friend of a friend had raised the political point about chocolate in Dresden at Easter 1986. The *good-quality* chocolate *Osterhasen* were only on sale for hard currency in the Intershops. My acquaintance

Sweet seller, from Jacques Le Hay, Recueil de Cent Estampes
Representant Differentes Nations du Levant, *Paris 1714*

wondered out loud what sort of children would grow up, seeing these eggs through the shop windows but not being allowed to have them, but only something markedly inferior, made for domestic consumption. Children with a sense of them and us, I guessed, a notion which seems to us as socially antiquated as life above- and below-stairs. A chocolate for us and a chocolate for them. Even between *countries* in Eastern Europe there's a chocolate hierarchy. I was given some chocolate once in Yugoslavia for helping a Serbian woman dodge the Romanian customs. The word that came to mind when my daughter and I tried it later in the hungry privacy of our Romanian hotel room was 'debased'. It was far removed from the real thing. Yet the Serbian woman was taking it in multiple quantities to sell at a weekly barter market just inside the Romanian border. In that country there was none at all.

Oriental-style pastries and sweetmeats

Cafés in the north of Yugoslavia have an Austrian or Italian character and it is not until one reaches Serbia and Bosnia that the Oriental style takes over. The coffee is Turkish, sweet, short and boiled, served with a glass of water. The pastries with nuts or fruit are rich in fat and thickly coated in syrup. A number of them are well-known in Britain as Greek or Cypriot, such as *baklava*, consisting of thin layers of pastry folded around nuts and immersed in syrup, and *kadaif*, fried honey-coated pastry vermicelli. At lunch-time in the streets of the bazaar in Old Sarajevo mainly women and girls congregate to chatter and eat two cakes apiece. Outside the cake shops narrow shelves provide minimal extra seating. Coffee waiters hurry through the streets with laden trays, serving customers rather than tables. Their domain appears to be the whole street.

The pastry for Balkan *pâtisserie* is usually *banitsa* or flaky pastry, sweetened and sometimes fried, or filled with dried fruit or *crème pâtissière*, or poppy seeds, or honey or nuts, and often in a sticky bath of syrup. The lightest confection is made with ground almonds, icing sugar and beaten egg, which is baked in small cakes and sprinkled immediately out of the oven with rose-water. A quick home-made sweetmeat is to fry crustless slices of bread or milk loaf in oil, drain them, dip them in a syrup of sugar and water, sprinkle them with cinnamon and serve them immediately. The only time I could face trying this was for a late breakfast and even then it was too much. Baked apples with a very sweet filling are nicer, as are thin strudels. Choosing at random from an *à la carte* menu, we had a delicious breakfast of custard cakes, plum juice and mint tea one morning in Sofia, which seemed to be far more representative of the Bulgarian national food style than the German breakfast we were offered in our hotel.

In the larger Romanian towns, just as in parts of Yugoslavia, the Oriental tradition in sweetmeats is accompanied by Viennese and French-style cakes, and there are strong influences from other cuisines – Hungarian, German and Russian – which have become native. The cafés therefore serve cappuccino, Turkish and French-style coffee and the mixture of pastries reflects the same range. Within Eastern Europe it is however an outstanding feature of Romanian cuisine that they insist sweet things be sweet and savoury savoury.

Sugar pies

In Lezhe, northern Albania, very slim waiters served us these 'pies' followed by cubes of chilled watermelon. The cakes are a kind of shortbread anointed with thick sugar syrup, and they crop up as far afield as Bosnia and Lebanon.

180 g (6 oz) butter	*For the syrup:*
350 g (12 oz) plain flour	350 g (12 oz) sugar
1 egg yolk	2 tablespoons lemon juice
1 tablespoon sugar	
a pinch of salt	

Rub the butter into the flour, add the egg yolk, sugar and salt, and knead into a stiff dough. Form with the hands into 12 round cakes 2–3 cm (1–1½ inches) thick, place on a greased baking tray and bake in a preheated hot oven for 8–10 minutes. Boil the sugar in 1 cup of water until it forms a syrup, add the lemon juice and while the syrup is still hot pour it over the cakes on a serving plate. Most of the syrup will be absorbed by the time the cakes are cool, but any left in a pool should be served with them.

Halva

This a sweetmeat popular since medieval times and enjoyed in countries as far apart as Poland and India. Further back, the Romans ate something similar made with pine nuts and honey. *Halva* was originally made with rice and is related to the Oriental rice desserts such as *malebi* (see p. 381). Nowadays it is made with semolina or ground nuts in various consistencies. Bars of *halva* as firm as nougat and sweeter than sugar, easy to manufacture and store, are found throughout Bulgaria, most of Yugoslavia, Albania and Romania, often with the flavour of almonds or sesame, mixed with honey. George Lang's Hungarian version is appropriately called *Turkish Honey*. Modern versions may be coated with chocolate.

The joy and enthusiasm of the citizens continued to grow and spread in the surrounding villages. In the early days of October, Arif Beg ordered a great feast for the completion of the bridge . . . the feast, in which anyone could take part, lasted two days. The Vezir's health was celebrated in meat and drink, in music, dancing and song; horse and foot races were arranged, and meat and sweetstuffs divided amongst the poor. On the square which linked the bridge with the market place, *halva* was cooked in cauldrons and served piping hot to the people. That *halva* even got as far as the villages around the town and whoever ate it wished good health to the Vezir and long life to his buildings. There were children who went back 14 times to the cauldrons until the cooks, recognizing them, drove them away with their long wooden spoons. One gypsy child died after eating too much hot *halva*.

Ivo Andric, *The Bridge over the Drina*

This was the scene drawn by the Yugoslav novelist Ivo Andric, set in Turkish-occupied Bosnia. The Vizier built a famous bridge over the river Drina at Visegrad and when it was built *halva* was ladled out as a mass treat. In this semi-liquid form it was probably made with semolina and the following recipe on a minute scale is enough to give four people a taste of something similar.

$\frac{1}{4}$ cup sugar
2 tablespoons butter
50 g (2 oz) semolina
2–3 tablespoons chopped mixed nuts
powdered cinnamon and blanched almonds, to decorate

Boil the sugar and $\frac{1}{2}$ cup water together to make a light syrup. Melt the butter in a heavy pan, add the semolina, stirring, and cook for a few minutes, till golden. Mix with the syrup and nuts, take the pan from the heat, cover with a damp cloth and leave to stand over a very low heat or in a warm oven for 15 minutes. Transfer to small wetted ramekins and press down. Either decorate the *halva* in these pots or, having wetted the moulds first, then chilled them, turn the *halva* out on to small plates to serve, accompanied by strong black coffee.

Other densely textured, rich Oriental sweetmeats from the Balkans include some made with the boiled cream, *kaimak*. This is dried a little, cut into squares, sprinkled with sugar and then folded into triangles. It is a more formal presentation of the top of the boiled milk which Ion Creanga used to skim off with his finger from the plates of *kaimak* his mother put out to set.

A sweet 'salami' is made from Austria to Romania with chocolate and nuts. No less an establishment than Capşa in Bucharest specialized in this confection, which it called a 'chocolate ingot', though the generally low quality of chocolate nowadays must make it undesirable. The fate of chocolate marzipan has gone the same way.

More reliable is *lokum* or Turkish delight, prized from Albania to Bulgaria. Bulgaria has no rival in producing the rose-water that gives this soft jelly its distinctive scent. *Lokum* is often

lemon juice and pour over the triangles. Leave to soak in well and serve cold.

Chestnut fingers

500 g (1 lb) chestnut purée
1 tablespoon rum
½ cup icing sugar, or to taste
flour
oil for frying
icing sugar for dusting

Mix together the chestnut purée, rum and sugar to taste and, with wet hands, shape into small oblongs about 8 cm (3 inches) long and 2 cm (1 inch) thick. Roll in flour and fry carefully in hot oil. Sprinkle with icing sugar while still hot. These Bulgarian 'fingers' have an authentic Oriental taste, are very quickly made and quite delicious with plenty of strong Turkish coffee. Beware only of their fragility in the frying pan. Either deep-fry them or turn them with the help of two wooden spatulas.

Jams and compotes

The preserves made with fruit from Eastern Europe are worth looking out for in British shops because invariably they contain a high proportion of fruit and have an excellent flavour at an inexpensive price. In the production there is a painstaking regard for quality. In Poland the jam is graded, the first-class stuff sent abroad and the second-class retained for home use. Perhaps this is insulting to the citizens of Poland, but actually the second-class produce is marvellous. It comes complete with stalks and pips and has the quality of an excellent home-made jam. I would seek it out in preference to any other if I only had access. Cranberry preserves/blueberry jam of the kind that is only satisfactory when it comes from Central Europe is essential to the authentic filling of Czech sweet leavened buns and doughnuts. Similar praise deserves to be heaped on bottled fruit compotes, especially blackcurrant, redcurrant and plum, which are never too sweet. These bottled berries are the ones to use as a compote with the various meat and poultry dishes that call for them. (Our apple sauce and cranberry sauce from a jar would also be called a compote.)

Plum preserves

A preserve that is harder to find in this country though well worth buying is a Czech *povidlo* of plums. In principle to make this fruit cheese neither sugar nor water is used. Rettigova adds some grated lemon peel and a knob of butter to her *povidlo* of fresh plums or stoned prunes and if the desired thickness can't be acquired she permits a spoonful of breadcrumbs or fine sugar. Prunes, though, do need to be soaked first in plenty of water, otherwise the result will be treacle. An American friend living in Vienna with a discerning tooth for sweet things wrote to say that *Böhmische Palatschinken*, which are thin pancakes rolled around this jam and topped with sour cream, should be included in this book.

The Balkan equivalent to this thick plum cheese is, in Serbian, *pekmez*. Robin Howe remembered his Yugoslav hostess having several jars of it in her kitchen, which she and her children used to spread on brown bread and butter and eat with a glass of cold milk. The high-quality plums in Czechoslovakia and Yugoslavia are of course also used to make *slivovica*.

Cherry preserves

German and Central European housewives also used to make a cherry jam the dry way. Though it appeals today for health reasons, the economic reason for making jam without added sugar was that in a good harvest the amount of sugar needed to preserve the whole glut cost far more than the fruit. The cherries are stoned, the stones and kernels crushed and these boiled in a little water, which is then strained and poured over the fruit. The jam is then simmered with frequent stirring for about three hours, until very thick. A little more water may be added to prevent burning.

Dulceaţa/slatko

The very sweet preserves that are served with coffee in the Balkans form the traditional welcome to guests, corresponding to the Slav welcome of bread and salt. Both habits are found in different parts of Romania and Yugoslavia, according to whether the Central European and Russian or the southern and Balkan influence is stronger. Anisoara Stan, idealizing her Romanian childhood and the folk heritage she left behind when she went to live in America, soliloquized:

And what child could ever forget the famous pantries, which were the pride of every Romanian housewife? There were rows and rows of jars of dulceata, compote, marmalade and syrups. The fruits were picked at full ripeness and the flavours couldn't be improved upon. And the colours of the jars seemed to blend in a harmony, like the colours of their beautiful and graceful costumes that they create from a rich imagination and then make with their own hands.

It is a custom in every Romanian home, whether it be rich or humble, to serve the sweet dulceata to anyone who comes to visit them. . . . This wonderful tradition has been passed along from mother to daughter from ancient times. It is carried out with dignity and sincerity. To serve or partake of the dulceata is a duty having religious overtones.

Herbert Vivian was certainly struck by some imperative on the same occasion:

Whenever you pay a call in Servia, a tray is immediately brought in with a dish or two of slatko, a stand for spoons with two compartments (one full and one empty), and a number of glasses of water. The tray is generally handed by a pretty daughter of the house, or, as a special compliment, by the hostess herself. ... You are expected to take a spoonful of preserve and drink a sip of water. If you are a novice, you may observe an amused smile watching you to see if you understand the procedure or are about to commit a gaucherie, such as replacing your spoon in the wrong compartment or even in one of the glasses of water. In poor places lumps of sugar and tumblers of water are served instead of preserve. Very soon after the slatko comes another tray with little cups of Turkish coffee and more glasses of water.

Servia: The Poor Man's Paradise, 1897

The fruits used to prepare *dulceaţa/slatko* include green grapes, cherries, wild strawberries, apricots, raspberries, green plums, green hazelnuts and walnuts, gooseberries, melon and rose petals. The recipes are common to all the Balkan countries. So too is the philosophy of *litze*, observed by Alec Brown in Yugoslavia. This is the overriding importance of the look of these preserves in their jars, their colour and refractive power when brought to the table.

Rose-petal jam

The rose-petal jam in Bulgaria comes from the famous Valley of the Roses and is associated with the town of Kazanluk. In the same way as Mrs Stan was charmed by the ancientness and abiding visual beauty of the *dulceata* tradition, Charles Salaberry, a Frenchman travelling through the country at the end of the eighteenth century, felt antiquity stretching out a hand to the modern day when he regarded Kazanluk's miles of blossoms:

Kazanluk, Europe's garden of roses, lies at the foot of the Haemus mountain. Fruit trees of every sort are to be seen all around here: it looks as if the township is situated amidst an enormous orchard. The roses are planted in rows, much like vineyards. In Spring the aroma of this enchanting flower saturates the air for over a league around. Kazanluk, where is your Theocritus or Anacreon? He would have brought Venus to watch over the picking of the precious flower. ... Pluto would have abducted a Persephone and the Kazanluk roses would have caused the strawberries of Enna to fall into oblivion.

If you try making rose-petal jam at home you will have the unctuous pleasure of collecting the fragrant, moist, silky petals from the garden. Sadly, the result of boiling them up with sugar and water is neither so satisfying nor so aromatic. The translucent coral colour is most impressive.

Watermelon preserve

This jam is well-known in the Balkans. In their day it was the speciality of the Lipovani sect living in the Danube Delta.

1 kg (2 lb) watermelon
2 kg (4 lb) sugar
2 vanilla pods
juice of 2 lemons

Remove the outer rind of the melon but leave the inner part, which will give this jam the necessary sharpness of all good *slatko*. Cut the fruit into 2 cm (1 inch) cubes and boil in water for 10 minutes. Strain off the water, add fresh cold water and boil again until nearly soft. Strain again. Meanwhile, make a syrup with the sugar and fresh cold water. When this is ready add the drained watermelon and cook slowly with vanilla and lemon for about 20 minutes. Leave to cool overnight, with the pan covered with a wet cloth, then pour into jars and seal.

Green fig preserve

1¼ kg (2½ lb) green figs, about the size of a walnut	juice of 6 lemons 3 kg (6 lb) sugar 2 vanilla pods

Peel the figs, discard the stalks, prick each twice with a needle and drop in cold water. Bring to the boil, strain, replace with fresh water and reheat. Do this 5 times, adding the juice of 1 lemon to the water the last time. When the figs are soft remove them with a draining spoon. Make a syrup with the sugar and some water in a separate pan, add the figs and cook until thick, adding the juice of the remaining lemons and the vanilla before the end. Finish as for watermelon preserve, above.

Bulgaria makes an aubergine jam which I have not tried.

Fruit preserved in alcohol

This activity, which occupies a place between jam making and the distillation of sweet fruit liqueurs, has never found much enthusiasm for its product in Britain. But it is greatly liked in Central Europe, where fruits such as cherries, plums and apricots in spirits are a treat to taste and to look at. Once again they are objects whose *litze* is important.

In Germany these fruits acquire a rich, dark, closeted identity. The *Römertopf*, one of those hideous outsize ceramic jars with lift-off lids, like elongated soup tureens, which now find their way into our chain stores at Christmas, is made for the job. It looks like a cross between a Victorian aspidistra pot and a Bavarian toby jug. Filled with alcohol it will conserve fruit for many months and should be left to rest at least two months in a cool place before the fruit is eaten. The idea is to add different fruits through the summer as they ripen.

Put $\frac{1}{2}$ litre (1 pint) rum or brandy in a deep stone jar with 500 g (1 lb) sugar, stir and add 500 g (1 lb) raspberries and another 500 g (1 lb) of sugar. Stir from the bottom. Cover while waiting for other fruits to ripen. Add currants, ripe cherries, greengages, plums and blackberries, always adding the same weight of sugar each time plus enough brandy or rum to cover and stirring from the bottom. Gooseberries are not recommended, as their skins toughen. Cover tightly and keep cool.

WINES AND SPIRITS AND OTHER BEVERAGES

❦❧❦

The best authority in English, which is also very witty and readable, is R. E. H. Gunyon's *The Wines of Central and South-Eastern Europe* (1971), which more than deserves reprinting. I can only append a few comments and tastings of my own. In general, the East European countries stand out for their high production of sweet wines, which are in demand at home and in Russia. These wines are often of a high quality, and anyone looking for a good value alternative to Sauternes, Barzac, Monbazillac, etc. would do well to scan the Hungarian, Bulgarian and Yugoslav lists. Since the Eastern marketing eye has turned towards the West, however, the past few decades have seen a steady growth of well-made dry wines, both red and white. Hungary and Bulgaria have an immensely attractive range now widely available in the United Kingdom.

Hungary

❦❧

The Romans planted vineyards along the north shore of Lake Balaton that were taken over by the Arpad dynasty in the ninth century. A distinctive feature of the region is the double heat of the hot sun above and the volcanic soil below. Many of the whites are fruity, made from the Riesling and Sauvignon grapes. For good quality, everyday drinking the Chardonnay from the Balaton region is dry, elegant and distinguished. It also keeps

436

well once opened. The standard Balaton meal is, alas, a medium Riesling with a mixed grill.

Slightly further north the furmint grape, a native species, produces a crisp, ripe-tasting wine of about the same sweetness as Riesling from the slopes of Mount Somló, an extinct volcano.

A few miles above Lake Balaton from the prized Badacsonyi region come sweet vintage white varietals, Tramini and Sauvignon Blanc, aged in cask then bottle.

The other major region exporting to the West is Villany, in the south of the country, by the Yugoslav border. Of the reds, both the Merlot and the Cabernet Sauvignon are reliable dry varietals true to type.

The old British favourite from the Eger region in the north, near Tokai, is Egri Bikaver (Bull's Blood), but this, having greatly declined, is no longer a good bet.

'*Minöségi Bor*' on the label designates a quality wine and is the minimum standard one is likely to find in Britain. In Hungary the *vin ordinaire* from the Great Plains is the everyday drink, sometimes diluted with mineral water.

Tokai, the Hungarian dessert wine, is the product of 20 km of small villages in the north, from Szerences to the Czech frontier and into Slovakia, where it loses its right to the famous name. It is made with the furmint grape and, coming in all degrees of sweetness, may be drunk at both the beginning and end of a meal. At the top end of the scale Tokai Aszu is the product of nobly rotted grapes. According to the epicure of a past generation, Francis Cunnynghame, Tokai is a stimulant in times of illness or weakness because of its phosphorus content. It made its mark in Georgian England as the drink of the king. I like Károly Gundel's idea of a dash of Tokai in chicken consommé.

The wine-producing areas of Eastern Europe

N D

U S S R

Carpathian

Dniester

Siret

A

Tokaj

ecen

Cotnari

Iasi

Oradea

Cluj

Tirnaveni

ad

Mures

Nicoresti

Focsani

R O M A N I A

Transylvanian Alps

Dealul Mare

ANAT

Arges

Ploesti

Pitesti

Dragascani

Bucharest

Murfatlar

Constanta

Wallachian Plain

Segarcea

Danube

Svishtov

Novi Pazar

Varna

RBIA

Morava

Niš

Sukhindol

Lyaskovets

Preslav

Black

ovo

Balkan Alps

Sofia

Karlovo

Sungulare

Sea

B U L G A R I A

Stara Zagora

Grudovno

Plovdiv

Maritsa

Skopje

Asenovgrad

T U R K E Y

B O S N I A

Melnik

Istanbul

G R E E C E

Yugoslavia
🐗

Serbia produces nearly half the wine, followed by Croatia with just over a third, and Slovenia and Macedonia with just under a tenth. Croatia includes most of the Dalmatian coast, where the cultivation of wine goes back to the ancient Greeks, though because of the Turkish occupation the greater part of the country was viticulturally retarded until this century. The best-known, best-selling Yugoslav wine in Britain is the Laski Riesling, an Austrian-style white wine on the sweet side, made in Slovenia, in the northern part of Croatia and in eastern Serbia, close to Hungary. Riesling grapes were introduced by the Austrians in the nineteenth century. These 'medium' wines with a large following have an average character that is forgettable. Like Hungary and Bulgaria, Yugoslavia produces Sauvignon and Traminer varietals of greater interest, grown in the ancient viticultural area of Fruska Gora, overlooking the Danube in Vojvodina. These are among the host of foreign vines planted since World War Two, alongside the Central European Furmint, Grüner Veltliner, and Muskat-Ottonel.

The products of the purely native vines are of varying quality and the variety ensures interest if not certain pleasure. The Muslim region of Herzegovina, with its capital in Mostar, raises vines among the mosques on very rocky soil and under an intense sun. It exports the locally bottled very light dry white, Zilavka, which I have seen described as 'ethereal honey' though my bottle in a magnificent rambling hotel in Sarajevo was only very pale, and with hardly a hint of sweetness. A dry white or yellow Plavac from Slovenia, Istria and Dalmatia is also worth pursuing, and Posip is said to be the finest white in the country, though I have not tried it.

Among the reds, known in Serbo-Croat as 'black wine', the smooth, dry, full-bodied Teran of the Istrian Peninsula is very attractive, neither as distinctive nor as eccentric as the prized Dingac growing on the steep slopes between the two Adriatic resorts, Šibenik and Dubrovnik. Dingac, which almost warrants the description black, attains extraordinary strength from its roots in volcanic soil and is often drunk diluted. It has a noticeable sweetness. Postup, produced from a single vineyard in the same area, the Peljesac Peninsula, is free of obvious sugar but seems to me too powerful to be subtle. All these deeply coloured, massive wines are made with the Plavac Mali grape, including Faros, a wine produced exclusively on the island of Hvar. Dionis, a Merlot with many years of life, is by contrast a softer, full-bodied wine comparable with a characterful claret. Bottled in Yugoslavia and exported inexpensively it is worth looking out for.

Prosek is Yugoslavia's tawny-coloured dessert wine, a naturally sweet wine high in alcohol, resembling marsala. It is pressed from sun-dried grapes all down the Adriatic coast and drunk like Tokai as an aperitif, long or short, chilled or with ice, or at room temperature after dinner.

Dry and medium sparkling white wines are produced from a blend of Riesling and indigenous Smederevka grapes.

We are likely to hear and see more of the better-quality Yugoslav wines in future, including some from lesser-known regions like Montenegro.

Czechoslovakia

Not enough wine is produced in Bohemia, Moravia and Slovakia to generate an export trade worthy of the name, but the dry and fruity wines of these slopes, made from the Sylvaner, Traminer, Riesling, Müller-Thürgau and Pinot Gris grapes, are often fragrant and refreshing, with a dedicated following amongst those who have tasted them locally. The first vines were planted in present-day Slovakia by the Romans. The Pinot Gris goes under the Czech version of its Austrian name, Rulandske. The Sylvaner produces a sweeter, flowery wine. Bratislava, the Slovakian capital, on the Danube and a mere sixty miles from Vienna, is famous for its old wine cellars where such wines can be enjoyed at their best. Prices by West European standards are inexpensive and excellent value for the quality offered. In Moravia the wines are all white, Austrian-style. The Bohemian whites from the area around Melnik can be compared to hocks.

A few dry red wines are produced from the Cabernet Franc grape on the slopes of the Little Carpathians in west Slovakia, which I have not been able to taste. The centre of the growing area producing mainly white wines is Modra, north of Bratislava.

Poland
❧

Grapes were cultivated in Cracow in south-west Poland in the twelfth century, but Polish wine production never grew into a large enterprise. Queen Bona, who came from Lombardy, tried to revive it when she married the Polish king in the sixteenth century, but the winters were too cold. Poland fell back on fruit wines sweetened with honey, and on mead, for drinking after a meal, while beer, of which there were apparently 468 varieties, accompanied food. Today wine is imported, generally from other East Bloc countries, but it is interesting to note that the style of drinking, at least in Fukier's in the centre of Old Warsaw, resembles that of an Italian café. The wine is served by the large tumbler, with no more pretension than beer. Wines in restaurants are imported from Romania, Bulgaria and Hungary.

Albania
❧

Red and white wines are produced on state vineyards from the north to the south of this mountainous country. What reached our tables was classed as 'first' or 'second' quality, respectively 70p and 40p a bottle at 1987 prices. The red varietals, Merlot and Shesh Izi, bottled under the state label Albavin, were dry, full-bodied table wines, unexceptionable everyday drinking with only the rare edge. The one white I tasted, a Riesling from the Adriatic coastal region behind the port of Durres (Durazzo), had a resinous, concentrated taste, dark-gold colour and high alcohol content, in other words it was not at all true to type. Like the Greek, Egyptian and Central Asian wines it makes its presence felt and requires a particular palate to enjoy it. Very little Albanian wine leaves the country.

Romania

৩৭৫

Romania has excellent wines. Almost impossible to find in this country, but worth trying on holiday, are a dry, fragrant white from Murfatlar, near the Black Sea, and a Merlot from among the full-bodied reds grown in the Carpathian foothills. Chardonnay, Riesling, Pinot and Muscat grapes are all cultivated in this fertile region. British importers say they have tried and failed to get these wines to our tables, with little help from Bucharest.

Dmitri Kantemir, describing Moldavia in the seventeenth century, pointed to the excellence of the vines between Cotnar and the Danube, which continues today. It is an area of very high yield once again cultivated by the Romans. The sweet unctuous Cotnar wines were 'said to be better than fine European wines, even better than Tokai' after four years acquiring a luscious density and a misleading colour for a mature wine:

The strongest drinker is hardly able to drink a third glass without becoming drunk; but he will have no headache. The wine has a quite special colour one doesn't find with other wines, that is, green; and it becomes greener with age.

Today's Cotnar wines are produced from a blend of four native vines including Feteasca and Graşa (= furmint). Odobesti and Nicoresti not far away comprise the largest wine-growing area today.

Further north Bessarabia, though very dry and hot, also produced good wine in Kantemir's day, before it was overrun by the Turk, 'the one contemptuous of wine'. Nowadays Moldavian wine is one of the jewels of Soviet and Romanian viti-culture.

Wine is also produced in the far west of the country, the Banat (Banat Riesling). Near Timisoara is the wine village of Rekas, where we drove to sample the Cabernet Sauvignon in humble conditions. The lights went out in the village bar and stayed out for an hour, but no one seemed to mind. This dry full-bodied wine is of such a high quality much of it goes to Bucharest.

In south Romania a distinguished growing region is the River Olt Valley, which has been producing a prized sweet white wine from the market village of Dragaşani, near Slatina, for over a century. An Austrian traveller of the 1880s, Rudolf Bergner, gave a joyful description of wine production in this poor, picturesque region where there were 'everywhere men stamping, women picking and children surrounded by wasps'. The vineyards were owned then as today by the state.

Not for export again, but very enjoyable, is Romanian dry white sparkling wine, champagne-style. There is also a local vermouth, Pelinu.

Bulgaria

Bulgaria is rapidly becoming the best-known exporter of wines to the United Kingdom, wines which are of a high quality and good value. Huge investment in the industry that was held back by five centuries of Muslim rule has pushed it into fifth place as a capacity exporter, after France, Italy, Spain and Portugal. The overseas market has entirely developed since the last war, when the vast, privately owned vineyards which had often been owned and run by foreigners, were nationalized and modernized with expertise from California. The Californian touch shows in the big, velvety dark-hued reds which are matured in oak and look and taste to many palates like blackcurrant. That consensus is perhaps faintly discouraging as to the prospect of a very individual style making its mark, but it is excellent for securing general appeal and high sales. The Western market, started from scratch, was carefully studied. The unwitting buyer is unlikely to pick off the shelf a sweet red wine from Bulgaria by mistake, as can happen with Hungarian and Yugoslav products. Very reliable among the reds and often highly impressive are the Cabernet Sauvignon and in second place the Merlot; of the whites the Chardonnay is the driest and finest, followed by the Sauvignon. Produced from single native vines are two mighty wines with a long life: Mavrud and Melnik. They have reached their maximum potential when they appear as Reserve wines, estate bottled and numbered. This powerful category is worth noting, for these vintage wines can easily overwhelm a delicate meal.

Under the Mehana brand name a very acceptable blended *vin ordinaire*, dry red or white, is available. Under the same label 'medium' wines for the British market are also on sale, as well as a rich and fragrant dessert wine (Mehana sweet white).

The Wine Law of 1973 imposed a strict quality control along French lines. '*Controliran*' designates a high-quality wine particularly characteristic of its region.

Bulgaria also exports a competitive dry sparkling Chardonnay. If this is the 'Bulgarian champagne' marketed at home as Iskra, it is very like the dry Russian product.

German Democratic Republic

Wines are produced in Saxony and Thuringia, but are not exported. My only tasting was disastrous. My local host would have preferred a wine imported from West Germany, but none was available.

Lunch at a Polish inn, from Daniel Chodowiecki, Von Berlin Nach Danzig, 1773

Spirits

Vodka has been the Polish peasant drink for centuries. A young man wishing to propose to a girl sent his friends to her with vodka to see if she would drink. It has moved up the social ladder in the past hundred years. According to a Polish proverb the best comes from Gdańsk. Apart from the basic spirit, vodka is also the generic term for all kinds of flavoured spirits, such as with caraway seed (*kminkowka*) and with a special dried grass (*zubrowka*). Vodkas with fruit are generally sweet.

Țuica is the dry colourless Romanian plum brandy famous for its after-smell 'like liquid compost'. It 'makes one smell like a still'. It propped up the foreign community in pre-war Bucharest, according to Olivia Manning's *The Balkan Trilogy*. I tested it walking in the snow and found it an excellent nip. A fair amount of home distillation goes on in contemporary Romania. We acquired ours in unlabelled litre wine bottles.

Travarica and *orehovica* are amongst the distillations less well-known outside Yugoslavia and much appreciated at home. Both are considered 'healthy', the first made with herbs and faintly greenish in colour, the second made with green walnuts and lemon rind. The plum brandy, *slivovica*, is milder than the Romanian *țuica* and like all the Yugoslav spirits is considered as a quick pick-me-up during the day and an accompaniment to café snacks rather than something saved for the end of a meal. This use is instructive, especially when travelling. You can be sure of getting a reasonable *slivovica* at the railway station buffet.

Mastika is the Macedonian grape spirit with aniseed that turns cloudy when served, as is customary, with water. Mastic is the resin through which the spirit is distilled and gives the spirit its distinctive taste. It is widely available in Yugoslavia, Bulgaria and Albania.

Other beverages

Mineral water has been drunk 'for centuries in Central and Eastern Europe. The cult of taking the curative natural waters once or twice a year in spas from Marienbad in Bohemia to Baile Herculane in western Romania and Bourgas on the Black Sea has been followed since Roman and in some cases in Bulgaria since Thracian times. Only one step further is to put this water in bottles and move it around the country. Like the cult of wine, the cult of water also went into abeyance under the Turks. East European mineral waters are beginning to appear in the United Kingdom, with Yugoslavia leading the way.

Airan is a cooling cocktail of yoghurt and sparkling mineral water you may be served in Bulgaria. It resembles the Indian *lassi*.

Braga is the Romanian equivalent of *kvas*, the Russian bread beer, except that it is sweet. Made of fermented bran, it used to be offered by itinerant sellers with barrels on their backs, or from stationary wagons. It was welcomed as being cooling without being chilled.

Stockists

These are specialists who may be able to help with particular inquiries. They also run mail-order services.

> Wines of Westthorpe Ltd,
> Unit L-22,
> Park Avenue Estate,
> Sundon Park,
> Luton, LU3 3AE

Vitkovitch Brothers,
Little Mostar,
Virgil Street,
London, SE1 7EF
Tel. 01-261 1770

Teltscher Brothers Ltd,
West India Dock,
Prestons Road,
London, E14
Tel. 01-987 5020

The Albanian Shop,
Betterton St,
London WC2

From Siklossy Lasziō, Svabhegy, *Budapest 1929*

BIBLIOGRAPHY

Recipe collections

The recipes in this book are largely taken or adapted from the following authorities:

Brizova, Joza, and Maryna Klimentova, *Czech Cuisine*, Collet's, London 1985

Cholcheva, Penka Ivanova, *Suvremenna domashna kukhnia*, Sofia 1975

Czerny, Zofia, *Polish Cookbook* (revised edition), Warsaw 1975

Dor, Doina, *La Cuisine de nos grands-mères roumaines*, Paris n.d.

Encyclopedia of European Cooking, edited by Musia Soper (2nd revised edition), Hamlyn, London 1969

Europäische Spezialitäten, Cologne 1972

Fialova, Juliana A., and K. Styblikova, *Ceska kuchyne*, Prague 1987

Frank, Kato, *Cooking the Hungarian Way*, Hamlyn, London 1963

Grum, Andreja, *Slovenske narodne jedi*, Ljubljana 1976

Howe, Robin, *Balkan Cooking*, André Deutsch, London 1965
     German Cooking, André Deutsch, London 1953

Ivacic, Ivan, *Kuharska knjiga*, Maribor 1978

Kniga za vseki den i vseki dom Domakinska entsiklopediya, Sofia 1973

Das Kochbuch von Goethes Grossmutter, herausgegeben von Manfred Lemmer, Leipzig 1980

Kovi, Paul, *Paul Kovi's Transylvanian Cuisine*, New York 1985

Kramarz, Inge, *The Balkan Cookbook*, New York 1972

Lambley, Hanne, *The Home Book of German Cookery*, Faber, London 1979

Lang, George, *The Cuisine of Hungary*, Penguin, London 1985

Lemnis, Maria, *Old Polish Traditions in the Kitchen*, Warsaw 1979

Levai, Vera, *Culinary Delights*, Budapest 1983

Macnicol, Fred, *Hungarian Cooking*, Penguin, London 1978

Marin, Sanda, *Carte de bucate*, Bucharest 1956

Marperger, Paul Jacob, *Vollständiges Küch und Keller-Dictionarium*, Hamburg 1716, reprinted Munich 1978

Nelson, Kay Shaw, *The Eastern European Cookbook*, New York 1972

Novac-Markovic, Olga, *Yugoslav Cookbook*, Collet's, London 1984

Ochorowicz-Monatowa, Marja, *Polish Cooking*, translated and adapted by Jean Karsavina, Deutsch, London 1960

Polish Cookbook, Culinary Arts Institute, Illinois 1978

Polvay, Marina, *All Along the Danube*, New Jersey 1979

Rettigova, Magdalena Dobromila, *Domaci kucharka spolu s ukazami z belatriskheho dila M. D. Rettigove a ctenim jeji osobnosti*, Prague 1986

   Kucharska kniha (14th edition), Prague 1921

Ridgeway, Judy, *The German Food Book*, Martin, Cambridge 1983

Rosicky, Mary, *Bohemian-American Cookbook*, Omaha, Nebraska, 1915

Schmaeling, Tony, *German Traditional Cooking*, Ware 1982

Stan, Anisoara, *The Romanian Cook Book*, New Jersey 1951

Food history, restaurant guides and gastronomic memoirs

Album literar gastronomic, Bucharest 1982

Hamm, M., *Coffee Houses of Europe*, with an Introduction by George Mikes, Thames and Hudson, London 1980

Hering, Richard, *Hering's Dictionary of Classical and Modern Cookery*, translated and edited by Walter Bickel (16th revised edition), Giessen 1970

Newnham Davies, N., *The Gourmet's Guide to Europe*, London 1908

Root, Waverley, *Food*, New York 1980

Schiedlausky, G., *Tee, Kaffee, Schokolade*, Munich 1961
Ukkers, W. H., *The Romance of Coffee*, New York 1948
Wechsberg, Joseph, *Blue Trout and Black Truffles*, Gollancz, London 1953
    The Lost World of the Great Spas, Weidenfeld and Nicolson, London 1979

Wine

Gunyon, R. E. H., *The Wines of Central and South-Eastern Europe*, Duckworth, London 1971

Travel

Alexander, Nora, *Wanderings in Yugoslavia*, Skeffington, London 1936
Baerlein, Henry (ed.), *Bessarabia and Beyond*, Methuen, London 1935
    In Old Romania, Hutchinson, London 1940
    (ed.), *Romanian Oasis*, Frederick Muller, London 1948
Berger, Florence K., *A Winter in the City of Pleasure, or, Life on the Lower Danube*, Bentley, London 1877
Bergner, Rudolf, *Rumänien*, Breslau 1887
Edwards, Lovett F., *Introducing Yugoslavia*, Methuen, London 1954
Hall, Donald John, *Romanian Furrow*, Methuen, London 1933
Hodgson, R., *On Plain and Peak*, Constable, London 1898
Kantemir, Demetrii, *Beschreibung der Moldau*, Frankfurt and Leipzig 1771
Kohl, Johann Georg, *Reise nach Istrien, Dalmatien und Montenegro* (2 vols.), Dresden 1851
Labbé, Paul, *La Vivante Roumanie*, Paris 1913
Lindsay, Jack, and Maurice Cornforth, *Rumanian Summer*, Lawrence and Wishart, London 1953
Mackintosh, May, *Rumania*, Robert Hale, London 1963

Parkinson, Maude, *Twenty Years in Roumania*, Allen and Unwin, London 1921

Pittard, Eugène, *La Roumanie*, Paris 1917

Sitwell, Sacheverell, *Roumanian Journey*, Batsford, London 1938

Stratilesco, Tereza, *From Carpathian to Pindus*, Fisher Unwin, London 1906

Vivian, Herbert, *Servia: The Poor Man's Paradise*, Longmans, London 1897

Fiction

Andric, Ivo, *The Bridge over the Drina*, translated by Lovett F. Edwards, Allen and Unwin, London 1959

Creanga, Ion, *Recollections from Childhood*, translated by A. L. Lloyd, Lawrence and Wishart, London 1956

Erben, Karel Jaromir, *Panslavonic Folk-lore*, translated by W. H. Strickland, New York 1930

Grass, Günter, *The Flounder*, translated by Ralph Manheim, Secker and Warburg, London 1978

Mickiewicz, Adam, *Pan Tadeusz, or, The Last Foray in Lithuania*, translated by George Rapall Noyes, J. M. Dent, London 1917

Nemcova, Bozena, *The Grandmother*, translated by Francis Gregor, Chicago 1891

Reymont, Ladislas (Wladislaw), *The Peasants*, translated by Michael H. Dziewicki, Jarrolds, London 1925–6

Vazoff, Ivan, *Under the Yoke*, translated by Edmund Gosse, Heinemann, London 1894

INDEX